SETTING
NATIONAL
PRIORITIES

SETTING NATIONAL PRIORITIES

The 2000 Election and Beyond

HENRY J. AARON
ROBERT D. REISCHAUER

EDITORS

BROOKINGS INSTITUTION PRESS
Washington, D.C.

Library of Congress Cataloging in Publication data

Setting national priorities : the 2000 election and beyond /
Henry J. Aaron and Robert D. Reischauer, editors.
    p.   cm.
Includes bibliographical references and index.
   ISBN 0-8157-7402-8 (cloth : alk. paper)—ISBN 0-8157-7401-X
(pbk. : alk. paper)
   I. Aaron, Henry J.   II. Reischauer, Robert D. (Robert Danton),
1941– 1. Political planning—United States.   2. United
States—Politics and government—1993–
   JK468.P64 S46 1999
   302'.6—dc21   99-006854
                                                             CIP

9 8 7 6 5 4 3 2 1

Typeset in Minion

Composition by
Harlowe Typography
Cottage City, Maryland

Printed by
R.R. Donnelley and Sons
Harrisonburg, Virginia

ℬ THE BROOKINGS INSTITUTION

The Brookings Institution is an independent organization devoted to nonpartisan research, education, and publication in economics, government, foreign policy, and the social sciences generally. Its principal purposes are to aid in the development of sound public policies and to promote public understanding of issues of national importance.

The Institution was founded on December 8, 1927, to merge the activities of the Institute for Government Research, founded in 1916, the Institute of Economics, founded in 1922, and the Robert Brookings Graduate School of Economics and Government, founded in 1924.

The Board of Trustees is responsible for the general administration of the Institution, while the immediate direction of the policies, program, and staff is vested in the President, assisted by an advisory committee of the officers and staff. The by-laws of the Institution state: It is the function of the Trustees to make possible the conduct of scientific research, and publication, under the most favorable conditions, and to safeguard the independence of the research staff in pursuit of their studies and in the publication of the result of such studies. It is not a part of their function to determine, control, or influence the conduct of particular investigations or the conclusions reached.

The President bears final responsibility for the decision to publish a manuscript as a Brookings book. In reaching his judgment on competence, accuracy, and objectivity of each study, the President is advised by the director of the appropriate research program and weighs the views of a panel of expert outside readers who report to him in confidence on the quality of the work. Publication of a work signifies that it is deemed a competent treatment worthy of public consideration but does not imply endorsement of conclusions or recommendations.

The Institution maintains its position of neutrality on issues of public policy in order to safeguard the intellectual freedom of the staff. Hence interpretations or conclusions in Brookings publications should be understood to be solely those of the authors and should not be attributed to the Institution, to its trustees, officers, or other staff members, or to the organizations that support its research.

Foreword

TWENTY-NINE YEARS ago, *Setting National Priorities: The 1971 Budget* appeared, the first of what has become a signature series of the Brookings Institution. The early editions of *SNP* provided hard-to-find analyses of the major national choices that budget debates resolved. These volumes helped inspire members of Congress who wrote and passed legislation establishing the Congressional Budget Office. Commentary on public policy is now readily available, but too little of it reflects the balanced examination of policy alternatives based on solid scholarship that remains the hallmark of this series.

On the eve of the new century, the range of decisions awaiting fresh vision and creative leadership is unusually large. For the first time in more than two decades Americans will have a chance to decide how to deal with a problem many thought they would never face—what to do with prospective budget *surpluses*. The economy is extraordinarily prosperous, with high employment and low inflation. The two major parties have articulated dramatically different visions of how the nation should respond to this opportunity. The electorate's choice between these visions will shape economic and political life in the United States well beyond the term of office of the president to be selected in November 2000. However they decide, American voters will set national priorities for the year 2000 and beyond. The need for good information and balanced judgments is therefore particularly urgent. This book is intended to help meet that need.

Three research divisions at Brookings and outside scholars collaborated to produce this book. The editors, Henry J. Aaron and Robert D. Reischauer, as well as authors Gary Burtless, William Gale, Bruce Katz, and Isabel V. Sawhill, are members of the Economic Studies program. Paul C. Light and Thomas E. Mann are, respectively, current and former directors of the Governmental Studies program. Michael O'Hanlon is a member of the Foreign Policy Studies program. The other authors are I.M. Destler (University of Maryland), John J. DiIulio Jr. (University of Pennsylvania), Donald F. Kettl (University of Wisconsin), Paul R. Portney (Resources for the Future), Diane Ravitch (New York University), and James Sly (Center on Budget and Policy Priorities).

Theresa Walker, Deborah Styles, and James Schneider edited the manuscript, and Jennifer Eichberger, Carole Plowfield, and Takako Tsuji verified it. Shanna Rose provided research assistance for the project, and Kathleen Elliott Yinug and Kara Chessman provided administrative assistance. Joanne Lockard proofread the book, and Robert Elwood prepared the index.

This project was partially supported by the Bruce and Virginia MacLaury Chair.

The views expressed in this volume are those of the authors and should not be ascribed to the trustees, officers, or other staff members of the Brookings Institution or any other organizations with which the authors are associated.

MICHAEL H. ARMACOST
President

September 1999
Washington, D.C.

Contents

Figures

ROBERT D. REISCHAUER

1

The Dawning of a New Era

T HE DEBATE OVER national priorities at the century's end is occurring in an environment markedly different from that of the past
twenty years. The nation's economy is unusually strong and surprisingly resilient in the face of considerable weakness and instability
abroad. Partly because of the strong economy, the overall federal budget is in surplus after almost three decades of large and intractable
deficits. Projections by both the Office of Management and Budget
(OMB) and the Congressional Budget Office (CBO) suggest that surpluses will continue for at least the next two decades if current tax and
spending policies are not significantly changed. Furthermore, many of
the issues that dominated past policy debates—such as the deficit, the
cold war, and welfare—have receded or disappeared.

This new environment should promote both a reexamination of
current national priorities and debate on an agenda for the nation's
future. With neither major political party having a lock on the Senate,
the House of Representatives, or the White House, and a presidential
election without an incumbent up for reelection only months away, a
full and open discussion of national priorities is needed. The dawn of
a new century—which the United States enters as the world's preemi-
nent economic, military, intellectual, and cultural power—underscores the importance of this debate.

The Economy

The performance of the U.S. economy as of the summer of 1999 is superlative in almost every way. Since the 1990–91 recession, real output has expanded at an annual rate of 3.1 percent. Rather than slowing, growth picked up as this expansion, the longest of the century during peacetime, has matured. Between the first quarter of 1997 and the second quarter of 1999, economic growth has averaged 3.9 percent. Productivity growth, which slowed markedly after 1972, has accelerated modestly during the second half of the 1990s. Just as the reasons for the earlier slowdown are not well understood even now, the causes and permanence of the recent pickup in productivity growth remain matters of debate. Increased investment in plant and equipment, improved worker training, the cumulative experience of a maturing labor force, relentless efforts of management to promote efficiency, and new computer and communications technologies are among the possible explanations for the improvement in productivity.[1]

To the envy of the rest of the world, the U.S. economy has been a job creation machine. Some 133 million Americans were employed in June 1999, up 16 million from a decade earlier. The fraction of the adult population with jobs—67 percent during the first half of 1999—was the highest of the post–World War II period. The overall unemployment rate, which has been below 4.5 percent since November 1998, is lower than at any time in three decades. African American unemployment, which was over 14 percent in 1992, had fallen to 7.3 percent in June 1999, still far higher than the white rate, but lower than it has been since separate rates were first tabulated in 1972.

With labor markets tight, the fruits of economic prosperity have begun to be shared broadly. From the mid-1970s until the mid-1990s, many types of workers—men without a college education and younger and minority workers in particular—experienced fairly steady declines in their real earnings. Women and highly educated men held their own during periods of economic slack and did modestly well when the econ-

---

1. A portion of the improvement is attributable to refinements that have been made in the methodology used to measure inflation. For an evaluation of the increase in productivity see Gordon (1999).

omy was strong. After the 1990–91 recession, the incomes of those at the top of the distribution began to grow rapidly. Real median family incomes began to rise after 1993 and by 1997 had surpassed, for the first time, the previous peak reached in 1989. The fraction of the population classified as poor fell from 15.1 percent in 1993 to 13.3 percent in 1997—a marked improvement, although well above the 11.1 percent low point reached in 1973.

Inflation has dropped to levels not seen on a sustained basis since the first half of the 1960s. Modest increases in hourly compensation, faster productivity growth, fiercely competitive markets awash in inexpensive imports, and improvements in the measurement of consumer prices have all helped keep inflation low. Since 1991, the consumer price index (CPI) has risen at an average annual rate of 2.8 percent and, for the two years ending in June 1999, it rose at an annual rate of under 2 percent. For all practical purposes, inflation as of mid-1999 was not a concern of consumers, workers, or businesses.

The Budget

For two successive years the unified budget—the "off-budget" accounts of social security and the U.S. Postal Service plus the government's other or "on-budget" accounts—has been in surplus. These fiscal 1998 and 1999 surpluses are the first back-to-back surpluses since 1956–57. The 1999 surplus—at over 1 percent of GDP—was the largest relative to the size of the economy since 1951. Both OMB and CBO project that, if spending and tax policies are not changed, the surpluses will grow to exceed 3 percent of GDP—more than $400 billion—by 2009. While the surpluses to date have been attributable to an excess of social security receipts over that program's expenditures, growing surpluses are projected to emerge in the rest of the budget over the next few years.

How Was the Deficit Dragon Slain?

The speed and extent to which persistent deficits have morphed into projected surpluses have left policymakers, economists, and an incredulous public scratching their heads and searching for explanations. Among the more important is a decade of sensible fiscal policy. Congress passed, and two presidents signed three major multiyear deficit reduction packages—in October 1990, August 1993, and August 1997. When enacted, these omnibus bills were estimated to reduce deficits during the first five years after implementation by $482 billion, $433 billion, and $118 billion. The first two packages balanced tax increases with spending reductions. Tax increases made up 49 percent of the combined deficit reduction of these two packages, reductions in spending the balance.[2] The Taxpayer Relief Act of 1997 (TRA97), a component of the 1997 deficit reduction package, reduced revenues by $92 billion over the 1998–2002 period, but the Balanced Budget Act of 1997 (BBA97), another element of the package, more than offset this revenue loss with $210 billion in spending reductions.[3]

In addition to provisions affecting taxes and spending, the three deficit reduction packages erected procedural barriers to future deficit-increasing spending and tax legislation. The Budget Enforcement Act of 1990 (BEA), a component of the 1990 deficit reduction package, established caps or limits on so-called discretionary spending for fiscal years 1991–95.[4] If Congress appropriated more than these caps allowed, the law required OMB to bring spending down to the limit by proportionately reducing or "sequestering" spending authority in each discretionary account.

To impose fiscal discipline on tax and mandatory spending legislation, the BEA created the pay-as-you-go (PAYGO) mechanism. Under it, the sum of the fiscal impacts of all tax and mandatory legislation enacted since the deficit reduction package was approved could not increase the deficit for any fiscal year. If, at the start of the fiscal year, the PAYGO scorecard—as the tally sheet is called—indicated a transgression, OMB was required to offset the breach by sequestering a handful of mandatory programs according to a complex set of rules.

2. This division excludes debt service savings, which should be prorated proportionately between tax increases and spending reductions.

3. The refundable portion of the EITC and child tax credit are included in the estimate given for reduced revenues as is the revenue increase associated with the boost in cigarette taxes that was included in the BBA97.

4. The term "discretionary spending" refers to budgetary resources provided through the appropriation process. Direct, mandatory, and entitlement spending refers to activities in which the authority to commit budgetary resources is controlled by authorizing, rather than appropriation, legislation. General Accounting Office (1993).

To accommodate unforeseen developments, the BEA provided that the spending caps and PAYGO scorecard would be automatically adjusted to reflect any spending increase or revenue loss associated with legislation that both Congress and the president designated as "emergency" in nature. The 1993 and 1997 packages extended the discretionary spending caps to cover fiscal years 1996–98 and 1999–2002; rebased the PAYGO scorecard, and modified, in minor ways, the procedures governing the discretionary spending limits and the PAYGO mechanism.

The discretionary spending caps and the PAYGO restraint proved remarkably effective. Between 1990 and 1998, real (inflation adjusted) discretionary spending was reduced by 11 percent. Concerned about triggering a PAYGO sequester, lawmakers took care to offset revenue losses and increases in mandatory spending in the legislation they approved by enacting cuts in other mandatory spending programs and increases in revenues. While Congress approved "emergency" spending or tax cut legislation each year, the amounts were modest and responded to genuine exigencies such as floods, earthquakes, hurricanes, terrorism, and military and humanitarian crises like Bosnia and Kosovo. Although free to place the "emergency" designation on any spending or tax legislation, lawmakers did not significantly abuse this authority until 1999 when they confronted the unrealistically tight fiscal spending caps established by the 1997 deficit reduction package.

The strong economy is a second important reason why large budget deficits have given way to growing surpluses. The Federal Reserve deserves much praise for its deft handling of monetary policy, which has played an important role in sustaining the economic expansion. Chairman Alan Greenspan convinced financial markets early in the 1990s that the Fed would act quickly to squelch any renewed inflationary pressures. He also implied that the central bank would offset the fiscal restraint inherent in Congress's deficit reduction packages with easier monetary policy if an economic slowdown threatened, a development he considered unlikely. Having gained the confidence of financial markets and lawmakers, the Fed's actual monetary policy allowed the economy to expand well beyond the limits that the central bank, in its official statements, suggested were consistent with price stability. In the mid-1990s, the Fed, along with most public and private sector economists, said that inflationary pressures could be expected to build if the unemployment rate fell much below 6 percent. But with inflation low and stable, the central bank allowed the expansion to continue and did not boost interest rates even though the unemployment rate fell, first below 5 percent and then below 4.5 percent.

Numerous other factors contributed to the economy's good performance. The distortions and imbalances that had characterized the economy during the late 1980s and early 1990s—for example, overbuilding in the real estate sector, weakness in the savings and loan and banking industries, sectoral adjustments caused by defense downsizing, exploding health care costs, and growing budget deficits—had worked themselves out by the mid-1990s. Low inflation created a more predictable environment for business decisionmaking. A strengthened dollar reduced import prices, which pushed U.S. companies to seek greater efficiencies. Burgeoning investment opportunities in the communications, biotechnology, and computer industries also helped to energize the economy.

It would be difficult to overstate the contribution of the strong economy to the improved budget outlook. In January 1993, CBO projected that GDP for 1999 would be $8,275 billion; by July 1999 its estimate for that year had grown to $8,964 billion. With a bit over one-quarter of increases in GDP accruing to the government as higher revenues, the $689 billion GDP improvement boosted revenues. So have unexpected changes in the composition of GDP. Corporate profits and wage and salary disbursements—two relatively highly taxed components of national income—grew over the 1990s as a fraction of GDP, rather than remaining roughly the same as most forecasters had predicted.[5] The strong economy also held down spending for such programs as unemployment insurance and welfare.

Lady Luck also contributed to the dramatic turnaround in the budget outlook. Just as virtually all unexpected developments during the

5. In January 1993, CBO projected that the growth of economic profits and wage and salary disbursements would average 5.7 and 4.8 percent, respectively, over the 1992–99 period. Its July 1999 projections estimate the growth rates of these two components over this period were 10.1 percent and 5.7 percent.

previous two decades had unfortunate fiscal repercussions, almost everything broke right from a budget perspective during the 1990s. The peaceful collapse of the Soviet empire justified significant reductions in the defense budget and made the painful consequences of defense downsizing politically acceptable. Without this downsizing, compliance with the discretionary spending caps would probably have been impossible because policymakers, in fact, showed no consistent ability to cut domestic discretionary spending. Defense spending fell 26 percent between 1990 and 1999 while discretionary spending devoted to domestic programs rose 24 percent.[6] Only in the 1996 budget—the first approved after Republicans gained control of both houses of Congress—did real spending on domestic programs fall.

The slowdown in the growth of employer health care costs, which began in the early 1990s, was a second serendipitous development with budgetary consequences. After more than two decades of double-digit increases, the growth of employers' health care costs slowed to a crawl as benefit managers energetically shifted workers into managed care plans that bargained aggressively with providers for lower fees and increased employee premiums and cost sharing. With a lag, these savings contributed to higher profits and wages, which boosted federal revenues because both are taxable while employer-paid health care premiums are not.

The concentration of the income gains among those with high incomes during the first half of the 1990s, while unfortunate from the majority's perspective, was another bit of budgetary good fortune that boosted government revenues and lowered deficits. Over the 1989 to 1995 period, 61 percent of the aggregate increase in income accrued to the richest tenth of households. Because the wealthy face higher-than-average tax rates and the 1990 and 1993 deficit reduction packages boosted those rates, the revenue gain realized by the government was greater than it would have been if the income gains had been more equally distributed.

---

6. Real discretionary spending for international programs fell 19 percent over the 1990–99 period. *Budget of the United States Government, Fiscal Year 2000, Historical Tables*, table 8.2.

The soaring stock market also helped lower the deficit. Equity prices rose far more than the improved outlook for corporate earnings and the reductions in inflation and interest rates could justify.[7] Whether this run-up turns out to have been a speculative bubble or a sustainable revaluation of equities, it has unexpectedly boosted tax collections. Tax payments on realized capital gains, which averaged $29 billion a year between 1990 and 1993, shot up to an estimated $78 billion a year from 1997 through 1999. Furthermore, the soaring stock market has encouraged many to exercise stock options, which during the 1990s have become an increasingly important form of compensation, particularly in the high-tech sectors of the economy. Income realized from exercising options is mostly taxed at ordinary rates, not at lower capital gains rates, providing another unexpected boon to federal revenues.

The dark clouds that have filled the economic skies of Japan, most of Europe, Korea, Southeast Asia, and much of Latin America in recent years have had a silver lining for the United States. With excess industrial capacity and weak currencies, foreign producers supplied the American market with inexpensive imports that helped hold down U.S. prices. Economic weakness abroad also depressed demand for many raw materials and basic commodities, helping to keep prices low and the Fed's inflationary concerns in check despite the U.S. boom. The price of oil, in particular, fell from $20 a barrel in 1990 to $8 in December 1998.

Finally, an unexpectedly sharp slowdown in the growth of medicare and medicaid spending has helped the budget outlook. Medicare spending grew 11.3 percent a year and medicaid outlays expanded at the annual pace of 17.1 percent between 1989 and 1995. The slowdown in private sector health care cost growth, together with legislative changes, particularly those enacted in the BBA97 reduced projections of the growth of medicare and medicaid spending to an estimated 5.2 and 6.1 percent, respectively, over the 1997–99 period. In fact, medicare spending barely rose, climbing less than 0.5 percent annually over this period. Aggressive efforts of the Health Care Financing Administra-

---

7. Between January 2, 1990, and July 1, 1999, the Dow Jones average rose 294 percent, the Standard and Poors 500 index by 284 percent, the Wilshire 5000 by 264 percent, and the New York Stock Exchange index by 229 percent.

tion to root out inappropriate and fraudulent charges, lower inflation, and underestimates of the severity of the BBA97 cuts may explain the sharper-than-expected slowdown. Medicaid spending growth slowed to an estimated 5.7 percent rate over the 1997–99 period. One explanation for this unanticipated slowdown is that the number of welfare recipients who are categorically eligible for medicaid has fallen more than was expected in the wake of the 1996 welfare reform act.[8] The rolls of the Temporary Assistance for Needy Families (TANF) program, which replaced Aid to Families with Dependent Children (AFDC), declined 40 percent and medicaid rolls fell by 14 percent between 1996, when the welfare bill was signed, and December 1998.

How Likely Are the Projected Surpluses?

Clearly, many factors—some attributable to policy decisions, others to luck—have transformed the gloomy budget outlook that prevailed in 1990 into the bright projections of 1999. But how realistic are these projections? Should discussions of future priorities assume that growing surpluses will be available to support new spending, tax cuts, or reductions in federal debt?

In the summer of 1999, OMB and CBO both projected that unified budget surpluses would cumulate to $2.9 trillion over the fiscal 2000–09 period if current policies were not changed (table 1-1). These projected surpluses would be significantly larger than the deficits accumulated over the 1988–97 period ($1,840 billion) but a bit less than the sum of the deficits incurred over the 1980–97 period ($3,097 billion). Just under two-thirds of the surpluses—about $1.9 trillion—projected for the next decade would be contributed by the social security program in the so called off-budget accounts. The surpluses in the balance of the budget—the on-budget accounts—would amount to about $1 trillion over the decade.

All such projections depend critically on assumptions about the performance of the future economy, the course of spending and tax legislation, and myriad noneconomic factors that affect the budget,

---

8. Most of those leaving the welfare rolls or not seeking welfare under the reformed system are thought to be eligible for medicaid benefits but, for a variety of reasons, do not enroll. For a discussion of this issue see Mann (1999).

Table 1-1. *Summer 1999 Budget Projections for Fiscal Years 1999–2009*
Billions of dollars

Budget review	Fiscal year projections			
OMB June 1999 mid-session review	1999	2000	2009	2000–09
Baseline total surplus[a]	$99	$142	$473	$2,926
On budget	−25	5	240	1,083
Off budget	124	137	233	1,843
CBO July 1999 budget update	1999	2000	2009	2000–09
Baseline total surplus[a]	$120	$161	$413	$2,896
On budget	−4	14	178	996
Off budget	125	147	235	1,901
Baseline assuming discretionary spending grows with inflation				
Total surplus	$120	$128	$274	$1,947
On budget	−4	−19	39	46
Off budget	125	147	235	1,901

Sources: OMB (1999); CBO (1999b); Crippen (1999).

a. Assumes that discretionary spending through 2002 does not exceed the caps established by the BBA97 and that after 2002 discretionary spending increases with inflation.

including such seemingly remote developments as state medicaid policy decisions and college tuition adjustments that would affect the revenue loss from the Hope and Lifetime Learning tax credits created by the TRA97.

Projecting the course of the economy two years out, let alone a decade into the future, is hazardous. Fortunately, accurate forecasts of the precise pattern of future business cycles are not essential if all one is seeking is a rough estimate of the likely budget situation over the course of a decade. If the average rates of economic growth, inflation, unemployment, and interest prove close to those assumed, the impact of the economy on the overall budget situation will be pretty much as projected.[9] In this respect, the economic assumptions used by OMB and

9. CBO estimates that after a decade (by 2009) a 0.1 percentage point lower annual rate of economic growth would reduce the projected surplus by $40 billion, a 1 percentage point higher inflation rate would increase the projected surplus by $117 billion, and a 1 percentage point higher interest rate would reduce the projected surplus by $20 billion. CBO (1999a, appendix C).

CBO seem reasonable.[10] While uncertain, they are similar to the consensus view of private sector economic forecasters. The projections of large and growing budget surpluses are, therefore, not the product of unduly rosy economic assumptions.

The same cannot be said, however, of the assumptions that the budget offices have made about the likely course of spending and tax policy. In accordance with the conventions of budget projections, the budget offices assume that tax policy and mandatory spending programs remain unchanged. This assumption is reasonable because the tax code and these programs do not have to be reauthorized periodically.

In the case of discretionary spending, which must be appropriated each year, the conventions of budget projections assume that such spending will stay within the legislated caps and will grow at the rate of inflation after the spending limits established in the BBA97 expire at the end of 2002. These assumptions are highly unrealistic. For them to be realized, Congress and the president would have to reduce real discretionary spending over the 2000–02 period by an average of 8 percent below the amount required to maintain 1999 levels of discretionary spending.[11] By 2002 spending would be almost 12 percent below the amount needed to maintain discretionary programs at their 1999 levels in the face of inflation. To maintain current real per capita discretionary spending would require 19 percent more discretionary spending in 2009 than the budget projections assume will be provided.

Faced with budget surpluses, neither Congress nor the president is likely to enforce such restraint on discretionary spending. Recent actions of lawmakers give no reason to question this judgment. Confronted by stringent discretionary spending caps for 1999, lawmakers broke the limits by designating some $21 billion as "emergency" discre-

10. Over the 1999–2009 period, CBO expects economic growth, inflation, unemployment, and interest rates to average 2.4, 2.5, 5.2, and 5.5 percent, respectively. The comparable assumptions underlying the OMB projections are 2.4, 2.5, 5.1, and 5.6 percent.

11. This represents a comparison of the discretionary spending caps with the 1999 spending level, including emergency spending, adjusted for inflation. Crippen (1999).

tionary spending.[12] To be sure, real discretionary spending was reduced some 11 percent between 1990 and 1998, but as noted previously, all of this reduction was in the defense accounts. Currently, the administration and most members of Congress from both parties now support increased real defense spending. If defense spending were just maintained at the 1999 real levels, nondefense discretionary spending would have to be reduced 18 percent below 1999 levels by 2002 to comply with the spending caps.

Achieving the much less ambitious goal of holding the growth of total discretionary spending roughly to the rate of inflation would reduce from $996 billion to a mere $46 billion the cumulative surplus projected by CBO for the non-social security portion of the budget over the 2000–09 period, and unified budget surpluses over this period would shrink from $2.9 trillion to $1.9 trillion (table 1-1). Meeting even this goal will be hard enough given population growth, expectations raised by budget surpluses, spending pressures built up from a decade of fiscal restraint, and the expiration of the spending caps after 2002.

The New Fiscal Policy Goal

Whether the cumulative non-social security surpluses over the next decade are close to $1 trillion or less than $50 billion is very important for discussions about national priorities. Between January 1998 and July 1999 a profound, but little noticed, shift occurred in the focus of fiscal policy. From 1969 until the president's 1998 state of the union address, lawmakers were primarily concerned with balance—or lack thereof—in the *unified* budget.[13] Merely achieving

12. If the supplemental appropriation approved in the spring of 1999 (P.L.106-31) and the 1999 outlay effects of the emergency appropriations for 1998 (P.L. 105-174) are added to the emergency appropriations contained in P.L. 105-277, the fiscal year 1999 budget contains $34.2 billion in emergency budget authority that will result in $18.9 billion in emergency outlays. Roughly $5 billion of these totals was disaster assistance to farmers, which is normally considered a mandatory, rather than a discretionary, spending.

13. Before 1969 there were separate "administrative" and "trust fund" budgets. Congress paid most attention to the administrative budget which differed from the current unified budget in several respects, the most important being that it excluded the social security program. The unified budget concept came from recommendations presented in the *Report of the President's Commission* (1967).

balance in the unified budget seemed unattainable for most of this period.

When lawmakers enacted the 1997 deficit reduction package, they cherished the hope that it would lead to tiny overall surpluses in 2002 and 2003—$1 billion and $5 billion—and larger ones thereafter. Yet many were skeptical because they considered the deep discretionary spending cuts required by the package to be unlikely, the sharp reductions in medicare's payments to providers to be unsustainable, and the packages's accounting gimmickery to be ephemeral.

Had history unfolded as lawmakers expected, a debate would probably have begun around 2001 concerning the uses to which the projected *unified* budget surplus should be put. But the budget situation quite unexpectedly improved so much that surpluses in the *non-social security accounts* became virtually certain before 2002 if tax and spending policies were left unchanged. Faced with this new budget reality, President Bill Clinton pledged in his 1998 state of the union address to "save social security first," before agreeing to any significant tax cuts or spending increases. Republicans agreed with the need to strengthen social security and, in spring 1999, responded to the president's challenge by offering various mechanisms—so-called lock box proposals—designed to ensure that all of the surpluses generated by social security would be devoted to reducing public debt. The president then endorsed this objective in his June 1999 *Mid-Session Review of the Fiscal 2000 Budget*. The upshot is a new consensus—that fiscal policy should aim to prevent deficits in the non-social security, or *on-budget*, accounts of the government.

If this consensus holds, what happens to discretionary spending will determine how much the nation will have available for cutting taxes, reforming entitlement programs, or reducing public debt below the level that will result if social security surpluses alone are devoted to this purpose. If the very tight lid on discretionary spending assumed in the budget offices' projections were sustained, close to $1 trillion would be available over the next decade to reduce taxes, expand and strengthen social security and medicare, or pay down debt. But such a policy would require significant reductions in discretionary programs, thereby setting priorities in a particular way. If discretionary spending grows at the rate of inflation, "on-budget" surpluses will almost vanish. In that case, lawmakers will not be able to cut taxes or strengthen entitlement programs unless they are willing to renege on their commitment to use all of the projected social security surpluses to pay down national debt. Similarly, if aggregate discretionary spending is permitted to grow more rapidly than inflation—say to accommodate increased procurement and readiness needs in defense, to boost funding for health research, or to augment spending on transportation infrastructure—taxes will have to be raised, entitlement programs cut, or social security surpluses diverted from debt repayment.

The Issues

In short, the budget debate *is* the debate on national priorities. The strong economy and arrival of the first budget surpluses since 1969 have transformed the debate. No longer do budget deficits and what to do about them dominate policy discussions. The end of deficits has freed policymakers to address new issues and confront old problems in ways that may cost more than was considered prudent in the lean and hungry deficit years.

The strong economy has reduced the importance of perennial issues involving personal economic security. Tight labor markets have allayed workers' concerns about finding or holding a job. With real wages rising across the board, concern over growing income disparities has abated. Nonetheless, income differences remain large, and the low earnings of the unskilled keep alive the debate about how much to raise the minimum wage. Although relatively low mortgage interest rates and rising incomes have pushed homeownership rates to an all-time high, homelessness remains a significant problem.

Cold war security matters have faded from the agenda, but Russia remains a potent and dangerously unstable nuclear power. New concerns have emerged, including potential threats from North Korea, Iraq, and other rogue states; regional conflicts on the Indian subcontinent and in the Balkans; civil wars in Africa; international terrorism; and economic instability in parts of Asia and Latin America that could affect otherwise sound economies.

Some divisive problems of the 1970s and 1980s have lost salience during the 1990s. Dropping rates of violent and property crime, which fell in 1998 to the lowest level since the government began collecting such data in 1973, has dulled the partisan and ideological edge of debates over criminal justice policy.[14] Welfare, long known as the Middle East of domestic policy, has become a back burner issue. The Personal Responsibility and Work Opportunity Act of 1996—the welfare reform legislation that replaced the Aid to Families with Dependent Children (AFDC) entitlement program with the Temporary Assistance for Needy Families (TANF) block grant program for states—resolved many of the more controversial matters, at least for a time. The unexpectedly sharp drop in the welfare rolls also helped to defuse the issue. By the end of 1998, the number of AFDC/TANF beneficiaries was down 46 percent from the 1994 peak; the number of food stamp recipients declined 33 percent over this period. In addition, the problem of teen pregnancy, which for years seemed to be unyielding, diminished modestly during the 1990s; between 1990 and 1996, the teen pregnancy rate fell by 17 percent.[15] Finally, the fiscal pressures that for many years led states and localities to beg Washington for federal assistance have eased dramatically. In fact, over the past several years, most states have boosted spending faster than inflation and cut taxes.

To be sure, hardy perennials of past debate remain at the forefront of policy discussions today. The large number of school dropouts and inadequately educated graduates remains troubling for a nation that hopes to lead the world during the twenty-first century. As a result, debate continues over the role the federal government should play in improving schools. The environment is far cleaner than it was a decade or two ago, but global warming, urban congestion, and suburban sprawl have joined pollution on the policy agenda. The number of Americans lacking health insurance continues to grow despite a slowdown in the growth of health premiums and record high employment, which is the source of insurance coverage for most people.

Free for the first time in three decades of the numbing effects of deficits, policymakers have turned their attention to several fundamental questions that will help to define the role of the public sector

14. U.S. Department of Justice (1999).

15. Alan Guttmacher Institute, "Teenage Pregnancy: Overall Trends and State-by-State Information," April 1999 (http//www.agi-usa.org [September 2, 1999]).

in the twenty-first century. Foremost among these is the question of what to do about social security and medicare, which provide income support and medical insurance for the aged and disabled. Action is essential to avoid financial insolvency during the first half of the twenty-first century when the baby boom generation retires. With surpluses projected for the non-social security accounts, a new financing option—adding general revenues to payroll taxes to support these social insurance programs—has emerged. Proposals to "privatize" these programs have also become part of the debate.

Projected surpluses have also revived tax cuts as a politically viable option. This debate is really about the appropriate size and scope of government. Federal receipts are estimated to reach 20.6 percent of GDP in 1999, the highest since the wartime year 1944 when receipts hit 20.9 percent of GDP. For some this is proof that tax burdens are too high and should be reduced. Others disagree, pointing out that the ratio is unusually high because the economy is booming, realized capital gains (which generate tax revenues but are not part of GDP) are soaring, and the nation is running surpluses for the first time in three decades, surpluses that should be used to pay down debt and strengthen the government's ability to meet the fiscal challenges it will face when the baby boom generation retires.

Chapter Summaries

While many of the problems of the previous two decades have dissolved or been reshaped by the nation's newfound prosperity, the new century holds sufficient challenges to test the imagination, creativity, and courage of American leaders to set national priorities for the year 2000 and beyond. The remaining chapters in this volume, which are summarized below, deal with some of the major issues facing policymakers and the nation at the turn of the century. These chapters lay out the dimensions of the problems and the policy options available for addressing them.

National Security and Foreign Aid

Spending on national defense is a smaller fraction of GDP—3 percent—than at any time since the outbreak of World War II. Real defense spending is about 25 percent below the average of the 1980s. Yet the annual U.S. defense budget of roughly $280 billion accounts for about one-third of global military outlays and is roughly five times larger than that of any other country. Russia and China together account for just over 10 percent of global spending, and the "rogue states" of Iran, Iraq, Libya, Cuba, and North Korea together spend less than 2 percent. However, as Michael O'Hanlon explains in chapter 2, U.S. defense spending is not necessarily excessive. The United States is the only country with major military commitments throughout the world, and its desire to prevail decisively with low casualties requires a substantial edge over potential foes.

After a decade of defense downsizing, most observers call for some increase. The debate is over how much. After a decade of small procurement budgets, the armed forces need to replace weapons and other hardware that are fast wearing out. Personnel cuts, base closures, and other economies may provide some small offsetting savings but with most of the post–cold war downsizing complete, there is little room for further savings in these areas.

While an increase in real defense spending would almost certainly be required to meet current procurement plans, that increase may not materialize if overall discretionary spending is held to the president's proposed fiscal 2000 budget or to the even more stringent congressional budget resolution for fiscal 2000. So the Pentagon may have to find ways to tighten its belt. Modest further cuts in manpower, as well as a partial restructuring of the military to help it handle the strains of frequent peacekeeping and crisis management operations, may be possible if the United States decides to maintain the capability to fight a two-war scenario less demanding than the two nearly simultaneous Desert Storm-like wars built into current plans. Furthermore, O'Hanlon suggests that the increase in procurement costs could be held down if the Pentagon refurbished existing systems or replaced them with similar equipment, rather than upgrading to far more expensive, next-generation weapon systems. In addition, the military should take advantage of the computer and electronics revolutions and purchase better munitions, communications systems, unmanned aerial vehicles, and advanced computer systems.

Like defense, the international affairs accounts have been cut deeply during the 1990s, although the end of the cold war did not measurably reduce the requirements for diplomacy or foreign aid. O'Hanlon acknowledges that foreign aid is often wasted but notes that recent research has confirmed that aid provided to countries with sound macroeconomic policies demonstrably increases their economic growth and reduces poverty. He suggests that the U.S. aid budget should be restored to roughly 1980s levels—an increase of about $3 billion annually—and focused on countries committed to reform.

International Trade

I. M. Destler notes a paradox in U.S. trade policy. During the 1970s and 1980s, the U.S. economy was troubled by inflation and high budget deficits. Nonetheless Congress gave successive presidents power to continue to negotiate reduced tariffs and liberalized trade rules with other countries under so-called fast-track authority, which required Congress to accept or reject the negotiated agreement without amendment. In the 1990s, by contrast, the economy is extremely robust, with stable prices and high employment. Increased trade and international competition have made large contributions to current U.S. economic strength. Yet Congress has denied President Clinton fast-track authority. It is vital to the future economic health of the United States, Destler argues, that Congress restore this authority.

When President Clinton entered office, the North American Free Trade Agreement (NAFTA) and global trade liberalization under the so-called Uruguay round of the General Agreement on Tariffs and Trade had already been negotiated. He fought hard for and won congressional ratification of both agreements, although the NAFTA success came only after the United States negotiated "side agreements" on labor and environmental issues. But since then, Congress has balked at extending "fast-track authority," thereby making it impossible for the president to bargain effectively with foreign governments, which are unwilling to commit to agreements that the U.S. Congress may subsequently modify. The disagreement derives from conflict between two groups in Congress. One fears that further trade liberalization will produce undesirable side effects—such as pressure on the wages of low-skilled U.S. workers, loss of U.S. employment, or unfair competition by foreigners with low labor or environmental standards. The other is unwilling to "encumber" trade negotiations with such matters, which they see as extraneous.

Meanwhile, the U.S. merchandise trade deficit has ballooned as the U.S. economy has boomed and the economies of its major trading partners have languished. The rising trade deficit has intensified concerns about the linkages among trade, labor standards, and the environment. Destler argues that these "trade and . . ." issues are real and must be addressed to reassure concerned members of Congress that such issues will not be neglected as the nation pursues freer trade.

The continued pursuit of trade liberalization is important because the U.S. economy is enormously flexible and gains much from the specialization that trade abets. It is no coincidence that the United States is exceptionally open and exceptionally rich. Besides making Americans better off, trade negotiations are an important component of U.S. political leadership, particularly in Latin America and China. And trade policy has substantial *domestic* political importance, as it symbolizes American attitudes toward engagement in the global economy.

To break the logjam, Destler calls upon President Clinton to initiate a three-pronged national dialogue. Working groups would be established to identify the specific negotiations to be authorized; to address labor, environmental, and other trade-related issues; and to design ways to help Americans who lose from globalization. The purpose of this effort would be avowedly political. Destler believes that common ground exists for additional trade liberalization, a process that has served the nation well for nearly half a century. Immediate approval of fast-track authority would be useful, but it is not necessary. What is needed urgently, Destler believes, is political leadership to begin the dialogue that will rediscover the currently silent, free trade majority.

The Future of the Family

Despite the nation's prosperity, children are increasingly at risk of growing up in economically or socially impoverished environments, which are associated with poor educational outcomes, high crime rates, and poor life prospects. Isabel V. Sawhill reports that almost one-third of children are born out-of-wedlock. Half of all marriages end in divorce. An estimated 60 percent of all children born in the 1990s will spend some time in a single-parent family. A higher proportion of young children than in the past live in one of two types of families: those started by poor, teenaged, unwed mothers who lack a high school degree and those headed by relatively affluent, well-educated married parents in their twenties or thirties. This bifurcation in family environments is already contributing to growing income inequality and could cast a dark shadow on the future. The increase of single-parent families has contributed importantly to the growth of child poverty and to escalating public costs for welfare, health care, social services, housing, and other forms of assistance.

Sawhill considers a variety of public policies to strengthen family ties, including changes in tax laws, benefit programs, and divorce laws; child care or other subsidies that might provide additional support to those raising children; and efforts to discourage people from having children before they are ready. She argues for reducing the marriage penalty in the earned income tax credit, for education to prepare people for marriage, for better child support enforcement, and for after school programs to reduce early childbearing.

Because full-time motherhood entails significant economic sacrifices for all but the affluent, child care subsidies can simultaneously improve the lot of single, working mothers and help vulnerable children enter school more ready to learn.

In the end, Sawhill emphasizes that government policies aimed at strengthening families are likely to have modest direct effects. But these direct effects are often amplified by the new messages such policies embody and by the tendency of even small changes in behavior to create their own momentum through a shift in cultural norms. Failure to recognize these indirect effects in the past may have made the tone of the policy debate in this area overly pessimistic about what government and nongovernment efforts can accomplish.

Income Inequality

Economic inequality has increased substantially during the past two decades. Adjusted for inflation, the average income of the one-fifth of families with the lowest incomes actually shrank between 1979 and 1997. But increased income disparities have not been driven solely by falling incomes of those at the bottom or by spectacular gains of those at the top. Rather, inequality has increased throughout the income distribution. Gary Burtless explains that this trend should concern the nation because growing disparities threaten political and social cohesion and could harm public health.

The sources of the increase in inequality are complex and not fully understood. Burtless estimates that greater earnings disparities, particularly among men, are responsible for roughly one-third of the increased inequality. The declining prevalence of husband-wife families accounts for another one-fifth. About one-eighth is related to the increased tendency of high-earning men and high-earning women to be married to each other. One-third of the increase in inequality is related to miscellaneous factors such as the growing inequalty and importance of nonwage income and a decline in the effectiveness of government assistance for the poor.

As Burtless explains, however, these explanations are mechanical. The underlying causes of growing inequality include technological change and globalization, which have boosted the demand for and wages of skilled and educated workers, and the erosion of family bonds. Why divorce has become more common and out-of-wedlock childbearing has increased remains largely a mystery.

Policy has not stood still in the face of the growing inequality. In recent years, low-income Americans have seen their income tax liabilities reduced or eliminated, and those with earnings have received more generous rebates from the earned income tax credit (EITC). Health insurance coverage for low-income children has been greatly expanded through medicaid and the Children's Health Insurance Program (CHIP). The availability of cash welfare benefits for low-income, working-age persons who are not disabled has been reduced and benefit levels have been cut.

Burtless judges that the United States is more likely than other advanced nations to accept increased inequality. Despite our limited tolerance for public sector action in this area, he urges that more should be done. Jobs paying a wage slightly below the minimum wage should be provided to some long-term unemployed and those being forced off the welfare rolls by time limits. A basic health insurance package should be generated for all children. Since health benefits constitute a significant share of total compensation for low-wage workers in firms that provide their workers with such coverage, this policy should boost the demand for and wages of such workers.

Providing Security for the Elderly and Disabled

Over the next four decades, the U.S. population will age rapidly. The population age 62 and over will double, and that age 85 and over will more than triple. The burden on future workers, from whose production must come the consumption for elderly and nonelderly alike, will increase. The aging population will also strain public budgets, particularly those of the social security and medicare programs.

Social security, which provides pensions to some 44 million elderly and disabled individuals, is enjoying surpluses now that are projected to continue for more than two decades. But the program faces a projected long-run deficit, necessitating some significant reforms before the exhaustion of the trust fund reserves, now anticipated in 2034. The sooner steps are taken to strengthen the program, Henry J. Aaron and Robert D. Reischauer argue, the easier and less disruptive they will be.

The authors examine three broad categories of reform: replacement of the current system in whole or in part with mandatory, individually owned savings accounts modeled on Individual Retirement Accounts (IRA), over which workers would exercise a good deal of control; replacement of the current system in whole or in part with mandatory, individually owned savings accounts modeled on 401(k) accounts, over which workers would have limited control; and strengthening the current system without reliance on individual accounts. They reject the approaches that rely on individual accounts, largely because such accounts cannot ensure basic income to retirees, their spouses, and dependents—the primary purpose of social security. Individual accounts would force workers to bear risks they are poorly positioned to handle and would be expensive to administer.

Projected budget surpluses have led members of both parties to propose using general revenues to strengthen social security. Aaron and Reischauer contrast three plans: President Clinton's proposal to divert surpluses to the social security trust fund and to invest a portion of those revenues in private equities; a proposal crafted by the chairman of the Committee on Ways and Means to use surpluses to finance deposits into individual accounts; and a bipartisan congressional proposal that would use surpluses only to ease the transition to a new system with individual accounts.

Medicare, which provides health insurance for the elderly and disabled, faces projected insolvency in 2015. Although the program has been an unquestioned success, it suffers from several deficiencies. Foremost among these is the program's outdated benefit package, which does not cover outpatient prescription drugs or cap out-of-pocket expenditures.

Three broad approaches have been proposed to reform medicare. The first is to strengthen and modernize medicare by expanding the benefit package, letting market forces rather than administrative mechanisms set the prices for services other than hospitals and physician services, and restraining the growth of hospital and physician fees through traditional mechanisms. A second approach would have government contribute up to a maximum amount toward the purchase of health care from the traditional fee-for-service system or a private health plan. Competitive defined benefits or "premium support," as this approach is called, would introduce competition that its advocates hope will dampen cost growth. Finally, some would like to replace medicare by diverting payroll taxes into savings accounts for each age group. These deposits plus investment earnings would be used to buy health insurance coverage during that age group's retirement.

A majority of the Bipartisan Commission on the Future of Medicare, as well as the president in his July 1999 medicare proposal, endorsed variations on the premium support approach. Both plans would let participants choose a benefit package that covers prescription drugs. The costs of such coverage would be subsidized for many or all participants. As Aaron and Reischauer explain, the plans put forward by the president and the majority of the commission illustrate how difficult it is to both deal with the deficiencies of the current medicare program and take steps to restrain the growth of its costs. They conclude that payroll taxes will almost certainly have to be raised or general fund support increased to sustain the program.

Long-term care is an important and expensive need of many of the elderly and disabled for which medicare provides only limited assistance. Medicaid is the nation's largest single source of support for such care, but only for those with low incomes and assets. Middle-income families must deplete their resources before they are eligible for the program. Substantial inequities exist because the generosity of medicaid's long-term care services varies significantly from state to state. The authors point out that there are no easy ways to help people pay for long-term care. The social insurance approach would be very costly, while tax subsidies to encourage people to buy long-term care insurance would likely be ineffectual.

Reischauer and Aaron conclude that failing to act soon will cause a problem that is manageable, if difficult today, to become unmanageable and divisive in the future.

Taxes

Despite seemingly endless tinkering over the years, almost everyone concurs that the tax system could be improved. Unfortunately, agreement about the nature and severity of the problems or what to do about them is elusive. After describing why federal taxes are so complex, how tax burdens are distributed, and the ways taxes affect economic growth, Henry J. Aaron, William Gale, and James Sly examine proposals for large tax cuts. They describe several arguments advocates make to justify tax cuts—that the government is taking in excess revenues, that Americans are overtaxed, that tax cuts would effectively reduce the size of government, and that cuts would promote economic growth—and show the weakness of each claim. Nonetheless Congress passed a large tax cut in the summer of 1999, which the president had neither signed nor vetoed as this book went to press. Should the bill become law, it would cut national saving and lavish large tax cuts on the wealthiest households. The authors argue that if taxes are to be cut, there are alternatives that would provide more relief to middle-income households and simplify the tax code more effectively than the proposal passed by Congress.

The chapter describes and evaluates different ways to modify the current tax system. Aaron and Gale focus on the panoply of targeted provisions that narrow and complicate the tax base, require increased rates on routine economic activities, mask true tax burdens and effective tax rates, and rarely achieve their goals. For the most part, the objectives sought through targeted provisions would be better addressed through direct expenditures, a course that would simplify and improve public understanding of the tax code. Better than adding to the menu of such special provisions—an approach that has many supporters in Congress and in the administration—would be curtailing them. For example, it would be possible to reduce complexity directly by converting deductions to 15 percent tax credits and using the revenue to cut rates or, if taxes are to be cut, by raising the standard deduction. They list other structural simplifications that could relieve many households of the need to file a tax return.

Expansive claims have been made on behalf of various fundamental tax reform plans that would replace the current system with a flat-rate consumption tax, with no credits or deductions. Fundamental reform retains many advocates although its popularity has waned since the mid-1990s. Radical reform would be subject to the same political constraints or trade-offs that currently plague tax policy. In particular, claims that fundamental reform could simplify taxes and spur economic growth are overstated because many superficially appealing simplifications would produce untoward consequences. Curtailing deductions for mortgage interest and charitable contributions, for example, could cause declines in housing prices and charitable donations. Furthermore, complex provisions to ease the transition would be inescapable. As a result, tax rates would be higher than flat tax supporters acknowledge.

Incremental reform is less dramatic but more promising. Specific steps could ease compliance and enforcement, finance rate cuts, and promote economic growth. Because every tax reform creates losers as well as winners, selective tax reductions would help make reform politically palatable. For that reason, as well as for reasons of fiscal prudence, large tax cuts at this time would be unwise. The nation should instead husband its resources—not only to meet problems related to population aging but also to accumulate a down payment on genuine tax reform.

Education

Since the mid-1960s, federal elementary and secondary education policy has aimed to ensure equality of opportunity. It has contributed significantly to the removal of legal barriers based on race, poverty, ethnic origin, and handicap. Yet, Diane Ravitch emphasizes, student performance is quite disappointing. U.S. students lag behind those in most other countries—particularly at the secondary education level—and do not measure up to domestic standards. The performance of black and Hispanic students is particularly disappointing.

A starting point for raising educational achievement is improving the qualifications of teachers, many of whom have neither a major nor a minor in the subject they teach. The federal government should support programs to strengthen teachers' knowledge of their academic field and help states develop instruments to test teachers' subject-matter knowledge.

The governance of education is undergoing major change in response to widespread bureaucratization and poor student performance. One strategy for change is the introduction of competition and market pressures. A prime example is income-tested vouchers—scholarships that poor parents can use to pay for tuition at public or nonpublic schools. Vouchers command headlines and raise blood pressure among advocates and opponents alike. Evidence of the educational outcomes of voucher programs remains a matter of intense dispute. Meanwhile, the proliferation of charter schools is revolutionizing educational governance. Charter schools are public schools that agree to be held accountable for results in exchange for autonomy on how those results are produced, as well as waivers from most regulations other than those governing health, safety, and civil rights. They are popular, in part, because they promise to reduce bureaucratic micromanagement, trim overhead costs, and dedicate a greater proportion of funds to actual instruction. Contract management represents another modification of traditional school governance. The actual effects of each of these innovations in school governance are far from settled.

In this environment, it would be premature for the federal government to promote any one approach to school governance, but the need for experimentation and evaluation is clear. For that reason, Ravitch argues, the federal government should make sure that aid provided under such federal programs as Title I, special education, and bilingual education follow the student, thereby removing any bias in federal policy toward current school governance. The federal government should also streamline regulations that now require costly and burdensome bookkeeping by school districts to comply with federal grants for elementary and secondary education, special education, and handicapped students.

The bilingual education program has been a particular disappointment. It was intended to help students who speak a language other than

English—usually Spanish—make the transition into English language instruction. In fact, it often obstructs acquisition of fluency in English. The drop-out rate of Hispanic students is higher than that of any other major group. Ravitch argues that the federal program should be rechristened as the English-language Literacy Program and that federal grants to states and school districts should emphasize that the primary goal of the program is to help children gain proficiency in English.

Head Start is at once the most popular educational program and, in Ravitch's view, the most poignant lost opportunity. Enrollments are high and growing, and congressional support is overwhelming. The program provides important health, nutrition, social, and psychological services to poor children. But Head Start teachers are not well trained to help children gain an educational head start. Additional Head Start spending, Ravitch maintains, should go to boost teachers' salaries and improve their training rather than to increase enrollment. By setting educational standards for preschool children, the Head Start program could better fulfill the promise of its name.

The major challenge of federal elementary and secondary education policy is to operate effectively within the limitations of the federal role imposed by the fact that federal spending constitutes only 10 percent of the roughly $300 billion spent on such education. Primary responsibility for precollege education under our constitutional system resides with state and local governments. But the federal role, if limited, is nonetheless vital. The issue of testing is illustrative. The federal government cannot and should not set educational standards for hundreds of thousands of schools and tens of millions of students. But it can and should, Ravitch maintains, set achievement standards for those who receive federal financial aid to attend college. In this way, the federal government could send a clear message that "achievement counts" and bolster the efforts of parents and teachers to improve education throughout the United States.

Metropolitan America

The dominant trend in metropolitan America is rapid decentralization. Outer suburbs have attracted population and employment, leaving behind many central cities and their adjoining older suburbs. In recent years, citizens and public officials have come to recognize that these growth patterns impose high costs—congestion, loss of open space, and school overcrowding in the newer suburbs, and poverty, fiscal distress, and lack of job growth in the older communities—and that a range of federal and state spending, tax, and regulatory policies are contributing to these patterns. Bruce Katz explores the metropolitan agenda that is emerging in reaction to these problems, an agenda the author hopes will reshape urban and suburban growth.

In some areas, new metropolitan coalitions are emerging. These coalitions are pursuing a range of policy reforms at the regional and state levels to curb sprawl and promote reinvestment in older communities. These reforms include the enactment of state growth management statutes, tax and bond initiatives to acquire open space, "smart growth" legislation to steer infrastructure funds toward older communities, pooling of metropolitan resources to promote fiscal equity between jurisdictions, and the creation of new metropolitan entities to govern issues of regional concern.

Katz argues that the federal government should support this new metropolitan agenda in several ways. It should modify existing policies that facilitate sprawl and concentrate poverty. It should instill metropolitan governance or, at a minimum, metropolitan thinking into a wide range of federal programs and policies. The administration of federal transportation, homeownership, affordable housing, and work force programs should reflect the fact that they have metropolitan effects. Finally, the federal government should investigate whether particular parts of metropolitan areas are treated fairly in the allocation of federal resources, particularly those that create wealth and leverage private sector investments.

Crime

Until the 1960s, congressional conservatives, especially those from the South who feared civil rights legislation, stymied active federal involvement in fighting crime. Then, starting in the 1960s, Congress passed not only civil rights legislation but also a lengthy series of bills to fight violent crime, improve information on crime, provide financial assistance to crime-fighting activities in states and localities, control gun sales, build prisons, and establish mandatory sentencing. The reason for this legislation was obvious—crime was on the rise, and the electorate was frightened and angry. Today crime rates are falling, in part for demographic reasons, in part because of more stringent law enforcement, and in part because of changed social and economic conditions. John DiIulio Jr. argues that it is time for the federal government to take stock of the role it has assumed in fighting crime. Furthermore, he believes that the federal government should not extend the law enforcement initiatives it has adopted in recent years.

One clear success for federal policy has been improvement in the accuracy of crime statistics, although further improvements are possible and desirable. Crime continues to be undercounted, as it always has been. The solution, unsurprisingly, is more money and more public support for data-gathering efforts by the responsible agencies: the Bureau of Justice Statistics and the Federal Bureau of Investigation.

Perhaps the most striking developments in criminal justice in recent years have been the proliferation of prisons (both federal and state), the large increase in the number of inmates, and the increased average duration of incarceration. Contrary to the beliefs of some, violent criminals, not petty drug offenders, make up most of the increased prison population, although even now, many violent offenders never spend time in prison. Growing rates of incarceration have contributed in some measure to the fall in crime rates, for the simple reason that while in prison inmates cannot commit crimes against the general population.

However, with roughly two million people in prison, it is time to recognize that measures other than a further increase in the prison population are in order. Putting violent and habitual offenders behind bars is one thing; insisting that every convicted felon spend every sentenced minute behind bars is quite another. In particular, incarceration of drug offenders without treatment is bad social policy. DiIulio reiterates a recommendation he made in the 1992 edition of *Setting Domestic Priorities*: the federal government should mandate that all state correctional systems provide drug treatment programs similar to those offered prisoners in the federal system, and that the federal government fully pay for these programs. DiIulio also recommends that the federal sentencing grid for drug offenders be replaced by antidrug policies and advisory guidelines that restore a degree of judicial discretion to federal judges in drug cases. The federal government should also provide support for intensive, coerced, community-based abstinence programs for all probationers—state and federal—with a history of substance abuse.

DiIulio devotes particular attention to the problem of youth crime. While it has diminished in recent years, he is not sanguine about the future. The population in the crime-prone late teens will increase, and crime may also rise. "Getting tough" on juvenile offenders—that is, treating them like adult criminals—has not had a major effect on how young offenders are actually treated, in large part because no state has had the stomach to treat more than a few young people in this fashion. For now, the best federal policy, in DiIulio's view, would be to monitor juvenile crime rates and let states and localities determine how best to deal with juvenile offenders. In the end, DiIulio believes, the nation should acknowledge the ancient wisdom that chronic delinquency usually has its origins in early childhood experiences; that most juveniles who engage in frequent or serious crimes against persons and property usually come from families characterized by violence and dysfunction; that the presence of loving, responsible adults to teach children right from wrong reduces criminal propensities among youth; and that the absence of such adults makes it more likely that children who might otherwise simply be aggressive will become criminals.

The Environment

Paul R. Portney reviews the progress that has been made and the problems that remain in environmental policy thirty years after the creation of the Environmental Protection Agency (EPA) and Council on Environmental Quality and the expansion of the Clean Air Act of 1963. Without question, the quality of the ambient environment has improved. The nation's rivers, lakes, and coastal waters are cleaner now than in the past. As Portney points out, environmental policy owes its successes to broad and consistent public support for environmental protection. Nevertheless, significant problems remain, particularly in nonpoint source pollution, such as runoff from farms and city streets.

As government involvement in regulating the environment has increased, so too has the size and budget of the EPA, the United States' largest regulatory agency. But as Portney explains, most of the cost of environmental regulation is paid not by government but by those who must comply with federal rules and regulations. These costs are large,

difficult to measure, and outside fiscal restraints, but should be balanced against the considerable economic and social benefits of a cleaner
environment.

Environmental policy has evolved in several directions that Portney
finds promising. It has moved from prescriptive, technology-based regulation to market-oriented approaches that give polluters incentives to
clean up. It has increased emphasis on environmental reporting, which
has added to public information about emissions. Many businesses
have reacted to the disclosure of this information by voluntarily reducing their pollution to show that they are good stewards of the environment. Finally, the EPA is increasingly sharing responsibility for
environmental issues with other government departments and with
state agencies. Because state regulatory capacity has increased and the
nature of many environmental problems are localized, Portney suggests
that a thoughtful reappraisal of "who should do what" in the environmental arena is in order.

The complex and controversial issue of global climate change is likely
to be a major focus of environmental policy in the coming decades.
Portney believes that it will be difficult to persuade Congress to move
aggressively because of uncertainty about global warming trends and
the high cost of modifying emissions that are thought to promote
warming. Nevertheless, the consequences of global warming could be
very serious and difficult to reverse. It is therefore urgent to narrow
the uncertainty about the size of this problem and the costs of addressing it and to develop a consensus around appropriate remediation.

The Changing Shape of Government

During the past fifteen years, the federal bureaucracy has undergone the
most dramatic reshaping in administrative history. Deep cuts have been
made in both the civil service and defense contractor work forces. Overall, federal employment has been reduced by almost 400,000 positions.
The cuts have been much deeper in the Department of Defense than
in the domestic agencies. They also have been deeper at the bottom of
the pyramid of government jobs than at the top.

As Paul Light explains, these cuts reflected no administrative strategy
other than reducing the total headcount of the federal civil service. For
the most part, the work force was downsized through attrition. No

work force planning system existed to enable those responsible for downsizing to identify jobs peripheral to the government's core missions. As a result, the cuts were not targeted on deadwood, inefficiencies, or duplicative activities. By cutting as much muscle as fat, the downsizing may well have undermined the federal government's ability to meet its future missions.

Pressures for further downsizing are likely to reappear following the 2000 presidential election, as candidates vie with one another over who can cut government most. Care is warranted to ensure that additional force reductions do not jeopardize government's ability to provide essential services and reduce even further the public's faith in the public sector.

Restructuring Government

Shortly after taking office, the Clinton administration launched a major effort to "reinvent" the federal government. The administration pledged "a government that works better and costs less." Despite cynical observations of many critics, the administration not only downsized the federal work force but also reshaped the government through tactics ranging from procurement reform to improved customer service.

But, as Donald Kettl points out, substantial work remains undone. The civil service was not reformed because the administration calculated that it stood little chance of moving such legislation through Congress. Instead, the administration concentrated on what it—and millions of federal workers—could do on their own. The result was an incremental strategy in which, according to Kettl, Vice President Al Gore took strong, consistent, and surprisingly personal leadership.

As the "reinventing government" process unfolded, the administration found itself caught in tough political battles over the size of government. While the work force was smaller, government spending continued to grow, and citizens gained little sense that government was "smaller." And while the performance of many government programs unquestionably improved, some agencies, like the Internal Revenue Service (IRS), suffered embarrassing attacks for its poor service. Despite its enormous efforts, the administration won few political kudos, according to Kettl. However, the inescapable pressure to improve the government's productivity—squeezing more services out of less money—has made reinvention a permanent movement. Indeed, that truth frames the basic dilemma of the reinvention movement: elected officials can expect little political gain, even when progress is clear. Public perceptions may be influenced more dramatically by failures, such as the IRS's abuse of taxpayers, than by the successes, which are rarely flashy or newsworthy. At the same time, politicians have little alternative but to continue the reinvention effort.

Campaign Finance Reform

No aspect of our democracy is subject to more withering criticism than the manner in which election campaigns are financed. Yet few areas of policy seem less amenable to consensus building and legislative resolution. Thomas E. Mann describes the collapse of the comprehensive campaign finance regulation enacted in reaction to the scandals surrounding the 1972 election. By 1996 the money chase was unbridled. The author analyzes the chronic problems with money and politics—politicians' need for money, conflicts of interest, inequities in access and influence, the lack of competition, and weak enforcement—and the more critical ailments associated with soft money and election-oriented issue advocacy.

Mann critically reviews three ambitious proposals for reforming the system—full public financing, complete deregulation, and a jurisprudential alternative to the Supreme Court decision, *Buckley* v. *Valeo*, which ruled that legislated limits on campaign spending were unconstitutional. He then outlines a more incremental agenda that would adjust the current regulatory system rather than replace it. That agenda includes abolishing or strictly limiting soft money, making election-oriented issue advocacy subject to federal regulations regarding contributions and disclosure, raising contribution limits to account for the inflation since the limits were established, freeing political parties to play a more active and constructive role on behalf of their candidates, providing public subsidies to congressional candidates, improving disclosure of contributions and expenditures, and strengthening enforcement of existing laws.

Reformers face daunting political obstacles to enacting new campaign finance law: politicians' self-interest, low public salience, partisanship, potential Senate filibusters, and limits imposed by the courts.

In addition, conflicts among desirable goals produce legitimate disagreement over how best to proceed. Under these circumstances, Mann
concludes that the best hope is not a solution to the campaign finance
problem but a continuous effort to manage it as well as possible, given
the complex constraints, rapidly changing environment, and the other,
sometimes competing, goals of the political system.

References

Congressional Budget Office. 1999a. *The Economic and Budget Outlook: Fiscal
    Years 2000–2009*.
———. 1999b. *The Economic and Budget Outlook: An Update* (July 1).
Crippen, Dan L. 1999. "Statement on the Mid-Session Review of the Fiscal
    Year 2000 Budget before the Senate Committee on the Budget, July 21."
    106 Cong. 1 sess. Government Printing Office.
General Accounting Office. 1993. *A Glossary of Terms Used in the Federal Bud-
    get Process*, revised (January).
Gordon, Robert J. 1999. "Has the "New Economy" Rendered the Productivity
    Slowdown Obsolete?" Paper prepared for the CBO Panel of Economic
    Advisors meeting (June).
Mann, Cindy. 1999. *Promoting Medicaid Enrollment for Children Who Are
    Moving In and Out of the TANF System*. Washington: Center on Budget and
    Policy Priorities (March).
Office of Management and Budget. 1999. *Mid-Session Review, Budget of the
    United States Government, Fiscal Year 2000* (June 28).
Report of the President's Commission on Budget Concepts. 1967. Government
    Printing Office (October).
U.S. Department of Justice. 1999. National Crime Victimization Survey for
    1998.

PART I

The International Challenges

MICHAEL O'HANLON 2

Defense and Foreign Policy: Time to End the Budget Cuts

SPENDING ON NATIONAL DEFENSE and international affairs is down sharply from cold war levels. Nonetheless, the United States retains— without close rival—the strongest and most influential military force in the world. With the end of the cold war, continued large defense expenditures might seem unwarranted. But they are needed if the United States is to remain capable of deterring, and if necessary defeating, aggressors around the world. Even if the United States were not militarily dominant, peace would probably endure among the world's major Western powers. But without U.S. power, Persian Gulf oil supplies could be jeopardized, more countries would feel the need to acquire nuclear weapons (because they would not be able to count on the United States to help preserve stability in their neighborhoods), and the likelihood of war would increase in such places as the Korean peninsula.

Concluding that U.S. military strength is desirable does not answer the question of how much the United States should spend on its armed forces. Many are now arguing that U.S. military responsibilities require increased defense spending. Such increases, however, are unnecessary. Although the Pentagon's current plans for purchases of advanced

The author appreciates the contributions of Julien Hartley, Brian Finlay-Dick, and Dov Zakheim to this chapter.

weaponry would require increased spending, those Pentagon plans are too ambitious for an era in which no country has, or is likely in the medium-term future to have, the potential to challenge American military supremacy. In this environment, simpler equipment will frequently do. Moreover, rapid advances in electronics and in precision munitions mean that the United States can, in many cases, improve its military capabilities impressively without buying "next-generation" fighter aircraft, ships, and submarines that often cost twice as much as systems now in use.

It is fortunate that maintaining U.S. global military commitments is possible without major spending increases because the added defense spending the president and some members of Congress have been promoting in 1999 may not come to pass. Democracies at peace seldom launch military buildups—particularly when their armed forces are already the best and most expensive in the world by far. The desire of Republicans to cut taxes and of Democrats to raise spending on such functions as education and the environment place competing demands on available resources and thereby jeopardize increases in defense spending. In fact, despite all the pro-Pentagon rhetoric, real defense spending in 2000 will probably be less than it was in 1999. Increases planned for future years may not actually be requested when those future years roll around.

Cuts in spending on foreign aid and diplomacy have already gone too far. They have declined proportionately by nearly as much as defense since the end of the cold war, although the fall of the Soviet Union cut the Pentagon's global responsibilities far more sharply than it reduced the costs of diplomatic representation and U.S. interests in providing foreign assistance. Because expenditures on these accounts are less than one-tenth of those on defense, they can be increased by a hefty percentage without causing major fiscal strain.

Advocates of many national interests will seek a piece of any budget surplus that is not devoted to reducing national debt. Other chapters in this book show that some increases in domestic spending are warranted. At the same time, foreign policy activities are too important to slight and do have a fair claim to a modest piece of the anticipated surplus.

The Budget Facts

After constituting more than half of federal outlays in the early cold war decades, total U.S. spending on foreign policy has declined sharply.

Figure 2-1. *U.S. Spending on National Defense, 1962–2004*

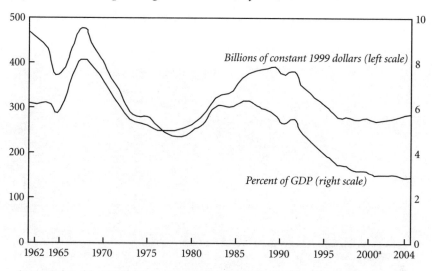

Source: *Budget of the United States Government; Historical Tables, Fiscal Year 2000,* pp. 118, 120.
a. Figures from 2000 onward are the president's estimates based on the fiscal year 2000 budget proposal.

Spending on foreign policy now constitutes just one-sixth of total federal spending, down from 10 percent of GDP in the Eisenhower, Kennedy, and Johnson years to just over 3 percent today.[1] National security spending in 1999, including the nuclear weapons activities of the Department of Energy, was about $280 billion, $50 billion (all figures in constant dollars unless otherwise noted) less than the cold war average (1951 through 1990) and almost $100 billion less than the 1980s levels (figure 2-1). Proportional cuts in international affairs spending—the sum total of development aid, UN dues and other fees, U.S. overseas diplomatic missions, overseas broadcasting, and security aid to places like the the Middle East, Bosnia, and Russia—have been nearly as large in the 1990s as those for defense (figure 2-2). Total spending in 1999 was $19.6 billion, down from an average of $21 billion since the 1960s and nearly $25 billion in the 1980s (all figures in constant 1999 dollars unless otherwise noted).

1. Foreign policy spending is not defined officially anywhere in the federal budget. In this chapter, I treat it as the sum of the national defense or "050" and international affairs or "150" budget functions.

Figure 2-2. *U.S. Spending on International Affairs, 1962–2004*

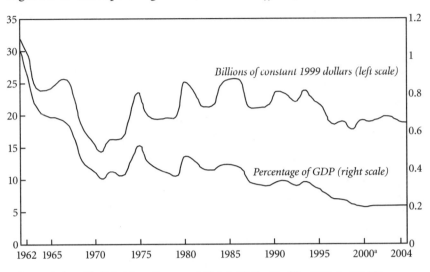

Source: *Budget of the United States Government, Historical Tables, Fiscal Year 2000,* pp. 117, 120.
a. Figures from 2000 onward are the president's estimates based on the fiscal year 2000 budget proposal.

Over the next five years President Clinton's year 2000 budget calls for an increase in annual defense spending to $295 billion but a decrease in outlays for foreign aid and diplomacy to just over $18 billion a year. The intended increase in defense spending dates from early 1999, when the Clinton administration boosted real defense outlays by $112 billion for the years 2000 through 2005.[2] It may not be enough to fund the Pentagon's weapons modernization agenda, however.

U.S. Military Strategy Today

The United States has no close rival as the world's dominant military power. Its defense spending is at least four times that of either Russia or China and remains more than 80 percent as large as during the cold war (table 2-1). Why is it necessary to spend so much?

2. That is to say, the 2000 budget plan contains $112 billion more in scheduled spending than the 1999 plan it superseded. Of the total, $84 billion reflects increases in nominal projected budgets, while $28 billion flows from reduced estimates of future inflation rates.

Table 2-1. *Global Distribution of Military Spending, 1998*

Countries	Defense spending (billions of dollars)	Share of global total (percent)
United States and its major security partners		
United States	270.5	33.7
NATO (not including the United States)[a]	185.8	23.2
Major Pacific allies[b]	64.1	8.0
Other allies[c]	34.0	4.2
Other friends[d]	53.0	6.6
Others		
Russia	64.0	8.0
China	36.6	4.6
"Rogue states"[e]	13.4	1.7
Remaining Asian countries	48.5	6.0
Remaining European countries	12.5	1.6
Remaining Middle Eastern and North African countries	11.4	1.4
Others[f]	8.4	1.0
Global total	802.2	100.0

Source: International Institute for Strategic Studies ([IISS], 1998, pp. 293–300); O'Hanlon (1998a, p. 29).

a. NATO total includes Poland, Hungary, and the Czech Republic.

b. Japan, South Korea, and Australia.

c. New Zealand, Thailand, Philippines, and the Rio Pact countries minus Cuba (including all South American countries except Belize, Guyana, and Suriname, and also four Caribbean islands or island groups: the Bahamas, the Dominican Republic, Haiti, and Trinidad and Tobago).

d. Austria, Finland, Ireland, Sweden, Switzerland, Israel, Egypt, Jordan, Kuwait, Oman, Qatar, and Saudi Arabia.

e. Cuba, North Korea, Iran, Iraq, and Libya.

f. Principally African and Caribbean countries.

The answer is that the United States is the world's only global military power, and it is in the nation's—and the world's—interest that the United States remain a global power. It is both costly and vitally important for the United States to keep strong alliance relationships in good working order, retain the capacity to respond to serious crises or wars wherever they might occur, and be prepared to use the nation's armed forces to promote values that undergird American society and foreign policy. The fact that the United States alone accepts such a broad range of responsibilities means that direct comparisons of its defense budget with those of other countries are of limited value.

The regions of most immediate security concern to the United States are the Persian Gulf and Korean peninsula. The United States and many other countries are heavily dependent on Persian Gulf oil. They also have a major interest in restraining nuclear proliferation and preserving general stability on the Korean peninsula. These are also places where Washington has long-standing security commitments to valued and loyal allies.[3] In neither of these regions would any future conflicts likely require as many American forces as Desert Storm. But a war in either place could prove challenging, particularly if an adversary used weapons of mass destruction or obtained the ability to impede the U.S. military's deployment to the conflict through effective use of cruise missiles, sea mines, or terrorism.[4]

Major conflicts could also arise elsewhere. A war against China over Taiwan would pose enormous dangers. The odds of such war will be smallest if the United States continues to pledge to defend Taiwan only against unprovoked attack, in my judgment. A stronger U.S. commitment to Taiwan might embolden Taiwan to move toward independence and needlessly create a situation fraught with danger. Regardless of the deterrence policy adopted, however, U.S. military capabilities should remain robust enough to prevail in this contingency even as China modernizes its armed forces.

U.S. military strength also helps create and sustain a climate of stability and trust among the major powers. Much is often made of the fact that democracies tend not to go to war and that the United States should therefore continue to do what it can to promote democracy in as many countries as possible. But an equally compelling lesson of history is that international systems featuring only one or two major aggregations of power tend to be the most stable. They reduce the paranoia countries feel about their neighbors and potential rivals and mitigate the pressures many countries might feel to build their own nuclear weapons arsenals. The current dominance of the Western alliance— with two-thirds of all military spending and four-fifths of world

3. Vickers and Kosiak (1997); O'Hanlon (1998a),
4. Krepinevich Jr. (1996).

Table 2-2. *U.S. Military Personnel Overseas*
Thousands

Region	1989[a]	1998	Percentage change
Germany	249	70	−72
Other European countries	71	42	−41
Europe, afloat	21	4	−81
South Korea	44	37	−16
Japan	50	40	−20
Other Pacific	16	1	−94
Pacific, afloat, including			
southeast Asia	25	18	−28
Latin America/miscellaneous	34	48	41
Total	510	260	

Source: Cohen (1999, app., table C-2).

a. Figures for 1990 are not used because they reflect the Desert Storm buildup. Therefore, 1989 figures are used as a more typical late cold war benchmark. All figures are for the ends of the respective fiscal years (September 30).

economic production—is conducive to international stability and should be sustained.

The U.S. military is an important factor contributing to the maintenance of a peaceful international system. With its overseas deployments and commitments the United States holds together an alliance system of dozens of countries (table 2-2). If the United States did not play an active role, the alliance system would exist more on paper than in real military terms. And paper alliances are often paper tigers when the chips are down.

The U.S. Military Today

Current U.S. defense policy is based on the 1997 *Quadrennial Defense Review* (QDR).[5] It fine-tuned earlier Clinton and Bush administration defense reviews with similar strategic frameworks (though the Bush review kept a force 15 percent larger and more expensive). This review, led by William Cohen, examined a wide range of military scenarios to assist in determining defense spending and force structure for the U.S.

5. Cohen (1997).

Table 2-3. *Department of Defense Personnel*
Thousands

Personnel	1990	1999	QDR[a]	Percent change, 1990–99	Percent change, QDR goal versus 1990
Total active duty	2,069	1,390	1,360	–33	–34
U.S. Air Force	539	366	339	–32	–37
U.S. Army	750	480	480	–36	–36
U.S. Navy	583	372	369	–36	–37
U.S. Marine Corps	197	172	172	–13	–13
Selected reserves	1,128	877	835	–22	–26
Civilians	1,102	724	640	–34	–42

Sources: Cohen, (1999, app. table C-1; 1997, p. 31); O'Hanlon (1998a, p. 7).
a. 1997 *Quadrennial Defense Review.*

defense establishment. The most demanding plausible scenario was a situation in which wars occurred simultaneously on the Korean peninsula and in the Persian Gulf region. But the need to be able to sustain an overseas presence in Europe, Japan, and the Western Pacific, to maintain a nuclear force, and to continue a vigorous research and development program also drive up defense requirements and costs.

Under the QDR, U.S. military force levels will soon be a full one-third smaller than they were during the cold war. The active duty force will decline to 1.36 million from over 2 million troops in 1990 (table 2-3).[6] Most major parts of the force structure are declining anywhere from 25 percent to 45 percent (table 2-4). The QDR calls for streamlining several major military modernization programs but canceled none. For example, the U.S. Air Force's F-22 Raptor fighter program was cut by about 100 planes to 339 aircraft. Comparable proportionate cuts were made in the U.S. Navy's cheaper but less technologically capable F/A-18 E/F Super Hornet fighter and attack jet, which is now to number somewhere between 550 and 785 planes. The U.S. Marine Corps V-22 tilt-rotor transport aircraft program is now to involve 360 rather than 425 planes (the Pentagon's plans for each of these programs in 2000 is shown in table 2-5).

6. Cohen (1997, p. 31).

Table 2-4. *Major Elements of U.S. Military Force Structure*

Service unit[a]	1990	1999	QDR plan[b]
U.S. Army			
Active divisions	18	10	10
Reserve brigades	57	42	30
U.S. Navy			
Aircraft carriers (active/reserve)	15/1	11/1	11/1
Air wings (active/reserve)	13/2	10/1	10/1
Attack submarines	91	56	50
Surface combatants	206	116	116
U.S. Air Force			
Active fighter wings	24	12+	12+
Reserve fighter wings	12	7+	8
Reserve air defense squadrons	14	4	4
Bombers (total)	277	190	187
U.S. Marine Corps			
U.S. Marine expeditionary forces (active/ reserve)	3/1	3/1	3/1

Sources: Cohen (1999, chp.5; 1997, pp. 30, 33); Ferry (1995, pp. 275, D-1); IISS (1990, pp. 17–27); O'Hanlon (1998a, p. 13).

a. The typical division contains three brigades as well as additional combat and support equipment; a U.S. Marine expeditionary force is composed of a division plus an air wing.

b. 1997 *Quadrennial Defense Review.*

The QDR recognized that the Department of Defense still maintains too many bases. Although the number of military personnel is down more than 30 percent, the number of major domestic bases is being cut only 20 percent. The QDR therefore rightly recommended closing more bases—two more rounds, in 1999 and 2001, on top of the four rounds undertaken since 1988—and privatizing various defense support functions. Faced with congressional resistance to these base closures, the Pentagon has since proposed that subsequent rounds occur in 2001 and 2005. Some in Congress have correctly criticized the Clinton White House for politicizing the base closure process by electing to keep open two facilities that had been slated for closure. Nevertheless, Congress ultimately must authorize these fifth and sixth rounds. There is no serious military argument against additional base closings, and the Pentagon badly needs the

Table 2-5. *Proposed Funding for Major Platforms, RDT&E and Procurement Funding, Fiscal Year 2000*

Millions of dollars

Service unit	Number	Total request
U.S. Air Force		
C-17 Transport	15	3,561.9
F-16 Fighter	10	440.8
F-22 Fighter	6	3,074.3
B-2 Bomber	. . .	374.6
E-8 Joint STARS Aircraft	1	483.0
Milstar satellite	. . .	361.3
JPATS	21	121.7
Joint strike fighter (RDT&E only)[a]	. . .	235.4
Total		8,653.0
U.S. Army		
AH-64D helicopter	. . .	773.5
RAH-66 helicopter	. . .	427.1
Total		1,200.6
U.S. Navy (includes U.S. Marine Corps)		
DDG-51 destroyer	3	2,928.0
New attack submarine	n/a	1,105.7
F/A 18E/F fighter	36	3,066.3
Trident II ballistic missile	12	537.0
E-2C early warning aircraft	3	411.6
JPATS[b]	8	45.1
Joint strike fighter (RDT&E only)[a]	. . .	241.5
Total		8,335.2

Source: Office of the Undersecretary of Defense (1999b).
a. Research, development, test, and evaluation.
b. Joint primary aircraft training system.

nearly $3 billion a year in savings that will result when they are completed.

The Pentagon should implement additional reforms that promise to save money too, but achieving these savings will be slow and tedious. Privatization will not be a panacea for the upcoming defense budget crunch, as the Pentagon itself has increasingly acknowledged in the last year.[7] Reforms in procurement of weapons and other supplies are

7. Office of the Secretary of Defense (1999).

also needed, and some have already occurred. For example, inexpensive defense purchases can now be made directly through the use of special credit cards rather than necessitating elaborate paperwork trails. Commercial electronics and communications systems are generally technologically ahead of defense-specific systems these days and can often be incorporated into the force at lower cost. But large savings should not be expected. Modern weapons are innately expensive. Acquisition reform is needed, but it too is incapable of putting the Pentagon's books in balance.

Readiness

In the course of 1998, military readiness—always a hot-button issue politically—became a major subject of contention between the Clinton administration and Congress. Ultimately concern over the matter galvanized political momentum in favor of an increase of nearly $9 billion in the 1999 defense budget (though only about a third of that money was focused on readiness; much of the rest was a response to the Kenya and Nairobi terrorist bombings and was focused on improving intelligence).

The term "military readiness" is used in different ways. The simplest standard of readiness is whether an individual unit measures up to its own potential. Readiness does not refer to the overall size or structure of the armed forces. Nor does it refer to the way that weapons are being acquired although some refer to weapons acquisition as a means of ensuring long-term readiness. The term "readiness" refers to immediate and near-future capabilities. The personnel budget, as well as the budget for operations and maintenance, influences readiness most directly.

The military uses many indicators to monitor readiness. All are keyed to determining whether the military has enough of the right kinds of people in the right jobs; if those people have serviceable equipment on hand; and whether personnel are being provided the resources and training they need to perform their tasks at a specified standard. These measures indicate that the readiness of U.S. armed forces remains very good—as evidenced by the excellent performance of troops in Bosnia, Iraq, and recently Serbia—but is subject to some severe strains. Most of these strains concern military personnel, but a few are also

showing up in equipment and infrastructure.[8] The war against Serbia
is exacerbating some of these problems but has had less effect so far
(as of May 1999) than a decade of difficult missions elsewhere. These
problems demand attention from policymakers and justify much of
the $112 billion budget increase that the president proposed for the
years 2000 through 2005 in his fiscal year 2000 budget submission to
Congress.

For example, the armed services are having increasing trouble
attracting good people into their ranks. About 200,000 recruits are
needed annually—down about one-third from the cold war. The U.S.
Navy fell short of its recruitment goals in 1998. While the other three
services achieved at least 99 percent of their goals, the navy attracted
7,000 fewer sailors than its goal, achieving only 88 percent of its target.
Largely as a result, some navy ships not on deployment are considerably
less ready for combat than they have been in recent years: specifically,
only 50 percent of those ships not deployed to sea at a given moment
are considered ready for most or all possible missions, down from 70
percent a decade ago. Similar problems afflict other services. This fact
means that some stateside units would require weeks or in some cases
months of preparation before being fully deployable for war.

Retention rates are also falling, an additional threat to readiness. The
proportion of recruits who leave the service before completing their
first three years of service has risen from 28 percent in the 1980s to 35
percent. This trend increases the number of personnel gaps and the
general sense of flux in many units. Pilot shortages are becoming
serious as fewer pilots reenlist than in the past. The U.S. Air Force was
1,000 pilots short of its official goals in early 1999 and expected to be
1,400 short late in the year, a 10 percent shortage. Other services are
also experiencing pilot shortages. Unless reenlistment rates increase, the
problem will get worse. Transferring pilots from desk jobs can help
but only if the problem does not keep getting worse. The origin of the
problem includes competition from a strong and high-paying civilian
airline industry and fatiguing and tedious missions to patrol the skies of
Iraq and Bosnia, as well as other taxing missions.

8. O'Hanlon and Wilson (1999).

Some equipment is in its worst shape in a decade. The proportion of U.S. Air Force aircraft that are *not* mission capable now exceeds 25 percent, up from 20 percent in the late 1980s and 15 percent in the early 1990s. The proportion of U.S. Marine Corps equipment that is not mission capable has risen to 15 percent from 10 percent just five years ago.

Funds for the upkeep of bases are inadequate. As a result, commanders must choose between letting bases deteriorate and raiding operating accounts to maintain facilities, which forces cutbacks in training. Many U.S. Army units have been forced to reduce tank training hours about 20 percent, forcing cancellation of some large exercises at the battalion level and above.

While the trend is in the wrong direction, readiness is hardly poor. Today's military is far better than the "hollow force" of the 1970s. The armed forces have never been better educated or more experienced. About 99 percent of enlisted personnel are high school graduates. Ninety-four percent of officers are college graduates. Both fractions are all-time highs. Recruits remain skilled and well educated. About 94 percent of recruits in 1997 and 1998 had high school diplomas, and 68 percent scored above the national average on the armed forces aptitude test. These numbers are slightly better than they were in the 1980s, although a bit below levels in the early and mid-1990s when they averaged almost 97 percent and 73 percent respectively.

Peacetime casualty rates are at an all-time low. Accidental death rates have dropped by about one-quarter since the 1980s. Overall safety rates improved in 1998 for the third consecutive year and are now their best ever in most services. These trends reflect well on the quality of equipment but even more on the caliber of the men and women of the armed forces who are operating and maintaining the equipment.

Training funds remain adequate for first-to-fight units. Although operations like those in Bosnia, Iraq, and Serbia can interrupt training, Pentagon budgets are still providing adequate resources for units based in key regions overseas or slated to rapidly reinforce those forward units in the event of a crisis (table 2-6).

Some QDR initiatives should soon bear fruit. For example, the U.S. Air Force is adding 5,000 people to so-called low-density/high-tempo specialties such as security forces, civil engineering units, communica-

Table 2-6. *Training Rates*

Service unit	Year					Percentage change 1990–99
	1990	1996	1997	1998	1999	
U.S. Air Force						
Flying hours per crew per month, fighter/attack aircraft	19.5	20.0	19.3	17.0	17.7	−9.2
U.S. Army						
Flying hours per crew per month	14.2	13.9	14.5	11.4	11.5	−19.0
Annual tank miles	800.0	618.0	654.0	630.0	703.0	−12.1
U.S. Navy						
Flying hours per tactical crew per month	23.9	22.8	21.1	20.2	22.1	−7.5
Ship steaming days per quarter:						
Deployed fleet	54.2	50.5	50.5	50.5	50.5	−6.8
Nondeployed fleet	28.1	29.6	28.0	26.8	28.0	−0.4

Source: Office of the Undersecretary of Defense (1999a).

tions units, and crews for airborne warning and control aircraft that have been severely overworked. The Pentagon, recognizing that today's frequently deployed forces often need time at home even more than they need extra training, has scaled back joint-service exercises by about 25 percent. Similarly, downturns in the mission-capable rates of key equipment should soon be at least partly redressed by increases in funding for spare parts that began in 1997.

The overall picture of U.S. military readiness is mixed. Today's soldiers, sailors, airmen, and marines remain individually as good as, if not better than, they have ever been. But, collectively, military readiness has slipped somewhat and is still slipping. Some steps to reverse these trends have already been taken and should mitigate the problems. But more needs to be done in military compensation, equipment repair and maintenance, and training. The president's recent $112 billion initiative earmarked roughly the correct amount to these areas—about $84 billion of the total, with some $36 billion devoted to military and civilian personnel and $49 billion to operations and maintenance accounts focused on training, bases, and equipment. This increase should go far toward solving the problem—if the funds are actually appropriated by Congress. The political risk that they may not materialize motivates the proposals for cutbacks in weapons modernization and certain other Pentagon accounts described below.

Weapons

U.S. military equipment stocks and weapons arsenals remain by far the best in the world, with no serious competitor even on the horizon. But they are aging. In addition, they may have certain vulnerabilities that can be increasingly exploited by future adversaries. In fighter versus fighter or tank versus tank confrontations, U.S. forces will remain dominant. The risks lie in technologies such as cruise missiles that could render U.S. ships, bases, and troop concentrations more vulnerable as these technologies spread.

Sizable weapons purchases are necessary in the near future. Large equipment purchases of the late 1970s and 1980s enabled the United States to enjoy a "procurement holiday" in the 1990s. During the 1990s, the U.S. military has bought few fighter aircraft and submarines, only a modest number of combat ships, and virtually no tanks. But the holiday is drawing to a close. Two- or even three-decade old equipment must soon be replaced or refurbished. Not every system need be replaced, but the overall condition of equipment is cause for concern. For example, the average age of the air force and navy tactical combat aircraft is increasing about a half a year per calendar year. (The typical lifetime of aircraft is about twenty years.) These trends will continue through 2005 despite the introduction of new F-22 Raptor and F/A-18 E/F Super Hornet aircraft.[9] The average age of the attack helicopter fleet will exceed the desired lifetime of twenty years before 2005.[10]

How to replace this aging weaponry poses some difficult trade-offs. The Pentagon seems normally to prefer to buy large numbers of new and improved types of equipment. This approach is needlessly expensive for reasons set forth below.

9. Pierrot and Vines (1997).
10. Lussier (1995, pp. 15–27).

Buying Adequate National Defense on $275 Billion a Year

Can the United States sustain an adequate national defense establishment even if annual defense spending remains at or a bit below its current level, $280 billion? How can the U.S. armed forces, already very busy around the world and one-third smaller than they were in the cold war, become sufficiently leaner and more efficient to squeeze out funds for new or refurbished equipment while maintaining continuous effectiveness?

A series of cutbacks and weapons program changes would reduce the Pentagon's required annual spending level by almost $25 billion. With these economies, a $275 billion annual budget will permit improvements in equipment and readiness, support one or two modest operations like those now under way in Bosnia and the Persian Gulf, and fund the deployment of a light national missile defense in a few years.

A more economical equipment modernization agenda than the Pentagon now envisions would save $10 billion and enable the United States to meet its defense objectives. Carefully targeted cuts in force structure would save nearly $15 billion a year. Those force cuts would be made possible, in turn, by changes in the Department of Defense's two-war strategy, naval overseas presence operations, and nuclear posture. These calculations presuppose that Congress will approve two further rounds of base closures and encourage other Pentagon economies. There is no serious military argument against allowing the Pentagon to adopt such reforms.

What Two-War Strategy Makes Sense?

The Department of Defense currently employs a "two-war"—or to be more specific, a "two–Desert Storm"—approach to force planning. Some type of two-war strategy does make sense. Iraq's Saddam Hussein and North Korea's Kim Jong-II could plausibly cause overlapping crises or even wars. Nonetheless, the Pentagon's current two-war concept is unnecessarily cautious and pessimistic. The Pentagon's image of regional war follows a more or less standard script, regardless of where that conflict is assumed to occur. First, allied and forward-deployed U.S. forces are assumed to be attacked and to prove incapable of fending off the initial assault, losing substantial territory in the process.

Next, initial U.S. reinforcements would over several weeks allow combined allied forces to stop further losses, set up a strong defense, and begin to weaken enemy forces largely through air power and other long-range weapons. Finally, after roughly three months, enough heavy ground reinforcements would have arrived to permit a major ground counteroffensive to evict enemy forces from allied territory and possibly to invade the adversary's own territory.

Some critics see the two-war concept as mechanistic and artificial, not a serious strategy for fighting a war. That is a bit unfair, as the United States does face at least two well-armed foes in important parts of the world—Iraq and North Korea, to say nothing of Serbia—each with aggressive designs against important U.S. friends and interests and a recent track record that raises the real possibility of war in the near future. So some type of two-war strategy does make sense.

Instead of the two–Desert Storm model, however, the Pentagon could prudently adopt what might be called a one and one-half Desert Storm model—what could be viewed, perhaps more aptly, as a "Desert Storm plus Desert Shield" approach. Desert Shield was the 1990 U.S. deployment intended to protect Saudi Arabia from any Iraqi attack. It involved about 200,000 troops (before reinforcements began arriving in preparation for Desert Storm). Desert Storm, by contrast, employed half a million American troops to force Iraqi troops out of Kuwait. The one and one-half Desert Storm approach would still require about 90 percent as many active duty forces as current plans do, because it would need to include a cushion for peacekeeping missions and for war fighting insurance. (Added backup would exist in the U.S. Army National Guard, which retains almost as many combat force units as the active army but would send less than 20 percent of its combat units to war under the two–Desert Storm plan.)[11] But cutting about 100,000 active duty members of the U.S. Army, U.S. Air Force, and U.S. Marine Corps—a 10 percent troop cut—would lower spending by more than $10 billion and do much to get the Pentagon out of its budgetary fix (the U.S. Navy is considered in the following section).

Such a plan makes sense for three reasons. First, a 200,000-strong Desert Shield force would be extremely effective. Once deployed, it

11. Lussier (1997, pp. 8–12).

could defend such allied territory and key military infrastructure as bases and airfields against virtually any armored threat the United States might face in the world today. U.S. commanders felt confident that they could have defended Saudi Arabia with such a force once it was deployed in October of 1990. Its air power component, nearly as large and capable as that of a Desert Storm force, could wreak havoc on an enemy's military and industrial infrastructure and even carry out some offensive operations.[12]

The odds of deploying such a Desert Shield–like force in time to prevent significant loss of allied territory in a future conflict are continually improving. The U.S. military has stored more equipment in the Persian Gulf and northeast Asian regions since the end of the cold war than in the past. It has also increased its fast sealift capacity. The United States routinely keeps about 37,000 troops in South Korea and roughly 20,000 in the Persian Gulf region. The U.S. Army keeps brigade sets of equipment in South Korea and Kuwait, another afloat at Diego Garcia in the Indian Ocean, and lead elements of a fourth in Qatar. Marine brigade-equivalent sets are prepositioned at sea at Diego Garcia, Guam, and the Mediterranean.[13]

Second, the Iraqi and North Korean militaries are notably weaker than they were several years ago and have little prospect for getting much stronger anytime soon. This fact increases the odds that a Desert Shield force, together with regional friends of the United States, could prevent any significant loss of allied territory in a future conflict. It also means that, though the full 400,000 U.S. troops anticipated under the QDR for either major war could prove necessary under truly pessimistic assumptions, it is more likely that 200,000 to 300,000 U.S. troops would suffice even for large-scale counteroffensives and occupations. Iraq's forces are now only about half the size and strength they were before Desert Storm.[14] North Korean armored forces are even

12. Gordon and Trainor (1995, pp. 123–41); Scales (1994, pp. 121–28).

13. Schmidt (1997, pp. 36, 40).

14. International Institute for Strategic Studies (IISS) (1990, p. 105), and IISS (1997, p. 127). For measures of capability that factor in equipment quality as well as quantity, see O'Hanlon (1995, p. 43).

more obsolescent than Iraq's, and their readiness has been declining with their country's economic conditions.[15]

Third, its recent economic troubles notwithstanding, South Korea's armed forces are much improved and getting better. South Korea, together with the U.S. Army's 2d Infantry Division and forward-based American airpower, could wreak great damage on the North Koreans and stop any assault well north of Seoul with high confidence of success (even though they could not prevent serious damage to Seoul from long-range North Korean artillery and missiles). Although it possesses less armor than North Korea, the Republic of Korea's technological edge evens out the overall military balance of tanks, artillery, airplanes, and other heavy equipment between the two countries according to the best quantitative gauges available. If South Korea's superior readiness is also considered, the South undoubtedly possesses net superiority over the North.[16]

The military force of the Republic of Korea is well structured to stop any invasion attempt. Historically, attackers attempting to penetrate directly through densely prepared defensive positions like South Korea's have usually advanced at most a couple of kilometers a day—even when they were not technologically outclassed by their opponent.[17] But modern air power is so deadly and the United States is able to fly combat jet reinforcements to the region so quickly that such a slow advance—even if feasible—would be about as bloody and futile as were most attacks against entrenched troops during World War I.

North Korean chemical weapons, commandos deploying through tunnels, and forward-deployed, dug-in artillery could admittedly complicate the battle. But the allies are reasonably well protected against chemical attack. North Korean commandos would have a hard time deploying in enough strength to fundamentally alter the course of battle

15. For what little is publicly available about the Pentagon's expectations for a future Korean war and its operations plan 5027, see Oberdorfer (1997, pp. 313–25); for a more detailed assessment of the Korean military balance, see O'Hanlon (1998b).

16. Dupuy (1990, p. 108). Dupuy examines a wide body of historical battle outcomes and estimates that such readiness factors can at least double combat capability.

17. Helmbold, (1990, pp. A-278–94, A-318–22); Posen, (1986, p. 114).

at front lines. And radar-guided allied artillery would be much more accurate than North Korean guns.

Offensive operations would require far larger forces. If the United States and allies ever decided to overthrow Saddam Hussein or Kim Jong-Il, large U.S. forces would probably be needed. Iraqi and North Korean soldiers might fight fiercely in urban settings in defense of their homelands. Also, war could occur in other places where the United States has important interests yet is less well prepared to respond quickly. For these reasons, keeping the capability for a single Desert Storm–like war, as well as smaller deployments elsewhere, is critical. But planning for two overlapping Desert Storms seems excessive.

Overseas Naval Presence and Crisis Response

The U.S. Navy currently maintains carrier battle groups in the Persian Gulf, Mediterranean Sea, and western Pacific region nearly continuously. Brief gaps in coverage occur routinely, and extended gaps can occur during crises. In the 1997–98 dispute between the United States and Iraq over weapons inspections, for example, the carrier *Independence*, which normally was homeported in Japan and deployed in northeast Asian waters, traveled to the Persian Gulf. A similar event unfolded during the war against Serbia. But a fleet with eleven active and one reserve battle group can generally maintain this coverage nearly continuously.

This is how the U.S. Navy's deployment arithmetic works. The navy regards a carrier homeported in Japan as "deployed" at all times even when it is in port. Otherwise, it takes about five carriers in the fleet to keep a continuous deployment of one carrier overseas. This five-to-one ratio reflects the fact that ships homeported in the United States deploy for six months at a time, some of which is spent in transit. Once home, another six-month period is used largely for changes of assignment and classroom teaching and other forms of preparation. An additional six-month period is devoted to training exercises at sea but in home waters. Ships must also undergo major overhauls every few years that reduce the duty cycle further. During the cold war, this practice posed no major problem because the country wanted a large carrier fleet in case of war with the Soviet Union. But today it drives the size of the U.S. Navy.

The U.S. Navy has begun to rotate crews through airlift while leaving ships forward deployed, but so far only for ships with small crews. However according to a concept developed at the navy's own think tank, the Center for Naval Analyses, crew rotations by airlift are probably feasible even for large ships with large crews, such as destroyers, which could remain forward-deployed for perhaps one and one-half to two years.[18] Eventually, the same approach might be extended to aircraft carriers. Crews would train on one set of ships in stateside waters, then fly overseas to deploy on another. By this scheme, the navy's deployment efficiency ratio would roughly double, so that only two and one-half ships would be needed, on average, to sustain a continuous overseas presence rather than today's five. Because efficiency cannot be increased so easily for such other missions as crisis response and regional warfighting, crew rotation by airlift would not imply a 50 percent cut in the navy. But it could reduce the number of carrier groups by one-quarter to one-third and ultimately save $5 billion a year.

Implementing this approach would be logistically and operationally difficult. Several thousand sailors at a time would need to fly to an overseas port to relieve a crew of similar size. Since every ship in the fleet is somewhat different from every other—even vessels of the same type and class—a core crew would probably need to remain on the ships during this transition to ensure a smooth handover. The U.S. Navy would need reliable access to ports with sufficient berthing space for ships and hotel or barracks space for thousands of servicemen and servicewomen. These challenges are significant but solvable.

With this approach, the U.S. carrier fleet might be reduced from twelve to eight vessels. The Pentagon says it would need eight to ten carriers to deal with two overlapping regional wars. This number should be sufficient for all plausible contingencies. The regional commander in Desert Storm requested four carriers. In any war in northeast Asia the United States would almost surely enjoy ample access to land bases in South Korea and Japan; and the 1997 revision to the U.S.-Japan Defense Cooperation Guidelines provides for access to an increased number of airfields in Japan should a crisis arise. In a war against China over Taiwan, it is doubtful that Taiwan would need much help to repulse a

18. Morgan (1994, pp. 1–9).

Chinese amphibious assault, at least at any time in the next decade or so, given the inherent difficulty of an amphibious operation and Taiwan's air superiority over China.

Should China elect instead to blockade Taiwan's commercial sea trade, the challenge could be more complex. China could certainly scare away many commercial vessels and upset stock markets in Taipei with missile salvos or even with submarine attacks against a number of ships trying to run a declared blockade. However, its lack of air cover for any extended blockade would doom its navy to eventual destruction. Even a small flotilla of two to three U.S. aircraft carriers would be ample to achieve air dominance anywhere in the vicinity of Taiwan and to launch essentially unopposed attacks against Chinese surface vessels. In the waters north, east, and south of Taiwan, China would have difficulty attacking the carriers with submarines or any other weapon in its current arsenal or that it is likely to acquire for many years into the future.[19]

Nuclear Forces

The United States needs to retain a small nuclear deterrent but should take steps to reduce the risk of unintended nuclear war. Three changes in U.S. nuclear policy should be made soon to advance both objectives. The steps include a reduction in the size of the nuclear deterrent, changes in the character of offensive nuclear forces, and deployment of a "light" nationwide missile defense if that becomes technically feasible. Though desirable on military grounds, these steps are unlikely to save money.

As a first step, the United States should immediately and unilaterally reduce its offensive nuclear arsenal to the target set in the START II (Strategic arms reduction talks) negotiations—3,500 strategic warheads. The Russian Duma has not yet ratified START II, but Moscow and Washington have already made plans to move onto START III and cut back to force levels of around 2,000 warheads after START II is ratified. Even a 2,000-warhead force may be more than Russia can afford in the next decade. Although some might view such a cut as unilateral disarmament, an unconditional U.S. decision to reduce its forces to START II levels right away would save money here, relieve pressure on

19. Gill and O'Hanlon (1999).

Russia to spend money on nuclear weapons that would be better put to other uses, and improve the climate of relations between Washington and Moscow. President George Bush took similar unilateral steps in 1991 when the United States reduced certain types of nuclear weapons and changed the deployment patterns of others. The B-1 fleet, now envisioned for conventional missions, would remain a hedge against indefinite Russian nonratification of the START II Treaty. In any event by retaining the ability to place it in dual-capable service, the United States could, if necessary, restore its strategic warhead count to about 5,000.

Moscow and Washington should also move away from hair-trigger alert. As Brookings analyst Bruce Blair has observed, both countries could launch weapons at the other within seconds or minutes, an extremely dangerous posture in light of the poor state of repair of Russian nuclear forces, warning radars, and satellites. Even if both countries abandoned this posture, neither country would be vulnerable to a surprise first strike because both retain the capacity to launch sea-based missiles from submarines or land-based missiles from partially surviv-able concrete silos.[20] The United States should be prepared to reduce the alert status of its nuclear forces, unilaterally if necessary, in order to build trust and induce Russian reciprocity. After all, the alertness of Russian forces is declining willy-nilly as its forces fall into disrepair.

Congress recently has taken steps to pass a bill making it U.S. policy to deploy a national missile defense system when it becomes techno-logically feasible. The bill also states that the effect of missile defense on U.S.-Russian relations should be taken into account before any decision to deploy, but indicates a strong predilection to deploy regardless of diplomatic consequences. Earlier, the president had added $6.6 billion to his future years defense program (the budget plan through 2005) to fund such a deployment. Hence, even though no production and deployment programs have been formally approved, both the president and Congress are moving to build the country's first nationwide missile defense system.

This policy makes sense for a world in which the major missile threat to the United States is no longer posed by a huge Soviet force, but by

---

20. Blair, Feiveson, and Von Hippel (1997, pp. 74–81).

such forces as those of North Korea or, perhaps, of a renegade Russian commanding a submarine or a group of land-based missiles. The 1972 Anti-Ballistic Missile Treaty did not reflect a belief at that time in either the United States or the Soviet Union that missile defenses were inherently undesirable but rather the view that they would have been wasteful (because larger offensive forces could overwhelm them). Residual elements of these strategic considerations remain, but they must be weighed against the desirability of protection against a missile threat from a country like North Korea, whose 1998 long-range missile launch surprised the U.S. intelligence community.

Missile defense critics often belittle defenses against one type of nuclear delivery vehicle because an adversary might circumvent a missile defense system by smuggling a warhead into the United States in a suitcase or on a ship. Although such arguments contain a kernel of truth, U.S. measures to stop illicit materials from entering the country by airplane, ship, or land vehicle might well thwart a country trying to deliver a warhead against American territory through these means. Moreover, delivering a warhead by these means is slow, while missiles are very fast. In some wartime settings, time is critical. Missile defense critics are on stronger ground when they point to the technical difficulty of creating defenses that can work well—not only against individual missiles but also against barrages of many missiles, some of which may release not only warheads but also dozens or hundreds of decoys. Nonetheless, many of these problems may well be solved in the coming years, particularly against the fairly limited missile threat that a country such as North Korea would probably be capable of developing.

Weapons Purchases—and a Revolution in Military Affairs?

The aging of U.S. weaponry will oblige the Pentagon to boost spending on procurement. Current Pentagon plans call for an increase from $45 billion to an annual average of at least $70 billion (in constant 1999 dollars) in the next decade.[21] The cost of modernization need not be so high, if the United States is willing to undertake a program emphasizing relatively low-cost advanced munitions, communications, computer, and reconnaissance systems, which would reduce the need for

21. O'Hanlon (1998a, pp. 36–41).

purchasing such very costly major weapons "platforms" as advanced fighter jets.

Two considerations justify this more economical approach. First, the United States is so far ahead of potential adversaries that it does not need to worry about maximizing its technological excellence in every facet of weapons modernization. Rather than buy a large number of F-22 or "Raptor" fighter jets at more than $100 million a copy, for example, the nation can instead buy a modest number of those advanced planes—and replace the rest of the aging F-15 fleet with new $50 million F-15s instead. Second, electronics and computer technologies are advancing so fast that we can make important improvements in military capabilities by emphasizing new systems that feature them. These include advanced precision-guided munitions, unmanned aerial vehicles, and "real-time" information grids that tie weapons together on the battlefield and allow them to fight much more synergistically than before.

Some defense experts are so excited about improvements in these technologies that they are promising a revolution in military affairs— a transformation in the way wars are fought as revolutionary as that arising from tanks and air power (the blitzkrieg), carrier and submarine warfare, and nuclear weapons. With the demise of great-power military competition, it is argued, the United States should take the near-term risk associated with reducing the size or readiness of its current force in order to hasten the deployment of a new type of military. A nine-member congressionally appointed National Defense Panel, in its December 1997 report, expressed the view that a revolution in military technology and tactics is imminent and called for an added $5 billion to $10 billion a year to acquire systems that would facilitate a "transformation strategy."[22]

These analysts, however, often oversell the purported revolution. And they are vague about what it amounts to. For example, the National Defense Panel wants to expand spending on intelligence, space warfare, urban warfare, information operations, and weapons featuring greater agility, stealth, speed, and firepower. Alas, nearly every next-generation weapon system fits one of these categories. Moreover, the

---

22. National Defense Panel (1997, pp. 23, 49, 59, 79–86).

apostles of a revolution in military affairs sometimes lack historical perspective. For half a century, military technology has been undergoing rapid technological change, with the introduction of helicopters, infrared sensors, laser-guided bombs and rangefinders, phased-array radars, high-performance jet engines, stealth technology, autonomous and accurate cruise and ballistic missiles, and reconnaissance satellites. The consequences for strategy and warfare have been far reaching. It is not clear that the current technical changes have larger tactical implications than did past advances. Past technological changes caused evolutionary, but not revolutionary or discontinuous, change in battlefield tactics. Furthermore, bad weather, dense foliage, and smoke often degrade the effectiveness of the sensors on which future weapons will depend. These weapons may be vulnerable to such enemy countermeasures as flares, acoustic jammers, and other simple devices. At this point, few of the supposedly revolutionary weapons have yet been tested under battlefield conditions.[23] And, even if they work nearly as well as some claim, it will remain hard to detect distant soldiers armed with light weapons (as we have recently seen in Kosovo) and harder still to distinguish friend from foe, so that old-fashioned ground patrols and human intelligence networks will remain necessary.

Nonetheless, the revolutionaries are right about at least one thing: we can benefit greatly from improvements in electronics and computers. Investments in systems featuring advanced information processing capabilities and electronics can generally be made reasonably inexpensively. Other types of defense technology are not advancing as fast. With such an approach, we can modernize a great deal, and keep the weapons inventory young, safe, and reliable—with a procurement spending level around $60 billion rather than $70 billion or more.

U.S. Allies

Together, the military budgets of NATO Europe, Japan, and other U.S. allies equal that of the United States, and their total forces considerably exceed those of the United States. Unfortunately, most U.S. allies do not spend their defense resources very effectively given the demands of the current world. They are simply not very good at moving large

23. Murray (1997, pp. 69–76).

numbers of forces far from their national territories and then supporting them there in austere conditions. During the cold war, when Europe
was the main potential battlefield of concern to NATO, and when Japan
and Germany were still wrestling with the immediate legacy of World
War II, our allies' limited abilities to project power outside their borders
mattered less than they do now. Major U.S. allies in Europe would have
provided roughly half the total NATO combat force for a major ground
war with the Soviet Union, for example.

In Desert Storm, however, the Western allies provided less than
10 percent of the total force, and they could do little better today in a
major war. The *Quadrennial Defense Review* assumes absolutely no contribution to a war in the Persian Gulf or Korea from a major Western
ally other than the Republic of Korea. Many allies would offer valuable
bases, intelligence, special forces, and general political support. But
the only other major Western ally that could provide significant combat
forces to a future war in timely fashion is Great Britain.[24]

To rectify this situation, the Europeans need not spend more money
on defense. By cutting their forces, abandoning conscription militaries
with short tours of duty (many, including Germany and for the time
being also France, still rely on the draft), and buttressing their logistics
and transport capabilities, the European countries in aggregate could
become a major global military partner of the United States for operations in places like the Persian Gulf. The United States could not absolutely count on strong allied support, since it cannot dictate the security
decisions of sovereign nations. But today, the allies cannot help very
much, even if they want to do so.

The direct costs of admitting new members to NATO are small. The
military threat to these countries is small and does not require significant expenditures by the United States. Some outlays are needed to integrate Polish, Czech, and Hungarian communications and air traffic
control systems with those of other NATO members, to improve a base
or two, and to conduct occasional multilateral exercises. The current
U.S. position is that costs to the United States would be only about half
a billion dollars in all over roughly a decade and that the total costs to
the alliance would be about $1.5 billion. Whether or not the precise

24. Eland (1996, pp. 28–50); O'Hanlon (1997).

figures are correct, the direct costs are certainly modest. The only significant questions regarding NATO expansion are political, including, for example, the effect on relations with Russia.

International Affairs

The budget for international affairs is every bit as complex as that for defense. The following discussion focuses on three issues of particular current budget or policy importance: UN funding issues, U.S. aid to the Middle East, and development aid.[25]

As noted earlier, total U.S. spending on international affairs has declined and is projected to continue falling. Although some economies remain achievable, the argument is strong for restoring international spending to at least its cold war average, which would imply an increase in annual spending of about $3 billion. The end of the cold war did not substantially reduce the size or importance to the United States of the problems these expenditures are designed to address. A lessened need to provide security aid to countries in NATO's southern tier and direct international broadcasting into communist states has been roughly balanced out by new needs: to support democratic and economic transitions in former Warsaw Pact regions, to conduct peacekeeping and conflict recovery efforts in places like Bosnia, and to assist larger numbers of refugees around the world (table 2-7).

Development Aid

The United States has been giving foreign aid for a half century to help the world's poorer countries address their humanitarian needs and to

25. Other issues, such as enhanced nuclear security programs within the former Soviet republics or transition assistance that might someday be provided North Korea as part of a major arms control and economic reform plan for the Korean peninsula, could also lead to new demands for funds. But I shall not explore these issues here. Both hinge so strongly on the actions of other countries that they cannot be regarded as options for U.S. policy alone. On the nuclear problem, see CSIS (1996, pp. 4–6, 45–49); Ellis and Perry (1997, pp. 14–22) make several modest and reasonable suggestions for increased spending on nuclear security. They also point to the potential to spend billions of dollars helping Russia destroy its chemical weapons stocks, but that is clearly a nonproliferation goal of lesser concern than nuclear security. On Russia's economy, see Gaddy and Ickes (1998, pp. 53–67). On North Korea, see Mazarr (1998, pp. 91–97), and Almeida and O'Hanlon (1999, pp. 58–72).

Table 2-7. *The U.S. International Discretionary Account, 1999*

Billions of dollars

Type of spending	Estimated outlays
Development aid	
Multilateral aid	
Development banks	1.43
Voluntary contributions to international organization	0.29
Bilateral aid	
Development assistance	1.82
Economic support funds	2.20
Food aid	0.82
Refugee assistance	0.69
Peace Corps, other	0.98
Subtotal	8.23
Other foreign assistance	
Aid to Central/Eastern Europe, Former Soviet Union	1.01
Foreign military financing	3.85
Narcotics control	0.33
UN peacekeeping	0.33
Foreign information and exchange activities	1.21
Subtotal	6.73
Bilateral and multilateral diplomacy	
State Department	3.09
International organizations	1.00
Subtotal	4.09
Business	
Export-Import Bank, other	0.59
Subtotal	0.59
Grand total	19.64
Addendum: Aid funded out of the U.S. military budget	
Nunn-Lugar CTR aid to Former Soviet Union[a]	0.42
U.S. military costs in indirect support of UN-authorized operations	
(principally Bosnia and Iraq)	2.80

Sources: *Budget of the United States Government, Fiscal Year 2000*, pp. 316–17; O'Hanlon and Graham (1997).

a. Cooperative threat reduction.

promote their economic development. Should it continue to do so? If so, what is the best way to do the job?

Many critics of aid claim that overseas assistance is no longer needed as a major instrument of foreign policy. They point to the large volume of private capital now flowing to developing countries—roughly

$130 billion in 1996. Those numbers greatly exceed the $55 billion in aid given by all official donors combined that year.[26] Although flows of private capital can be volatile, as the drop-off in investment to Asia in the second half of 1997 illustrates, there is good reason to expect the amount of private capital to increase.[27] However, most developing countries do not receive much private capital from abroad, and many do not gain a great deal from global trade either.[28] Twenty of the world's 166 developing countries—mostly in East Asia and South America—receive 95 percent of all private investment while most official aid flows to Africa, the Middle East, and South Asia.[29]

Critics also argue that aid does not work. Some of their criticisms are valid and should cause changes in the way aid is allocated and administered. But aid has done a good job in improving certain basic health and education indicators in the past several decades. Aid has supported child immunizations, greater availability of rehydration salts and nutritional supplements, and provision of clean drinking water. These and other efforts have reduced by more than 50 percent since 1960 the proportion of children in developing countries who die before reaching their fifth birthday. Partly as a result of increased contraceptive availability, now employed by 55 percent of the world's married couples, the fertility rate is down from five to three children per woman over that same period—a much more economically and environmentally sustainable growth rate.[30]

To be sure, aid does little to spur growth if countries pursue poor economic policies. It can even slow growth if it cushions economic elites and retards economic reform.[31] But aid does speed growth where recipient governments adopt good policies. Two studies have estab-

---

26. Michel (1998, pp. A1–A4).
27. World Bank (1997a, pp. 19–22).
28. O'Hanlon and Graham (1997, p. 35).
29. World Bank (1997a, pp. 1–32, 140–43).
30. World Bank (1997b, pp. 1, 59).
31. For example, in the early 1990s countries in Africa with poor economic policies were still receiving more aid per capita than those with good policies. See O'Hanlon and Graham (1997, pp. 70–71). For evidence that recipients' policies are still not adequately scrutinized by donors, see CSIS Task Force on the Multilateral Development Banks (1998, p. 5).

lished that aid adds nearly half a percent a year to economic growth after controlling for other factors in countries with sound economic policies.[32] Donors should be selective and limit aid to basic humanitarian relief and grass-roots projects in countries unable to benefit substantially from it, while providing it fairly generously to reformist governments.

Led by the multilateral organizations, donors have been trying to be selective in their aid disbursements for at least a decade. But they have often done so in ways that swamp weak bureaucracies in developing countries, requiring recipients to satisfy dozens of specific conditions in detail. Despite these conditions, donors often continue to provide funds even when many of the critical requirements are not satisfied.[33] Donors should instead declare that they will preferentially support countries with low inflation rates, modest-sized public sectors, small government deficits, dependable property rights, generally open trade regimes, and reasonable exchange rates. Ample room for debate exists on the specifics, as has been made clear in the wake of the Asian economic crisis of 1997. But the need for solid core economic fundamentals is beyond dispute.

Huge increases in foreign aid, as proposed by some individuals and organizations including the UN General Assembly, are neither needed nor desirable.[34] But the case for some increase is strong.

Official aid should be confined to activities to which private investment cannot be expected to flow, such as public health, education, debt relief, some types of national infrastructure, or high-risk loans to small entrepreneurs. Capital for projects that are expected to produce tangible marketable returns should be left to the private investors who are better positioned to make the myriad tough-minded decisions that should govern the allocation of capital.

The UN goal that donors provide 0.7 percent of their gross domestic product for developing countries is excessive. The average donor nation now gives less than 0.3 percent of GDP; the United States gives about 0.12 percent. But an increase in global aid by about 50 percent—

---

32. Burnside and Dollar (1996); Bruno and Easterly (1996).
33. For a related critique, see Van de Walle and Johnston (1996, pp. 102–03).
34. O'Hanlon and Graham (1997, p. 82).

from $55 billion to $80 billion a year—could provide added support for debt relief for poor countries in Africa, primary education and primary health care, family planning services, construction of infrastructure, recovery from conflicts, help for the poor when countries adopt painful economic reforms, and narrowly targeted environmental programs. The U.S. share of such an increased world aid budget would be $3 billion to $4 billion a year.

The United Nations

Congress has tried in recent years to force the Clinton administration to seek lower dues at the United Nations. This policy is sensible on the whole. Dues are based on each nation's share of world GDP. But the United States plays a unique role as global military power and international stabilizer. This role entails sizable direct expenditures. It is reasonable, therefore, for the United States to pay a smaller percent of its GDP as dues for other international activities than do other countries. Although the United States gives a smaller percent of its GDP as official development assistance than does any other country in the Organization for Economic Cooperation and Development (OECD), it spends more of its GDP on foreign policy broadly defined than all of its major allies. That is a consequence primarily of the size of its defense budget—which not only allows the U.S. military to protect the United States but also to protect allies, back up peacekeeping operations, and provide humanitarian relief in crises.

However, Congress has recently pushed a legitimate point too far. It keeps holding up payment of even a scaled-back tally of U.S. dues, most recently over the matter of family planning overseas.

The Clinton administration bears some of the responsibility for the impasse over payment of UN dues. Thoughtful compromises with Congress on the family planning and abortion issue could have accommodated congressional concerns without weakening UN support for overseas family planning efforts. For example, in places where numerous organizations are able to provide family planning services, the United States could fund only those groups that do not lobby on behalf of abortion policy. It is one thing, pro-life members of Congress might argue, for the United States to reach pro-choice abortion policies through the democratic process for its own citizens, however much those pro-life members might themselves disagree with the laws. But that does not mean that the U.S. government needs to financially support adoption of specific policies on abortion rights by foreign countries. Unfortunately, the Clinton administration has not sought out such compromises.

Aid to the Middle East

Reducing grant aid to Egypt and Israel to 1980 levels or less would reduce U.S. spending by at least $1 billion dollars a year. Israel, with a per capita income similar to that of countries in southern Europe, is by far the world's wealthiest recipient of significant amounts of development assistance. Egypt's poor current economic policies preclude the productive use of aid.

Halving current economic aid—about $2 billion a year—would free these resources for better use elsewhere. Military and economic aid combined to the two countries would drop from $5 billion to $4 billion.

Conclusion

National security and international affairs accounts (along with interest payments) are the only major federal budget categories on which real spending has declined in the 1990s. The end of the cold war provided a compelling rationale for significant cuts in defense, but the cuts have gone far enough. On the whole, total real spending for defense should be maintained at 1999 levels, and outlays for diplomacy and aid should increase about $3 billion annually.

The spending increases now planned for the Pentagon result largely from an excessively ambitious weapons modernization agenda that is neither necessary nor politically plausible. But even if its weapons plans are scaled back, the Pentagon will need to retain its current real funding levels.

It is often said that democracies in peacetime tend toward isolationism. That may be true, but with a few billion more dollars devoted to foreign policy in the years ahead, the United States can be reasonably confident that it will have the resources to maintain a vigorous and successful foreign policy not unlike that which won the cold war and helped usher in the greatest waves of global economic growth and democratization in world history.

References

Almeida, Pedro, and Michael O'Hanlon. 1999. "Impasse in Korea: A Conventional Arms-Accord Solution?" *Survival* 41 (Spring): 58–72.

Blair, Bruce G., Harold A. Feiveson, and Frank N. von Hippel. 1997. "Taking Nuclear Weapons Off Hair-Trigger Alert." *Scientific American* 277 (November): 74–81.

Bruno, Michael, and William Easterly. 1996. "Inflation's Children: Tales of Crises That Beget Reforms." Paper presented to the American Economics Association annual meeting (January).

Burnside, Craig, and David Dollar. 1996. "Aid, Policies, and Growth." Washington: World Bank.

Cohen, William S. 1997. *Report of the Quadrennial Defense Review.* U.S. Department of Defense.

———. 1999. *Annual Report to the President and the Congress.* U.S. Department of Defense.

Congressional Budget Office. 1991. "Costs of Operation Desert Shield." CBO staff memorandum. Washington (January).

CSIS Task Force Report. 1996. *The Nuclear Black Market.* Washington: Center for Strategic and International Studies.

CSIS Task Force on the Multilateral Development Banks. 1998. *The United States and the Multilateral Development Banks.* Washington: Center for Strategic and International Studies (March).

Dupuy, Col. Trevor N. 1990. *Attrition: Forecasting Battle Casualties and Equipment Losses in Modern War.* Fairfax, Va.: HERO Books.

Eland, Ivan. 1996. "The Costs of Expanding the NATO Alliance." Washington: Congressional Budget Office (March).

Ellis, Jason D., and Todd Perry. 1997. "Nunn-Lugar's Unfinished Agenda." *Arms Control Today* (October): 14.

Gaddy, Clifford G., and Barry W. Ickes. 1998. "Russia's Virtual Economy." *Foreign Affairs* 77 (September–October): 53–67.

General Accounting Office. 1997a. *U.N. Peacekeeping: Issues Related to Effectiveness, Cost, and Reform*, NSIAD-97-139.

General Accounting Office. 1997b. *Bosnia Peace Operation*, NSIAD-97-132.

Gill, Bates, and Michael O'Hanlon. 1999. "The (Mostly) Hollow Chinese Military." *National Interest* (Summer): 55–62.

Gordon, Michael R., and Bernard E. Trainor. 1995. *The Generals' War: The Inside Story of the Conflict in the Gulf.* Little, Brown and Company.

Helmbold, Robert L. 1990. "A Compilation of Data on Rates of Advance in Land Combat Operations." Research Paper CAA-RP-90-04. Bethesda, Md.: U.S. Army Concepts Analysis Agency (February).

International Institute for Strategic Studies (IISS). 1990. *The Military Balance 1990–1991.* Oxford, U.K.: Brassey's.

———. 1997. *The Military Balance. 1997/98.* Oxford, U.K.: Oxford University Press.

———. 1998. *The Military Balance. 1998/99.* Oxford, U.K.: Oxford University Press.

Kosiak, Steven. 1999. "Cost of Allied Force Air Campaign: Day 15." Center for Strategic and Budgetary Assessments (April 8).

Krepinevich Jr., Andrew F. 1996. *The Conflict Environment of 2016: A Scenario-Based Approach.* Washington: Center for Strategic and Budgetary Assessments (October).

Lussier, Frances, M. 1995. *An Analysis of U.S. Army Helicopter Programs.* Washington: Congressional Budget Office (December).

———. 1997. *Structuring the Active and Reserve Army for the 21st Century.* Washington: Congressional Budget Office (December).

Mazarr, Michael J. 1998. "Korea: A Time to Be Bold?" *National Interest* (Spring): 91–97.

Michel, James H. 1998. *Development Co-operation: 1997 Report.* Paris: Organization for Economic Cooperation and Development.

Morgan, William F. 1994. *Rotate Crews, Not Ships.* Alexandria, Va.: Center for Naval Analyses (June).

Murray, Williamson. 1997. "Thinking about Revolutions in Military Affairs." *Joint Forces Quarterly* (Summer): 69–76.

National Defense Panel. 1997. *Transforming Defense: National Security in the 21st Century.* Arlington, Va. (December).

Oberdorfer, Don. 1997. *The Two Koreas: A Contemporary History.* Addison-Wesley.

Office of the Secretary of Defense. 1999. *Defense Reform: Partnering for Excellence.* Department of Defense.

Office of the Undersecretary of Defense (Comptroller). 1999a. *National Defense Budget Estimates for FY 2000 (Green Book)* (February).

———. 1999b. *Program Acquisition Costs by Weapon System* (February).

O'Hanlon, Michael. 1995. *Defense Planning for the Late 1990s: Beyond the Desert Storm Framework.* Brookings.

———. 1997. "Transforming NATO: The Role of European Forces." *Survival* 39 (Autumn 1997): 5–15.

———. 1998a. *How to Be a Cheap Hawk: The 1999 and 2000 Defense Budgets.* Brookings.

———. 1998b. "Stopping a North Korean Invasion: Why Defending South Korea is Easier than the Pentagon Thinks." *International Security* 22 (Spring): 135–70.

O'Hanlon, Michael, and Carol Graham. 1997. *A Half Penny on the Federal Dollar: The Future of Development Aid.* Brookings.

O'Hanlon, Michael, and Jerre Wilson. 1999. "Shoring Up Military Readiness." Policy Brief 43. Brookings (January).

Perry, William J. 1995. *Annual Report to the President and the Congress*. U.S. Department of Defense (February).

Pierrot, Lane, and Jo Ann Vines. 1997. *A Look at Tomorrow's Tactical Air Forces*. Washington: Congressional Budget Office (January).

Posen, Barry R. 1986. "Measuring the European Conventional Balance: Coping with Complexity in Threat Assessment." In *Conventional Forces and American Defense Policy*, edited by Steven E. Miller, 79–120. Princeton University Press.

Scales, Jr., Robert H. 1994. *Certain Victory: The U.S. Army in the Gulf War*. Washington: Brassey's.

Schmidt, Rachel. 1997. *Moving U.S. Forces: Options for Strategic Mobility*. Washington: Congressional Budget Office (February).

Van de Walle, Nicolas, and Timothy A. Johnston. 1996. *Improving Aid to Africa*. Washington: Overseas Development Council.

Vickers, Michael G., and Steven M. Kosiak. 1997. *The Quadrennial Defense Review: A Strategic Assessment*. Washington: Center for Strategic and Budgetary Assessments.

World Bank. 1997a. *Private Capital Flows to Developing Countries: The Road to Financial Integration*. Oxford University Press.

———. 1997b. *Health, Nutrition, and Population*. Washington: World Bank.

I. M. DESTLER 3

Trade Policy
at a Crossroads

U.S. TRADE POLICY during the past twenty-five years is marked by paradox. It is widely thought that the United States, like other nations, finds it harder to liberalize trade when its economy is weak than when it is strong. Yet, from 1974 through 1994, when the performance of the U.S. economy was mediocre, trade liberalization proceeded apace, extending a trend that dated back half a century. In the past five years, the performance of the U.S. economy has been exemplary, but trade liberalization has stagnated because of disagreement over the goals of future negotiations.

The United States needs to break the current political deadlock. Further reduction of trade barriers will promote expanded trade and investment, enhancing U.S. economic performance many years into the future. And it can reinforce U.S. international economic leadership worldwide.

Trade and Economic Performance, 1974–99

During the two decades from 1974 through 1994, the U.S. economy experienced two "oil shocks," double-digit inflation in 1973–74 and

The author is grateful to Russell Harrison for research assistance and to Susan Schwab for her helpful critique.

1979–80, twelve-digit budget and trade deficits in the 1980s, the highest unemployment since the Great Depression in 1982, slowed productivity growth, stagnation in workers' take-home pay, and sharply increasing economic inequality.[1] Despite these woes, the United States maintained and reinforced its open-market international trade policies with the 1973–79 Tokyo Round under the General Agreement on Tariffs and Trade (GATT) and the 1986–94 Uruguay Round, and the North American Free Trade Agreement (NAFTA) with Canada and Mexico. Throughout this period, the United States also pressed its trading partners for unilateral reductions in trade barriers on specific products and for broader market liberalization as part of efforts at comprehensive economic reform.

In the past five years, the performance of the U.S. economy has improved strikingly. Inflation and unemployment are at or near their twenty-five-year lows. Productivity and workers' real incomes are rising. The budget has moved into surplus. The Federal Reserve Board chairman finds the current economic expansion "as impressive as any I have witnessed in my nearly half-century of daily observation."[2] Aside from the merchandise trade deficit—discussed later—the usual obstacles to trade liberalization have receded.

Yet U.S. trade policy has been on hold since the beginning of 1995. The reason is the expiration of "fast-track" negotiating authority, under which every president since Gerald Ford has been authorized to submit legislation implementing trade agreements to Congress for an up-or-down vote within ninety days. President Bill Clinton failed to win renewal in 1994 and did not submit a new proposal to Congress for three years thereafter. When he finally did so in 1997, the House of Representatives spurned his request. No president had suffered a comparable defeat on trade since the United States inaugurated its trade liberalization policy during the Roosevelt administration.

U.S. producers and consumers are exceptionally well positioned to gain from the increased global trade that further trade liberalization will generate. But no agenda for reducing trade barriers can be credi-

---

1. See chapter 5 in this volume.
2. Testimony of Alan Greenspan on June 10, 1998, before the Joint Economic Committee quoted in the *Washington Post*, June 11, 1998, p. C1.

ble in the year 2000 and beyond unless it is formulated in light of the political forces that doomed President Clinton's efforts.

Success after Success:
NAFTA, the Uruguay Round, and Beyond

President Clinton inherited two landmark trade initiatives: NAFTA, signed by President George Bush in 1992, and the Uruguay Round of global negotiations, initiated in 1986. In a dramatic uphill battle, Clinton won congressional approval of NAFTA in November 1993 but only after negotiating side agreements with Canada and Mexico on labor and environmental issues. His U.S. trade representative, Mickey Kantor, closed the Uruguay Round deal a month later, and Congress approved its implementing legislation in a lame-duck congressional session in December 1994.

Both policy steps were unprecedented for the United States. NAFTA committed the United States to remove tariffs and most other import barriers with its northern and southern neighbors. The GATT-Uruguay Round agreement reduced a record number of trade barriers and included a record number of countries. It also created a permanent global institution, the World Trade Organization (WTO) with strengthened dispute settlement procedures. The United States concluded the year 1994, moreover, with two major new trade liberalizing commitments. In November, leaders of the Asia Pacific Economic Cooperation (APEC) forum, meeting in Bogor, Indonesia, committed themselves to free trade among themselves by 2010 (2020 for the less developed members). In December, Western Hemisphere nations meeting in Miami pledged negotiation of a Free Trade Area of the Americas (FTAA) by 2005.

In the years that followed, the WTO fostered further trade liberalization. An *Information Technology Agreement* (ITA) was negotiated in 1996 and went into effect on July 1, 1997. It provided for reciprocal elimination of tariffs on information technology products by countries constituting at least 90 percent of global trade in these products. Under an *Agreement on Basic Telecommunications Services,* concluded in February 1997, sixty-nine nations, constituting 91 percent of global telecommunications revenues in 1995, made commitments to liberalize regulation and improve market access in a sector long characterized by heavy-handed governmental restrictions. An *Agreement on Financial Services,* negotiated in December 1997, opened markets starting in 1999 that generate 95 percent of global revenues in such areas as banking, securities, insurance, and financial data. In addition, the WTO's newly established Dispute Settlement Understanding (DSU), was off to a credible start, aided by procedures that (unlike those of its predecessor, the GATT) did not allow defendant nations to block adverse decisions. The United States became the most active complainant and usually prevailed.[3]

The cumulative effect of freer trade on the American economy has been enormous. Between 1970 and 1998, total U.S. exports of goods and services have risen from 5.5 percent to 11.3 percent of gross domestic product. U.S. companies are increasingly dependent on foreign markets for increased sales, particularly in high-technology industries where the United States enjoys a significant advantage. Imports have also risen, from 5.4 percent to 13.0 percent of GDP, as U.S. consumers and producers have shifted to activities in which they enjoy a comparative advantage and bought goods that can be produced more cheaply abroad.[4]

The Failure to Extend Fast Track

Since the Uruguay Round, U.S. negotiators have been hamstrung by the expiration of fast-track authority. This law makes credible the promises of U.S. negotiators to reduce U.S. trade barriers in exchange for market-opening commitments by U.S. trading partners.[5] Fast track

3. There were two highly publicized losses: one ("Kodak-Fuji") involving access to the Japanese market for photographic film and the second addressing the GATT-consistency of U.S. laws restricting shrimp imports from nations whose fleets do not protect turtles.

4. *Economic Report of the President, 1999,* pp. 326–27; Council of Economic Advisers (1999, p. 1).

5. Section 111(b) of the Uruguay Round Agreements Act of 1994 did provide residual proclamation authority for the president to reduce tariffs to zero in certain negotiations carried over from the Uruguay Round. It was under this authority, for example, that the administration could implement the tariff reductions in the Information Technology Agreement (ITA) described above. See U.S. House of Representatives (1997, p. 187).

resolves a bedrock constitutional dilemma: while the president and executive branch can negotiate all they like, Congress passes trade legislation and ratifies treaties. Other nations know, from experience, that an unfettered U.S. Congress will not necessarily honor executive promises. Accordingly, they generally refuse to bargain seriously on broad-ranging commitments to open markets unless U.S. negotiators can credibly promise that Congress will ratify the resulting agreements.

When negotiations were limited to tariffs, Congress could grant the president advance authorization to reduce rates within a specified range if trading partners did likewise. When negotiations shifted to nontariff barriers, or to "free trade agreements" providing preferential treatment to particular countries, Congress could no longer give advance approval, because it could not know the details in advance. Foreigners worried that after they had made concessions Congress might not honor the resulting deal, changing its content through amendments or refusing to vote at all. Fast track commits Congress to vote, within a fixed time period, on legislation as submitted by the president to implement specific trade agreements. No amendments are allowed, though legislators can—and do—influence how the legislation is drafted.

Congress first granted fast-track authority in 1974 and has renewed it five times. Without it, the Tokyo and Uruguay Rounds, the U.S.-Canada Free Trade Agreement, and NAFTA would have been impossible to negotiate. When APEC members and the Western Hemisphere nations agreed to free trade in 1994, the prevailing assumption was that the U.S. president would be given fast-track authority to carry out his nation's side of the bargain. A similar expectation underlay agreement in the World Trade Organization to negotiate further reductions in trade barriers, and the United States is hosting the November–December 1999 WTO Ministerial Conference, which aims to set the agenda.

But President Clinton is now in his fifth year without fast-track authority, and near-term prospects for its renewal are poor.[6] Congress has denied a president with a good trade record and an even better

6. The longest previous lapse lasted seven months, from January to August 1988.

economy authority it had granted four predecessors who served in less favorable times. The troubles began in 1994, when U.S. Trade Representative Mickey Kantor proposed a broad, seven-year fast-track extension as part of the Uruguay Round implementing legislation.[7] Kantor proposed to build on the NAFTA side agreements and mend trade policy relations with wounded Democratic constituencies by making "labor standards" and "trade and the environment" two of the seven "principal trade negotiating objectives" for which fast track would be employed. Representatives of business objected vehemently, as did free-trade Republicans. They had accepted the NAFTA side agreements with reluctance, and they saw an effort to address these subjects in the body of trade agreements as, at best, a waste of U.S. negotiating leverage (since few other nations favored their inclusion), and, at worst, a route to new government regulation. The administration tried to find language acceptable to both groups, but it failed and decided not to include any fast-track extension in the Uruguay Round implementing bill lest its enactment be endangered.

After Republicans took control of Congress in 1995, the House Committee on Ways and Means, under its new chairman, William R. Archer (R-Tex.), reported a fast-track bill out of committee in September. But sporadic negotiations with Kantor, centering on the labor-environment language, were unsuccessful, complicated by the administration's determination to avoid a fight with organized labor in the months before the 1996 election. The administration never presented a draft bill of its own.

Once President Clinton was re-elected, the prospects seemed better. He clearly wanted to proceed, and the Senate majority leader, the Speaker of the House, and the Senate Finance Committee leadership joined Archer in pressing for a White House proposal in early 1997. But differences over labor and environmental standards had hardened. Many Democrats wanted these issues to be central to future trade negotiations. How, they asked, could a government that had fought hard to prevent piracy of movies and compact disks fail to defend worker rights, which were at least equally relevant to trade? Almost all Republicans took the opposite position. They wanted severe limits on

7. For the story through summer 1997, see Destler (1997, pp. 16–27).

extending fast-track coverage to labor and environmental issues, because they believed that agreements in these areas would be dubious public policy and would waste bargaining leverage best devoted to commercial objectives. Organized business joined Republicans and withheld active support for fast-track legislation until they could see just what Clinton would propose.

The president was sympathetic to linkage of trade with workers' rights and the environment. Such linkage would please important Democratic constituencies, build on the precedent of the NAFTA side agreements, and broaden potential domestic support for any resulting new agreement. But it was hard to see, in practice, how trade negotiations could advance these causes. The Clinton administration had been pressing the trade-labor connection within the WTO since it came to office. It had met strong international resistance, particularly from developing nations that saw the trade-labor—and often trade-environment—linkage as disguised protectionism. Moreover, no plausible fast-track bill was likely to win labor support—or even neutrality—and more than token linkage would risk provoking opposition from business and needed Republicans.

Faced with a dilemma, Clinton fiddled away most of 1997, while fast-track supporters burned. More charitably, he delayed until September, after other priority issues were out of the way, and only then decided on the specific language his fast-track bill would contain. In the end, he deferred to the Republican majority and proposed legislation with severe limits on coverage of labor and environmental issues, presumably counting on his persuasive powers to bring victory, as they had with NAFTA. Business community supporters also waited until they were sure Clinton's bill would not be too labor-environment friendly.

In contrast, adversaries did not wait. House Minority Leader Richard A. Gephardt (D-Mo.) circulated a twelve-page "Dear Democratic Colleague" letter in February proposing to "limit any grant of fast track authority . . . to bilateral negotiations with Chile or to remedy the flaws in the NAFTA."[8] Organized labor, on which Democratic candidates were increasingly dependent for campaign funds, sent a clear message that it would allocate campaign contributions to reward—or punish—

8. Richard A. Gephardt, February 26, 1997, p. 7.

members based on their stand on fast track.[9] The *Global Trade Watch* project spearheaded by *Public Citizen*, an organization that had unsuccessfully fought NAFTA, exploited the statutory requirement that the administration issue a report on that agreement's first three years to issue a counter-report, *The Failed Experiment: NAFTA at Three Years;* sponsoring organizations included the labor-backed Economic Policy Institute and the Sierra Club.[10] They blamed NAFTA for fouling of the environment on the U.S.-Mexico border and bilateral trade imbalances allegedly costing hundreds of thousands of jobs. Moreover, they declared that "NAFTA and globalization generally have changed the composition of employment in America [toward] lower-paying services industries."[11] The message found a ready audience among House Democrats who seemed to believe that the president had abandoned many of their causes in the summer 1997 budget deal struck with Republicans. And since the administration presented only a rather general trade policy agenda, persuading members of Congress that action was urgent proved impossible.

Arguments like those of *Public Citizen* did not dominate the debate, but they eroded the advantage that free traders had traditionally enjoyed—the presumption that free trade promotes the general interest against narrow protectionist forces and the general belief that the case for free trade was right—even among legislators driven to vote otherwise. In the end, despite assiduous eleventh-hour presidential lobbying, approximately four-fifths of House Democrats indicated that

9. During their thirty-eight-year control of the House, Democrats had received substantial contributions from business interests who preferred Republicans ideologically but wanted access to power. With Republicans now in control, business could now put its money where its heart was.

10. *Public Citizen* showed it had learned from its rather shrill efforts against NAFTA and the Uruguay Round. Instead of attention-getting arguments that mobilized the faithful but tended to alienate the undecided, the organization centered its attack on perceived problems with NAFTA (if you liked NAFTA, you'll love fast track), the alleged diminution of legislative power ("Congress loses the authority and the ability to shape [trade] issues"), and the exclusion of most trade-related labor and environmental issues from coverage under the legislation. Public Citizen, "Questions and Answers about Fast Track Negotiating Authority" (http://www.citizen.org/pctrade/fasttrack/ftqa.htm [June 18, 1999]).

11. Public Citizen website (http://www.citizen.org [June 18, 1999]).

they would oppose the legislation.[12] Facing a likely defeat, the White House asked Speaker Gingrich first to delay the vote and then to adjourn for the year without it. Gingrich complied. The president initially pledged to resubmit his proposal in 1998, and when he did not do so, the Speaker brought it to a vote anyway in September, over Clinton's objections: one of his motives was to divide Democrats in the run-up to the midterm congressional election. The result was a debacle for trade liberalization: the bill failed by 243 votes to 180, with only twenty-nine Democrats (out of 200) in favor.

Anxiety over Globalization

U.S. markets remain open. Trade continues to expand. The U.S. economy is exceptionally strong. But U.S. trade policy is in serious trouble. The core reason is that trade has hurt some Americans even as it has helped many others, and Americans differ over how to respond.

Linkage with Labor and the Environment

"Globalization"—the growing engagement of the United States with the world economy—has favorably affected most Americans. Foreign competition has contributed to the flexibility and innovativeness of U.S. companies and promoted price stability, which helps American consumers. But not everyone has gained, and the process has generated widespread anxieties, which critics have fanned.[13]

Caught in the middle are many Democrats who worry about the increase of income inequality, the weakening of labor unions and of workers' bargaining position generally, and the perceived adverse effect of economic activity on the environment. Globalization may be inevitable and mostly beneficial, but it inflicts losses on some workers and industries—including important Democratic constituencies. To make matters worse, these Democrats believe that programs to

---

12. A softer count of Republicans had 160 (70 percent) in favor, with more perhaps available. By contrast, fast track won a procedural vote in the Senate by 68–31, with majorities of both parties in favor.

13. For a comprehensive treatment of the economic issues, written for a broad audience, see Burtless and others (1998).

compensate losers and help them become winners—the trade adjustment assistance (TAA), for example—are ineffective and underfunded. They feel, with some justification, that globalization undercuts the historic American social bargain regarding capitalism—that markets should be kept free, but a social safety net should protects the losers.[14]

These Democrats generally favor strengthening the social safety net in the United States but are sympathetic to arguments that global labor and environmental standards are also necessary. It follows that the United States should be as aggressive in bargaining about human conditions in other societies as it is in bargaining about intellectual property rights. Trade policy, these Democrats hold, should be linked to issues traditionally outside its domain.

The pressure for linkage has intensified as the United States has moved to supplement global trade liberalization with the negotiation of regional free trade areas (FTAs). When the United States is considering a special economic relationship with a specific country or group of countries, many members of Congress—and of the broader society—insist on considering issues outside the commercial arena, such as whether the country is a democracy and respects human rights. Focus on a specific country gives concreteness to such issues as the impact of trade on jobs, labor standards, and the environment. In the case of NAFTA, for example, pollution across the border clearly affects U.S. residents. And a free trade agreement with a lower-wage country can intensify the fears of American workers that employers will move production to Mexico, a threat they regularly make in bargaining with labor.

Gephardt's "Dear Democratic Colleague" letter of February 1997 played unabashedly to this interest in linkage, suggesting almost peremptorily that other nations should shape up in just about every area of social policy if they want to negotiate trade deals with the United States. Such issues resonate with a broad range of advocacy groups usually identified with liberal Democrats. Republicans have opposed linkage on labor-environment issues, which plays mainly to Democratic constituencies. But Republicans are increasingly sympathetic to linkage on issues pressed by the religious right—including, for example, reli-

14. For a persuasive analysis of some ways that it has, see Rodrik (1997).

gious freedom legislation threatening sanctions against China or seeking to tie replenishment of International Monetary Fund reserves to policies on abortion and family planning. The "values conservatives" who champion this sort of linkage will make their weight felt in congressional primaries and throughout the 2000 presidential campaign. This linkage also weakens potential support for trade liberalization.

For all these reasons, the "trade and ..." issues, playing on Americans' broader anxieties over globalization, have blocked fast track since 1994. They pose the greatest impediment to trade liberalization for the current president and the next one.

Is Traditional Protectionism Dead?

Traditional business protectionism, by contrast, has been weaker since the Uruguay Round than it was in the years after the Kennedy and Tokyo Rounds, despite the rising overall U.S. merchandise trade deficit, up from $133 billion in 1993 to $247 billion in 1998 and an estimated $300 billion in 1999.[15] In the early Clinton years, the quantity of imports increased less rapidly than their value, as the U.S. dollar depreciated relative to currencies of its major trading partners. Between April 1995 and August 1998, however, the trade-weighted real value of the dollar rose 33 percent, driven importantly by the Asian financial crisis and the collapse of confidence in Japan.[16] This brought about a decline in import prices, so that the quantity of imports grew more during this period than the dollar figures show. The ratio of the volume of U.S. merchandise imports to the volume of goods production—a useful indicator of the pressure of imports on U.S. producers—shot up from 29.0 percent in the second quarter of 1995 to 36.2 percent in the third quarter of 1998. This increase is roughly equivalent, proportionately, to the rise of that ratio during the hyperstrong dollar period of the early 1980s.[17]

15. U.S. Department of Commerce (1996b, p. 11; 1999, p. 15).

16. As measured by the nominal broad index of the Federal Reserve Board, the dollar rose from 90.04 in April 1995 to 120.14 in August 1998, declining thereafter to 116.91 in May 1999. Calculations in the text are based on that index.

17. Between 1982 and 1984, the period of most rapid rise during that decade, the ratio of merchandise imports to goods production went from 18.9 percent to 23.3 percent. This comparison uses 1982 dollars as a base while that in the text employs

In the 1980s, the result was a major upsurge in protectionist pressure. In the 1990s, the story has been different: only one prominent anti-import campaign by a major industry, steel.[18] If more industries do not follow in response to the sharp rise in imports, then it will be reasonable to conclude that traditional business protectionism has been reduced to a shadow of its former self, victim of the same forces of globalization that have brought the "trade and. . ." issues to prominence.

Nonetheless, the trade deficit is still a burden for advocates of trade liberalization. Thus the year 2000 presidential election will play out in a trade policy environment less auspicious than that in which fast track failed in late 1997. Yet the arguments remain strong for renewing the sixty-five-year-old U.S. policy of leadership in international trade liberalization. This policy not only improves American economic welfare but also brings strong international and domestic political benefits.

Trade Liberalization: Multiple Reasons to Persist

The economic case for trade rests on the gains from specialization. As individuals, families, communities, or nations, we trade because we can obtain more of the goods and services we want if we produce what we can do comparatively well and use the proceeds to buy what others are comparatively good at making or doing. Lowering import barriers increases opportunities to trade and thus the gains from trade. Gains from trade liberalization are typically small at first but cumulate over time. The benefits grow because trade encourages each nation to deploy its resources, human and material, in activities offering the greatest returns. International competition also stimulates innovation, leading to increased productivity and increased global output.

It is no accident that the United States, generally regarded as an exceptionally open economy, leads all major industrial nations in

---

1992 dollars. All are calculated from U.S. Department of Commerce (1996a, p. 16; 1998, p. 16). See *Economic Report of the President* (1991, pp. 295, 309; 1999, p. 339). For the trend through the 1980s, see Destler (1995, pp. 205–06).

18. In March 1999, the House voted 289–141 in favor of a steel quota bill, but the legislation faced strong opposition in the Senate and a White House veto threat.

income per person.[19] The benefits of economic openness are available to any nation and have been captured by many. The diversity and flexibility of the U.S. economy, however, may give this nation particular advantages in today's fast-changing world marketplace, as exemplified by the growing dominance of U.S. companies in the emerging computer software industry and the resurgence of U.S.-based automobile production with the adoption by U.S. companies of new technologies and reformed management and labor practices.

When the United States liberalizes trade through negotiations, it can increase its gains by getting other nations to reciprocate. They benefit from unilateral liberalization, and many have undertaken it in the past fifteen years. But trade negotiations can lock in these reforms by incorporating them in international agreements. And since trade barriers in many low- and middle-income countries remain substantially higher than those of the United States, bargaining them down toward zero can bring asymmetric gains for U.S. producers. Such nations are often willing to make such reductions in exchange for ensured access to the world's largest market—if the United States is in a position to negotiate with them.

The United States benefits particularly from further reduction of trade barriers in concert with its major trading partners—Canada, Mexico, and the countries of Europe and the Pacific Rim—since trade with them has a large base on which to build.[20] Economic gains are also maximized in global negotiations under the auspices of the WTO, because the preponderance of U.S. trading partners reduces trade barriers with each agreement.

Besides making Americans better off, trade negotiations are an important component of U.S. political leadership. Economic exchange contributes, on balance, to more cooperative overall relationships, despite intermittent conflicts that the United States and foreign press

---

19. U.S. per capita income ranks first after adjustment for purchasing power. For the economic case for trade in fuller form, see Burtless and others (1998, esp. chap. 2).

20. In 1998, 85 percent of total U.S. merchandise trade (exports plus imports) was with Mexico and Canada (32 percent), western Europe (22 percent) and the Pacific Rim—East Asia, Australia, and New Zealand (31 percent). Calculated from U.S. Department of Commerce (1999, pp. 18–22).

like to label "trade wars." The political gains from U.S. trade policy leadership enhance relations with the European Union, the G-7 advanced industrial countries, and the APEC nations.

U.S. leadership in trade liberalization is particularly important in relations with Latin America. U.S. trade with Western Hemisphere nations outside NAFTA is growing rapidly but still amounts to only two-thirds of U.S. trade with Mexico alone.[21] However, democratization and economic reforms have brought most Western Hemisphere nations to view deepening of engagement with the United States, and with one another, as beneficial. This attitude reverses a longstanding insistence on "nonintervention in internal affairs" and national economic autonomy. The 1994 Miami Summit of the Americas issued a declaration pledging cooperation on a broad range of issues, including democracy, education, health, and drug trafficking. The Free Trade Area of the Americas agreed upon there, however, is widely viewed as the capstone of the new hemispheric agenda.[22] It is the area of hemispheric action where this nation has the most to offer directly, and hence it is a powerful source of U.S. leverage—particularly on economic issues, but beyond them as well.

Of first-order political *and* economic importance is U.S. trade with the People's Republic of China. That nation has achieved astonishing gains in living standards over the past quarter century as it has liberalized trade, investment, and overall economic activity. Along with these economic gains have come significant increases in the day-to-day autonomy, if not in political democracy, for its citizens. But although Maoist totalitarianism is a thing of the past, continuing political repression has exposed the policy of economic engagement adopted by both Presidents George Bush and Bill Clinton to severe domestic criticism from the left—and increasingly from the right. Nonetheless, economic and cultural exchange remains important in encouraging the ongoing liberalization of Chinese society. Here fast track is not central. The goal is to bring China into compliance with WTO standards and thereby facilitate its entry into the organization. Chinese Premier Zhu

---

21. U.S. Department of Commerce (1999, pp. 18–22).
22. Feinberg (1997).

Rongji made major concessions to this end in spring 1999 negotiations with President Clinton, but the outlook remains murky, with a plethora of other China issues and episodes complicating the picture.

Finally, trade policy has substantial domestic political importance for Americans. Trade policy symbolizes American attitudes toward engagement in the global economy. By acting affirmatively, Americans embrace opportunities presented by globalization and express confidence about their capacity to handle them. Ambivalence and stalemate send the opposite message. Moreover, trade policy has been a matter of bipartisan consensus since the 1950s, with all presidents backing trade expansion and both parties turning out similar, overwhelming majorities as recently as the Uruguay Round vote of 1994.[23] Restoring that consensus is important for effective policy in the future. Furthermore, international trade negotiations remain the primary means of shaping the terms of globalization, with the twenty-first century goal of replicating at the international level the grand capitalist bargain that Americans crafted in the twentieth. Americans can and should debate their negotiating priorities, but they should not fail to engage in such negotiation. To do so would deprive the United States of the opportunity to shape the specifics of the globalization that is coming, whether the United States is ready or not.

Breaking the Stalemate

The U.S. government needs the fast-track trade negotiating authority it has lacked since 1994. Without fast track, the president and his successor will be unable to negotiate significant new trade agreements, and their hands will be tied in their exercise of broader international economic leadership.

Congress failed to pass fast track in 1997, and the House voted decisively against it in 1998. The prime reason was an inability to find common ground on how to address trade-related labor and environmental matters. Behind the differences lay anxiety over globalization, concern over a future beyond Americans' control, and specific worries about the

---

23. On that vote, roughly two-thirds of both Democrats and Republicans voted yes in the House, and three-quarters did so in the Senate.

impact of open international markets on cherished domestic values and institutions. These concerns are nowhere near strong enough to cause Congress to repeal existing trade agreements, but they can bar new ones.

Much of this argument has been symbolic. There are no important new trade-related labor and environmental understandings within reach if only Congress would authorize their pursuit. Thus many in the trade policy community see these issues as a no-win diversion, a move into territory guaranteed to stir domestic controversy with little chance of international achievement. Yet trade does affect the plight of workers. Trade does affect the environment. If ways are not found to address legitimate concerns about these effects, advocates of these causes will oppose trade liberalization. So not to treat these issues invites further polarization. Moreover, it is self-contradictory to argue simultaneously how important trade has become to people's lives and then to declare it illegitimate to deal with trade's impact on a wide range of values.

At the same time, as free trade advocates emphasize, the trade agenda can easily become overloaded with related issues on which prospect of meaningful agreement is slight because there exists neither domestic or international consensus nor an established mode of international negotiation. Seeking to do everything may ensure doing nothing. And for some in the labor-environment coalition, blocking new trade action may in fact be the real objective.

For these reasons, it made sense to fast-track supporters in 1997 to try to pass legislation that largely excluded labor and environmental issues. But with the failure that fall, and the devastating defeat the following September, it makes sense no longer. The present choice is clear: compromise on these issues or a continuing trade policy stalemate.

Little time remains to the Clinton administration. And though the president gave the need for trade compromise prominent attention in his January 1999 State of the Union address, little progress has been evident since then. Therefore, though one should not rule out the possibility that Congress will enact new fast-track legislation during the remainder of his term, it is prudent to assume that it will not. So it is time to start planning for 2001, to lay the trade policy groundwork for the next administration and Congress.

If the United States is to resume its role as a leader in the fight for trade liberalization, the constituency for trade policy must be enlarged by addressing public concerns about trade's impacts. A national dialogue must take place on how best to respond to these concerns. The president could launch such a dialogue during his remaining time in office. President Clinton, working with Republican and Democratic congressional leaders to the extent feasible, should reiterate his personal support for broad trade-negotiating authority and his hope that it can be enacted on his watch but declare also that the current controversy makes this task very hard. Therefore, if he could not get a law passed, he would at least like to prepare the bipartisan political ground for his successor.

However it is initiated, such a trade policy dialogue should address three related issues, ideally with a working group established for each one: the specific negotiations to be authorized; means for addressing labor, environmental, and other trade-related issues; and means for coping with the costs of globalization to Americans who are hurt. It should engage a broad range of groups in order to seek consensus, with an emphasis on those inclined to seek a middle ground.

A working group on the specific negotiations to be authorized could address global and regional negotiations. The group could be led by the current U.S. trade representative or by a previous holder of that office who commands bipartisan respect. The global issues gained new salience for the United States with President Clinton's decision to host the November-December 1999 WTO ministerial meeting in Seattle, and the group should consider whether to continue the WTO's recent emphasis on sectoral negotiations on such issues as intellectual property, services, and agriculture, or to move toward a comprehensive new "millennium" trade round.

Regional issues have attained increased urgency with the decision, taken at the Santiago summit in April 1998, to launch the actual negotiations for a Free Trade Area of the Americas. This issue has become controversial because it provokes debate on NAFTA and its legacy. If they wish future trade authority to include the FTAA, the administration and other fast-track advocates must step up and make a stronger case about the benefits of NAFTA than they have done to date.

A second group could address the hot-button issues of trade-related labor and environmental issues. It should be headed by a senior figure outside the administration known for sympathy to these causes and to trade liberalization. The chair should come from outside the trade establishment because executive branch and congressional trade leaders, historically successful against industry-based protectionism, are not well suited to brokering these issues.[24] Their primary constituents are in the business community, and they lack credibility with environmentalists and with organized labor. The group should include representatives of the business, labor, and environmental communities who are prepared to be pragmatic about one another's perspectives and to explore how much they might be accommodated.

This group should begin by developing a short list of major labor and environmental problems associated with trade, determine which problems matter most to whom, and then examine means for addressing them. The objective would be an agenda for international negotiating goals and means acceptable to most Republicans and attractive to many Democrats. Some of these goals might be pursued through trade negotiations. Many would be better addressed through separate, perhaps parallel, negotiating tracks, but steps could be taken to modify international trade rules so that they would not block enforcement of multilateral environmental and labor agreements. The group would almost certainly propose relaxation of the language in the 1997 bill restricting fast-track coverage of labor and environmental issues.[25]

A final group would address the costs of globalization to Americans who are hurt by economic changes that result from increased trade. Its head might be a current or former member of Congress who is sympathetic to these problems. The Clinton administration's lack of a strong program to help the trade losers has seriously weakened its position on trade liberalization. Moreover, domestic trade adjustment assistance for workers is more effective in responding to their losses than are any conceivable agreements on foreign labor standards.

The choice is between broad programs to help workers hurt by all economic changes and assistance only for those deemed to have been injured by trade. Broad programs are fairer—why compensate workers hurt by trade but not by technology?—and avoid the thorny prob-

24. For further development of this argument, see Destler (1998a, pp. 121–46).
25. For some constructive suggestions, see Charnovitz (1998).

lem of determining the cause of each specific job loss. But they are expensive and have less bite in the trade debate. Unfortunately, trade adjustment assistance has lost credibility because appropriations have been small and worker retraining is perceived to be ineffective. A possible alternative would be a program of "earnings insurance" offsetting a portion of workers' losses in pay that result from trade-liberalizing agreements.[26]

The purpose of such a dialogue is political—to broaden support for trade policy steps that enhance Americans' overall welfare and to address trade's oft-disruptive impacts on American society. It could be launched in any number of ways: members of Congress might take the lead if the president were disinclined. It could also lead to any one of a number of policy outcomes. One possibility would be enactment of a relatively narrow fast-track bill for those negotiations enjoying the broadest support, such as sectoral negotiations under the WTO, with dialogue continuing on the thornier issues. A second possibility would be simultaneous enactment of broad fast-track authority with a new program or programs to assist those hurt by trade and economic changes. Yet another outcome could be a law combining immediate fast-track authority for certain negotiations with an expedited procedure under which the president could seek it for others.[27] Finally, the result could be a law reflecting a grand compromise on the labor-environment issue, with business accepting a removal of prohibitions and advocates recognizing limits in the labor and environmental reforms achievable through trade agreements. Realistically, one would hope to build a consensus approach that would eventually win the support of most but not all national environmental groups and some labor sympathizers, but probably not the American Federation of Labor–Congress of Industrial Organizations.

Although immediate congressional approval of comprehensive fast-track negotiating authority would be best for U.S. trade policy, such an outcome is neither likely nor essential. What is essential is for the president, Congress, and key interest groups to engage in a process that

26. For this and other options, see Litan (1998).
27. On this and others ways the fast-track law could be reconfigured, see Destler (1998b).

leads, step-by-step, to negotiating authority for the president and to realistic measures to address the concerns of critics. It may well be that this entire consensus-building process will have to await the inauguration of the next president. But it would be far better if constructive trade policy dialogues begin now and are maintained through the 2000 elections, because the presidential primaries may well work in the opposite direction as Democrats compete for union favor and Republicans seek endorsement by values conservatives.

Anxieties over globalization have brought stalemate to the U.S. trade policy agenda. But the exceptional current condition of the American economy offers an unusually favorable climate for addressing these anxieties. If not now, when?

References

Burtless, Gary and others. 1998. *Globaphobia: Confronting Fears about Open Trade*. Washington: Brookings, Progressive Policy Institute, and Twentieth Century Fund.

Charnovitz, Steve. 1998. "Labor and Environmental Issues." In *Restarting Fast Track*, edited by Jeffrey J. Schott, 55–68. Special Report 11. Washington: Institute for International Economics (April).

Council of Economic Advisers. 1999. *Economic Indicators*. Government Printing Office.

Destler, I.M. 1995. *American Trade Politics*, 3d ed. Washington: Institute for International Economics and Twentieth Century Fund.

———. 1997. *Renewing Fast-Track Legislation*. PA 50. Washington: Institute for International Economics (September).

———. 1998a. "Congress and Foreign Trade." In *The Controversial Pivot: The U. S Congress and North America*, edited by Robert A. Pastor and Rafael Fernandez de Castro, 121–46. Brookings.

———. 1998b. "Fast Track: Options about the Process." In *Restarting Fast Track*, edited by Jeffrey J. Schott, 41–52. Special Report 11. Washington: Institute for International Economics.

Feinberg, Richard E. 1997. *Summitry in the Americas: A Progress Report*. Washington: Institute for International Economics.

Litan, Robert E. 1998. "Reducing Anxiety about Trade Agreements." In *Restarting Fast Track*, edited by Jeffrey J. Schott, 71–83. Special Report 11. Washington: Institute for International Economics.

Rodrik, Dani. 1997. *Has Globalization Gone Too Far?* Washington: Institute for International Economics.

U.S. Department of Commerce, Economics and Statistics Administration. 1996a. "News: U.S. International Trade in Goods and Services." (December).

————. 1996b. "News: U.S. International Trade in Goods and Services." (June).

————. 1998. "News: U.S. International Trade in Goods and Services." (October).

————. 1999. "News: U.S. International Trade in Goods and Services." (June).

U.S. House of Representatives. Committee on Ways and Means. 1997. *Overview and Compilation of U.S. Trade Statutes*: 1997 ed. Government Printing Office (June).

PART II

The Societal Challenges

ISABEL V. SAWHILL

4

Families at Risk

MOST PEOPLE are worried about the breakdown of the family and hold strong views on what to do about it. Unfortunately, people are strongly at odds. Opinions differ on how important it is for mothers to remain at home to rear children, how much damage—if any—results from the birth of children to unmarried parents, how important fathers are to the development of children, and the appropriate roles for men and women. Since people disagree along several dimensions, the range of opinions is enormous. Some want to restore the traditional life-long, two-parent, one-earner family as the norm. Others believe marriage has been oversold or is no longer viable for men without jobs. Most people do not fall cleanly into either camp. They view recent changes in the family as both liberating for women and troublesome for children who increasingly are growing up in families where one parent is absent or both are working.

Public concerns about the family express themselves in the political arena through debates about the so-called marriage penalty under the personal income tax, child care subsidies for working parents, divorce

The author thanks Maya MacGuineas, Shannon Smith, Laura Chadwick, and Caleb Patten for their assistance with this chapter. Andrew Cherlin and William Galston made especially helpful comments on an early draft.

laws, and restrictions on welfare benefits for children born out of wed-lock. Proposals would advance different and sometimes conflicting objectives. Raising barriers to divorce would strengthen the traditional family. Subsidizing child care would make work easier for single parents or for two-earner couples, nontraditional modes of family life that have emerged in the past few decades.

Whatever one's values, the evidence is clear. Families are under stress and children are increasingly at risk of growing up in economically or socially impoverished environments that are associated with poor educational outcomes, high rates of crime, and poor life prospects. Direct assistance to such families, especially high quality child care and early education, can create a better start for such children. However, existing government programs that provide more income or other supports to families and children are costly and are fighting demographic trends so strong that even substantial amounts of aid will do little to improve children's prospects unless changes in norms and values lead their parents to behave differently. Public and private efforts to promote a different set of behaviors may have modest direct effects, at best. However, because even small changes in behavior may be socially contagious and lead eventually to a shift in norms and attitudes, such efforts are worth pursuing.

Families under Stress

Family life has changed in all industrialized countries during the past half century. New technologies have improved occupational prospects for women, permitted substitution of commercial for home-produced goods, and enhanced control over fertility. These developments have enabled more women to work outside the home and improved their status. The greater economic independence of women has contributed to higher divorce rates and more childbearing outside of marriage. All of these trends have fostered a shift in attitudes that has reinforced the initial effects of technology.[1]

The effects of these changes on family life have been benign in many respects for adults, but they have been problematic for children. Women—and many men—have been freed from restrictive roles.

---

1. Fuchs (1988, chap. 2); Spain and Bianchi (1996, chap. 4); Goldin (1990).

Women have experienced greatly improved career opportunities outside the home. But other developments have caused widespread concern (table 4-1).[2] Almost one-third of children are born out of wedlock. Half of all marriages end in divorce. Seventy percent of all children under 18 have working mothers, and as many as 60 percent of all children born in the 1990s will spend some time in a single-parent family.[3] Mothers employed outside the home work longer hours than women did in the recent past to meet the demands of work and home. Poverty and other social problems among children have increased with the growth of single-parent families. The life prospects of children appear increasingly unequal, and society is bearing some of the costs formerly borne by families.

Consequences for Adults

Not so long ago, divorced men and women were stigmatized, and children born out of wedlock were called "illegitimate." Such mores and women's economic dependence often trapped people in unhappy or abusive relationships. But marriage also has many benefits. Married people are healthier, live longer, earn more money, and accumulate more assets than the unmarried, even after adjusting for the tendency of those with better prospects to get and remain married. Couples can also live more cheaply together than they could separately.[4] The sharp decline of marriage in impoverished inner-city communities, where women head more than half of all families with children, has exacerbated the problems commonly found in such communities.[5] As shown in figure 4-1, two minimum wage jobs provide an after-tax income of $21,000 a year, not perhaps enough to eliminate hardship but above the official poverty thresholds for families consisting of two adults and three or fewer children.

2. These trends have been evident in virtually all industrialized countries, although they have proceeded at different paces. Between 1960 and 1990, the largest changes in the labor force participation of women occurred in Canada, the United States, Australia, Sweden, and the United Kingdom. Smaller increases were experienced in France, Germany, and Italy. Spain and Bianchi (1996, p. 101).

3. Furstenberg and Cherlin (1991, p. 11).

4. Waite (1995) reviews this literature. The wealth effects are from a study by Smith (1994), and the male wage effects are from Daniel (1994).

5. Of the families living in census tracts (1990) where the poverty rate was higher than 40 percent, more than half were headed by women. Mincy and Wiener (1993).

Table 4-1. *Indicators of Family Change, 1950–96*

Indicator	1950	1960	1970	1980	1990	Most recent
Labor force participation rate of women with children younger than 18[a]	18.4	30.4	52.9	56.6	66.7	70.2[b]
Divorce rate[c]	10.3	9.2	14.9	22.6	20.9	19.5[b]
Percent of all births out-of-wedlock	4.0	5.3	10.7	18.4	28.0	32.4[d]
Percent of children younger than 18 in single-parent[b] families	n.a.	9.1	11.9	19.7	24.7	27.9[b]

Sources: Labor force participation of women: 1950: Bureau of the Census (1974, p. 341, table 552); 1960–96: U.S. House of Representatives (1998, p. 662, table 9-2); divorce rate: 1950–70: Bureau of the Census (1974, p. 66, table 93); 1980–96: Bureau of the Census (1998, p. 111, table 156); births out of wedlock: 1950–80: Bureau of the Census (1984, p. 70 table 97); 1990–97: Ventura and others (1999, table C); children in single-parent families: 1960–96: U.S. House of Representatives (1998, p. 1245).

n.a. Not available.

a. Rates for 1950 and 1960 are for married women with children only. Rates for 1970 exclude never-married women.

b. 1996.

c. Divorce rate is per 1,000 women over 15 years old.

d. 1997.

Some analysts blame the decline of marriage, especially among urban African Americans, on the lack of well-paid jobs for men. However, marriage rates have fallen almost as much among well-educated as among poorly educated black men and almost as much among the employed as the unemployed or poor. Furthermore, statistical analysis indicates that the decline in earnings or employment prospects among black men cannot explain more than about 20 percent of the changes in black family structure since 1960.[6]

In the meantime, greater job opportunities have enabled women to earn more money. Although these opportunities allow couples to enjoy

6. Ellwood and Crane (1990); Lerman (1989); Mare and Winship (1991); McLanahan and Casper (1995). These relationships work in both directions. As we have seen, men who are married do better in the labor market that those who are not. Indeed, it is increasingly argued that marriage has a socializing and stabilizing influence on men that we ignore at our peril. And several recent studies tend to support this view. Daniel (1994); Wilson (1993, p. 172); Waite (1995); Akerlof (1998).

Figure 4-1. *Marriage as an Antipoverty Strategy*

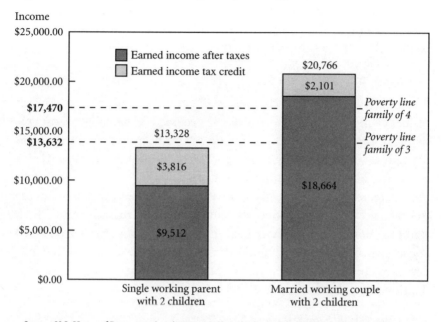

Source: U.S. House of Representatives (1998, p. 899); Joint Committee on Taxation (1999). Assumes minimum wage of $5.15 an hour.
a. Author's calculations based on the 1999 tax, poverty, and EITC levels.

higher incomes, they also create stresses in the family. Employed married women are working longer hours than ever. Although women spend fewer hours on household chores and child care than in the past, and men's contribution has increased from about five to about ten hours a week over the past twenty years, women still do twice as much work as men in the home.[7] As a result of this "second shift," employed married women work about fifteen hours more each week overall than their husbands do.[8] In opinion surveys, a majority of both men and

7. Spain and Bianchi (1996, p. 169). Bianchi and Spain employ data from household surveys of families from the 1980s. According to Robinson (1997), new survey data about household work from working men and women in the 1990s do not differ substantially from the 1980s data.

8. Hochschild (1989, p. 3). The housework and child care gap is largest (more than twenty-four hours a week) when the oldest child in the family is three years old or younger. Scarr (1992, p. 220). And the amount of housework done by men is relatively unresponsive to the share of income provided by their wives. Akerlof and Kranton (forthcoming). See also Spain and Bianchi (1996, pp. 169–70).

women (but more of the latter) say there is too much pressure to "have it all—marriage, family, and a successful career." And about a third of both sexes think the country would be better off if men and women went back to the traditional roles they had in the 1950s.[9]

Consequences for Children

Many believe that recent changes in the family—the most important influence in young children's lives—have been responsible for an epidemic of problems affecting the nation's youth, from juvenile crime to drug abuse. Child poverty, abuse and neglect, juvenile crime, and violence have all risen over the past few decades (table 4-2). Over this same period, teens have become more sexually active, resulting in an increase in pregnancies and early, out-of-wedlock births. Drug use among high school seniors appears to have peaked in the 1980s and to have declined subsequently. Child health and infant mortality have improved. Children are completing more years of schooling, but indicators of academic achievement are relatively flat.

The Growth of Single-Parent Families

Among the forces increasing poverty and other social problems among children, one trend seems especially deleterious—the growth of single-parent families. Children raised by only one parent experience more psychological and behavioral problems and are less successful in school than are children raised by two parents. These problems are partially because of the lower incomes typically received by such parents, but roughly half of the difference remains even after adjusting for economic circumstances. According to one study, increasing the number of years that school-age children spend in an intact family (from eight and one-half years to ten years) would improve later attainment as much as eliminating poverty for this same age group.[10]

Although powerful evidence indicates that growing up in single-parent families is linked with a host of problems, people who remain in stable marriages may differ from those who do not. These differ-

---

9. *Washington Post,* Kaiser Family Foundation, Harvard University Survey Project (1998, pp. 29, 57).

10. Haveman and Wolfe (1994, pp. 246–48).

ences—some of which are difficult to measure—could contribute to differences in outcomes for their children. If so, encouraging marriage or making divorce more difficult will make less difference for children than current studies suggest. A British study that followed children from birth to age 33 found that part of the negative effect of divorce on children's mental health resulted from factors that predated the dissolution of their parents' marriage, although divorce precipitated further behavior problems or depression that persisted into early adulthood.[11] Judith Wallerstein, who has intensively studied children whose parents divorced, finds that feelings of abandonment and fear of failure in their own relationships plague the children.[12] These findings have led many observers to conclude that, though divorce may be the best solution for deeply troubled marriages, divorce laws have gone too far in the direction of liberating adults from marriages that in the past would have been preserved "for the sake of the children."[13]

The economic effects of changes in family structure are especially clear. From 1970 to 1997, child poverty rose from 15 to 20 percent. If family composition had not changed, the child poverty rate would have remained virtually unchanged (figure 4-2).[14]

More Working Mothers

Most people once believed that children are better off if their mothers care for them full time. Such common wisdom justified cash assistance to low-income mothers so that they could stay home with their chil-

---

11. Cherlin, Chase-Lansdale, and McRae (1998). This study uses both a so-called growth curve and a fixed-effects model to control for characteristics of an individual or her or his family that may affect mental health either before or after divorce and thus help to reveal the "true" effect of the divorce event itself. In a comparison of children whose parents divorced when they were 7 to 22 years of age to those from intact families, the former scored 0.11 standard deviations higher at age 7 on an index of behavior problems, anxiety, or depression but 0.25 standard deviations higher by age 33.

12. Nordlinger (1998, p. 29).

13. Amato and Booth (1997, p. 220) claim that less than a third of all divorces are high-conflict situations.

14. See Lerman (1996). He found that the growth of single-parent families explained all of the increase in poverty among children between 1971 and 1989 (even after adjusting for the fact that currently unmarried women are less likely to find husbands who are as successful as the men that are already married).

Table 4-2. *Indicators of Child Well-Being, Selected Years, 1960–1997*

Indicator	1960	1970	1980	1990	Most recent
Percent of children in poverty[a]	29.6	15.1	18.3	20.6	19.9[b]
Median income of families with children[c] (1997 dollars)	28,996	40,013	41,666	42,035	43,545[b]
Reports of child abuse and neglect[d] (in thousands)	n.a.	60.0	785.1	1,767.7[e]	2,050.8[f]
Juvenile crime rate (delinquency case dispositions per 1,000 youth aged 10–17 years old)	20.1	32.3	38.3	51.5	60.7[g]
Violent crime arrest rates for youth under 18 (per 100,000)	58[h]	101	163	184	231[i]
Infant mortality rate (per 1,000 births)	26.0	20.0	12.6	9.2	7.2[f]
Death rates of children, 5–14 years old (per 100,000)	46.6	41.3	30.6	24.0	21.9[f]
Drug use among high school seniors (percent using in past month)					
Cocaine	n.a.	1.9[i]	5.2	1.9	2.4[j]
Alcohol	n.a.	68.2[i]	72.0	57.1	52.0[j]
Marijuana	n.a.	27.1[i]	33.7	14.0	22.8[j]
Cigarettes	n.a.	36.7[i]	30.5	24.0	21.9[f]

Sources: Children in poverty: Bureau of the Census, *Historical Poverty Tables—Persons, Table 3* (http://www.census.gov/hhes/poverty/histpov/hstpov3.html [June 17, 1999]); median income: 1980–97: Bureau of the Census, *Historical Income Tables—Families: Table F-10* (http://www.census.gov/hhes/income/histinc/f10.html [June 22, 1999]); 1960, 1970: calculated with data from *Historical Income Tables-Families*, (http://www.census.gov/hhes/income/histinc/f09.html [June 22, 1999]); child abuse: 1970: Sawhill (1992, p.149, table 5-1); 1980: Bureau of the Census (1984, p. 182, table 301); 1991: Bureau of the Census (1993, p. 209, table 340); 1996: Bureau of the Census (1998, p. 227, table 374); juvenile crime rate: 1960, 1970: Bureau of the Census (1984, p. 193, table 322); 1980: Bureau of the Census (1993, p. 208, table 337); 1990, 1995: Bureau of the Census (1998, p. 226, table 371); violent crime arrest rate: U.S. Department of Heath and Human Services (1998, p. 197, table SD1.6); infant mortality rate: 1960, 1970: Bureau of the Census (1974, p. 60, table 84); 1980–96: Bureau of the Census (1998, p. 98, table 134); child death rate: 1960–90: U.S. House of Representatives (1998, p. 1279, table G-23); 1996: Federal Interagency Forum on Family and Child Statistics (1998, p. 83); drug use among high school seniors: "Monitoring the Future Study," University of Michigan, *Data Table 4: Long-Term Trends in Thirty-Day Prevalence of Various Types of Drugs for 12th Graders* [http://www. isr.umich.edu/src/mtf/pr98t4.html [June 17, 1999]); teen sexual activity rate: 1970–90: Moore, Driscoll, and Lindberg (1998, p. 19); 1997: Kann and others (1998, table 26, p. 70); teen pregnancy rate: 1970–90: U.S. Department of Heath and Human Services (1999, p. 341, table SD 4.5A); 1995: Ventura, Mathews, and Curtin (1998, p. 2); teen birth rate: 1960–90: U.S. Department of Heath and Human Services (1999, p. 349); 1997: Ventura and others (1999, table 3); percent of teen births out of wedlock: 1960–90: figures adapted from Child Trends, *Facts at a Glance* (October) (http://wwwchildtrends.org/faag97.htm [June 22, 1999]); 1997: Ventura and others (1999, p. 42, table 17); high school completion: National Center for Education Statistics

Table 4-2. (*continued*)

Indicator	1960	1970	1980	1990	Most recent
Percent of teens who are sexually active[k]	n.a.	29.0	47.0[l]	55.0	48.4[b]
Teen pregnancy rate[m]	n.a.	9.6[n]	11.0	11.5	10.3[g]
Teen birth rate[m]	8.9	6.8	5.3	6.0	5.2[b]
Percent of teen births that are out of wedlock	15.0	30.0	48.0	68.0	77.8[b]
Proportion of people who have completed 4 years of high school by 25–29 years of age	60.7	75.4	85.4	85.7	87.4[b]
SAT scores[o]					
Verbal	543[p]	537	502	500	505[j]
Mathematics	516[p]	512	492	501	512[j]
National Assessment of Educational Progress scores:					
17-year-olds					
Reading	n.a.	285.2[q]	285.5	290.2	286.9[f]
Mathematics	n.a.	304[n]	299[r]	305	307[f]
Science	n.a.	305	283[r]	290	296[f]

(1998, p. 17, table 8); SAT scores: 1960–90: College Entrance Examination Board (1998, table 1); 1998: National Center for Education Statistics (1998, p. 146, table 132); NAEP scores: National Center for Education Statistics (1998; p. 127, table 109; p. 136, table 120; p. 144, table 128).

n.a. Not available.

a. This child poverty figure is for all children under 18. The child poverty rate in figure 4-2 is for related children in families under age 18 and is slightly lower.

b. 1997.

c. Median income of families with one or more children was not recorded before 1974, so median income figures were estimated with expected value formula, using data about families with specific numbers of children for 1970 and 1960.

d. Data are now kept on substantiated cases of child abuse, as well as reports. Substantiated incidences are fewer than the numbers above, but no data on substantiated reports exist before 1990.

e. 1991.

f. 1996.

g. 1995.

h. 1965.

i. 1994.

j. 1998.

k. Percent of females 15 to 19 years old who report having had premarital sexual intercourse.

l. 1992.

m. All rates are for women 15 to 19; pregnancy rate is the percent of teens who were pregnant, and birth rate is the percent of teens who gave birth.

n. 1973.

o. The SAT test was changed in 1995. Previous years' scores (back to 1967) have been recalibrated so that they are comparable with the 1996 scores.

p. 1967.

q. 1971.

r. 1982.

Figure 4-2. *Child Poverty Rate, 1970–97*

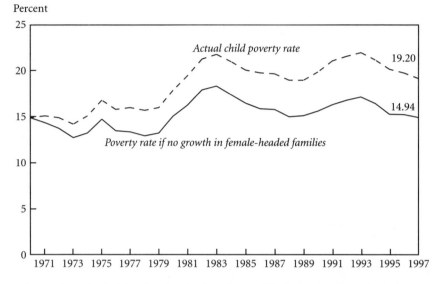

Percent

Actual child poverty rate

19.20

Poverty rate if no growth in female-headed families

14.94

1971 1973 1975 1977 1979 1981 1983 1985 1987 1989 1991 1993 1995 1997

Sources: Author's calculations based on data from Bureau of the Census, data from *Historical Poverty Tables, table 10* (http://www.census.gov/hhes/poverty/histpov/hstpov10.html [June 4, 1999]) and *table 3* (http://www.census.gov/hhes/poverty/histpov/hstpov3.html [June 4, 1999]).

dren. And this belief continues to weigh heavily with many mothers who are considering going to work for pay.

The most recent research offers some comfort to two-earner families. It finds that the quality of the home environment matters a great deal, but that the amount of time a mother spends in the home or out of it makes little difference even for very young infants and toddlers. These findings are somewhat surprising and may not be the last chapter in the story of children with working mothers. Studies done in the late 1980s or early 1990s consistently showed that regular, nonmaternal care during the first year of life led to insecure attachment and was not, on balance, in the best interests of children.[15] A more recent study of 1,364 children born in 1991, which involved extensive and ongoing observations of children interacting with both child care providers and their own mothers and careful efforts to adjust for the tendency of different

15. For a review of this earlier literature and a full set of citations, see NICHD Early Child Research Network (1994).

types of families to select different child care settings, found that whether infants and toddlers received care from mothers or other caregivers made little difference.[16]

Children's Life Prospects: Increasingly Unequal?

Many women have adjusted to the new environment of greater choice by delaying marriage and childbearing and having fewer children or none at all. With fewer children, these women can invest more time and money in each child than mothers could in the past. Other women, particularly those with little education, continue to have children early. But increasingly they bear them out of wedlock and go on welfare.[17]

The result of these choices is that more young children than in the past live in one of two types of families: those headed by poor, teenaged, unwed mothers who lack a high school degree and those headed by relatively affluent, well-educated married couples in their late twenties or thirties. In 1974, 3 percent of all children under the age of seven lived in the first kind of family while 11 percent lived in the second kind.[18] By 1996 the proportion in the first group had almost doubled in size while the proportion in the second group had almost tripled.[19]

Children born into such disparate circumstances have very different life prospects. This bifurcation in family life is already contributing to growing income inequality and could have larger effects in the future.[20] Children of school age whose mothers delay childbearing until they have finished high school, get married, and are at least twenty years old are one-tenth as likely to be poor as those whose mothers have not done these three things (figure 4-3). Other research points to a strong relationship between early family environments and a child's later edu-

16. NICHD Early Child Care Research Network (1994, 1997).

17. Among women who were married and at least 20 years old at the time of their first birth in the late 1970s, 18 percent ended up on welfare in the subsequent ten years. If the mother was unmarried and under 20, however, the proportion ending up on welfare was 81 percent. O'Neill and O'Neill (1997, p. 28).

18. More specifically, these children faced at least three out of the four environmental risks or opportunities mentioned.

19. These data are from the Panel Study of Income Dynamics. Details available on request from the author.

20. Lerman (1996) for example, finds that changes in family structure can explain about half of the increase in income inequality between 1971 and 1989.

Figure 4-3. *Circumstances of Birth and Subsequent Poverty Rates of School-Age Children*

Poverty rate 7–12 years old (percent)

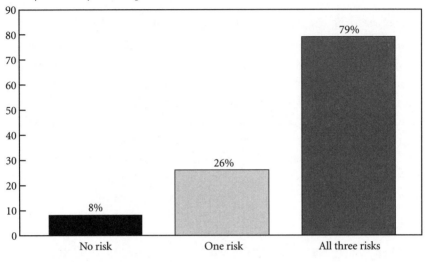

Source: Zill and Nord (1994, pp. 18, 25).
Risks defined:
No risks: Child born to married parents, mother age 20 or older and at least a high school greaduate.
One risk: Child born to a mother who is either unmarried, a teenager, or lacking a high school degree.
Three risks: Child born to a mother who is unmarried, a teenager, and lacking a high school degree.

cational achievement, chances of becoming a teen parent, and hours worked in early adulthood.[21] Children have always benefited from their parents' economic and social position. What is new is not an inequality of prospect but the growing importance of one reason for that inequality: the increasing prevalence of fatherless homes.

Public Costs

These trends in marriage and the family have affected public budgets. I estimate that the growth of single-parent families between 1970 and 1996 increased spending on welfare and food stamps by $229 billion or about $9 billion a year. This number would be increased if one added the costs of medicaid, social services, housing, and other forms of assis-

21. Haveman and Wolfe (1994); McLanahan and Sandefur (1994).

tance. It would be reduced if one recognized that not all of these women would have escaped poverty if they had married or delayed childbearing. But there is little doubt that sizable costs have been shifted from families to public budgets.

What Should Be Done?

These changes in the family have elicited strong but diverse responses from different parts of the political spectrum. Cultural conservatives want to restore traditional two-parent families—a mother who stays home to care for children and a father who works for pay. They typically advocate sexual abstinence until marriage, laws that discourage divorce and out-of-wedlock childbearing, and support for stay-at-home mothers as great as that for the employed. They believe that welfare and other government social assistance have undermined the family and would drastically curtail or end such assistance. Families, not government, they assert, should be responsible for raising children.[22]

Cultural liberals, in contrast, argue that new family forms are legitimate and, in any case, are here to stay. A few view marriage as an atavistic, patriarchal institution and celebrate the freedom that has enabled many women to escape abusive or dependent relationships. Most accept and support marriage but also favor assistance for single mothers. Liberals believe that declining demand for low-skilled workers, exacerbated by racial discrimination, is primarily responsible for declining earnings among the least skilled. The solution, according to this group, lies not in what they see as the futile effort to restore traditional families but in an effort to deal with economic disadvantage. Toward this end, government should assist families of all types in their child-rearing roles because children are a collective responsibility and government alone can discharge this collective responsibility.[23]

These political tensions are hardly surprising, given the enormous transformations in attitudes and behaviors that have occurred in a relatively short period. In the 1930s, Americans by a ratio of 4 to 1 disapproved of married women working outside the home. By the late 1980s, these attitudes had completely reversed—four times as many Ameri-

22. Ashcroft and others (1996).
23. Hochschild (1991).

cans approved as disapproved of women working for pay.[24] At the same time, the public's greatest concern is that parents are spending too little time with their children.[25]

In short, most Americans embrace neither the liberal nor conservative positions in full. Most do not want to turn back the clock to a time when divorce was highly stigmatized and women were restricted to domestic roles. They want to preserve a safety net for single-parent families and provide extra help to poor children. But they believe that parents are ultimately responsible for their children's well-being, see merit in increasing the proportion of children being raised by two married parents, and are open to public or private initiatives that promise to achieve these objectives. The real question is whether effective interventions exist.

What Can Be Done?

Proposals to strengthen families have taken many forms. Changes in tax and benefit programs or in divorce laws can be designed to encourage marriage. Child care or other subsidies can provide direct assistance to families raising children. Encouraging teenagers to delay childbearing and enforcing parental obligations to pay child support are aimed at fostering more responsible parenting. Finally, messages matter. Government policies or nongovernmental initiatives in all of these areas may influence values and norms in ways that are not immediately evident but affect behavior over the longer term.

Encouraging Marriage

One way to encourage marriage is to provide incentives through tax or benefit programs that favor married over unmarried individuals. Three aspects of public policy are the subjects of current debate: amendments to the tax laws to deal with the so-called marriage penalty, legislation to curb the antimarriage bias in the welfare system, and measures to make divorce more difficult to obtain.

---

24. Yankelovich (1994, p. 34).
25. Yankelovich (1994, pp. 35–36).

THE MARRIAGE PENALTY. Marriage usually raises or lowers the combined taxes of the couple. Such penalties and rewards are inescapable in a family-based tax system with progressive rates. The personal income tax system typically provides a marriage bonus to traditional families in which one spouse works full time and earns most of the family's income and the other spouse works part time, if at all. Taxes are lower for such couples than they would be for the two spouses separately because lower tax rates apply to couples than to a single person with the same income.

Two major groups experience marriage penalties, however. First, low earners may lose eligibility for the earned income tax credit (EITC) if they marry.[26] For example, a single mother with two children qualifies for as much as $3,816 if she has a minimum wage job and earns around $10,000 a year. But if she marries another earner with a similar income, she loses almost half of the EITC as well as other benefits, making marriage a very expensive proposition.[27] This tax provision encourages poorly paid men and women who have a child to cohabit rather than marry.[28] One way to solve the problem is to allow a higher standard deduction for two-earner couples that recognizes the extra costs and work effort associated with holding down two jobs. This would reduce the amount of taxable earnings assumed to be available and thus the phaseout of the EITC that now occurs between incomes of $12,000 and $31,000 a year.

Second, couples who have approximately equal earnings or who both have high earnings are likely to pay more in tax if married than they would if single. For example, if two $40,000 earners marry, their tax bill will increase by about $1,400 (assuming both claim the standard deduction).[29] At higher earnings, the penalty is larger. Chapter 7 examines solutions to these and other marriage tax questions.

26. The maximum credit can be earned at incomes between $9,540 and $12,460 in 1999 and is reduced by 21 percent of earnings above $12,460, phasing out entirely at an income of $30,580 for a family with two children.

27. Not all families face a marriage penalty: if a mother with little or no income marries someone with a minimum wage job, the family is eligible for a larger EITC. For more evidence on marriage penalties, see Steurle (1997).

28. One-third of nonmarital births overall in the United States are to cohabiting couples according to Larry Bumpass. Haaga and Moffitt (1998, p. 20).

29. Congressional Budget Office (1997, p. 4).

Although marriage penalties and bonuses are inescapable under a progressive, family-based income tax, the evidence indicates that they do not have major behavioral effects. Although tax incentives may cause couples to shift wedding dates to minimize taxes, it is not clear that they have a more permanent effect. For one thing, the complexities of the law make it difficult for people to even know how marriage will affect their tax bill. And for another, any marriage penalty or bonus is not likely to loom large in the decision to marry. The few studies that exist on this topic have not produced consistent results but suggest that the effects of the marriage penalty on behavior are probably small to nonexistent.[30] Of course, it can be argued that as a matter of policy and simple fairness, society should never penalize marriage even if the penalties have little or no direct impact on behavior.

THE WELFARE SYSTEM. The welfare system pays benefits to women who have children outside of marriage but not to childless women or, except under special circumstances, to married woman.[31] In 1997, for example, a typical poor mother with two children received a benefit package equal to roughly $8,300 a year.[32] The 1996 welfare reform law, the Personal Responsibility and Work Opportunity Reconciliation Act (PRWORA) dampened but did not eliminate these incentives by setting limits on the duration of benefits, requiring the mother to work after two years, requiring teen mothers to live at home or in another supervised setting, and allowing states to deny benefits to teenage unwed mothers and to women who have another child while on welfare.[33]

---

30. Alm and Whittington (1996); Sjoquist and Walker (1995).

31. Since 1990, states have been required to offer AFDC to needy two-parent families but under a requirement that one parent is unemployed and has a work history. These families account for only 7 percent of the caseload nationally. U.S. House of Representatives (1998, pp. 400, 423).

32. U.S. House of Representatives (1998, p. 418). The benefit package includes food stamps and the maximum AFDC-TANF benefit for the median state in January 1997 for a three-person family. Such families are also eligible for medicaid and may also receive some form of housing assistance.

33. Under the waivers granted before enactment of the new law, fifteen states had implemented a so-called family cap. After the passage of the Personal Responsibility and Work Opportunity Reconciliation Act (PRWORA), twenty-two states had family caps. Five of these states offer some form of assistance for the additional child,

The availability of welfare is only one of the many reasons why single women have children. Most such pregnancies are unintended and occur among women who have few good alternatives. At the same time that out-of-wedlock births skyrocketed in the 1970s and 1980s, real benefit levels in the welfare system declined, suggesting that no simple and direct relationship exists between benefit levels and birth rates. Still, that the safety net existed at all may have contributed to the trend, and some studies suggest that it has had a modest effect.[34]

All of the research to date is based on the welfare system that existed before the 1996 reform. No one yet knows how people will react to the new law, which permits states to implement widely varying rules. The statute makes clear the congressional interest in encouraging marriage, provides new funding for abstinence education programs, and promises large bonuses to states that reduce out-of-wedlock births without increasing abortions. Most important, it has made welfare, and thus unwed motherhood, as a life choice much more difficult.

Discouraging Divorce

By the end of the 1980s, all states had enacted "no-fault" divorce laws. Under these laws either spouse may end a marriage for any reason—even if the other contests it—and waiting periods are relatively short—typically six months.[35] American divorce law is now more lenient than that of most European countries, where longer waiting periods are typically required, especially in contested cases.[36] Although polls indicate that the public believes divorce should be made more difficult to obtain, few states have restricted divorce so far.[37]

---

either through partial cash benefit increases, vouchers for food and clothing, or cash benefits to a third party (a community group or church) on behalf of the child. Delaware is the only state with plans to deny benefits completely to minor mothers who have a child. Gallagher and others (1998, pp. VI8–VI10).

34. Haaga and Moffitt (1998, p. 7); Acs (1995, p. 53). Some evidence says that effects exist for white but not for black women. As one would expect, the effects also appear to be stronger among low-income women whose pregnancies are intended.

35. Only two states (New York and Mississippi) require mutual consent, and in forty states a divorce can be obtained after separation of one year or less.

36. Furstenberg and Cherlin (1991, p. 98).

37. Nordlinger (1998, p. 26).

Louisiana offers couples the option of choosing "covenant" marriage, which requires the couple to undergo counseling before marriage and divorce and which grants divorce only after a two-year separation, except in cases of adultery, abuse, abandonment, or conviction of a felony. The law is new, and few couples have yet taken these more restrictive vows. But it will be important to evaluate its long-term effects, as couples may be under considerable pressure to choose the more binding set of ties. Other proposals to strengthen marriage through changes in divorce laws have included longer waiting periods, a return to more fault-based systems, and requirements for counseling—especially when divorces involve children or are contested. These proposals recognize that relatively permissive laws do not serve everyone's interests in such cases.

Until recently most studies suggested that changes in divorce law had little or no effect on divorce rates because changes in the law reflected rather than caused changes in behavior.[38] However, several recent studies suggest that liberal laws have increased divorce.[39] Although permissive laws may lead some people to treat marriage cavalierly, they enable others, women in particular, to escape from abusive relationships. And while children are better off in a well-functioning family with two supportive parents, they are better off in a single-parent home than in a conflict- or abuse-ridden two-parent home. For these reasons, few would favor a return to the fault-based system of the 1950s. But many people believe it is time to discourage divorce among those whose marriages may simply be less than ideal rather than deeply troubled.

The best way to prevent divorce is to help marriages succeed. Premarital testing and counseling that identifies potential incompatibilities can cause couples to reconsider their decision to marry. Marriage education aims to teach couples better communication or conflict-reduction skills that can help marriages succeed. Participants in one such education program—Prevention and Relationship Enhancement

38. See, for example, Peters (1986, pp. 437–54); Allen (1992, pp. 679–93); Peters (1992).

39. Nakonezny, Shull, and Rogers (1995); Honeycutt (1997). Honeycutt finds that each year of exposure to a liberal, no-fault divorce environment decreased the likelihood that a child lived with both biological parents by about 1 percentage point. She controls for fixed effects across both states and years.

Program or PREP—had divorce rates one-third lower than those not participating at the end of five years. At the end of twelve years results were still positive but smaller and not statistically significant.[40] This program suggests the desirability of further efforts by schools, religious congregations, and other community institutions to educate couples on the need to prepare for the responsibilities of married life.

Child Care

Mothers of more than three-fifths of children under six years of age are employed. In 1994 a relative (often the father) cared for almost half of these preschoolers. Another 37 percent received some form of organized day care. Nine percent were in school (typically nursery school), and a small proportion received in-home care from a babysitter or nanny (figure 4-4). Many older children of working mothers also receive after school care, but 7 to 10 percent of these children are on their own and constitute the nation's "latch key kids."[41]

Child care is costly. In 1998 the federal government spent an estimated $12 billion through such major programs as grants to states, child care tax credits, and Head Start (table 4-3). Good estimates of state spending are not available but probably add $1 or $2 billion to the total. Parents spend another $25 billion or more. A family with an employed mother and a preschool-age child spent an average of $79 a week in 1993 or about $4,000 a year. Care that meets standards proposed by the National Academy of Sciences or the National Association for the Education of Young Children can cost far more. For low earners, these costs are especially burdensome—families making less than $14,400 a year spend 25 percent of their income on child care. Even families making more than $54,000 spend 6 percent.[42]

40. Russo (1997, p. 38).
41. Hofferth and others (1991, pp. 36, 67).
42. On state spending, see Jones, Ross, and Kerachsky (1998, table 1. 2). The $25 billion estimate of parental spending is for 1993 (latest available) and is calculated from U.S. Census Bureau, table C2: Weekly Child Care Costs Paid by Families with Employed Mothers: 1985–1993 (http://www.census.gov/population/socdemo/child/cctab2.txt [June 4, 1999]). Estimates of day care costs for preschool children and the share of income devoted to this expenditure are from Casper (1995, table 3). Estimates of the cost of high-standard care are from Maynard and McGinnis (1992, p. 193).

Figure 4-4. *Form of Child Care for Preschool Children with Working Mothers, Fall 1994*

Percent

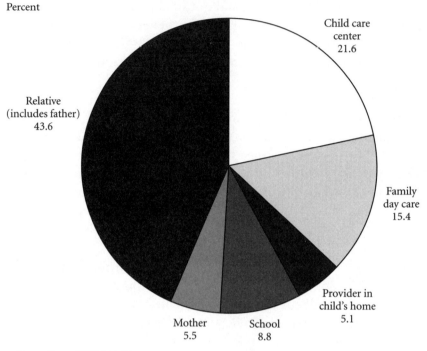

Source: Casper (1998, table 2).

While child care helps working mothers cope with their dual roles, it can also improve the well-being of the next generation. In 1997, almost one-quarter of children under the age of six lived in poor households. Many of these children—and not a few from families with higher incomes—come to primary school not ready to learn. Many never catch up with their peers as they move through the formal educational system. High-quality child care or its close though more expensive cousin—early childhood education—can help prevent these deficits (see chapter 8 for a proposal to convert Head Start into such a program).

Recent reviews of the literature evaluating child care and early education programs suggest that good programs produce a variety of pos-

Table 4-3. *Federal Expenditures on Child Care and Early Childhood Education, 1998*

Program	Description	Fiscal year 1998 outlays (millions)
Child Care and Development Block Grant	Block grants to states to subsidize child care expenses for families with working parents and income less than 85 percent of the state median.	$3,122
Child and Dependent Care Tax Credit	Nonrefundable tax credit for employment-related expenses for the care of a dependent child under 13.	$2,485
Head Start	Early childhood education and development services for low-income preschool children.	$4,346
Dependent Care Assistance Plan	Up to $5,000 for dependent care may be excluded from the employee's income.	$1,325
Social Services Block Grant (SSBG)	Block grants to states that may be used for social services at the state's discretion.[a]	$366
Other	Even Start, IDEA Infants and Toddlers, IDEA Preschool Grants, 21st Century Community Learning Centers.	$959
Total[b]		$12,603

Sources: Congressional Research Service (1999, pp. 2–5); Jones, Ross, and Kerachsky (1998); *Budget of the United States Government, Fiscal Year 2000.*

a. States used almost 15 percent of SSBG funds for child day care in fiscal year 1995. The number reported is 15 percent of the total.

b. Does not include the Child and Adult Care Food Program, which was $1.6 billion in fiscal year 1998.

itive results as children mature.[43] Higher-quality child care affects sociability, cooperation, self-control, and language development, although the effects of higher-quality child care are modest and not as important as a child's home environment in affecting these outcomes. More intensive early education programs that provide a continuum of services have bigger effects. The children experience improved school achievement, lower grade retention, fewer special education courses, and reduced crime. The best results come from those interventions that begin early, include children from the most disadvantaged homes, and provide intensive education and other services over a lengthy period. In the most successful programs, social benefits that can be monetized greatly exceed program costs, with net savings to the government from $13,000 to $19,000 a child.[44]

Research showing that children's brains develop extremely rapidly before age three strengthens the view that education—not just custodial care—could be of particular benefit to very young children. The importance of early education is increasingly recognized at the state level where public funding of preschool programs is catching on, though at an uneven pace. Other countries also recognize the need to provide children with an educational experience from an early age. In France and Italy, for example, nearly all children three to five years old are enrolled in publicly funded preschools. But perhaps parents themselves provide the most telling indicator of the importance of early education. Families are enrolling their children in preschool programs in record numbers (figure 4-5). In fact, the proportion of children from affluent families enrolled in preschool is twice that of those from families with more limited incomes. The federal government's Head Start program serves only about 40 percent of eligible poor children. Thus, the children who most need a head start are not always getting it.[45]

Indeed, an important issue in federal support of child care concerns whether subsidies should be targeted on lower-income families. The federal government's major child care program provides grants to states

43. Karoly and others (1998); Barnett (1995); Reynolds and others (1997); NICHD (forthcoming).

44. Karoly and others (1998, pp. 73–103).

45. Ripple and others (1999, p. 328).

Figure 4-5. *Percentage of Children Enrolled in Preschool, according to Household Income, 1995–96*

Household income

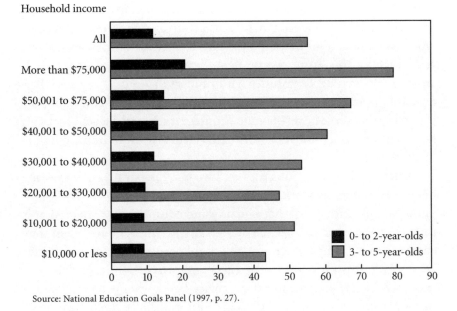

Source: National Education Goals Panel (1997, p. 27).

and targets families with incomes below 85 percent of the state's median. The block grant provides sufficient resources to serve roughly 10 percent of eligible children. Some additional low-income children are enrolled in Head Start, but typically only for part of the day and for one year (at age four). These targeted programs are supplemented by the child and dependent care tax credit (CDCTC) that provides up to $1,440 a year to a family with two children and is available regardless of the family income. The cost of these tax credits has grown five-fold since the mid-1970s. Forty-five percent of the credit goes to families with adjusted gross incomes above $50,000.[46] And because the credit is not refundable, it provides no benefits to most low-income families. For example, a single parent with two children would receive no benefit from the credit if her income were less than $27, 000.

46. U. S. House of Representatives (1998, p. 874); Internal Revenue Service (1998, p. 32).

The case for targeting any new child care subsidies on lower-income families is strong. Many single parents work out of necessity, not choice, and the new welfare system strengthens these incentives. Child care subsidies help make work pay for this group and can help vulnerable children enter school prepared to learn. One way to finance any new assistance for this group would be to limit eligibility for the existing child care tax credit to families with modest incomes—say, less than $60,000 a year. The savings—roughly $1 billion a year—could support programs that serve lower-income children or increased teacher salaries and training, which most experts believe are critical to improving the quality of care.[47]

Targeting child care subsidies on low-income families achieves the objectives of making work pay and keeping children out of harm's way, but unless the care is very high quality and educationally oriented, it is unlikely to compensate for the deficits many children face when they enter school. To improve children's school performance, research suggests, programs must intervene early and provide an intensive (and expensive) curriculum and other services over several years. For this reason, as many children as possible, but especially those from low-income homes, should be enrolled in a preschool or Head Start program that will help prepare them for school while simultaneously allowing their mothers to work.

Encouraging Responsible Parenting

Early, unintended childbearing and the failure of absent parents (usually fathers) to support their children are major factors in the increase of child poverty and impose significant social costs. Any society must strike a balance between supporting families that need help and encour-

---

47. Many child care centers are understaffed, and their staffs tend to be poorly paid. Currently, average salaries for center teaching staff are about $13,100 a year, and only 18 percent of child care centers offer full health benefits. Helburn and others (1995). Salaries are even lower for other types of providers. Those who operate family centers earn on average $9,500 a year after expenses, and unregulated providers are estimated to earn just over $5,100 a year after expenses (1996 dollars). Not surprisingly in light of such low salaries, annual turnover in child care centers is high, at roughly one-third (http://www.acf.dhhs.gov/programs/ccb/faq/workforc.htm [June 4, 1999]).

aging parental responsibility. Too little support exposes children and parents to avoidable hardship. Too much support permits people to behave irresponsibly without suffering the consequences. These considerations suggest more attention needs to be given to reducing teenage pregnancies and enforcing the child support obligations of absent parents.

REDUCING TEEN PREGNANCIES AND BIRTHS. Teen pregnancy and birth rates have been falling in the United States but remain higher than in other industrialized countries (figure 4-6). Teen pregnancy and birth rates have declined recently because teen sexual activity has fallen and use of contraception has increased, perhaps because of the fear of acquired immune deficiency syndrome (AIDS) and other sexually transmitted diseases, and perhaps because the pull of plentiful jobs in the mid-1990s and the push of welfare reform increased incentives to delay childbearing.[48] In addition, sexual mores have become more conservative. The proportion of college freshmen that agreed with the statement, "If two people like each other, it's all right for them to have sex even if they've known each other for a very short time" declined from 52 percent in 1987 to 42 percent in 1997.[49] Another survey found that the proportion of men approving of nonmarital sex increased from 55 to 80 percent between 1979 and 1988 but fell to 71 percent by 1995.[50]

The good news of the 1990s follows several decades during which teen pregnancy and childbearing became more common and more acceptable. As recently as the 1950s, a girl suffered real social penalties if she became pregnant outside of marriage. Forced marriages were common, and young girls refrained from intercourse before marriage for fear of becoming pregnant and being socially ostracized. Young men understood that they had to compete for women's affections by promis-

48. Between 1990 and 1995, the proportion of girls, 15 to 19 years old, who were sexually active declined from 55 to 50 percent. The proportion using contraception at first intercourse increased from 64 percent in the late 1980s to 76 percent in 1995. Most of this increase involved greater use of condoms. Other forms of birth control are little used by this age group. Moore, Driscoll, and Lindberg (1998, p. 27).

49. Rene Sanchez, "Survey of College Freshmen Finds Rise in Volunteerism," *Washington Post*, January 13, 1997, pp. A1, A6.

50. Ku and others (1998, pp. 258–59).

Figure 4-6. *Teen Birth Rates: The United States in Comparison with Other Countries*

Births per 1,000 women, 15–19 years old

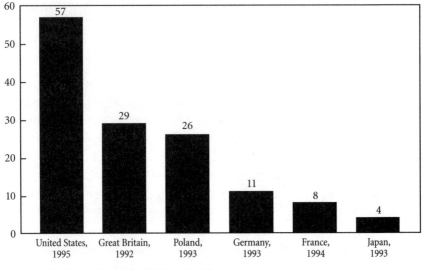

Source: Alan Guttmacher Institute (1998, p. 52–53).

ing marriage or at least commitment.[51] During the 1970s and 1980s contraception and abortion became more readily available. Women became more liberated and sexual mores changed dramatically. As a result, an increasing proportion of teens became sexually active. The trend was especially pronounced among very young teens (15 and

51. Akerlof, Yellen, and Katz (1996) believe that the change in attitudes or norms regarding early sex are the result of a "reproductive technology shock," which provided women with the means to control their fertility but in the process eroded women's bargaining power (since women now considered pregnancy and childbearing to be a woman's choice) and especially women's ability to insist on marriage in cases of pregnancy (shotgun marriages). Sexual activity without commitment thus became the norm. Men no longer had to promise marriage in the event of pregnancy in exchange for sex. These authors calculate that if the shotgun marriage rate had remained constant from 1965 to 1990, white out-of-wedlock childbearing would have increased only 25 percent as much as it actually has. Black out-of-wedlock births would have increased by 40 percent as much. This shotgun marriage effect may have been reinforced by the destigmatizing of sexual relations, pregnancy, and births outside of marriage, and for low-income women, by the availability of welfare.

under) and among those for whom sex had carried the strongest taboos in an earlier era: white, middle-class girls.[52]

The increase in sexual activity during the 1970s and 1980s was massive. If teens had not increased their use of contraception over this period, teen pregnancy rates would now be about 40 percent higher than they are.[53] If current behavior persists, roughly 40 percent of all girls in the United States will experience at least one pregnancy before age 20. For girls from low-income and minority families, the risk is much higher. About one-third of such pregnancies end with abortion, a small percentage by miscarriage, and about half lead to live births. Less than 3 percent of the babies are then put up for adoption.[54] The remainder must run the gauntlet of poverty and other risks confronting new single-parent families.[55] Women who bear their first child before age 20 have more children, complete less education, rely more heavily on welfare, and are less likely to marry than are women who defer childbearing. The children of teen mothers are sicker, more likely to be abused and neglected, less likely to graduate from high school, and more likely to be jailed and to become unmarried teenage parents than are children of older parents.[56]

Efforts to reduce teen pregnancy have traditionally centered on sex education, family planning services, and such youth development programs as mentoring, community service, and after school activities.

52. Besharov and Gardiner (1997).

53. National Campaign to Prevent Teen Pregnancy (1997, p. 8).

54. All of these estimates are quite rough, mostly because data on abortions are not very good and an indeterminate number of women have multiple abortions. People disagree on whether out-of-wedlock births or early childbearing is the larger problem. Some deplore out-of-wedlock births but see no problem with early births to young married women. Others see early births, even within marriage, as the larger problem based on research showing that teen marriages are highly unstable and teen mothers tend to be inferior parents.

55. National Campaign to Prevent Teen Pregnancy (1997, p. 17, note 13).

56. For more details on consequences, see Maynard (1997); Hoffman (1998); Hotz, McElroy, and Sanders (1997). Hotz and others used teen women who miscarried as a control group for those who had a birth and found that teen mothers actually earned more than those who delayed childbearing for two to three years because they worked more hours. However, they completed less formal education and spent more time as single parents than those who delayed.

The few careful evaluations find a mixed record of effectiveness.[57] Sex education is widely available but is often too little and too late to have much impact. The best curricula go beyond lessons on reproductive biology to include teaching adolescents the skills needed to handle relationships, resist peer pressures, and negotiate difficult situations. Condom distribution in schools is controversial but seems to have increased contraceptive use. Critics allege that it increases sexual activity as well, but the evidence does not support this claim.

Family planning clinics have given young women access to effective contraception—such as the pill—that might not otherwise have been available to them. Teenage use of contraception is on the rise but is still inconsistent, so that failure rates are high and unplanned pregnancies remain all too common.[58]

These efforts to educate adolescents about contraception have created intense controversy and provoked a backlash among conservatives, and even among some moderates, who want more emphasis placed on abstinence, especially for younger teens. Although most people believe that contraceptives should remain available to teenagers, polls report that more than 90 percent of the public believes that abstinence is the right standard for school-age youth.[59] In 1996 Congress provided $50 million a year for abstinence education programs. However, these programs have never been adequately evaluated, and many experts doubt that "just say no" campaigns by themselves will have much effect. If these or other funds are used for mentoring, community service, after school programs, or other youth activities, research indicates that this expenditure could make a difference. An evaluation of the Teen Outreach Program—a year-long community volunteer experience for high school students that is coupled with weekly teacher-facilitated group discussions about adolescent decisionmaking—indicates that partici-

57. Kirby (1997).

58. The Alan Guttmacher Institute (1994, pp. 34–37). Of the 72 percent of sexually active 15- to 17-year-olds who use some form of contraception, only 35 percent of condom users use one during every intercourse, and only 40 percent of those using the pill take a pill every day. As a result, about 75 percent of sexually active adolescent women are at risk of an unintended pregnancy.

59. Association of Reproductive Health Professionals and the National Campaign to Prevent Teen Pregnancy (1997, pp. 2–3).

pants in this program are less than half as likely to become pregnant as nonparticipants.[60]

Government programs are unlikely ever to make a large dent in early, out-of-wedlock childbearing unless social norms change. The greater availability of contraception and abortion during the past twenty-five years did not prevent an increase in teen pregnancies and births, especially those occurring out of wedlock. Hand in hand with the new technologies came greater social acceptance of early sex and increased adolescent sexual activity. In principle, contraceptives could prevent all teenage pregnancies and births outside marriage. In practice, they do not because teens are imperfect and inconsistent users of contraception. Even if the failure rate among teenagers were no higher than the 12 percent annual failure rate typical among condom users of all ages, roughly 40 percent of condom users could expect at least one pregnancy within four years. A policy of encouraging the recent trend toward delayed sexual activity while providing contraceptives to those who reject this advice holds greater promise of controlling pregnancies and births, even if it does not convey precisely the moral message on which many insist.

Enforcing Child Support Obligations

In efforts to curb teen pregnancy and birth rates, the role of men and boys has received insufficient attention. In 1997 only 31 percent of single mothers received any support from the child's father. Among never-married mothers, levels of support are even lower, in part because paternity is often not legally established.[61] If sex imposes few costs, young men may see little reason either to abstain or use contraception, which, by all accounts, they frequently resist.

---

60. Allen and others (1997, p. 735).

61. Sorenson and Halpern (1999). About half of young unwed fathers remain connected to their children, with many providing some support informally or erratically. But these connections typically decline over time. Lerman (1993, p. 35). By 1996 paternity had been established for 46 percent of all children under 18 born out of wedlock. In 1995 about 18 percent of never-married mothers received child support. U.S. Department of Health and Human Services (1997, pp. III-22–III-25).

Since 1975, Congress has enacted a series of laws, culminating in the 1996 welfare bill, intended to improve paternity establishment and the collection of child support. These laws allow the federal government to intercept tax refunds from fathers owing support, require wage withholding of new support amounts, and reduce judicial discretion by encouraging states to treat their child support guidelines as "presumptive" or legally binding in most cases. Welfare mothers who do not cooperate in the establishment of paternity can lose a portion of their grant, but at state discretion those who cooperate are allowed to keep some of the money collected rather than paying it to the state. States are required to establish arrangements for men voluntarily to acknowledge paternity through a simple civil process or in the hospital at the time of birth. In addition, states must keep central registries of paternities established along with child support orders and match these items against information on all new hires reported by employers. Applications for professional and other licenses must be accompanied by social security numbers to assist in tracking down absent parents, and licenses can be suspended in cases of nonpayment of support.[62] In 1998 Congress passed the Deadbeat Parents Act, which makes it a felony for parents to cross state lines to evade child support payments.

In fiscal year 1997, federal and state governments spent $3.4 billion on child support enforcement or $182 per case. One study suggests that the proportion of women receiving support has risen steadily and that the various enforcement tools put in place during the past two decades have contributed importantly to that progress. This progress is hard to see in the overall data because the rise in receipt rates for each subgroup of single mothers has been masked by a shift in the composition of the group to include a far higher proportion of never-married mothers for whom receipt rates have always been very low.[63]

Efforts to establish paternity and collect child support may cause boys and young men to act more responsibly. One study finds that the adoption of state programs such as genetic testing to establish paternity and presumptive child support guidelines reduces nonmarital birth rate (two years later) by 1.5 to 2.0 percentage points.[64]

62. Katz (1996, pp. 2700–01); Sorenson and Halpern (1999).
63. Sorenson and Halpern (1999).
64. Case (1998, pp. 212–13).

Changing the Culture

Technological change and economic incentives may have triggered the upheaval in the American family, but shifts in social mores and attitudes have amplified their effects. Social norms that once kept women at home now send them to work. Standards that once labeled sex before marriage as wrong now characterize abstinence until marriage as hopelessly old-fashioned. And acceptance has replaced the disapproval that once confronted women who bore children out of wedlock or divorced.

It is simply impossible to explain the magnitude of recent behavioral changes without invoking norms and community standards. No social scientist has been able to assign more than a small percentage of the change in marriage or out-of-wedlock births directly to measurable changes in economic incentives.[65] A newer body of work recognizes that behavior is influenced by the actions and attitudes of others.[66] People seek acceptance and approval by modeling their behavior on what others do or think. Children imitate their parents, peers, and celebrities and internalize their values. Once one acknowledges that people respond to the behavior of peers, friends, and relatives, changes in incentives can have large indirect effects through a process much like contagion.[67] A mother who observes that her neighbors have all gone to work will be more likely to seek a job herself. A teenager whose friends are sexually active may feel her popularity will be compromised if she abstains.[68] A couple whose marriage is troubled is likely to find

65. Aaron (1994) argues that economists have not taken the formation of preferences seriously, leading to impoverished and misleading models of behavior.

66. A number of economists are now beginning to model the way in which one person's behavior may be influenced by the behavior of others, how social norms or rules of behavior evolve, and some of the implications for public policy. See, for example, Glaeser and Scheinkman (1997); Akerlof (1997, 1998); Evans, Oates, and Schwab (1992).

67. Ellen and Turner (1997) and Dickens (1999) contain good reviews of the empirical literature. Although the literature suggests that individual behavior is partially explained by community environment, it is not clear whether this reflects the operation of social norms within these communities or simply the influence of individual factors that have not been well measured or the tendency of like-minded individuals to co-locate.

68. The powerful influence of group norms on behavior is nicely illustrated in a large-scale study of adolescent girls' likelihood of initiating sex and of becoming pregnant. The authors found that girls whose social network included a high proportion

divorce more acceptable if their best friends have just divorced. Through imitative behavior social trends create their own momentum. Such snowball effects can be good or bad. They may initially be positive and then overshoot some socially desirable optimum. The increased tolerance of diversity and respect for different lifestyles that many welcomed in the 1960s and 1970s may have become a threat to social cohesion and the well-being of the family in the 1990s. Finding the right balance is difficult and will always be controversial, but the decline of strong—or at least good enough—families has in recent decades put excessive burdens on other institutions and raised public costs.

If changes in social norms have weakened marriage and created greater poverty and behavioral problems among children, the question is what, if anything, can be done? Two kinds of experience suggest the cultural genie can be put back in the bottle. First, attitudes and norms are hardly immutable. Societies that become more accepting of certain behaviors in one era may become less so in another as they gain more experience with and information about the consequences of that behavior. Smoking is one dramatic example. The recent decline in sexual activity among teenagers may be another. Drug use has ebbed and flowed historically as knowledge of the consequences of particular forms of addiction has spread. Cycles in birth rates have long baffled demographers, falling unexpectedly during the Great Depression of the 1930s only to give way to the baby boom following World War II.[69] Even childrearing practices cycle as each generation corrects the errors of its parents and commits its own.

Second, when the time is ripe, these changes in norms and behavior can be inspired or catalyzed by both public policies and social movements or other nongovernmental efforts intended to modify or accelerate existing trends. The civil rights and feminist revolutions were fought and won not just in legislatures and courts but also in homes and neigh-

---

(over 75 percent) of "high-risk" peers at the time of the survey were more than twice as likely to become sexually active within eighteen months as those whose network included few "high-risk" peers (less than 25 percent), even after adjusting for a large number of individual and family characteristics that might influence both the outcome and the selection of one's friends. Bearman and Bruckner (1999).

69. Furstenberg and Cherlin (1991, p. 104).

borhoods or wherever people gathered to discuss these issues. More recently, if less dramatically, organized efforts to prevent drug abuse and drunk driving and to encourage seatbelt use appear to have had some success in changing attitudes.[70]

The 1996 welfare reform law has not just changed the rules for recipients but also the culture of the welfare office and most people's expectations about recipients' responsibility to work. How much these revised expectations are affecting behavior remains unclear, but the sharp decline in the caseload is hard to explain fully on any other grounds. Nongovernmental efforts to encourage marriage and responsible parenting are still in their infancy but gaining momentum.[71] The Million Man March, Promise Keepers, and the National Fatherhood Initiative are all working in highly visible, if sometimes controversial, ways to reengage men with their families. Community Marriage Policies that involve religious and other leaders in helping couples prepare for and sustain their marriages have now sprung up in eighty cities. New books, such as Maggie Gallagher's *The Abolition of Marriage* and Barbara Dafoe Whitehead's *The Divorce Culture* are changing the conversation as are such newly formed organizations as the National Marriage Project at Rutgers University and the National Campaign to Prevent Teen Pregnancy in Washington, D.C., along with the somewhat older and better-established communitarian movement.[72]

Organized action has a role to play, especially when it supports an emerging but unarticulated public consensus. Polls and focus groups suggest that the public is deeply disturbed by current trends. In this soil public and private initiatives can help the seeds of cultural change to take root.

References

Aaron, Henry J. 1994. "Distinguished Lecture on Economics in Government: Public Policy, Values, and Consciousness." *Journal of Economic Perspectives* 8 (Spring): 3–21.

70. Dejong and Winsten (1998).
71. For more details, see Nordlinger (1998); Family Impact Seminar (1998).
72. Gallagher (1996); Whitehead (1997).

Acs, Gregory. 1995. "Do Welfare Benefits Promote Out-of-Wedlock Child-bearing?" In *Welfare Reform: An Analysis of the Issues*, edited by Isabel V. Sawhill, 51–54. Washington: Urban Institute.

Akerlof, George A. 1997. "Social Distance and Social Decisions." *Econometrica* 65 (September): 1005–27.

———. 1998. "Men without Children," *Economic Journal* 108 (March): 287–309.

Akerlof, George A., and Rachel E. Kranton. Forthcoming. "Economics and Identity." *Quarterly Journal of Economics.*

Akerlof, George A., Janet L. Yellen, and Michael L. Katz. 1996. "An Analysis of Out-of-Wedlock Births in the United States." *Quarterly Journal of Economics* CXI (May): 297–317.

Alan Guttmacher Institute. 1994. *Sex and America's Teenagers.* New York.

———. 1998. *Into a New World: Young Women's Sexual and Reproductive Lives.* New York.

Allen, Douglas W. 1992. "Marriage and Divorce: Comment." *American Economic Review* 82 (June): 679–93.

Allen, Joseph P., and others. 1997. "Preventing Teen Pregnancy and Academic Failure: Experimental Evaluation of a Developmentally Based Approach." *Child Development* 64 (August): 729–42.

Alm, James, and Leslie Whittington. 1996. "Does the Income Tax Affect Marital Decisions?" *National Tax Journal* 48 (December): 565–72.

Amato, Paul R., and Alan Booth. 1997. *A Generation at Risk: Growing Up in an Era of Family Upheaval.* Harvard University Press.

Ashcroft, Senator John, and others. 1996. "Can Government Save the Family?" *Policy Review: The Journal of American Citizenship* 79 (September–October): 43–47.

Association of Reproductive Health Professionals and the National Campaign to Prevent Teen Pregnancy. 1997. "A Summary of the Findings from National Omnibus Survey Questions about Teen Pregnancy," by Princeton Survey Research Associates. Washington: National Campaign to Prevent Teen Pregnancy (May 2).

Barnett, W. Steven. 1995. Long-Term Effects of Early Childhood Programs on Cognitive and School Outcomes. *The Future of Children* 5 (Winter): 25–50.

Bearman, Peter, and Hannah Bruckner. 1999. *Power in Numbers: Peer Effects on Adolescent Girls' Sexual Debut and Pregnancy.* Washington: National Campaign to Prevent Teen Pregnancy.

Besharov, Douglas J., and Karen N. Gardiner. 1997. "Trends in Teen Sexual Behavior." *Children and Youth Services Review* 19 (5/6): 341–400.

Bureau of the Census. 1974. *Statistical Abstract of the United States: 1974.* U.S. Department of Commerce.

———. 1984. *Statistical Abstract of the United States: 1984.* U.S. Department of Commerce.

————. 1993. *Statistical Abstract of the United States: 1993*. U.S. Department of Commerce.

————. 1998. *Statistical Abstract of the United States: 1998*. U.S. Department of Commerce.

Case, Anne. 1998. "The Effects of Stronger Child Support Enforcement on Nonmarital Fertility." In *Fathers under Fire*, edited by Irwin Garfinkel and others, 191–215. New York: Russell Sage Foundation.

Casper, L. M. 1995. "What Does it Cost to Mind Our Preschoolers?" *Current Population Reports*. P70-52. U.S. Department of Commerce.

————. 1998. "Who's Minding Our Preschoolers?" (Fall 1994, Update) PPL-81. Washington: U.S. Bureau of the Census (http://www.census.gov/population/socdemo/child/p70-62/tab02.txt [June 4, 1999]).

Cherlin, Andrew J., P. Lindsay Chase-Lansdale, and Christine McRae. 1998. "Effects of Parental Divorce on Mental Health throughout the Life Course." *American Sociological Review* 63 (April): 239–49.

College Entrance Examination Board. 1998. *College-Bound Seniors, 1998*. New York.

Congressional Budget Office. 1997. *For Better or for Worse: Marriage and the Federal Income Tax*.

Congressional Research Service. 1999. *Child Care Issues in the 106th Congress*. Washington.

Daniel, K. 1994. "Does Marriage Make Workers More Productive?" Working Paper. Wharton School, University of Pennsylvania.

Dejong, William, and Jay A. Winsten. 1998. *The Media and the Message: The Use of the Mass Media to Communicate Public Service Messages, Lessons Learned from Past Media Campaigns*. Washington: National Campaign to Prevent Teen Pregnancy.

Dickens, William T. 1999. "Rebuilding Urban Labor Markets: What Community Development Can Accomplish." In *Urban Problems and Community Development*, edited by Ronald Ferguson and William Dickens, 381–46. Brookings.

Ellen, Ingrid Gould, and Margery Austin Turner. 1997. "Does Neighborhood Matter? Assessing Recent Evidence." *Housing Policy Debate* 8 (4): 833–66.

Ellwood, David T., and Jonathan Crane. 1990. Family Change among Black Americans: What Do We Know? *Journal of Economic Perspectives* 4 (Fall): 65-85.

Evans, William, Wallace E. Oates, and Robert M. Schwab. 1992. Measuring Peer Group Effects: A Study of Teenage Behavior. *Journal of Political Economy* (October): 966–91.

Family Impact Seminar. 1998. "Strategies for Strengthening Marriage: What Do We Know? What Do We Need to Know?" Washington.

Federal Interagency Forum on Child and Family Statistics. 1998. *America's Children: Key National Indicators of Well-Being, 1998*. Federal Interagency Forum on Child and Family Statistics. Government Printing Office.

Fuchs, Victor R. 1988. *Womens Quest for Economic Equality.* Harvard University Press.

Furstenberg, Frank F. Jr., and Andrew J. Cherlin. 1991. *Divided Families: What Happens to Children When Parents Part.* Harvard University Press.

Gallagher, Jerome L., and others. 1998. *One Year after Federal Welfare Reform: A Description of State Temporary Assistance for Needy Families (TANF) Decisions as of October 1997.* Washington: Urban Institute (May).

Gallagher, Maggie. 1996. *The Abolition of Marriage. How We Destroy Lasting Love.* Regnery.

Glaeser, Edward L., and Jose A. Scheinkman. 1997. *Measuring Social Interactions.* Harvard University, University of Chicago, and National Bureau of Economic Research.

Goldin, Claudia. 1990. *Understanding the Gender Gap: An Economic History of American Women.* Oxford University Press.

Haaga, John, and Robert A. Moffitt, eds. 1998. *Welfare, the Family, and Reproductive Behavior: Report of a Meeting.* Committee on Population, Board on Children, Youth and Families. National Research Council and Institute of Medicine. Washington: National Academy Press.

Haveman, Robert, and Barbara Wolfe. 1994. *Succeeding Generations: On the Effects of Investments in Children.* New York: Russell Sage Foundation.

Helburn, Suzanne W., and others. 1995. *Cost, Quality, and Child Outcomes in Child Care Centers: Executive Summary.* University of Colorado.

Hochschild, Arlie Russell. 1989. *The Second Shift: Working Parents and the Revolution at Home.* Viking.

————. 1991. "The Fractured Family." *American Prospect* (Summer): 106–15.

Hofferth, Sandra L., and others. 1991. *National Child Care Survey, 1990.* Urban Institute Report 91-5. Washington: Urban Institute.

Hoffman, Saul. 1998. "Teenage Childbearing Is Not So Bad After All . . . Or Is It? A Review of the New Literature." *Family Planning Perspectives* 30 (September–October): 236–39.

Honeycutt, Amanda Ann. 1997. "Marriage, Divorce, and the Impacts on Children: Using State Laws to Identify Causal Relationships." Ph.D. dissertation submitted to the faculty of the Graduate School of the University of Maryland at College Park.

Hotz, V. Joseph, Susan Williams McElroy, and Seth G. Sanders. 1997. "The Impacts of Teenage Childbearing on the Mothers and the Consequences of those Impacts for Government." In *Kids Having Kids: Economic Costs and Social Consequences of Teen Pregnancy,* edited by Rebecca Maynard, 55–94. Washington: Urban Institute.

Internal Revenue Service. 1998. *Statistics of Income Bulletin* 18 (Fall).

Joint Committee on Taxation. 1999. *Overview of Present Law and Issues Relating to Individual Income Taxes.* JCX-18-99 (April).

Jones, Pamela, Christine Ross, and Stuart Kerachsky. 1998. "Spending on Early Childhood Care Programs and Research: An Analysis of Federal

Departments, State Governments and Foundations." Princeton, N. J.: Mathematica Policy Research, Inc.

Kann, Laura and others. 1998. "Youth Risk Behavior Surveillance—United States, 1997." In *CDC Surveillance Summaries MMWR*, vol. 47, no. SS-3 (August).

Karoly, Lynn, and others. 1998. "Investing in Our Children: What We Know and Don't Know about the Costs and Benefits of Early Childhood Interventions." Santa Monica: Rand.

Katz, Jeffrey L. 1996. "Welfare Overhaul Law." *Congressional Quarterly* 54 (September 21): 2696–2705.

Kirby, Douglas. 1997. *No Easy Answers: Research Findings on Programs to Reduce Teen Pregnancy.* Washington: National Campaign to Prevent Teen Pregnancy.

Ku, Leighton, and others. 1998. "Understanding Changes in Sexual Activity among Young Metropolitan Men: 1979–1995." *Family Planning Perspectives* 30 (November–December): 56–262.

Lerman, Robert I. 1989. "Employment Opportunities of Young Men and Family Formation." *American Economic Review* 79 (May): 62–66.

———. 1993. "Unwed Fathers: Who They Are." *American Enterprise* 4 (September–October): 32–35.

———. 1996. "The Impact of Changing U.S. Family Structure on Child Poverty and Income Inequality." *Economica* 63 (Supplement): S119–S139.

Mare, Robert D., and Christopher Winship. 1991. "Socioeconomic Change and the Decline of Marriage for Blacks and Whites." In *The Urban Underclass*, edited by Christopher Jencks and Paul E. Peterson, 175–202. Brookings.

Maynard, Rebecca A. 1997. "The Study, the Context, and the Findings in Brief." In *Kids Having Kids: Economic Costs and Social Consequences of Teen Pregnancy*, edited by Rebecca Maynard, 1–22. Washington: Urban Institute Press.

Maynard, Rebecca, and Eileen McGinnis. 1992. "Policies to Enhance Access to High-Quality Child Care." In *Child Care in the 1990s: Trends and Consequences*, edited by Alan Booth, 189–208. Hillsdale, N.J.: Lawrence Earlbaum Associates.

McLanahan, Sara S., and Gary Sandefur. 1994. *Growing Up with a Single Parent. What Hurts. What Helps.* Harvard University Press.

McLanahan, Sara, and Lynne Casper. 1995. "Growing Diversity and Inequality in the American Family." In *State of the Union*, vol. 2, edited by R. Farley, 1–45. New York: Russell Sage Foundation.

Mincy, Ronald B., and Susan J. Wiener. 1993. *The Under Class in the 1980s: Changing Concept, Constant Reality.* Washington: Urban Institute.

Moore, Kristin Anderson, Anne K. Driscoll, and Laura Duberstein Lindberg. 1998. *A Statistical Portrait of Adolescent Sex, Contraception, and Childbearing.* Washington: National Campaign to Prevent Teen Pregnancy.

Nakonezny, Paul A., Robert D. Shull, and Joseph Lee Rogers. 1995. "The Effect of No-Fault Divorce Law on the Divorce Rate Across the 50 States and Its Relation to Income, Education, and Religiosity." *Journal of Marriage and the Family* 57 (May): 477–88.

National Campaign to Prevent Teen Pregnancy. 1997. "Whatever Happened to Childhood?" Washington.

National Center for Education Statistics. 1998. *Digest of Education Statistics, 1998.* Washington.

National Education Goals Panel. 1997. *Special Early Childhood Report.* Washington (October).

NICHD Early Child Care Research Network. 1994. "Child Care and Child Development: The NICHD Study of Early Child Care." In *Developmental Follow-Up: Concepts, Domains, and Methods*, edited by Sarrah L. Friedman and H. Carl Haywood, 377–96. Academic Press.

———. 1997. "The Effects of Infant Child Care on Infant-Mother Attachment Security: Results of the NICHD Study of Early Child Care." *Child Development* 68 (October): 860–79.

———. Forthcoming. "The Relation of Child Care to Cognitive and Language Development." *Child Development.*

Nordlinger, Pia. 1998. "The Anti-Divorce Revolution." *Weekly Standard* (March 2): 25–29.

O'Neill, Dave M., and June Ellenoff O'Neill. 1997. *Lessons for Welfare Reform: An Analysis of the AFDC Caseload and Past Welfare-to-Work Programs.* Kalamazoo, Mich.: W. E. Upjohn Institute for Employment Research.

Peters, H. Elizabeth. 1986. "Marriage and Divorce: Informational Constraints and Private Contracting." *American Economic Review* 76 (June): 437–54.

———. 1992. "Marriage and Divorce: Reply." *American Economic Review* 82 (June): 687–93.

Reynolds, Arthur J., and others. 1997. "The State of Early Childhood Intervention: Effectiveness, Myths and Realities, New Directions." *Focus* 19 (Summer–Fall): 5–11 (newsletter of the Institute for Research on Poverty of the University of Wisconsin-Madison).

Ripple, Carol H., and others. 1999. "Will 50 Cooks Spoil the Broth? The Debate over Entrusting Head Start to the States." *American Psychologist* 54 (May): 327–43.

Robinson, John P. 1997. *Time for Life: The Surprising Way Americans Use Their Time.* Pennsylvania State University Press.

Russo, Francine. 1997. "Can the Government Prevent Divorce." *Atlantic Monthly* (October): 28–42.

Sawhill, Isabel V. 1992. "Young Children and Families." In *Setting Domestic Priorities: What Can Government Do?*, edited by Henry Aaron and Charles Schultze, 147–84. Brookings.

Scarr, Sandra. 1992. "Keep Our Eyes on the Prize: Family and Child Care Policy in the United States, As It Should Be." In *Child Care in the 1990s: Trends and Consequences,* edited by Alan Booth, 215–22. Hillsdale, N.J.: Lawrence Earlbaum Associates.

Sjoquist, David L., and Mary Beth Walker. 1995. "The Marriage Tax and the Rate and Timing of Marriage." *National Tax Journal* 48 (December): 547–58.

Smith, J. P. 1994. "Marriage, Assets, and Savings." Working Paper. Santa Monica: Rand.

Sorenson, Elaine, and Ariel Halpern. 1999. "Child Support Enforcement Is Working Better Than We Think." *New Federalism Issues and Options for States,* series A, no. A-31.Washington: Urban Institute (March).

Spain, Daphne G., and Suzanne M. Bianchi. 1996. *Balancing Act: Motherhood, Marriage, and Employment among American Women.* New York: Russell Sage Foundation.

Steuerle, C. Eugene. 1997. "Taxation of the Family." Statement before the Committee on Ways and Means, U.S. House of Representative. April 15, 1997 (http://www.urban.org/TESTIMON/steuerly2.htm [June 4, 1999]).

U.S. Department of Health and Human Services. 1997. *Indicators of Welfare Dependence: Annual Report to Congress* (October).

———. Office of the Assistant Secretary for Planning and Evaluation. 1998. *Trends in the Well-Being of America's Children and Youth, 1997.* Washington: Child Trends.

———. 1999. *Trends in the Well-Being of America's Children and Youth, 1998.* Washington: Child Trends.

U.S. House of Representatives, Committee on Ways and Means. 1998. *Green Book.* Government Printing Office.

Ventura, Stephanie J., T. J. Mathews, and Sally C. Curtin. 1998. "Decline in Teenage Birth Rates, 1991–97: National and State Patterns." *National Vital Statistics Reports* 47 (12). Hyattsville, Md.: National Center for Health Statistics.

Ventura, Stephanie J., and others. 1999. "Births: Final Data for 1997." *National Vital Statistics Reports* 47 (18). Hyattsville, Md.: National Center for Health Statistics.

Waite, Linda J. 1995. Does Marriage Matter? *Demography* 32 (November): 483–507.

Washington Post, Kaiser Family Foundation, and Harvard University Survey Project. 1998. *Survey of Americans on Gender: Questionaire and Toplines.* Menlo Park, Calif.: Kaiser Family Foundation.

Whitehead, Barbara Dafoe. 1997. *The Divorce Culture.* Knopf.

Wilson, James Q. 1993. *The Moral Sense.* Free Press.

Yankelovich, Daniel. 1994. How Changes in the Economy Are Reshaping American Values. In *Values and Public Policy,* edited by Henry J. Aaron, Thomas E. Mann, and Timothy Taylor, 16–53. Brookings.

Zill, Nicholas, and Christine Winquist Nord. 1994. *Running in Place: How American Families Are Faring in a Changing Economy and an Individualistic Society.* Washington: Child Trends.

GARY BURTLESS

5

Growing American Inequality: Sources and Remedies

Tʜᴇ ᴜɴɪᴛᴇᴅ sᴛᴀᴛᴇs has experienced a startling increase in economic inequality over the past two decades. In the 1970s the pattern of strongly rising living standards that had prevailed for almost three decades after World War II came to an end for families at the bottom and middle of the income distribution. The average income of the one-fifth of families with the lowest incomes actually declined between 1979 and 1997. The incomes of those in the middle rose very slowly. Only at the very top of the income distribution did real incomes continue to climb at a robust pace during the 1980s and 1990s. While the strong economy of the past five years has boosted the incomes of families up and down the income scale, the incomes of those in the bottom fifth of the distribution remain more than 7 percent below where they were at the end of the 1970s.[1]

The author gratefully acknowledges the helpful research assistance of Stacy Sneeringer and Jane Kim and the suggestions of Brenda Szittya.
    1. The calculations are based on a comparison of the average income of families in the bottom one-fifth of the income distribution in 1979 and those in the bottom one-fifth of the income distribution in 1997. The comparison is made in constant dollars—that is, after subtracting the effect of inflation. Of course, the families at the bottom of the distribution in the two years are not the same. Many families with low incomes in a given year enjoy rapid income gains as their breadwinners move up

Trends in relative income over the postwar period are displayed in figure 5-1. The top line—which shows the ratio of the average cash incomes received by families in the top 5 percent and the middle 20 percent of the income distribution—provides a rough measure of the distance between the nation's most affluent families and families in the middle class. This measure, which is only approximate because the Census Bureau does not obtain reliable information about the incomes of households in the top 1 or 2 percent of the distribution, indicates that the gap between well-to-do and middle-class families generally declined from the end of World War II until the 1970s and then soared in the 1980s and 1990s. Part of the large jump between 1992 and 1993 was due to better measurement of rich families' incomes, but the relative income gap between middle- and high-income families almost certainly continued to increase after 1992.

The bottom line in figure 5-1—which shows the ratio of the average incomes received by families in the middle and bottom fifths of the distribution—reflects the distance between middle-income and poor American families. Bolstered by increased wages and better social security and welfare benefits, the relative position of the nation's poorest families improved through the early 1970s. Since the 1970s, their absolute incomes have declined, widening the gulf between poor and middle-income families. The estimates displayed in figure 5-1 imply that the increase in inequality has not been driven solely by worsening poverty among the poor or by spectacular income gains among the wealthy. Rather, it has been produced by growing disparities among Americans at every level of the income distribution.

Soaring inequality has not been confined to the United States. Rich nations around the world have experienced growth in inequality since the late 1970s.[2] In Canada and western Europe, the long-term rise in joblessness, especially among younger and less skilled older workers, has helped push up income disparities. The jump in income inequality

---

the wage ladder. Even taking account of this kind of individual income mobility, however, there is no doubt that the inequality of *lifetime* income has risen over the past two decades. For a clear introduction to these issues, see Gottschalk and Danziger (1998, pp. 92–111).

2. Smeeding (1998, pp. 194–217).

Figure 5-1. *Trend in Family Income Inequality: Ratio of Average Incomes of Well-to-Do and Middle-Class Americans and of Middle-Class and Poor Americans, 1947–97*

Average income of top 5 percent/
Average income of middle 20 percent

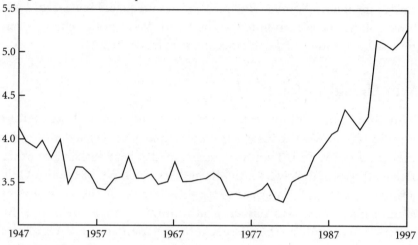

Average income of middle 20 percent/
Average income of bottom 20 percent

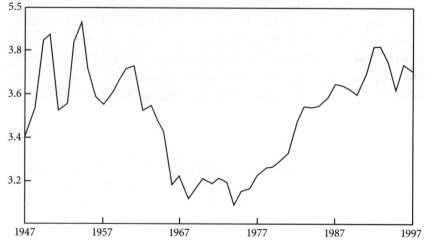

Source: Author's tabulations based on Bureau of the Census (1998b).

has been greater in the United States than in most other countries, however, and the increase in U.S. inequality occurred on top of a higher initial level of inequality.

This chapter addresses four broad questions raised by recent trends in U.S. inequality. Should we care? Why has inequality increased? How have policymakers responded to the trend? What policy changes can reverse the trend or make its consequences less painful?

Why Should We Care?

Why should the United States be troubled by increased inequality? On the whole, Americans are not particularly concerned about the income distribution. They are less persuaded than citizens of other rich countries of the need for public policies to temper inequality. Only about a quarter of Americans strongly agree that the government should guarantee each citizen a minimum standard of living. By contrast, over half of the populations in Japan and in each of five European countries strongly agree that the government has such a responsibility.[3]

Americans' distinctive views about economic inequality may stem from two related beliefs about the way a just society ought to operate and the way their own society actually functions. A large majority of Americans believe that individuals should bear primary responsibility for supporting themselves, whereas voters in other rich countries are much more inclined to believe that governments have an obligation to ensure that everyone is provided for. Large majorities of Americans also believe their society offers an equal opportunity for people to get ahead and think that hard work ordinarily translates into a better life. Residents of other rich countries are less likely to think their societies provide equal opportunity and more inclined to believe that differences in individual success are due to luck or personal connections rather than individual effort.[4]

---

3. On average among the six nations other than the United States, 64 percent of adults strongly agreed that the government should guarantee a minimum standard. Ladd and Bowman (1998a, pp. 103–13, 118–23).

4. Ladd and Bowman (1998a, pp. 118–22).

Given their views, why should Americans be concerned about the trend in inequality? One reason might be the threat that growing income disparities will undermine political equality and social cohesion. Even if they are indifferent about the abstract principle of economic equality, most Americans probably believe in the ideals of political and legal equality. But, as Arthur Okun observed, wide gaps in income and wealth can produce big differences in legal rights and political influence. "Money buys legal services that can obtain preferred treatment before the law; it buys platforms that give extra weight to the owner's freedom of speech; it buys influence with elected officials and thus compromises the principle of one person, one vote. . . . Even though money generally cannot buy extra helpings of rights directly, it can buy services that, in effect, produce more or better rights."[5]

The growing gap between the incomes of the rich, middle class, and poor and its consequences for the distribution of political influence may have contributed to Americans' dwindling confidence that their elected officials care very much about the views of ordinary people. In 1960, 25 percent of respondents agreed and 73 percent disagreed with the statement, "I don't think public officials care much about what people like me think." By 1996, 60 percent of respondents agreed and just 24 percent disagreed with the same statement.[6] The sharp decline in confidence in elected officials cannot be attributed to the state of the economy. The unemployment rate was slightly lower and per capita income much higher in 1996 than in 1960. About two-thirds of the drop in confidence occurred after 1968, a year in which income inequality was near its post–World War II low point.

A second reason for concern about rising inequality is the potential effect of growing income disparities on public health. Demographers and public health experts have found mounting, though controversial, evidence that greater inequality contributes to higher mortality rates and poorer health. Researchers have long recognized the powerful positive association between high income and good health. High-income people are healthier and live longer than poor people; rich countries have longer average life spans than poor ones. Only recently have

5. Okun (1975, p. 22).
6. See Ladd and Bowman (1998b, pp. 83–84).

analysts begun to investigate the consequences of economic inequality on health. Most studies now point to a strong link between mortality rates and inequality. Countries and communities with greater inequality have higher mortality rates than those with less inequality, even if the comparison is confined to countries or communities with similar average incomes and poverty rates. This finding suggests that it is not just low absolute incomes, but also large relative differences in income, that contribute to bad health and excess mortality among a nation's poorest citizens. Low-income Americans have death rates comparable to those in Bangladesh, even though absolute incomes, average consumption, and health-care spending are substantially higher among America's poor than they are in poverty-stricken Bangladesh.[7] The possible link between public health and inequality may help explain why a number of other rich countries with lower average incomes but substantially less inequality have longer average life spans and lower infant mortality rates than those of the United States.[8] If the benefits of U.S. income growth after 1979 had been more equally shared, it is possible that the average health and life spans of Americans, especially poor Americans, might have improved faster than they did.

The last and most obvious reason to care about inequality is simple humanitarian concern for people at the bottom of the distribution. Many of us would find repugnant a society in which some members suffer deprivation or extreme destitution while others enjoy all the luxuries that a prosperous economy can offer. With extensive media coverage of conditions among the inner-city poor and the super rich, it is impossible for Americans to remain ignorant of these disparities.

---

7. The relation between average life spans and inequality is examined by Duleep (1995, pp. 34–50). For proposed explanations of the link between inequality and population health as well as citations to the recent literature, see Kawachi and Kennedy (1997, pp. 1037–40). U.S. and Bangladesh mortality rates are discussed in Wilkinson (1998, p. 1611). A fascinating comparison of mortality rates among white and African Americans and people in China, Bangladesh, and Kerala, a low-income region of India, is in Sen (1998, pp. 1–25).

8. Bureau of the Census (1997, pp. 832–33, 839).

While acknowledging that the consequences of inequality often are unlovely, most defenders of American economic and political institutions point out that inequality plays a crucial role in creating incentives for people to improve their situations through saving, hard work, and investment in education and training. Some also note that wage and income disparities must occasionally widen in order to send correct signals to people to save more, work harder, change jobs, or increase their investment in education. Without the powerful signals provided by increased inequality, the economy would operate less efficiently and average income levels would grow less rapidly. In the long run, poor people might enjoy higher absolute incomes in a society in which income disparities are permitted to widen than one in which law and social convention keep income differentials small. According to this argument, widening inequality is in the best long-term interest of the poor themselves.

Even if it were true that the absolute incomes of the poor are higher in an economy that has more inequality, it does not follow that the poor are happier in such a society. Many people at the bottom may feel greater distress as the relative distance between their position and that of others in society increases. Living in a cramped apartment will seem more tolerable if the majority of people also live in crowded conditions than if most other people are comfortably housed. Being reduced to a scanty or unappetizing diet may represent a smaller hardship if one's neighbors also dine on meager fare.

For poor Americans, the theoretical advantages of greater inequality have failed to materialize over the past two decades. Their living standards have declined rather than improved, and their absolute incomes are *below* the incomes that poor people receive in most other rich countries with lower inequality. Among fifteen countries providing information to the Luxembourg Income Study, only low-income residents of the United Kingdom are worse off than the poor in the United States. People at the tenth percentile of the income distribution in the thirteen other countries have higher absolute incomes than a person at the same position of the income distribution in the United States. In thirteen of the fourteen countries other than the United States, average incomes are lower than the average U.S. income; in nine of the countries, the average income is 20 percent or more lower than it is in the United States.[9] Clearly, the efficiency advantages of growing inequality have not accrued to America's poor—at least not so far. To the extent that such advantages exist, they have been captured by Americans much further up the income scale, conspicuously widening the gaps between rich, middle class, and poor.

Why Has Inequality Increased?

Although informed observers may disagree on the social significance of inequality, they all recognize that it has increased. The reason for its rise, however, is hotly debated. Researchers do agree, however, on two key points.

First, greater inequality in family income is closely connected to growing disparities in workers' pay. Some, but not all, of the increase in wage disparity is associated with growing pay differentials based on workers' education, job experience, and occupational skill. Workers with limited skill have suffered declining real pay; workers with specialized competencies—including CEOs and superstars in sports, entertainment, and the professions—have enjoyed unprecedented wage gains. In short, the premiums that are awarded for worker skill are a principal reason for the growing inequality in wages.

Scholars also agree that shifts in family composition have reinforced the effects of widening wage inequality. The percentage of Americans living in single-parent families continues to grow while the fraction in married-couple families shrinks. This trend has increased the percentage of Americans, especially children, who are at high risk of being poor since single-parent families tend to have fewer wage earners and are thus much less likely to enjoy middle-class incomes.

In thinking about the sources of increased inequality it is useful to distinguish between mechanical explanations of the trend—such as

9. Smeeding (1998, p. 203). Smeeding's calculations refer to absolute incomes received in the early 1990s. Comparisons of average per capita income at purchasing power parities are based on Organization for Economic Cooperation and Development (OECD) estimates for 1997 (http://www.oecd.org/std/gdpperca.htm [June 2, 1999]).

growing wage disparities, the increase in single-parent families, and the like—and the deeper explanations that account for the economic and social forces behind these trends. In order to address the long-term problem of rising inequality, it is undoubtedly necessary to understand the underlying forces driving the trends; in other words, to be able to answer such questions as, "What is causing wage disparities to rise?" Nonetheless, it is illuminating to consider the mechanical explanations.

Mechanical Explanations

The leading mechanical explanation for widening income inequality has already been mentioned. Pay disparities have risen sharply, widening the gap between workers on successive rungs of the wage ladder. This development in turn has increased income differentials among poor, middle class, and well-to-do families. The trend in pay disparities has attracted intense scrutiny from journalists and economists, though it is doubtful whether this trend by itself accounts for most of the increase in family income inequality.

Hourly pay disparities jumped noticeably over the past two decades. Figure 5-2 shows the size of real—inflation-adjusted—wage gains or losses at successive deciles of the pay distribution.[10] The first decile wage earner receives hourly pay that is higher than wages earned by one-tenth of workers but lower than the wages of the other nine-tenths of workers; the second decile earner receives pay that is higher than two-tenths of workers but lower than the other eight-tenths; and so on. The figure shows wage changes for men and women separately. In one crucial respect the trend in hourly pay has been quite different for the two sexes. The typical male worker suffered a loss in real pay; most women got a raise. Because women earn substantially less than men, this implies that

---

10. The change in real hourly wages reflects the gain or loss in pay after the effect of inflation is subtracted. The estimated rate of inflation therefore has a significant effect on the estimates shown in figure 5-2. Historical price statistics have been criticized by some economists because they may exaggerate annual inflation, leading to an understatement of the true wage gains enjoyed by American workers over the past two decades. Even if these criticisms are accurate, however, the estimates of the trend in wage *inequality* are unaffected.

Figure 5-2. *Change in Real Hourly Earnings, by Decile, 1979–97*[a]

Percent change

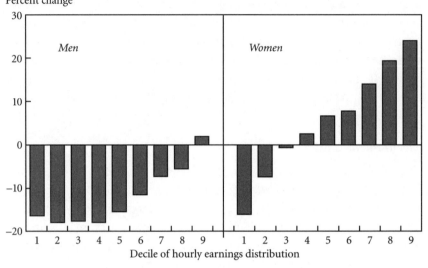

Decile of hourly earnings distribution

Source: Economic Policy Institute tabulations of Current Population Survey files.
a. Wage and salary workers between ages 18 and 64.

one badly paid group of workers did better than a group that initially ranked above them on the wage ladder. The gap between male and female pay shrank, reducing labor market inequality in one important dimension.

Both male and female workers saw pay disparities increase, however. Wages at the first decile fell 16 percent between 1979 and 1997, among both men and women. At the top end of the pay ladder, ninth decile wages rose 2 percent among men and 24 percent among women. Changes in annual earnings mirrored this pattern. Men at the bottom of the pay scale saw their annual earnings fall, while men at the top saw their annual pay increase. Among women, the gain in *annual* earnings for those at the top was substantially greater in percentage terms than their gain in *hourly* wages. Many women, especially those in high wage brackets, increased their weekly and annual hours of work, pushing up their annual pay faster than their hourly wages.

One way to assess the effect on overall *income* inequality of the rising disparity in wages is to calculate how much overall inequality would have changed if earnings disparities had remained constant. I have performed this calculation for the 1979 to 1996 period.[11] Clearly, income inequality would have increased more slowly if wage dispari- ties had remained unchanged. If earnings disparities among male heads of families had not increased between 1979 and 1996, the overall increase in inequality would have been about 28 percent smaller than it was. If earnings disparities among women who head families had remained unchanged over the same period, the observed increase in overall inequality would have been about 5 percent smaller.[12] If *both* male and female earnings inequality had remained constant after 1979, the observed increase in family income inequality would have been reduced by about one-third. In other words, even if there had been no increase in male and female earnings inequality after 1979, two-thirds of the observed increase in personal income inequality would have occurred. Most of the increase in overall inequality was therefore due to factors other than the growth of disparities in earnings.

One major factor was the shift in composition of American house- holds. More families now contain only a single adult member, and fewer contain married couples. This is an advantage for some middle- and high-wage single people because their incomes do not have to be shared with other family members. It is a distinct disadvantage, how- ever, for many low-wage single people with dependents because they are deprived of the potential wage contributions of a spouse. Income is distributed much more equally among people who are members of married-couple families than it is among people who are members of families where there is only one adult (possibly with child dependents). The fraction of adults and children living in married-couple house- holds shrank from 74 percent in 1979 to 65 percent by 1996. If the per- centage of Americans living in married-couple and single-parent families had remained unchanged over this period, the jump in inequality that occurred would have been about one-fifth smaller.

11. An appendix to this chapter describes how the calculation was performed. It also discusses the method used to measure income inequality and some limitations of the standard Census Bureau measures of income and inequality.

12. Female heads of family include married as well as single heads of families. In married-couple families, both the husband and the wife in the couple are considered heads of family. As is the case with male heads of families, female heads earn virtu- ally all of the labor income earned by adults of their gender.

Another trend that has pushed up income disparities is the rapid increase in labor force participation of women who are married to men with high incomes. The income gap between affluent, dual-income families and families in the middle and at the bottom of the income distribution has grown because women with high-wage husbands are increasingly likely to hold year-round jobs and to earn high annual incomes. Of course, employment rates have increased among nearly all groups of working-age women. But some of the biggest employment gains since 1979 have been among wives in families that would have high incomes even if the wife did not work. The extent of this development can be illustrated by examining the change in the employment rates and earnings of married women after dividing them according to their spouse's earnings.[13] Among women who were married to men in the top one-fifth of male earners, just 32 percent held a year-round job in 1979. In comparison, 41 percent of the women married to earners further down the male earnings distribution held year-round jobs in 1979. By 1996, 54 percent of women married to men in the top fifth of the male earnings distribution held year-round jobs. The employment rate of women married to men in the bottom four-fifths of the male earnings distribution increased as well (to 57 percent), but more slowly than it did among women married to men with high labor incomes. Women married to men in the bottom four-fifths of the male earnings distribution experienced earnings gains of 68 percent between 1979 and 1996; women married to men in the top one-fifth of male earners enjoyed earnings gains of 135 percent.[14]

The pattern of strongly rising earnings among women with high-income husbands has had a noticeable effect on the income distribution of American families. By far the most important source of income received by working-age families is wage and self-employment income. When the correlation between the earnings of husbands and wives increases, the income gap between dual-earner and other kinds of fam-

13. These calculations refer to wives in families where either the wife or husband is between twenty-five and fifty-nine years of age.

14. The calculated percentage changes take into account the gains experienced because more wives entered the work force and because wives who were employed earned higher wages.

ilies rises as well. This would be true even if the inequality of men's and women's wages remained unchanged.

The effect of the greater correlation between husband's and wive's earnings can be evaluated by freezing this correlation at its 1979 value and then calculating what the income distribution would have looked like in 1996.[15] If the correlation between the earnings of husbands and wives had remained unchanged, the rise in inequality would have been 87 percent of the actual change. In other words, 13 percent of the rise in overall inequality occurred because of the increase in the correlation between the earned incomes of husbands and wives.

A summary tabulation of the main mechanical causes of rising inequality is presented in table 5-1. The factors mentioned above account for about two-thirds of increased income inequality (see the top four items in table 5-1). The remaining one-third is explained by a variety of miscellaneous factors, including the growing inequality of nonwage sources of income, the declining effectiveness of government transfers in combating poverty among the very poor, and the increasing importance of some kinds of unearned income that are received disproportionately by the very affluent (such as interest and dividend income).[16]

Underlying Causes

Two underlying explanations for rising wage inequality dominate popular discussion—technological change and globalization. Most economists believe the best explanation for widening inequality is a shift in employers' demand for labor linked to the introduction of new kinds of production techniques. Innovative management practices and new technologies, such as personal computers and improved communications, have caused a surge in demand for highly skilled workers. Technological innovation has put competitive pressure on employers to change their production methods in ways that require a more entrepreneurial and skilled work force. Employers have persisted in hiring more highly skilled workers even though sharply rising wage differentials make this strategy more expensive than ever. The resulting

15. To hold the husband-wife correlation constant at the 1979 level, I adjusted earnings amounts in the 1996 census file to reflect the correlation pattern in 1979.
16. Burtless (1998).

Table 5-1. *Sources of Change in U.S. Personal Income Inequality,*
1979–96

Source of change	Percent explained[a]
Increased male earnings inequality	28
Increased female earnings inequality	5
Higher correlation of husband and wife earnings	13
Declining percentage of Americans in husband-wife families	21
Other	33

Sources: Author's tabulations of March 1980 and March 1997 Current Population Survey files.
a. Percentage of change in Gini coefficient explained.

surge in demand for highly skilled workers has pushed the relative wages of such workers up to a sixty-year high.

A more popular underlying explanation for rising wage inequality focuses on globalization—the growing importance of international trade, especially trade with the developing world. According to a common view, liberal trade with low-wage countries has harmed and threatens to impoverish low-skill and middle-class workers in the manufacturing, or tradeable goods, sectors of the U.S. economy. This argument was forcefully advanced by opponents of the North American Free Trade Agreement, who warned that free trade with Mexico and other poor countries would eliminate middle-class industrial jobs and undermine the wages of semiskilled U.S. workers.

Most economists who have studied the influence of international trade are skeptical of these claims. With few exceptions economists find little evidence that growing or liberalized trade is the main explanation for increasing wage disparities in the United States. Most would concede, however, that free trade has added to the downward pressure on the wages of less skilled workers and has contributed modestly to their decline.

Increased immigration and the changing characteristics of immigrants have played at least as big a role in depressing the wages of the less skilled. The effect of surging immigration on wages earned by people with very limited education has been particularly large because immigrants represent a large and growing percentage of workers with the lowest levels of education.

The leading explanations for wider pay disparities do not go far toward explaining increased income inequality, however. Neither technological change nor international trade can provide a *direct* explanation for most of the rise in U.S. income inequality. The reason is straightforward. Even if all of the growth in *wage* inequality were attributable to these two factors, far less than half of the recent rise in *income* inequality would be explained. Though the increase in wage inequality is the most important source of growing family income inequality, it directly explains only about a third of the recent rise in overall inequality (see table 5-1). Most of the increase is due to other factors—principally, demographic trends, changing patterns of work among partners in married-couple families, and growing inequality in the distribution of income from nonlabor sources. The disintegration of traditional family organization and changing gender roles have produced an increasingly affluent population of dual-working-spouse families and childless persons as well as a growing and relatively impoverished population of single-parent families containing children.

Some observers suggest that increased wage inequality directly or indirectly caused the recent changes in American family structure and the labor market role of women. While this is probably true to some extent, it is doubtful that the long-term trends in divorce, in out-of-wedlock child bearing, and in female participation in the job market can be traced to widening pay differentials. Each of the trends began or was well under way in the 1960s, when average wages were rising strongly and pay differentials were stable or shrinking. The divorce rate actually declined after 1979, when wage disparities began to soar. The increase in female participation in the labor force, especially among women married to men with high wages, seems linked to a long-term shift in the social and economic role played by women in western societies. This shift is occurring in France, Germany, and Sweden as well as the United States, even though pay disparities have not changed very much in these west European countries. Some struggling middle-class mothers may have been pushed unwillingly into the job market to supplement the declining wages of their husbands, but this trend should expand rather than shrink the middle class. As we have seen, two demographic and social trends have been much more important in recent years. Women who are married to men with high incomes have entered full-time employment in record numbers. And Americans have shifted toward living arrangements in which an increasing percentage of households contain only a single adult—and a single potential earner.

In sum, the trends in wages, family composition, and female work patterns during the past two decades have profoundly affected the relative well-being of two groups of Americans—the very affluent and the least skilled. Americans in the top tenth of the income distribution are better off relative to the middle class than they have been at any time since the Great Depression. In contrast, the share of all cash income received by families in the bottom fifth reached a postwar low during the 1990s. Even though poor families have enjoyed real income gains in the past few years, their 1997 incomes remained lower than they were at the end of the 1970s and in the 1980s. The adverse effects of recent distributional trends have been felt most keenly by households headed by people in their twenties and early thirties, especially people with limited education. Since these young adults are responsible for rearing a large percentage of the nation's children, the child poverty rate remained stubbornly high through most of the 1980s and 1990s.

Policy Responses

Though critics of U.S. social policy seldom mention the fact, policymakers have not stood still in the face of momentous changes in income distribution. The direction of policy has shifted noticeably since the early 1980s. The shift began when President Ronald Reagan tried to scale back and reorient welfare programs targeted on the working-age poor. His goal was to make the programs less attractive to potential applicants by making benefits harder to obtain and reducing the generosity of monthly payments. One important policy change, reversed by the 1990s, was to reduce benefits available to poor families with a working member. President Reagan thought welfare payments should be focused on the *nonworking* poor. He expected working adults to support themselves.

The steep decline in hourly wages of low-skill workers made this strategy increasingly untenable. Measured in inflation-adjusted dollars, the minimum wage fell more than 30 percent during the 1980s, and wages paid to unskilled young men fell almost as fast.[17] Few U.S. workers can support families on wages of $5 or $6 an hour.

President Reagan and Congress responded to this development by reforming tax policy toward low-income families and broadening eligibility for publicly financed health benefits. The Tax Reform Act of 1986 removed millions of low-income Americans from the income-tax rolls and increased the tax rebates low-income workers receive under the earned income tax credit (EITC). This tax credit was further liberalized by legislation passed in 1990 and 1993, which significantly increased the size of credits flowing to low-income breadwinners and their children. Spending on the credit increased ten-fold in the decade after 1986, reaching more than $21 billion by 1996 (see figure 5-3). Since the credit is payable to breadwinners even if they owe no federal income taxes, it has boosted the incomes of millions of families with extremely low incomes. The burden of federal payroll and income taxes once pushed millions of people into poverty. The generosity of the EITC now means that millions are lifted out of poverty by the federal tax system.[18]

The EITC is a distinctive U.S. innovation in policy toward the working poor, one that other rich countries may eventually adopt in a modified form. While most cash assistance for the poor is provided to people who do not work, the EITC is provided only to low-income people who *do* work. In 1998 the credit provided as much as $3,756 in refundable income tax credits to a breadwinner with two or more dependents. For a person working full time in a minimum wage job, the EITC can increase the worker's net earnings by nearly 40 percent. The increased generosity of the credit has offset all of the reduction in real hourly wages that low-wage workers with dependent children have suffered over the past two decades.

---

17. Bureau of Labor Statistics, "Value of the Federal Minimum Wage, 1954–1996" (http://www.dol.gov/dol/esa/public/minwage/chart2.htm [June 2, 1999]).

18. As recently as 1983, about 1.6 million persons in families with children were pushed into poverty by the burden of federal income and payroll taxes. By 1996 about 2.2 million people in such families were lifted above the poverty line by the federal tax system. U.S. Department of Health and Human Services (1998, p. III-17). These calculations are based on a nonstandard definition of poverty; see note 21.

Figure 5-3. *Expansion of the Earned Income Tax Credit, 1975–97*

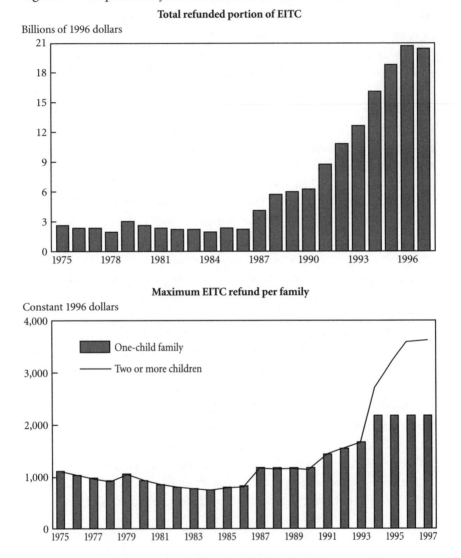

Total refunded portion of EITC

Billions of 1996 dollars

Maximum EITC refund per family

Constant 1996 dollars

One-child family

Two or more children

Source: U.S. House of Representatives (1998); *Budget of the United States Government, 1999.*

The idea behind the credit is to boost work incentives by increasing the incomes available to low-income breadwinners, particularly those who have children.[19] Instead of shrinking as a recipient's earnings grow, the credit rises, at least up to a limit. At low earnings levels the credit increases by 34 cents or 40 cents—depending on whether the worker has one or more than one dependent child—for each extra dollar earned by the breadwinner. Parents who have no wages are not eligible to receive the credit, so the credit provides a big incentive for unemployed parents to find work. Most labor economists who have examined the credit conclude that it has contributed to a sizable increase in job holding among unmarried mothers.

State legislatures and Congress have also tried to increase the attractiveness of work by boosting child-care subsidies available to working welfare recipients, former recipients, and other low-income single parents. Based on detailed analyses of spending patterns in thirteen representative states, the Urban Institute estimates that federal, state, and local spending on child care and early childhood development programs amounted to $631 per poor child in 1995.[20] Since many poor children do not have working parents and many others are not enrolled in early childhood programs, these programs probably provide more than $1,000 in subsidies per child to participating families with a working breadwinner. Although child care remains a big hurdle for many single parents who are seeking work, the increase in child care subsidies has reduced the hurdle a bit.

Congress has also liberalized eligibility requirements for medicaid, the primary public health insurance program for low-income Americans. Medicaid now offers benefits to a much broader population of low-income children with working parents. Until the late 1980s, publicly subsidized health insurance had been restricted mainly to welfare recipients. Working-age families with children were usually eligible for health protection only if the families were actually collecting cash assistance—aid to families with dependent children (AFDC) or supplemental security income (SSI). Children typically lost their eligibility for

19. Single workers without dependent children are eligible for a much smaller credit, one whose maximum value in 1999 is only $347.

20. Flores, Douglas, and Ellwood (1998, p. 38).

free health insurance when the family left public assistance because of work. Liberalization of medicaid in the late 1980s and early 1990s expanded the population eligibile for benefits to large numbers of children whose parents had modest earnings and were not currently collecting public assistance.

Ten state governments have created state earned income tax credits, and even more have established state programs to provide subsidized health insurance to members of working-poor families, including the adult breadwinners. In 1997 Congress passed legislation offering states generous federal subsidies to establish or enlarge health insurance programs for poor and near-poor families having children. Between 1998 and 2002 the federal government will provide more than $20 billion in matching subsidies for these new, state-sponsored children's health insurance programs (CHIP).

As policy has been reformed to expand tax credits and health benefits for the working poor, state and federal lawmakers have slashed the cash assistance available to the *non*working poor. General assistance, which provides cash aid to childless adults, has been scaled back in most states and eliminated in a few. AFDC was abolished in 1996 and replaced with temporary assistance to needy families (TANF). The new federal program places pressure on all states to adopt aggressive policies that would curtail cash benefits to poor parents who are capable of working. The head of each family on welfare is required to work within two years after assistance payments begin. Work-hour requirements are stringent, and states face increasingly harsh federal penalties for failing to meet them. The law stipulates that the great majority of families may receive benefits for no longer than five years, and it permits states to impose even shorter time limits. More than a dozen states have already done so.

Along with the strong economy, the new welfare law—and the new state welfare policies that preceded it—helped produce an unprecedented drop in the nation's child welfare rolls. Since reaching a peak in 1994, the number of families collecting public assistance for children has dropped more than 2 million, or 45 percent. No drop this large had occurred in the previous forty years (see figure 5-4).

On the whole, U.S. social policy has become much less generous to the nonworking (but working-age) poor, while it has become much

Figure 5-4. *Number of AFDC Cases, 1960–98*

Millions

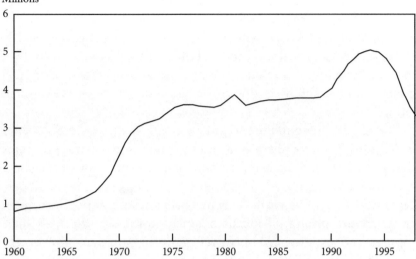

Source: U.S. Department of Health and Human Services.

more generous to the working poor. For many low-wage breadwinners with children, the increased generosity of the EITC, expansions in medicaid, new state-financed health insurance plans, and enlarged day-care subsidies have more than offset the loss of potential earnings due to shrinking hourly wages. The standard poverty statistics do not fully reflect this fact because they fail to account for most of the improvements in benefits.[21] At the same time, official poverty statistics fully reflect the drop in cash benefit payments that has been caused by cutbacks in the nation's main cash assistance programs.

The recent policy changes are having real economic effects in addition to offsetting the drop in wages. Poor breadwinners with children have been induced to enter the work force—and stay there. This can be seen in figure 5-5, which shows the changing work patterns of mothers rearing children under age eighteen. One line in the figure shows the

21. The standard poverty measure is based on families' pretax cash incomes. It therefore ignores income received from the EITC and improvements in family circumstances that occur because of better health insurance and more generous reimbursement of child care expenses.

trend in employment among married mothers currently living with their spouses; the other shows the trend among mothers who are separated from their spouses or divorced or who have never been married. Married mothers who live with their spouses have experienced a steady increase in employment over most of the past two decades. In contrast the trend in employment rates among divorced, separated, and never-married mothers showed little change for most of the period through 1994.

The relative trend in the two groups changed after 1994. Soon after EITC subsidies were liberalized and state public assistance programs were curtailed, employment rates among unmarried mothers began to soar; they have increased more than 10 percentage points (or 18 percent) in the past five years. This increase does not reflect a surge in employment among *all* mothers, since mothers living with their spouses have experienced only small gains in employment in recent years. The entry of divorced, separated, and never-married mothers and other disadvantaged new workers contributes to the downward pressure on wages of the least skilled. In effect, public subsidies to the working poor and cutbacks in welfare benefits to the nonworking poor have helped keep employer costs low and have encouraged U.S. companies to create millions of poorly paid jobs.

In contrast with policies in western Europe, the U.S. mix of harsh and liberal policies toward the working-age poor has spurred high employment, rapid job creation, and the expansion of a large and flourishing low-wage sector. While the combination is broadly consistent with popular American attitudes toward work and self-reliance, it would be much tougher to sell these policies in other rich countries.

Future Directions

Public policy toward low-income, working-age families has not stood still in the face of large shifts in the wage and income distributions. Policymakers have not left struggling families to cope with declining wages wholly on their own. More generous public programs have improved the circumstances of many low-income parents—if they can find jobs. But the new social policies have not been so generous that poor, working-age Americans have shared proportionately in U.S. prosperity.

Figure 5-5. *Employment-Population Ratio of Married and Unmarried Mothers*

Percent of population at work

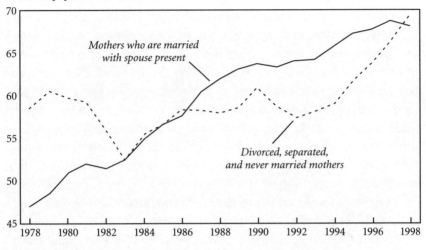

Source: Author's tabulations of unpublished data from the Bureau of Labor Statistics.

A different set of policies, such as those adopted in western Europe, would have produced different outcomes. Some differences, such as low poverty rates and high hourly wages, make western Europe a more pleasant place to live for the poor. But some side effects of European policies, particularly high unemployment, are very unwelcome. It is not obvious that most Americans, even liberals, would welcome the alternative outcomes or approve the policies needed to achieve them. Few U.S. voters favor giving undisguised cash transfers to people who are old enough and healthy enough to work. Yet the policies that prop up wages and incomes in western Europe include several that provide steady and generous transfers to able-bodied people who do not work.

While the current U.S. policy mix broadly reflects the preferences of American voters, it is haphazard and fails to reach some of the working poor who are most in need of help. Two policy reforms could improve the circumstances of working-age people who have suffered the worst reductions in hourly pay. The first would assure some of the long-term unemployed a job at a modest wage. The second would make work subsidies more uniformly available and would provide these subsidies in a form that most voters approve.

Since public assistance to the nonworking but able-bodied poor has been drastically curtailed, it makes sense to assure at least some poor adults that they will be able to find jobs at a modest wage, however bad the local job market. In some cases this may involve creating publicly subsidized jobs that pay a little less than the minimum wage. It seems particularly important to extend this offer to parents who face the loss of cash public assistance payments if they do not work. New state and federal welfare policies attempt to push nonworking parents into jobs by threatening to withhold assistance benefits from those who remain jobless. If voters and policymakers want unskilled parents to begin supporting themselves through jobs, they should guarantee these parents that some jobs will be available even when unemployment is high. A public-sector jobs program providing last-chance employment to some of the parents forced off the welfare rolls might cost between $7 billion and $11 billion a year.[22]

For poorly paid breadwinners who do find jobs, it is important to improve the rewards from working. One possibility is to make a basic package of subsidized health insurance available to all children and young adults. Many Americans regard health insurance for children as a fair and acceptable way to provide help to those in need.

Most health insurance for children is either publicly subsidized through medicaid or privately provided through employer health plans. When insurance is provided under an employer-financed plan, most of the cost to employers takes the form of lower cash wages paid to workers. Public assumption of some or all of the cost of a basic health package for children, even of those covered by employers, would encourage employers to boost the wages they pay to insured workers who have child dependents. This will have a greater percentage impact on the pay of low-wage workers, for whom health insurance represents a large fraction of compensation, than on the pay of high-wage workers.

22. This estimate is based on offering 500,000 to 750,000 public jobs that on average pay $5.25 an hour. A job held for a full year would thus pay $10,500. The administrative cost of the program is assumed to absorb roughly one-third of the direct wage costs. The wages paid to job holders would reduce the amount of food stamp and other public benefits that job holders would receive, but these public spending offsets are ignored.

About 15 percent of all children (and nearly one-quarter of poor children) currently lack health insurance.[23] For these children and their working parents, publicly subsidized child health insurance would directly improve their well-being and reduce out-of-pocket spending on medical care. A reform establishing such a program would substantially increase the reward inherent in working. Parents who do not work already qualify for free medical insurance for themselves and for their children under medicaid. Some lose this insurance when they accept a job that pays modest, but above-poverty-level, wages. If a public health insurance package is offered to *all* children, this penalty of accepting a job would be reduced or eliminated.

Guaranteeing a basic health insurance package for all the nation's children would not be cheap. In 1995 the cost of providing medicaid health insurance to 16.6 million youngsters on AFDC was $17.8 billion, or about $1,100 per child. Extending the same insurance to all 10.7 million youngsters under eighteen who are not covered by health insurance would boost the cost of the program by at least $11 billion. The gross cost would be far greater, because two-thirds of the nation's 72 million children are covered by private insurance plans.[24] Many would be withdrawn from such plans if a good, inexpensive public plan were available.

Conclusion

American economic progress over the past two decades has been very uneven. Families and workers at the top of the economic ladder have enjoyed rapidly rising incomes. Workers at the bottom have suffered a sharp erosion in their relative income position. In 1979, the American at the 95th percentile of the income distribution—5 percentiles below the very top—received an income that was three times the median income and thirteen times the income of an American at the 5th percentile. By 1996, the American at the 95th percentile received an income that was almost four times the median income and twenty-three times

23. Bureau of the Census (1998a, table 2).
24. Medicaid enrollments and outlays are reported in U.S. House of Representatives, Committee on Ways and Means (1998, pp. 972–75). For health insurance coverage statistics on children, see Bureau of the Census (1998a, table 6).

the income of the person at the 5th percentile. The income difference between Americans in the top 1 percent of the income distribution and other Americans grew at an even faster pace.

For many low-income workers, new public policies have helped offset the loss of wages with larger earnings supplements and better health insurance. Many low-wage workers have not benefited from these policies, however. Humane public policy would ensure that the most vulnerable Americans share fully in the nation's prosperity.

Appendix: Measuring Income Inequality

A standard statistic to measure overall inequality is the Gini coefficient, which ranges in value between zero and one. Zero indicates an income distribution in which all families or persons have the same incomes; one, a distribution in which all income is received by a single family or person. The Census Bureau has estimated the Gini coefficient of household income inequality back through 1967. Between 1967 and 1997 the Gini statistic ranged as low as 0.388 in 1968 and as high as 0.459 in 1997.[25] Most of the rise occurred after 1979. The Gini coefficient increased almost 14 percent between 1979 and 1997.

The Census Bureau's estimate of the Gini coefficient has two main shortcomings. It is based on an incomplete measure of household income, and it ignores differences in household size when comparing the incomes received by different households. The first problem arises because the standard census definition of income considers only pretax cash sources of income. It ignores realized capital gains, the effect of income and payroll taxes on spendable income, and noncash sources of income (such as employer-provided medical insurance, food stamps, and the flow of services from owner-occupied homes). The Census Bureau has tried to remedy this shortcoming by calculating the Gini coefficient under a variety of experimental income definitions that include capital gains and noncash income sources and that subtract estimated tax payments. When inequality is measured using the broadest definition of income, the general trend in inequality after 1979 is roughly the same as it is using the standard

25. Bureau of the Census (1998b, table B-3).

cash income definition.[26] Between 1979 and 1997 the Gini coefficient rose 14 percent under the cash income definition, while it increased 13 percent under the broadest income definition.[27] This implies that changes in the distribution of tax burdens and noncash income generally paralleled changes in the distribution of pretax cash income.

The second problem with the Census Bureau's measure of inequality is that it treats income received by different households as identical even if the number of family members differs. Most people recognize that it takes more money to support a large household than a small one. For example, the official poverty thresholds are based on the assumption that it takes twice as much income to support a family with four members as it does to support a single person who lives alone. Under this assumption, we should treat people in a four-person family as having income equivalent to that of a one-member household only if the four-person family has twice as much income as the single-person household. If the four-member family has less income, its members should be treated as receiving less "equivalent income" than the person in the single-member household.

The estimates of the changes in income inequality described in this chapter show the trend in overall inequality using the concept of equivalent personal income. This concept is based on the standard pretax cash income definition used by the Census Bureau, but it makes a family-size correction to reflect economies of scale in consumption enjoyed by people who live in families of different sizes. For a person in a single-person household, equivalent personal income is simply equal to the person's pretax cash income. For a person in a larger family, equivalent income is less than the family's pretax cash income because that income must be divided among two or more members.[28]

---

26. The alternatives are described in Bureau of the Census (1998b, pp. A1–A5).

27. Bureau of the Census, March Current Population Survey, table RDI-5, "Index of Income Concentration (Gini Index), by Definition of Income: 1979 to 1997 (http://www.census.gov/income/expermnt/rdi5.txt [June 2, 1999]).

28. My adjustment is based on the assumption that a family's income requirements are proportional to the square root of the number of family members. Thus the definition of equivalent income per person is $Y_E = Y_T/\sqrt{F}$, where Y_E = Equivalent income per person; Y_T = Total family income; and $\sqrt{F}$ = Square root of family size.

People who are members of the same nuclear family are treated as receiving an identical income. I measure inequality by ranking all persons represented in the census file according to their equivalent personal income and then calculate the Gini coefficient of income inequality. The trend in personal income inequality using this concept is similar to that of the Census Bureau's Gini coefficient of household income equality. Whereas the Census Bureau's estimate of household cash income inequality rose 13 percent between 1979 and 1996, my estimate of the Gini coefficient of equivalent personal income rose 15 percent, increasing from 0.348 to 0.400.[29]

The chapter provides estimates of how much inequality would have changed if earnings inequality had remained fixed. To estimate income inequality under the assumption that earnings disparities among male heads of families remained constant, I assume that every male head of family would keep his position in the 1996 male earnings distribution, but his labor earnings would be changed so that the 1979 distribution of relative male earnings is preserved. For example, if a worker is 10 percent from the bottom of the male earnings distribution in 1996, he is assigned the relative earnings he would have received if he had been 10 percent from the bottom of the earnings distribution in 1979. By "relative earnings" I mean the worker's earnings as a percentage of average male earnings. An overwhelming majority of working-age males are heads of family, and they earn virtually all labor income that is earned by adult males. Similar calculations were performed to see how much of the increase in inequality was due to growing earnings disparities among women who head families and how much was due to changes in the correlation of husband and wife earnings.

References

Bureau of the Census. 1997. *Statistical Abstract of the United States.*
———. 1998a. *Health Insurance Coverage: 1997,* Report P60-202. U.S. Department of Commerce.
———. 1998b. *Money Income in the United States: 1997.* Current Population Reports P60-200.

29. These calculations and the ones mentioned in the main body of the chapter are described in detail in Burtless (1999).

Burtless, Gary. 1998. "Technological Change and International Trade: How Well Do They Explain the Rise in U.S. Income Inequality?" In *The Inequality Paradox: Growth of Income Disparity,* edited by James A. Auerbach and Richard S. Belous, 60–91. Washington: National Policy Association.

———. 1999. "Effects of Growing Wage Disparities and Changing Family Composition on the U.S. Income Distribution." *European Economic Review* 43 (May): 853–65.

Duleep, Harriet Orcutt. 1995. "Mortality and Income Inequality among Economically Developed Countries." *Social Security Bulletin* 58 (Summer): 34–50.

Flores, Kimura, Toby Douglas, and Deborah A. Ellwood. 1998. *The Children's Budget Report: A Detailed Analysis of Spending on Low-Income Children's Programs in Thirteen States.* Assessing the New Federalism Occasional Paper 14. Washington: Urban Institute.

Gottschalk, Peter, and Sheldon Danziger. 1998. "Family Income Mobility— How Much Is There, and Has It Changed?" In *The Inequality Paradox: Growth of Income Disparity,* edited by James A. Auerbach and Richard S. Belous, 92–111. Washington: National Policy Association.

Kawachi, Ichiro, and Bruce P. Kennedy. 1997. "Socioeconomic Determinants of Health: Health and Social Cohesion: Why Care about Income Inequality?" *British Medical Journal* 314 (April 5): 1037–40.

Ladd, Everett C., and Karlyn H. Bowman. 1998a. *Attitudes toward Economic Inequality.* Washington: American Enterprise Institute.

———. 1998b. *What's Wrong: A Survey of American Satisfaction and Complaint.* Washington: American Enterprise Institute.

Okun, Arthur M. 1975. *Equality and Efficiency: The Big Tradeoff.* Brookings.

Sen, Amartya. 1998. "Mortality as an Indicator of Economic Success and Failure." *Economic Journal* 108 (January): 1–25.

Smeeding, Timothy M. 1998. "U.S. Income Inequality in a Cross-National Perspective: Why Are We So Different?" In *The Inequality Paradox: Growth of Income Disparity,* edited by James A. Auerbach and Richard S. Belous, 194–217. Washington: National Policy Association.

U.S. Department of Health and Human Services. 1998. *Indicators of Welfare Dependence, Annual Report to Congress.*

U.S. House of Representatives, Committee on Ways and Means. 1998. *1998 Green Book: Background Material and Data on Programs within the Jurisdiction of the Committee on Ways and Means.* Government Printing Office.

Wilkinson, Richard G. 1998. "Low Relative Income Affects Mortality." *British Medical Journal* 314 (May 23): 1611.

HENRY J. AARON
ROBERT D. REISCHAUER

6

Paying for an Aging Population

UNLIKE MOST PROJECTIONS of future developments, the aging of the American population can be forecast with near certainty. Barring calamity, the population age 62 and over will more than double (from 41 million to approximately 86 million) between the years 2000 and 2040; the population over age 85 will more than triple. The elderly, who make up about 13 percent of the population today, will constitute about 20 percent of the population by 2040. The precise fraction will depend on birth rates, immigration, advances in medical science, and personal behavior (including how little Americans exercise and how much they kill one another and themselves with guns, automobiles, and cigarettes). But the overall trend is inescapable—the American population will age rapidly during the next four decades.

Almost everyone is aware of this demographic fact. Americans also understand that, as the population ages, the elderly will consume an increasing share of the nation's output. But widespread confusion persists about what an aging population means for the two largest government programs serving the elderly (social security and medicare),

The authors would like to thank Jeanne M. Lambrew, Jeffery Lemieux, Edward Lorenzen, and Joshua M. Wiener for their comments on sections of this chapter. Shanna Rose and James Sly provided exemplary research assistance.

for the living standards of working Americans, and for private and government budgets. Hyperbole abounds. Young workers of today won't
receive any social security benefits! Medicare will go bust within two
decades! The burden of supporting the baby boomers when they retire
will leave the working population in sackcloth! Government budgets
again will be awash in red ink! Though sobering, the reality is not apoc-
alyptic, particularly if government and individuals take measured steps
now to prepare for this inevitable demographic change.

This chapter begins with a brief review of the demographic trends.
This review introduces two concepts that need to be kept distinct for a
full understanding of the economic consequences of population aging:
the government budget costs of rising obligations for social security,
medicare, and other programs serving the aged, and the impact of those
costs on household budgets and living standards. The chapter then analyzes the principal alternative approaches that have been suggested to
help prepare social security and medicare for their coming burdens. It
concludes with a brief examination of medicaid, a third major program
that the aging of the population will significantly affect.

Darling, We Are Growing Older

In 2008, the oldest of the baby boomers, the group born between 1946
and 1964, will turn 62 and become eligible for social security retirement
benefits. Three years later, they will turn 65 and start receiving medicare
benefits. Millions of them will already have been receiving social security disability and survivor benefits. In the decades that follow, increasing numbers of baby boomers will become eligible for the nation's
means-tested programs. Some who earned little during their working
years and who don't have a spouse's pension to rely on will have to turn
for support to the food stamp program and Supplemental Security
Income (SSI)—the means-tested cash assistance program for the aged,
blind, and disabled. As age and infirmities overwhelm their bodies and
medical expenses deplete their savings, many baby boomers will have to
depend on medicaid to help pay for their acute and long-term health
care needs. Elderly veterans, whose ranks will peak in the year 2000
and remain high for the next few decades, will draw increasing amounts

of assistance from veterans' disability compensation, pensions, and medical benefits.

By 2040 when all the baby boomers are of retirement age, nearly one-fourth of the U.S. population will be over age 62. The major change will be among those age 75 and older. Their ranks will have increased sharply to 11.4 percent of the population, as large as the share that was over age 62 in 1960 (figure 6-1). The young elderly—those between the ages of 62 and 74—will constitute only a modestly larger share of the population in 2040 than in 1990.

The Economic Burden of Dependents

All consumption—that of the elderly and the nonelderly—comes from the goods and services produced by current workers. The burden that workers bear to produce for others depends on the proportion of the population that is not working—the retired elderly, children, and non-working adults. As figure 6-2 shows, the proportion of the population that is economically inactive will reach a low point around the turn of the century. The reason is that children have constituted a steadily smaller proportion of the population since 1964 because birth rates fell after the baby boom. Despite a continuing drop in the proportion of children in the population, the share of the population that is economically inactive is projected to rise after 2000 because the proportion of retirees will increase, and adult (20 to 62) labor force participation rates will drift down as the average age of those in this group increases. On balance, the number of people each worker will have to support will rise about 6 percent between 2000 and 2040, and the number of adults each worker will have to support will rise by 14 percent.

Broad demographic trends do not adequately capture the economic effects of population aging because the size and distribution of the burdens imposed by different groups among the economically inactive population differ. For the most part, parents bear the daily living expenses of children. Their educational costs are mostly borne by state and local government. The health and income support costs of poor children are shared by the states and the federal government. In contrast, large portions of the income support and health costs of the

Figure 6-1. *Percentage of Population, 62 and over, 1950–2040*

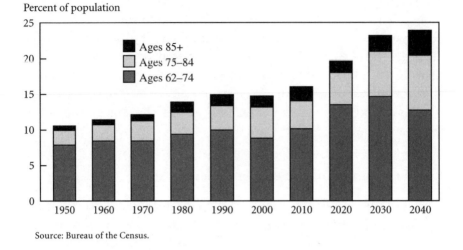

Percent of population

Source: Bureau of the Census.

elderly are borne by the federal government through the social security, SSI, and medicare programs. In addition, more than half of medicaid expenditures on behalf of the elderly and disabled with low
incomes is paid out of the federal budget; the remainder comes from
the states. Thus, as the population ages, the fiscal responsibility of sup-

Figure 6-2. *Ratio of Total and Adult Populations to the Labor Force*

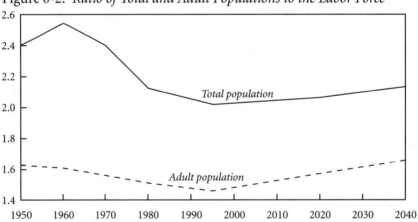

Source: Authors' calculations based on data from Office of the Actuary, Social Security Administration.

porting the economically inactive population shifts from families to governments and, within the public sector, from states and localities to the federal government. The anticipated difficulties of these fiscal redistributions, as much as the higher costs of the elderly relative to children, lie behind concerns about the aging of the American population.

Public Budgets

Whether a government program is financed by general revenues or earmarked taxes has profound political consequences. Policymakers concern themselves more strenuously with the long-run financial viability of entitlement programs supported by earmarked taxes than with entitlements financed through general revenues, even if the costs of such programs rise just as fast.

Earmarked payroll taxes are the primary receipts used to support both social security and the hospital insurance (HI) portion of medicare.[1] Receipts from these payroll taxes are deposited in trust funds from which program expenses are paid. If the balances are depleted, policymakers must raise taxes, cut benefits, or change the program's financing structure.

Almost since their inceptions, the social security and medicare actuaries have made long-term projections of the programs' expected revenues and expenditures. While both programs are currently running cash flow surpluses, the actuaries' projections reveal significant financial shortfalls between earmarked revenues and outlays that will grow over the long run. In the case of social security, earmarked tax receipts are expected to exceed the cost of benefits and program administration through 2013; total receipts, including interest earnings on the trust fund reserves, are projected to exceed program outlays through 2021, when reserves reach $4.5 trillion. Current projections indicate that social security will then have to begin drawing down its reserves to supplement program receipts in order to pay promised benefits.

1. The social security and medicare HI trust funds also receive income tax revenues attributable to including social security benefits in taxable income, interest earnings on trust fund balances, and other small general revenue payments as compensation for providing benefits to several small categories of beneficiaries who otherwise would not be eligible.

The financial pressures facing the hospital insurance component of medicare are more immediate. While social security's average cash surpluses are projected to exceed $100 billion a year over the next two decades, medicare is expected to run surpluses only through 2006, averaging less than $5 billion a year. The HI trust fund reserves are projected to peak at $155 billion at the end of 2006 and will be depleted by 2015 when expenditures will exceed revenues by a whopping 16 percent, and the gap will be growing fast. Adjustments will have to be made in the program's financing or expenditures several years before that date if large tax increases or abrupt benefit cuts are to be avoided.

The projected imbalances between the earmarked revenues that support social security and the HI portion of medicare and those programs' projected expenditures have generated concern and a vigorous debate over policies to strengthen the finances of these two programs or to change their structure. Although it is vital that the nation address the projected imbalances facing social security and medicare soon, the challenges elsewhere in the budget should not be overlooked. The costs of other entitlement programs, also of importance to the elderly—such as medicaid, SSI, food stamps, and veterans' programs—are also expected to rise rapidly over the next four decades. These programs also deserve attention even if projections of insolvent trust funds do not highlight their costs.

Although social security and medicare are both entitlement programs that serve the aged and the disabled, and both face projected long-term deficits, they differ markedly in nearly every other respect. Not surprisingly, the nation's options for strengthening these two programs for the future have little in common.

Social Security

Social security annually pays retirement, disability, and survivors benefits to 44 million elderly and disabled people. Monthly retirement benefits, which averaged $894 in 1998 for male workers, are based on each worker's highest thirty-five years of earnings. Benefits are financed largely by a payroll tax levied at the rate of 12.4 percent—half paid by workers, half by employers—on earnings up to a limit. The taxable wage ceiling, $72,600 in 1999, is raised each year at the same rate as the increase in average earnings. In addition, a small share of social security's income comes from income tax revenues on a portion of social security benefits received by middle- and upper-income beneficiaries that is included in taxable income.

Social security benefits have four distinguishing characteristics. First, they depend on each worker's earnings history, not on prices of financial market assets. As a result, older workers know with virtual certainty what their retirement pensions will be. Second, benefits are progressive. They replace a larger fraction of earnings for those whose average lifetime earnings were low than for those whose earnings were high, and they provide special benefits to workers' spouses and former spouses who have had limited or no participation in the paid labor force. Third, benefits are fully protected against erosion by inflation. And fourth, benefits are provided as joint-survivor annuities, which provide payments guaranteed to last as long as retirees and their spouses live.

By law, social security reserves—which are projected to reach $887 billion at the end of 1999—are invested only in assets guaranteed by the federal government. Most are held in safe but low-yielding Treasury securities.[2] Even at their projected maximum, in 2021, reserves will be much smaller than the amount that would have accumulated if each worker's payroll taxes had been deposited in a reserve and invested until the worker claimed benefits. The reason is that successive Congresses and presidents have used the reserves to provide those who retired during the program's first few decades with vastly larger benefits than their payroll taxes could have supported even if those contributions had been invested at market rates. If benefits had been limited to the value of taxes paid and interest earned on those taxes, poverty among the elderly

---

2. Social security reserves may also be invested in bonds of government agencies that are guaranteed by the federal government. Issues of eligible agencies include the Government National Mortgage Association, Export-Import Bank, Farmers Housing Administration, General Services Administration, Maritime Administration, Small Business Administration, Commodity Credit Corporation, Rural Electrification Administration, Rural Telephone Bank, and the Washington Metropolitan Area Transit Authority. The special issues in which nearly all social security reserves are invested carry the average interest rate on government bonds with a maturity of four years or more at the time the special issues are created. Special issues cannot be traded publicly but may be resold to the Treasury at par before they mature, if the social security trustees find that they need the funds.

would have been much higher than it was for decades after social security was enacted, and many more of the elderly and disabled would have been forced to turn to welfare programs for support. Whether the decision to pay generous social security benefits was wise or foolish, it cannot be undone. It has generated the so-called unfunded liability— benefit obligations to current workers and retirees that exceed accumulated reserves. This unfunded liability is the source of the projected deficit in social security, and all proposed reforms must come to terms with it one way or another.

The social security actuary has projected that revenues will fall short of expenditures by 2.07 percent of taxable earnings during the next seventy-five years. In other words, an immediate increase in the payroll tax rate or cuts in benefits equivalent to 2.07 percent of taxable payroll would be sufficient to close the gap between revenues and outlays projected over this period.[3] But neither a tax increase nor a benefit cut of this magnitude, which some might regard as modest, would be a viable solution to the program's long-run problem. These policies would result in larger surpluses and an even more significant buildup in reserves over the next few decades. But in 2075 reserves would be exhausted and expenditures would exceed revenues by more than 4 percent of payroll. Truly complete reform would not only eliminate the deficit as projected over the next seventy-five years but also leave the system's revenues and expenditures in rough balance at the end of that period and provide an adequate contingency reserve to deal with a temporary revenue shortfall that might accompany a recession.

While social security is not projected to face cash flow deficits for at least twenty years, there are two reasons why it is not too soon to address the long-run imbalance facing the program. First, any significant changes to the program will have to be phased in over a decade or two. Because most retirees and near retirees have a limited ability to

---

3. These estimates are based on the actuary's intermediate economic and demographic assumptions. Under more optimistic economic and demographic assumptions, the system remains in surplus indefinitely. Under more pessimistic assumptions the deficit is more than twice as large, and reserves would be exhausted in 2020. The terms "optimistic" and "pessimistic" refer to effects on the trust fund only. Paradoxically, higher inflation and shorter life expectancies are part of the "optimistic" assumptions because they improve the balance between revenues and expenditures.

adjust their lifestyles to accommodate reduced benefits, Congress has been appropriately loathe to enact benefit cuts affecting older workers or retirees. Younger workers will need fair warning that the rules of the game have changed. Unless needed to meet some immediate crisis, tax hikes are best introduced in small bites as they have been over the program's first sixty-five years during which two-thirds have been smaller than 0.2 percentage point. Second, demographic, economic, and budgetary conditions are almost certainly more conducive to reform today than they were in the past or will be in the future. In less than a decade, the fraction of the population receiving social security benefits will begin to climb, and the political constituency resistant to change will become ever more influential. With the economy strong, the unified budget in surplus, and the surpluses projected for the non-social security portion of the budget as yet uncommitted, the fiscal environment is unusually favorable for the consideration of a wide range of reform options.

What Are the Choices?

Proposed reforms fall into three broad categories: those that would replace the current system in whole or in part with mandatory, individually owned savings accounts modeled on Individual Retirement Accounts (the IRA option); those that would replace the current system in whole or in part with mandatory, individually owned savings accounts modeled on 401(k) accounts (the 401(k) option); and those that would fix the current system without reliance on individual accounts (fix the current system option).

THE IRA OPTION. Under this approach, the government would require individuals to establish and make deposits into special retirement savings accounts.[4] These deposits would be funded in one of three ways: by diverting a portion of the current payroll tax from financing social security (a carve out); by increased payroll taxes (an add on); or by tapping general revenues (drawing on the projected budget surpluses). Account holders would select their own fund managers and be free to invest in

---

4. An example of this approach is the Personal Securities Accounts plan put forward by five members of the Advisory Council on Social Security (1997, pp. 30–58).

stocks, bonds, mutual funds, insurance policies, real estate, or other approved assets. Social security benefits would be scaled back and, under some plans, eventually eliminated. Upon reaching retirement, people would withdraw funds from their accounts or, under some plans, would be required to convert the balances into an annuity. Most IRA-type plans would leave the basic framework of social security disability and survivors insurance in place but would scale back these benefits.

Advocates of this approach emphasize that people would own their accounts and would be free to invest the balances as they saw fit. These attributes, it is held, would spark workers' interest in saving for retirement, and private ownership would ensure that additions to the accounts increase national saving. Many claim that establishing personal accounts would raise the returns workers receive on their payroll taxes because the yield on the private securities in which the account balances would be invested is much higher than the low and declining implicit return workers will receive on their social security payroll tax contributions. As we explain later in this chapter, this assertion is incorrect.

Critics of the IRA option are concerned that many people would make poor investment choices and that administrative costs would be excessive. Those who invest unwisely or are merely unlucky in financial markets might be left with balances at retirement that are insufficient to support an adequate pension. Administrative and annuitization costs could reduce returns on investments significantly, undermining pension adequacy. Under the IRA-type system in Britain, for example, these costs are estimated to absorb an average of 43 percent of potential balances.[5]

THE 401(K) OPTION. Those who find the arguments advanced on behalf of personal accounts convincing yet harbor concerns about the IRA approach endorse the 401(k) option, which seeks to reduce these problems.[6] Under this approach, people would be required to invest their contributions in a few approved index mutual funds that would be heavily regulated or directly managed by the government. Pensions

5. Murthi, Orszag, and Orszag (1999).
6. An example of this approach is the Individual Accounts plan favored by two members of the 1994–96 Advisory Council on Social Security. See Advisory Council on Social Security (1997, pp. 30–34).

would be less variable across account holders than under the IRA option because the investment returns on all accounts would track broad financial market averages. Centralized management and passive investment would make administrative costs much lower than under the IRA option, although they would remain well above the estimated 0.9 percent administrative cost under social security. Most 401(k) type plans require that workers use their account balances to purchase annuities of at least a minimum size upon retirement.

FIXING THE CURRENT SYSTEM. Fixing the current system requires some combination of benefit cuts, payroll tax increases, higher returns on trust fund investments, or infusions of new revenues from other taxes.[7] Advocates of fixing the current system claim that personal accounts cannot reliably fulfill social security's primary purpose—providing ensured basic income to retirees and their spouses and dependents. The value of personal accounts would fluctuate with asset prices and each worker's investment decisions. The normal swings in financial markets will cause the account balances of new cohorts of retirees to vary considerably over relatively short periods even when all contributions are invested in index funds. For example, if the nation had had a personal account system in which all balances were invested in a total stock market index fund, workers retiring in 1977 would have received benefits that—measured as a share of average lifetime earnings—were less than half those of workers retiring in 1969.[8] If workers may select freely among assets, the

---

7. An example of this approach is the Maintain Benefits plan favored by six members of the 1994–96 Advisory Council on Social Security. See Advisory Council on Social Security (1997, pp. 59–97). See also Aaron and Reischauer (1998).

8. This calculation, provided by Gary Burtless, is based on simulations of working histories and pension fund contributions for average male workers who enter the labor force at age 22 and work for forty years. The text refers to workers who entered the labor force in 1937 and 1929. Workers experience the age earnings profile of employed men in 1995. Economywide real earnings grow 2 percent a year. Each worker saves 6 percent of earnings and invests those savings in a mixture of common stocks that yields the average dividend and capital gain of all listed securities in that year. The worker reinvests all dividends, which are free of individual tax when paid. At age 62, the worker converts his accumulated savings into an annuity based on the expected mortality experience of American men in 1995 and the interest rate on six-month commercial paper in the year when the annuity is purchased. All insurance company fees are ignored.

variations would be even larger. People whose accounts proved insufficient could become an added burden on welfare programs; cohorts whose pensions proved significantly smaller than the pensions received by those a bit older or younger would probably pressure government to compensate them for the market's poor performance.

Furthermore, if forced to rely on the balances in personal accounts, many people might outlive their assets and be forced to turn to SSI and food stamps for support. All would be exposed to inflation risk that would erode the value of their pensions as they grew older. The only way to avoid these risks would be for the government to require that personal account balances be converted at retirement into inflation-protected annuities similar to those provided by the current social security program. But this requirement would preclude leaving balances to heirs, one of the attributes of private accounts that proponents find most attractive.

Advocates of strengthening the current system point out that the claim made by some proponents of individual accounts—that returns would be higher if the nation switched from collective management of pension plans to private accounts—is simply wrong.[9] The pension returns that workers receive for their payroll taxes depend on three considerations: whether the pension plan builds reserves, what assets the reserves are invested in, and how cheaply the reserves are managed. On the first point, reserves can be accumulated in the social security trust fund just as well as in personal accounts. On the second issue, reserves held in the social security trust fund could be invested in assets similar to those that would be held by individual accounts if the restrictions on trust fund investment were relaxed. If the size of the reserves and the investment patterns were similar, reserve accumulation in the trust fund and in individual accounts would have similar *average* rates of return before administrative costs are deducted. Thus the claim that private accounts will boost returns must rest on the belief that the management costs of individual accounts would be lower than those of a centrally managed trust fund. In fact, however, administrative costs entailed in having private sector firms or the government manage more than 150 million individual accounts would be higher—possibly much

9. Geanakoplos, Mitchell, and Zeldes (1998).

higher—than those of managing the collective investment of a single social security trust fund account. The costs of managing individual accounts could range from .15 to 1.50 percent of account balances, while collective investment has been estimated to cost only .01 percent.

The Clinton Budget Initiative

In his January 1999 state of the union address President Bill Clinton proposed that bonds and other resources equal to 57 percent of the unified budget surpluses projected for the 2000–14 period be given to the trust fund to bolster social security's financial situation. This proposal was greeted with considerable criticism, in part because it appeared to credit the trust fund twice for a portion of the program's surpluses. In the mid-session review of the budget, the administration revised its approach and proposed that the social security surpluses be reserved to pay down the federal government's publicly held debt. To enforce this policy, the administration suggested that Congress adopt procedural restraints that would make it more difficult for Congress to pass tax or spending legislation that caused the non-social security accounts to be in deficit. The administration estimated that by the end of 2014, social security surpluses would be responsible for paying down $3.067 trillion of the $3.653 trillion public debt outstanding at the start of 2000.

The president also proposed that a portion of the surpluses projected for the non-social security budget accounts be credited to the social security trust fund after 2010. The amount transferred to the trust fund each year would be set to equal the projected interest savings the Treasury enjoyed as a result of the reduction in the public debt attributable to social security's surpluses. Over the 2011 to 2014 period, the administration estimates that these transfers, which represent general revenue support for social security, would amount to roughly $543 billion.

The additional resources provided to social security would be used to purchase equities for the trust fund until such holdings constituted about 15 percent of the trust fund's reserves. Thereafter, resources not needed to maintain that level of equity holdings would be invested in government securities similar to those traditionally held by the fund. The president recommended a number of institutional safeguards to allay widespread concerns that such stock market investment could lead to inappropriate government influence over private companies or politically motivated investment policies. He called for the creation of an independent board consisting of members with lengthy, staggered terms to oversee the private investment of reserves. The board would hire private fund managers, each of whom would invest a portion of the reserves passively in the broadest of stock index funds. The private managers would vote the trust fund's shares so as to maximize their long-run economic returns. These safeguards, the president believes, would insulate the trust fund's private sector investment activities from political influence.

Administration estimates suggest that the additional funds provided to the trust fund and the higher returns expected on equity investments would delay the trust fund insolvency from 2034 to 2053. These changes would close a bit more than two-thirds of social security's projected long-term deficit (table 6-1). Other measures—benefit cuts, increases in earmarked taxes, or additional general revenues—would be required to close the rest of the projected deficit. Although the president indicated his willingness to discuss such changes with congressional leaders, he did not make specific recommendations. The following changes are a few of the many possible ones that, when combined with policies presented in the mid-session review, would close the entire projected long-term deficit while keeping social security in its current form (table 6-1).

—Increase payroll tax base. The limit on earnings subject to social security payroll tax—currently $72,600 and indexed to the growth of average wages—could be raised. The current level encompasses roughly 86 percent of all earnings. Setting the limit at a level that covered 90 percent of earnings—$108,600 in 1999—would reduce social security's long-run deficit by more than one-quarter.[10]

—Accelerate increase in the "full benefits age" and raise this age along with increased life expectancy. The age at which retirees can obtain unreduced benefits will increase from 65 to 65 and 2 months for those turning 62 in 2000. This will be repeated in each of the next five years until the age reaches 66 for those turning 62 in 2005. After a twelve-year hiatus, the whole process will be repeated with the age at

10. Information supplied by Bill Piatt, Social Security Administration, August 1999.

Table 6-1. *Estimated Social Security Imbalance and Impact of the Clinton Plan and Selected Other Changes*
Percent of taxable payroll

Item	Trust fund balance, 75-year projection
Deficit projection in 1999 Trustees Report	−2.07
President Clinton's plan:	
Transfer of bonds to social security reserves and investment of 15 percent of reserves in equities	1.48[a]
Deficit remaining if Clinton plan is implemented	−0.59
Other possible changes	
Increase payroll tax base	0.57
Accelerate increase in "full benefits age" and index for increased life expectancy	0.49
Extend coverage to all newly hired state and local workers	0.21
Increase "averaging period"	0.25

a. This number reflects the administration's January 1999 estimates. It does not include adjustments made in the 1999 mid-session review.

which unreduced benefits are available for those turning age 62 after 2021 reaching 67. About 24 percent of the deficit could be eliminated if the increase to age 67 were accomplished by 2011—that is, by dropping the hiatus—and if this age were then increased gradually along with improvements in adult life expectancy.

—Extend coverage to all newly hired state and local workers. Roughly one-quarter of state and local government workers are not covered by social security payroll taxes, although most receive benefits upon retirement as the spouse of a covered worker or as a result of employment in covered jobs either before or after their state or local service. If all newly hired state and local workers were covered by social security, roughly 10 percent of the program's long-term deficit would be closed.

—Increase "averaging period." Retirement benefits are currently based on the average of each worker's highest thirty-five years of covered earnings. If the highest thirty-eight years of earnings were used to calculate benefits, benefits for future retirees would be cut by an average of 3.1 percent for male and 3.9 percent for female workers, reducing the program's long-run deficit by about 12 percent.

Other Measures to Encourage Retirement Saving

Social Security was designed to provide a secure source of basic retirement income that would be supplemented by employer- and union-sponsored pension plans and personal saving. The tax system has been used to encourage group pension plans since 1921 and individual retirement saving since 1962.[11] Businesses and individuals have made massive use of these saving incentives. Qualified employer pension plans hold assets totaling $7.5 trillion, and tax-favored individual accounts held balances of more than $2 trillion at the end of 1998.

In his fiscal year 2000 budget, President Clinton proposed to further encourage retirement saving by creating Universal Savings Accounts or "USA" accounts funded from part of the projected budget surpluses. While the president explicitly distinguished the USA accounts initiative from his social security reforms, his proposal is important for the debate over the future of social security because the USA accounts are similar to the personal accounts that are an integral component of many reform plans crafted by members of Congress.

Under the president's plan, the government would provide to eligible people—beginning in 2003—a refundable tax credit that would have to be deposited in a retirement saving account (USA account). When fully phased in, this credit would have a maximum value of $400 per person and would be available to those individuals and couples with at least $5,000 in earnings. The credit would phase out completely at incomes of $40,000 for individuals and $80,000 for couples.[12] In addition, starting in 2005 the government would match workers' voluntary contributions to their accounts. The match would be dollar-for-dollar, up to a limit of $325 in 2005, $300 in 2006–08, and $550 in 2009 and

11. Although the legislation and debate surrounding the first two of these provisions have stressed saving for retirement, balances in all tax-sheltered individual savings accounts are available at any time to people who are willing to pay ordinary income tax on withdrawals and a 10 percentage point penalty tax and without the penalty tax if certain conditions are met.

12. There would be no income limit for those lacking access to an employer-sponsored pension plan.

thereafter, for voluntary contributions made by low- and middle-income participants; lower match rates would apply to those with higher incomes.[13]

The investment options available for the USA accounts would be limited to a few broad-based funds similar to those offered to government employees in their Thrift Saving Plan. Withdrawals could not begin until the account holder reached the age of 65 but would otherwise be unrestricted. The maximum government transfer to a low- or middle-income couple that contributed voluntarily an additional $1,100 would be $1,900 a year—two $400 grants plus $1,100 in government matching payments. A couple who received the $800 annual grant starting at age 25, but made no voluntary contributions, would accumulate approximately $102,500 in 1999 dollars by age 65 if the account balance earned an average return of 5 percent a year (above inflation). If the same couple made the maximum voluntary contribution, their total balance would amount to approximately $380,500 by 65 years of age.

The Alternatives

Members of Congress have developed many social security reform proposals. One of the most prominent of these is the Social Security Guarantee (SSG) plan crafted by Bill Archer (R-Tex.), chairman of the Committee on Ways and Means, and Clay Shaw (R-Fla.), chairman of that committee's social security subcommittee. Under the SSG plan workers would be given a refundable tax credit equal to 2 percent of their earnings subject to the social security payroll tax. These credits would be deposited in qualified mutual funds whose portfolios would be 60 percent invested in stock index funds and 40 percent in corporate bonds. Annual fund administrative costs would be limited to .25 percent of account balances. Individuals would receive the higher of the benefits promised by social security or the annuity that could be supported from their SSG account balances. If the benefits promised by social security were higher, which would be true for virtually all workers, the SSG account annuity would be remitted in full to social

13. The president's plan would count deposits into 401(k) plans as contributions to USA accounts. The intent of this provision is to ensure that workers did not cut back on contributions to their employer-sponsored plans to gain the tax credit.

security, thereby bolstering the program's resources. Account balances of workers who died before reaching entitlement would be transferred to the accounts of their spouses, former spouses, or dependent children. If there were no potential social security liabilities of this sort, the balance would go, tax free, into the worker's estate.

Deposits in the SSG accounts would be funded from general revenues. While the social security actuary has estimated that the SSG plan would eliminate the program's long-run deficit under reasonable economic assumptions, the plan would subject the unified budget balance to something of a roller coaster ride. The plan would absorb virtually all of the surpluses projected over the next decade and then push the budget back into deficit. With time, the average SSG account balance would grow and an increasing fraction of the social security benefits paid to retirees would be offset by annuity remittances paid from the individual accounts to the trust fund. Toward the middle of the next century, the budget situation would turn around as a result of sharply growing offsets, permitting a payroll tax rate cut of 2.5 percentage points in 2050 and a further 1 percentage point in 2060.

The 21st Century Retirement Security Act (21st Century plan), another prominent proposal, has bipartisan support.[14] Under this "carve-out" plan, 2 percentage points of the current payroll tax would be diverted to support new Individual Security Accounts (ISAs). Workers could invest their account balances in a limited number of index funds that held stocks, bonds, or government securities. To keep administrative costs low, these funds would be managed in a fashion similar to the federal employees' Thrift Saving Plan. The government would contribute an extra $150 to the accounts of workers with low and modest earnings who voluntarily contributed at least $1 to their accounts and would match, on a one for two basis, these voluntary contributions up to $600 a year. All workers, no matter how high their incomes, would be permitted to make unmatched voluntary contribu-

14. The origins of this plan are to be found in the recommendations of the National Commission on Retirement Policy, a group that included members of Congress from both parties, leaders from the private sector, and policy analysts. Representatives Charles Stenholm (D-Tex.) and Jim Kolbe (R-Ariz.) have introduced H.R. 1793 in the House of Representatives. A similar, although not identical bill, has been introduced in the Senate by Judd Gregg (R-N.H.) and John Breaux (D-La.) as S. 1383.

tions of up to $2,000 a year. Owners of ISAs could withdraw their balances in a variety of ways when they retired or became disabled. Those choosing to withdraw the balance in a lump sum would have to use enough of the proceeds to purchase an inflation-indexed annuity that, when combined with the worker's reduced social security benefit, would at least equal the poverty threshold.

To close the long-run social security deficit—which the diversion of a portion of the payroll tax to fund ISAs would increase—the 21st Century plan would cut the benefits most for high earners but not at all for the lowest earners.[15] Furthermore, benefits would be calculated by dividing workers' total lifetime earnings over as many years as the worker had earnings by forty, rather than averaging workers' highest thirty-five years of earnings. Benefits would be cut across the board by accelerating the scheduled increase in the age at which unreduced benefits are paid and further raising the age at which unreduced benefits are paid to reflect improved life expectancy. The cost-of-living adjustment that protects benefits from erosion by inflation would be reduced to compensate for the upward bias assumed to be present in the consumer price index. Together, these changes would reduce social security benefits for the average wage worker retiring in 2040 at age 65 by roughly 39 percent. If, on average, future market returns are similar to those of the past, most participants will be able to offset these reductions with resources from their ISAs. The inevitable broad swings that characterize financial markets would mean that, at times, ISA pensions would not offset cuts in social security benefits for most workers.

To ensure that the reductions in social security's defined benefit do not impose undue hardship, the 21st Century plan would establish a new minimum benefit. Workers with twenty years of earnings would be guaranteed a social security benefit of 60 percent of the poverty level. This guarantee would rise for each year of work beyond twenty, reaching 100 percent of the poverty level for those with forty or more years of earnings.

---

15. Specifically, the Primary Insurance Amount (PIA) would be reduced gradually over the 2012–44 period, and the 32 percent and 15 percent PIA formula factors would be reduced gradually between 2006 and 2030 until they were 19.8 and 9.3 percent respectively. Stephen C. Goss and Alice H. Wade, "Estimated Long-Range OASDI Financial Effects of the 21st Century Retirement Security Act," memorandum to Harry C. Ballantyne, May 25, 1999.

The 21st Century plan would fully close social security's long-term deficit. While it would use projected budget surpluses to cover a portion of the transition costs, its reliance on surpluses would be small compared with that of the SSG plan. Moreover, because the plan would extend the temporary reduction in the COLA to the tax code and to most other indexed benefits, the non-social security surpluses would be augmented sufficiently to fully cover the transfers.

The Choices Ahead

With his 1998 state of the union pledge to "save social security first"— that is, to delay committing future budget surpluses to tax cuts or to increases in other government spending until measures were enacted to shore up social security's finances—President Clinton energized the debate over how best to reform social security and stimulated the development of many reform proposals. The most recent plans crafted by leading policymakers have shared several common themes. Foremost has been an increased willingness to use general revenues to support retirement pensions. Nevertheless, the nature and extent of the commitment of general revenues differs greatly from plan to plan. In addition, most reform proposals would create some type of individual account through which workers would save for their retirement. Under the president's approach, these accounts would be separate from the social security system; under most of the plans crafted by members of Congress, these accounts would be an integral component of a reformed social security program. In addition, recent proposals exhibit a growing reluctance to reduce benefits or raise taxes now or in the future. Some would guarantee retirement benefits no smaller than those provided under social security while others call for increased benefits.

Sharp substantive and political differences remain. Compromise will be difficult when there is no immediate crisis forcing legislative action and when legislative missteps could tip the balance of political power in the 2000 elections. Neither political party is likely to risk a blunder on an issue like social security that could give the other party a significant advantage for years to come.

The president and members of Congress elected in 2000 do not *have* *to* address the social security problem. Revenues are projected to cover currently promised benefits for more than two decades beyond the end of their terms. But the nation will be poorly served if its elected officials procrastinate. Options narrow as deficits become imminent because elected officials are properly reluctant to cut benefits or make other changes that would adversely affect people nearing retirement.

One fundamental choice before policymakers involves the extent to which projected budget surpluses should be used to strengthen the financing of the nation's mandatory pension system. The primary advantage of using general revenues to shore up social security is that this step would reduce the need to cut benefits or boost payroll taxes. However, general revenue financing might erode the contributory social insurance base of the program, which is a major reason for its overwhelming popularity. Furthermore, surpluses devoted to saving social security will not be available for other high-priority purposes, such as medicare, education, medical research, defense, and tax cuts.

The most fundamental decision facing policymakers is whether to replace, in whole or in part, the current defined benefit system—which provides progressive, fully inflation-protected benefits that do not fluctuate in value with asset prices—with a system of personal accounts that will inevitably lack some or all of those attributes but that will give people a heightened sense of ownership and control. A move to personal accounts will almost certainly affect the future distribution of retirement income and the political dynamic that sustains the mandatory pension system.

Who Gains? Who Loses?

Individual accounts, whether financed from the surplus or from carving out a portion of the payroll tax, raise the distributional question: what groups should benefit most? Under the president's approach, general revenues deposited in USA accounts would flow primarily to low and moderate earners. Under proposals that call for deposits proportional to earnings up to the social security earnings ceiling, a larger share of deposits would flow to upper-middle and upper-income workers. Under both approaches, high earners are likely to earn larger returns than low earners, because people with low incomes traditionally invest conservatively in relatively low-yielding assets such as bonds and money market instruments, while high earners invest proportionately more in higher-yielding assets such as common stocks. Such caution among low earners is understandable, because they usually have few assets, meager private pension coverage, and little experience with financial markets. But it means that unless deposits are progressive (as they would be in the president's plan and, to a lesser extent, in the 21st Century plan) or investment opportunities are severely constrained (as they would be in the SSG plan), the balances in the individual accounts of high earners at retirement are likely to be larger relative to their earnings than those in the accounts of low earners. If pensions from individual accounts replace, in whole or in part, the progressive benefits of the social security system, the net benefit to high earners will be even greater.

Policymakers should also consider the political dynamic that personal accounts will create as part of the government-mandated pension system. If workers are told that these accounts are their property, they are likely to demand control over investment decisions and disposition of account balances. The history of existing tax-sheltered individual savings accounts suggests that Congress would readily grant people permission to draw on these funds before retirement—for example, for college tuition, to buy a first home, to pay for medical care, or upon leaving a job. Similar pressures can be expected under any new system of personal accounts whether they are outside of the social security structure like President Clinton's USA accounts, or integral to a reformed system, like the SSG accounts. If account holders are given increased flexibility to control their account balances, some will dissipate their retirement assets through misfortune or misjudgment. Unless ensured retirement income—like social security's defined benefit— remains adequate, the number of people who find themselves with inadequate retirement incomes will grow.

Personal accounts could also create a political dynamic that erodes support for social security. As balances build up in personal accounts, people would come to rely less and less on social security. Many workers, particularly high earners, would compare the seemingly small returns on payroll taxes with the seemingly larger returns on personal accounts and conclude that they could do better if only social security were scaled back and their payroll taxes were transferred to their personal accounts. Support for social security among such workers would erode, putting in jeopardy the relatively generous benefits provided to low earners. If this process went far, even a guarantee that benefits would be as high as those promised currently by social security would become progressively harder to sustain.

The American public has before it two sharply different visions of government's role in supporting retirement income. The traditional view has been that ensuring basic income during retirement is a shared responsibility, one in which the inevitable risks should be broadly spread across all workers, and benefits should be distributed progressively. The alternative vision would give people ownership and control of their retirement accounts in return for agreeing to bear increased risk and to accept a less progressive distribution of benefits.

A critical question for both approaches concerns the wisdom of increasing transfers to the elderly at the very time when retirement of the baby boom generation threatens sharply increased budget costs not only for pensions but also for acute and long-term health care benefits. The apparent unwillingness to propose even modest benefit cuts means that future payroll and income tax payers will have to bear the full burden of supporting the growing ranks of the economically inactive elderly population.

Medicare

Medicare provides basic health insurance protection for the elderly and disabled. The program has two components: hospital insurance (HI, also known as part A) and supplemental medical insurance (SMI, also known as part B). Those who are eligible for social security disability benefits and those who are eligible for retirement benefits and are at least 65 years old are entitled to part A benefits, which cover inpatient hospital services, some skilled nursing facility and home health costs, and hospice care. Part A, which accounted for about 63 percent of total medicare spending in 1999, is financed largely by a 2.9 percent payroll tax paid—half by employees, half by employers—on all earned income. Tax receipts are deposited in a trust fund, and program expenditures can not exceed the balances in the fund.

Part A participants have the option of enrolling in part B, which covers physician visits, laboratory fees, outpatient hospital services, durable medical equipment, preventive services, some home health care, and other medical services. Because this insurance is highly subsidized, almost everyone chooses to enroll. Participants pay a monthly premium—$45.50 in 1999—that covers about one-quarter of the program's costs. General revenues cover the balance.

Most medicare beneficiaries receive care on a fee-for-service basis. Besides paying part B premiums, participants in fee-for-service medicare are responsible for a part B deductible of $100, a deductible for inpatient hospital services set at the cost of an average day in the hospital ($768 in 1999), and coinsurance on some part A and B services. Approximately one in six participants has chosen to receive care through one of the roughly 350 Medicare+Choice (M+C) health plans, (almost three-quarters of beneficiaries live in counties where these plans are available). While other plan types are permitted, almost all of these are managed care plans, such as health maintenance organizations (HMOs), independent practice associations (IPAs), or preferred provider organizations (PPOs). M+C plans are paid a fixed amount per month per enrollee that, subject to certain limits, is related to a blend of per beneficiary fee-for-service expenditures in the service area and in the nation, and the characteristics (age, sex, health risk, welfare status) of the enrollee. Most of these plans give their members, at no additional cost, benefits—such as routine physical exams, immunization, prescription drugs, vision and hearing care, and low cost sharing—that supplement medicare benefits.

Nearly all providers participate in medicare, thereby giving the elderly and disabled unfettered access to mainstream medical care. The fee-for-service component pays participating providers according to legislated fee schedules; providers serving members of M+C plans negotiate payment rates with the individual plans with which they contract. Both to ward off HI trust fund insolvency and to help balance the federal budget, Congress has periodically reduced the fee-for-service payment schedules. The most recent example of such legislation was the Balanced Budget Act of 1997 (BBA97), which at the time of passage was estimated to reduce the growth of medicare spending by $116 billion, or by about 9 percent, over the 1998–2002 period.

Medicare has been a great success but suffers from several deficiencies, which policymakers should address soon so that reforms can be implemented before retirement of the baby boomers creates additional strains. Foremost is the tendency for program costs to grow disturbingly fast. This problem is not unique to medicare. During the past two decades, per capita medicare spending has risen at roughly the same pace as health care spending for the nonelderly, nondisabled population. Nevertheless, as the capabilities of modern medicine expand and new and expensive diagnostic techniques and therapeutic procedures are introduced, cost pressures will increase. These pressures are likely to be especially intense among those, like the elderly and disabled, with chronic conditions and, for medicare, they will be compounded by the demographic stress of the aging baby boomers. Even after assuming that a substantial slowdown will occur in the historic rate of growth of per beneficiary medicare costs, the medicare actuary projects that spending will rise from 2.55 percent of GDP in 1999 to 5.25 percent in 2040; this 2.7 percentage point increase is even larger than the 2.43 percentage point rise forecast for social security. Under these projections, the HI trust fund will be depleted by 2015, and an ever-increasing fraction of general revenues will be needed to support part B.

A second problem facing medicare is that its benefits are outdated. Medicare offers benefits similar to those provided by employers in the mid-1960s. It does not cover outpatient prescription drugs, an ever more important and expensive component of modern health care. Nor does it provide protection against catastrophic costs, and therefore the deductibles, copayments, and costs arising from limits on coverage can easily become crushing. Medicare provides very circumscribed coverage for nursing home services, which, as the number of frail elderly with chronic conditions grows, will become an increasing concern. Finally, many believe that the bifurcated structure through which medicare benefits are provided makes little sense and offers undesirable opportunities for financial gaming. The division of services between parts A and B followed the distinction that employer-sponsored insurance of the 1960s made between hospital and medical services insurance, a distinction that has all but disappeared in the private sector. Because it persists in medicare, the program retains a confusing hodgepodge of deductibles and coinsurance rules. Furthermore, policymakers have been able to delay trust fund insolvency by shifting benefits from part A, where expenditures are limited by the trust fund balances, to part B, where there is an unlimited draw on general revenues.

The inadequacies of the basic medicare package have led almost all participants to seek supplementary coverage. In 1996, 30 percent received additional insurance through a former employer. Another 29 percent bought supplemental protection through so-called medigap policies. Medicaid filled in medicare's holes for an additional 16 percent. Eleven percent got additional benefits through an M+C plan.[16] Only 12 percent lacked some type of supplemental coverage.[17] The system of dual coverage through multiple types of supplemental policies is complex, confusing, inequitable, and costly both for providers and participants. If medicare beneficiaries received coverage through a single, more comprehensive policy, administrative costs would be reduced. Service costs would also be lower, because many supplementary policies provide first-dollar coverage that increases utilization, some of which is of marginal worth.

A third weakness is that fee-for-service medicare provides only limited encouragement for efficiency. Neither providers, who are paid on a per episode or service basis, nor participants, many of whom are shielded from cost considerations by supplemental insurance, face strong incentives to limit care to that which is cost effective. In addition, in many market areas, medicare pays more for durable medical equipment, laboratory, oxygen, and ambulance services than do other large insurers because these payments are set administratively rather than through market forces.

Finally, the availability and cost of medical services are becoming increasingly variable across geographic areas and among medicare participants. In some metropolitan areas, beneficiaries can choose between fee-for-service care and any of half a dozen or more M+C plans offering extra benefits. In others, participants may have only one or two M+C alternatives, or none at all. Those with supplemental policies provided by a former employer generally have extensive coverage at a limited cost, but this group is shrinking as employers curtail this fringe benefit. Those who must depend on a medigap policy face significant pre-

16. The importance of capitated plans—now called M+C plans—has increased since 1996. As of June 1999, 18 percent of enrollees were covered by such plans. Probably, the prevalance of employer-sponsored insurance has declined since 1996.

17. Most enrollees in M+C plans receive coverage in addition to the basic medicare package. These percentages reflect this fact.

miums—often around $1,500 a year—that are rising rapidly for much less comprehensive coverage.

The Alternative Approaches

Three broad approaches to medicare reform have emerged. The first is to strengthen and modernize the existing medicare program while preserving its basic structure. The benefit package would be extended to include outpatient prescription drug coverage, an out-of-pocket catastrophic expenditure limit, lower cost sharing for certain services, and broader coverage of preventive care—a package comparable to what most employers offer workers and their dependents. Such an expansion would reduce the importance of supplemental insurance, simplifying the system and lowering overall costs. To slow the growth of expenditures, medicare would let the prices it pays for lab services, oxygen, durable medical equipment, and similar items be set by competitive market forces rather than by administrative mechanisms. In addition, the restraints imposed on the growth of hospital and physician fees by the BBA97 would be extended when the current restrictions expire at the end of 2002, just as they have many times in the past.

Advocates stress that this approach would build on proven success and not subject a vulnerable population to risk or disruptive change. They also argue that strengthening the current structure does not depend on sophisticated new institutional arrangements and operational mechanisms that reforms described in the following pages would require.

Critics feel that under this approach cost growth will not be dampened, and inefficiencies and inequities will persist. Accordingly, two other reform approaches have emerged.

Under one approach—known as premium support or the competitive defined benefit approach—the government would contribute up to a maximum amount related to the cost of fee-for-service medicare, the cost of the average plan, or some other benchmark. Medicare fee-for-service and M+C plans would compete with one another. All would be required to offer a more adequate benefit package than provided currently. Participants selecting plans that charged less than the maximum amount offered by the government would pay reduced premiums, while those joining more expensive plans would be required to pay additional amounts. To hold down costs in fee-for-service medicare, the various cost-reducing measures encompassed in the previous approach would be adopted.

Advocates believe that this structure, which is similar to the federal employees' health benefit system, will lead participants to demand and plans to offer cost-effective, high-quality care and that competitive forces will slow cost growth. Opponents of this approach fear that the government will be unable to adjust payments it will make to plans to accurately reflect the differential health risks of their participants. If younger, healthier beneficiaries gravitated to a few low-cost plans and older, less-healthy ones joined other plans, the chronically ill might end up facing higher costs than they now confront. If the chronically ill chose fee-for-service medicare because it offered the widest and least constrained choice of providers, they might face relatively high costs, both for their basic medicare coverage and for their supplemental medigap policies. Opponents also question whether the benefits of competitive markets can be realized in the health sector. They believe that competition will result in lower quality and, possibly, deny needed services to those in low-cost plans. Furthermore, critics point out that a well-functioning premium support model requires adequate mechanisms not only to adjust plan payments for the differential health risks of their members but also to measure the quality of the different plans and to inform beneficiaries of the choices available to them.

The third approach involves prefunding future medicare benefits through individual or group accounts similar to those promoted by some social security reform proposals.[18] Medicare payroll taxes would be deposited in personal or group accounts for people of a given age cohort that would be invested in a mix of private and government assets. The tax rate for each cohort would be adjusted periodically to generate an account sufficient to buy insurance when the cohort reached retirement age. Government would make contributions on behalf of nonworkers and supplement the payments made by those with low earnings. Upon retirement, individuals would be required to purchase adequate insurance in a regulated individual insurance market. At a minimum, this coverage would consist of a catastrophic policy.

18. Gramm, Rettenmaier, and Saving (1998).

Advocates argue that it would make beneficiaries and providers more price conscious; that it would eventually eliminate medicare's unfunded liability; and that, by increasing saving, it would increase investment and economic growth. Skeptics see this approach as unworkable. To function efficiently, the individual insurance market would have to be reformed to ensure that plans could not discriminate against unhealthy persons. Mechanisms would have to be developed to pool or share risk so that plans that found themselves with disproportionate numbers of participants with expensive illnesses were not unfairly disadvantaged. Furthermore, large tax rate adjustments could become necessary if poor investment outcomes deplete account values or if advances in medical technology boost costs as a cohort nears retirement age.

The Bipartisan Commission on the Future of Medicare

The Balanced Budget Act of 1997 established a seventeen-member commission to analyze the problems facing medicare and report any findings and recommendations that at least eleven commissioners endorsed. The chairman, Senator John Breaux (D-La.), and the vice chairman, Representative William Thomas (R-Calif.), fell one vote short of the number required to make a plan that they crafted the official commission recommendation. Nevertheless, this proposal has considerable congressional support and represents a comprehensive, if somewhat skeletal, description of the sorts of changes that would be required to strengthen medicare for the long term. The Breaux-Thomas plan adopted a version of the premium support approach, under which the government's maximum contribution would be tied to the average price charged by all competing plans—both M+C plans and fee-for-service medicare. Participants who enrolled in an average-priced plan would pay a premium that covered 12 percent of the plan's costs— about the fraction of total medicare costs that part B premiums will cover in the future. Participants joining less expensive plans would face lower premiums, with no premium charged to those enrolling in plans charging 85 percent or less of the average. Those joining plans whose price exceeded the average would pay all the additional costs.

All plans would be required to offer both a standard and a high-option benefit package. The standard option would cover medicare's current mandated benefits although plans could, with approval of a newly established medicare board, vary benefits and cost-sharing requirements within specified limits. The high option would include a prescription drug benefit as well as a cap on catastrophic out-of-pocket spending. Those with incomes over 135 percent of the poverty line would bear the full additional cost if they chose this richer package. The federal government would, however, pay the high-option premium for those with incomes below this threshold if they joined plans whose costs were less than or equal to 85 percent of the national average of all high-option plans.[19]

The Breaux-Thomas proposal would unify parts A and B into a single trust fund, establish a single deductible that would be indexed to the growth of medicare costs, and impose 10 percent coinsurance on those services (except the first sixty days of inpatient hospital care and preventive care) for which no or lower coinsurance requirements currently are in force. The proposal also recommended that the age of eligibility for medicare be raised gradually along with the already scheduled increase in the age at which unreduced social security benefits will be paid. Those over 64 but below the higher eligibility age would be allowed to purchase medicare coverage without subsidy. Medicare would require additional resources over the long run even if the commission's modifications were adopted. However, the commission left unresolved whether the needed resources should come from higher payroll taxes, general revenues, or premiums.

Criticism of the Breaux-Thomas proposal focused on the recommended increase in the age of eligibility, which could expand the number of uninsured retirees, the possibility that fee-for-service medicare would have above-average costs forcing those who wanted to remain in this program to pay higher premiums, and concern that the high-option plans would be very costly and possibly unsustainable because, with voluntary participation, they would attract largely less healthy participants.

The President's Medicare Initiative

As part of the mid-session review of the fiscal year 2000 budget proposal, President Clinton unveiled a major four-pronged initiative to

---

19. If no such plan is available in an area, the government would pay the premium for the cheapest available high-option plan.

strengthen and reform medicare. The initiative included a premium support structure for private plans, a new prescription drug benefit, measures to modernize and restrain costs in the fee-for-service program, and an infusion of general revenues from the projected budget surplus to bolster the HI trust fund. Under the president's "competitive defined benefit" approach, those choosing the traditional fee-for-service medicare would continue to pay part B premiums. Participants in M+C plans that charged less than 96 percent of the cost of fee-for-service medicare would pay reduced premiums; those joining plans that charged 80 percent or less of the fee-for-service costs would pay no part B premium, a saving estimated to be $60 a month in 2003 when the competitive structure would be implemented.[20] Participants joining plans with costs over 96 percent of fee-for-service costs would pay the part B premium plus all costs above that threshold.

All plans would be required to submit bids based on their costs of providing the standard medicare benefit package, although M+C plans could price into their bids reduced cost-sharing requirements. The standard medicare benefit package would be modified to eliminate cost sharing on preventive services such as mammography screening, impose 20 percent coinsurance on clinical laboratory services, and increase the $100 part B deductible annually with inflation. M+C plans would be able to offer additional benefits, but they would have to market and price these supplements separately.

The prescription drug benefit proposed by the president is modest and, like the Breaux-Thomas approach, voluntary. Participants would face no deductible but would have to pay 50 percent coinsurance and a monthly premium (about $53 when fully phased in) set to cover half of program costs. The government would pick up both the premium and coinsurance costs for those with incomes below 135 percent of the

20. The actual reduction in part B premiums would be 75 percent of the difference between 96 percent of the cost of fee-for-service medicare and price charged by the plan. The government would take the remaining 25 percent as savings. Under current estimates of fee-for-service costs, the part B premium would be canceled at 80 percent of fee-for-service costs. If the estimates for total fee-for-service costs and part B costs are higher or lower than current estimates, the point at which the part B premium was absolved could be a bit higher or lower than 80 percent. National Economic Council (1999).

poverty line; those with incomes between 135 percent and 150 percent of poverty would face reduced premiums. The maximum annual benefit would be limited to $1,000 in 2002, the program's first year, and grow to $2,500 in 2008 when fully implemented.

All plans would have to offer as a high option the standard medicare package with the prescription drug benefit. Participants in M+C plans would receive their benefits through their plans, whereas those in fee-for-service medicare would receive benefits through a pharmacy benefits manager (PBM) or other private sector entity selected competitively in each region to provide this service. The PBMs could establish formularies and incentives to encourage the use of generic or less expensive drugs but "beneficiaries would be guaranteed access to off-formulary drugs when medically necessary."[21]

Although roughly 65 percent of medicare beneficiaries have some prescription drug coverage, virtually all beneficiaries would take up, directly or indirectly, the president's prescription drug option because it would be highly subsidized—half of the costs being paid by the government. Participation would also be spurred by the restrictions that would be placed on enrollment; beneficiaries could join only during their first year of medicare eligibility or when they lost coverage provided by their or their spouse's employer or former employer. Unsure what their prescription drug needs may be in the future, even the disabled and seniors with no current pharmaceutical expenditures would likely join. A partial government subsidy to employers that offer their retirees more generous prescription drug benefits would encourage these firms to continue coverage, rather than redesign their plans to offer only wrap-around benefits.

The president's proposal also includes measures designed to modernize fee-for-service medicare and restrain its costs. Medicare would be permitted to adopt techniques that private plans have used to restrain costs and improve care: incentives for participants to seek treatment for complex problems at institutions with proven track records of high-quality, cost-effective care; payment bundling for groups of services; a preferred provider option; encouragement of primary care case management and disease management; and arrangements to set pay-

21. National Economic Council (1999, p. 21).

ments through competitive bidding and negotiated prices. In addition, some of the payment restraints imposed by the BBA97 would be extended through 2009.

The president proposes to strengthen the HI trust fund with an infusion of general revenues from projected non-social security surpluses. Specifically, over the 2000 to 2009 period, the Treasury would issue to the trust fund $328 billion in special government securities in addition to those purchased with fund surpluses. Like the transfers made to the social security fund after 2010, these infusions would occur whether or not the surpluses materialize; that is, whether or not debt is actually retired. They will give the HI trust fund a claim on future general revenues and push off the date of insolvency to 2027.

Critics of the president's proposal point out that it would add a new and expensive benefit to an entitlement program that already faces insolvency. They also charge that it gives the Health Care Financing Administration (HCFA) too much flexibility, cuts payments to providers too deeply, and is unfair to M+C plans. The president's plan could also be criticized for being too timid in forgoing the simplification and efficiencies that could be realized from adopting a more adequate benefit package and an out-of-pocket expenditure cap—changes that would eliminate, for many, the need for supplementary insurance.

The Future

The future of medicare is more uncertain than that of social security. Both face retirement of the baby boom, but medicare must also cope with the uncertainties of advancing medical technology. Today's laboratory experiments and clinical trials will become tomorrow's routine care. These developments could conveivably lower costs but are far more likely to add—perhaps greatly—to tomorrow's medical bills.

Uncertainty surrounds not only medicare costs but also the institutional setting in which the program will operate. During the past decade and a half, new ways of providing coverage have emerged. Indemnity or fee-for-service care, which was the dominant form of insurance in the mid-1980s, has been replaced everywhere but in medicare by the bewildering acronyms of managed care—HMOs, HMOs with the option of service outside the HMO (so-called points of service plans), IPAs, and PPOs. Administrators are implementing mea-

sures of plan quality and encouraging evidence-based medical practice—concepts that were nothing more than the playthings of policy
analysts a decade ago. Per service, cost-based provider payments have
given way to prospective payment systems, bundled fee schedules, and
capitation. Providers, such as hospitals, nursing homes, and physicians,
have begun to consolidate into chains and ever larger group practices.
Because the situation is so fluid and medicare, which accounts for
nearly 20 percent of health expenditures, can strongly influence the
direction in which this institutional environment evolves, policymakers
should reform medicare in ways that preserve flexibility and are
reversible if developments warrant.

The similarities between the Breaux-Thomas proposal and the president's initiative suggest that a consensus may be developing over the
general form of structural reforms needed to strengthen medicare. Both
would rely on a premium support approach to determine payments to
plans and would have fee-for-service medicare and the M+C plans
compete. Both would provide fee-for-service medicare with added flexibility to enhance efficiency and extend BBA97 payment restraints. Both
would expand medicare's benefit package although neither would
establish a sufficiently comprehensive benefit package. Comprehensive
benefits are essential for real reform because without a package that
the vast majority of beneficiaries regards as sufficient, supplementary
policies will remain widespread, and the overall system of coverage
will remain needlessly complex, confusing, costly, and inequitable.
Under the president's approach, beneficiaries would continue to need
supplementary protection both from high out-of-pocket costs associated with the traditional services and the coinsurance required by the
pharmaceutical benefit and any expenditures above $5,000. The vol-
untary and unsubsidized nature of the Breaux-Thomas high-option
package could produce the same result, because those who anticipate
significant medical expenses would be more likely to enroll in the high-
benefit option, thus making it unaffordable for many. The problem
could be solved under the president's structure if a $3,500 to $4,500
cap on total (drug, hospital, and other) out-of-pocket expenditures
were added.

However, policymakers wishing to make medicare's benefit package
adequate face a dilemma resulting from increased costs. If beneficia-

ries are required to pay significantly higher premiums for the added benefits, those who already have such coverage through a supplemental policy provided at little or no cost by a former employer will, understandably, be upset. Deep subsidies can neutralize such opposition, but they would boost government costs and provide windfall relief to employers and individuals paying medigap premiums.

In the future, as in the past, medicare will face the challenge of cost control. But medicare's costs cannot be held down if per capita expenditures for the nonelderly, nondisabled population are soaring unless lawmakers are willing to impose heavy burdens on beneficiaries or cut provider payments to the point that few will be willing to participate and access will become a problem, as it is in medicaid. In the past, these responses have been mitigated by cross subsidies—that is, providers have been willing to accept lower payments from medicare and medicaid as long as commercial insurers paid higher fees. But in the new competitive environment, commercial insurers are increasingly unwilling to pay more than is required to cover the services used by their participants, all but eliminating the public sector's ability to hold down its program costs when systemwide costs are exploding.

The dirty secret of the medicare debate—which none of the participants has yet acknowledged—is that financing problems cannot be solved unless payroll taxes are greatly increased, premiums and cost sharing raised dramatically, or general revenue support sharply expanded. The choice among these financing approaches will determine who pays for the inevitable growth of medicare costs.

Beneficiaries could be required to contribute more for their coverage in one of three ways. Cost sharing (copayments and deductibles) could be raised. This would place most of the burden on those in the poorest health, who are also likely to have relatively low incomes and few assets. Alternatively, premiums could be raised across the board. While the part B premium is now set to cover one-quarter of that component's costs, when the program was established premiums covered one-half of part B costs. Across-the-board premium increases would hit sick and well, rich and poor alike. Of course, a $20 a month increase in premiums means much more to an elderly widow trying to make ends meet on only a $650 social security check, than to a couple whose private pension, social security, and dividend income amount to $3,000 a month. For this reason, many have proposed that only middle- and upper-income medicare beneficiaries be asked to pay higher premiums. When the president and the chairs of the bipartisan commission explored this approach, they met strong opposition from both members of Congress and interest groups. Many remembered the highly unpopular income-related premium imposed by the Catastrophic Care Act of 1988 which, in part because of this premium, was repealed eighteen months after enactment. Opponents argue that income-related premiums would subtly convert medicare into a means-tested welfare program and that upper-income people are already paying more than their share because the HI payroll tax is imposed on earnings without limit.

As premiums for medicare and supplementary insurance and out-of-pocket costs rise, policymakers must ensure that low- and moderate-income beneficiaries are not burdened excessively, relegated to second-class care, or denied access. During the past several decades, a loosely structured system has evolved to protect the low-income elderly and disabled. Medicare beneficiaries with very low incomes are eligible for medicaid, which supplements medicare with its much more comprehensive coverage. Those with incomes too high for medicaid eligibility but below the poverty threshold can have their part B premiums and cost sharing picked up by medicaid's Qualified Medicare Beneficiaries (QMB) program. Medicaid's Specified Low-income Medicare Beneficiaries (SLMB) program will pay the part B premiums of those with incomes between the poverty line and 135 percent of that level and the Qualified Individual (QI) provisions will cover a small portion of these premiums for those with incomes up to 175 percent of the poverty level. Some fourteen states have established programs that provide prescription drug coverage to low-income elderly.

For a variety of reasons, a substantial fraction of those who are thought to be eligible do not participate in these programs.[22] The stigma associated with welfare, the complexity of the application and recertification processes, and the failure of the HCFA and the states to inform seniors adequately about these options are some of the possi-

---

22. For estimates of participation rates see O'Brien, Rowland, and Keenan (1999, p. 9).

ble explanations for limited participation. As medicare reform increases the financial burden on beneficiaries, as it almost certainly must do over the next decades, the system for assisting low- and moderate-income participants must be rationalized and simplified. The subsidy schemes proposed in the Breaux-Thomas high-option and the president's drug benefit represent structures that, if expanded, could adequately address this problem.

Medicaid

Most people view medicaid as the program that pays for the acute health care needs of poor children and their parents. In fact, roughly 70 percent of medicaid beneficiaries fall into these categories. But medicaid outlays go primarily to support acute and long-term health care for the low-income elderly and disabled (including the blind). Although the elderly and disabled make up only 29 percent of beneficiaries, 73 percent of medicaid's vendor payments are made for their care. Of this total, acute care accounts for roughly 42 percent and long-term care, the balance.[23] Medicaid's acute care expenditures, for the most part, supplement medicare's benefits and pick up medicare's deductibles, coinsurance, and premium amounts.

Medicaid pays 40 percent of the nation's long-term care costs compared with 18 percent by medicare and 29 percent by individuals directly.[24] Private long-term care insurance pays only 7 percent of the total. Medicaid is the primary payer for more than two-thirds of nursing home residents and provides nursing homes with about half of their revenues.[25]

Medicaid is particularly important the very old. More than one-third of those 85 years old and over receive acute or long-term care benefits from medicaid. An estimated 43 percent of those who turned 65 in 1990 are expected to use some nursing home care before they die.[26] As the

23. U.S. House of Representatives (1998, p. 983).
24. Health Care Financing Administration, National Health Expenditure Projections 1998–2008 (http://www.hcfa.gov/stats/nhe-proj/proj1998/tables/default.htm [September 16, 1999]).
25. Komisar, Lambrew, and Feder (1996).
26. HCFA tables; Kemper and Murtaugh (1991, pp. 595–600).

population ages, the medicaid-dependent population will grow rapidly, straining federal and state budgets and highlighting the program's inequities.

States administer the program but pay only a fraction of the program's costs that varies with each state's per capita income—from 23 percent (in Mississippi) to 50 percent (in ten states) in fiscal year 2000.[27] The federal government pays the rest. Federal law sets minimum benefit and eligibility conditions, but states have wide latitude in setting provider payments, determining eligibility, and supplementing federally mandated benefits. As a result, long-term care expenditures per elderly beneficiary varied in 1994 from $17,776 in Connecticut to $3,267 in Mississippi, and acute care spending per elderly beneficiary varied from $3,914 in Rhode Island to $1,365 in Wyoming.[28] To limit their financial exposure for long-term care costs, states have restricted the growth of nursing home beds, held down medicaid reimbursement rates, and encouraged home and community-based care, which is sometimes less expensive than nursing home care on a per person basis.[29]

The fraction of the low-income elderly and disabled population eligible for medicaid benefits also varies greatly from state to state. Federal rules require that SSI recipients be covered. Some states also offer eligibility to the "medically needy," those aged and disabled whose resources and incomes are too high to make them categorically eligible but who meet higher state-set income and asset thresholds after their medical expenditures are taken into consideration. The other states make use of "special needs caps" under which nursing home residents with incomes up to a state-set limit that cannot exceed 300 percent of the SSI eligibility level can have medicaid pay for their care once they "spent down" to medicaid eligibility, which means that they have used all of their income except for a small personal needs allowance.

For those faced with lengthy stays in a nursing home, which cost roughly $50,000 on an annual basis, these options are important. Very high-income households can afford to pay long-term care costs them-

---

27. *Federal Register*, vol. 64, January 12, 1999.
28. Liska and others (1996, pp. 41, 58, 64).
29. Wiener and Stevenson (1998, pp. 81–100); and Coleman (1997).

selves and the persistently poor, who receive SSI benefits, can rely on medicaid. But most households retire with modest incomes and have assets that are sufficient to disqualify them from medicaid coverage but lack the resources to pay for more than a very short stay in a nursing home. Such families face agonizing financial choices when independent living is no longer physically possible. Some try to divest assets so that they qualify for medicaid. Others quickly deplete their income and assets and become eligible for medicaid. Of those first entering a nursing home as private pay residents, some 31 percent eventually end up with medicaid paying the bills.[30]

The deficiencies of the current system of paying for long-term care will become more apparent as the number of seniors grows. The population age 85 and older, one-quarter of whom are in nursing homes, will triple in size over the next four decades.[31] States with strong economies and robust revenue structures may be able to keep up with the need, but many states will find themselves overwhelmed and will take steps to reduce their financial exposure, possibly exacerbating existing interstate disparities in the availability of long-term care. More important than state fiscal pressures, however, is the personal anguish that families will suffer as assets shrink and the need to apply for means-tested benefits looms.

For years, policymakers have recognized the deficiencies of the current system of financing long-term care. They have not, however, agreed on a solution. Should policy encourage people to save when young so that most will be able to pay directly for their own long-term care should they need it? Or should people be encouraged to buy long-term insurance when they are a bit older by regulating and subsidizing the market for long-term care policies? Or should the nation develop a broad, publicly financed social insurance program like medicare that would help everyone obtain the long-term care they need? Or should policy build on the current system by improving the assistance available to households with incomes somewhat above current medicaid limits?

Even if policymakers agreed on the broad approach to take, disagreements would occur over the focus of any public subsidies and

30. Weiner, Sullivan, and Skaggs (1996).
31. Komisar, Lambrew, and Feder (1996, p. 11).

other details that would make legislative action difficult. For example, shallow public subsidies could be given to all those in need of long-term care, most of whom have needs that last a relatively short time. Or deeper support could be provided only to the minority with longer stays who have exhausted their own savings. Among the many details that would have to be resolved are the extent to which the systems of support for long-term and acute care should be integrated, the division of fiscal responsibility between the federal and state governments, and the relative emphasis placed on home and community-based versus institutional care.

Another inhibition to legislation is cost. Ensuring access to long-term care for a growing population of the very old would be expensive. Under a continuation of current policies, the total cost of all long-term care—home and community-based as well as institutional care—for the elderly is projected to increase from $123 billion in 2000 to $346 billion in 2040 in inflation-adjusted 2000 dollars.[32] Costs will be still higher if age-specific rates of disability do not decline 1.1 percent annually over the forty-year period, as currently assumed.

Any change in the current structure of paying for long-term care could cause a much more rapid growth in costs. Family, relatives, friends, and religious organizations now provide at home, without charge, much of the care the frail and the functionally impaired require. One estimate suggests that donated care amounts to 63 percent of the value of all care given.[33] If reforms made institutional care and formal home-health services affordable and widely accessible, many who are receiving informal care or are not receiving needed assistance, formal or informal, would increase their use of paid care.

Few lawmakers are currently advocating full-fledged social insurance for long-term care. Legislative proposals have been largely confined to using the tax code to encourage the purchase of long-term care insurance and to provide support to informal caregivers. The president, in his fiscal year 2000 budget, proposed a nonrefundable $1,000 tax credit for those with chronic conditions or the care giver with whom

32. Congressional Budget Office (1999).
33. Arno, Levine, and Memmott (1999). For another estimate, see U. S. Department of Health and Human Services (1998).

they live. The tax bill passed by Congress in August 1999 would permit taxpayers to deduct from their taxable incomes the medical care
component of premiums paid for long-term care insurance if such
insurance was not provided by their employer, allow employers to offer
long-term care insurance as an option in their "cafeteria" benefit plans,
and provide an extra personal exemption to taxpayers who provide
informal care to a related member of their household.

Even if enacted, such measures would accomplish little. The credits
and deductions are relatively small and would be of no value to the
many who have no tax liability. Less than half of all elderly households
have any income tax liability.[34] Deductions for long-term care insurance
premiums would provide a significant benefit only to those with the
highest incomes who face the highest marginal tax rates. Such households are likely to have the resources needed to pay out-of-pocket for
adequate long-term care. In any case, very few people choose to take out
such insurance policies, which typically are written for a maximum
daily benefit amount with a corresponding lifetime limit. While premiums are modest if the policy is written when the beneficiary is
55 years old, few middle-aged individuals regard protection against
the costs of long-term care as an immediate or pressing problem. When
the need becomes palpable, say around 65, premiums become quite
expensive—around $2,500 for a healthy individual.[35] Moreover, insur-
ers will not write policies for people of any age who exhibit signs of a
significant health risk.[36] In addition, consumers are dissuaded from
purchasing this insurance by the complexity and variation in the product and the uncertainty that surrounds their access to benefits, which
involves difficult judgement calls by the insurer.[37]

Conclusion

Helping families deal with the financial burden of long-term care will
become increasingly urgent over the next several decades. However,

34. Burman, Gale, and Weiner (1998, p. 642).
35. Coronel (1998).
36. Employee Benefit Research Institute (1995).
37. Lewin-VHI and Brookings Institution (1996); Alecxih and Lutzky (1996).

the lack of consensus about the best approach to the long-term care problem, combined with the high cost of certain options, places this issue well behind restoring financial balance to social security and medicare. Nevertheless, all are important elements of retirement security. The current economic, budget, and demographic environments present lawmakers with an unusual window of opportunity during which they should begin to address these problems that, left unresolved, will force themselves onto tomorrow's policy agenda, generating social and political conflict.

References

Aaron, Henry J., and Robert D. Reischauer. 1998. *Countdown to Reform: The Great Social Security Debate*. Century Foundation.

Advisory Council on Social Security. 1997. *Report of the 1994–96 Advisory Council on Social Security, vol. 1: Findings and Recommendations*. Washington.

Alecxih, Lisa Maria B., and Steven Lutzky. 1996. "How Do Alternative Eligibility Triggers Affect Access to Private Long-Term Care Insurance?" Washington: AARP Public Policy Institute (August).

Arno, Peter S., Carol Levine, and Margaret M. Memmott. 1999. "The Economic Value of Informal Caregiving." *Health Affairs* 18 (March–April): 182–88.

Burman, Leonard E., William G. Gale, and David Weiner. 1998. "Six Tax Laws Later: How Individuals' Marginal Federal Income Tax Rates Changed between 1980 and 1995." *National Tax Journal* 51 (September): 637–52.

Coleman, Barbara. 1997. "New Directions for State Long-Term Care Systems: Volume 4: Limiting State Medicaid Spending on Nursing Home Care." Washington: AARP Public Policy Institute (April).

Congressional Budget Office. 1999. "Projections of Expenditures for Long-Term Care Services for the Elderly" (March).

Coronel, Susan. 1998. *Long-Term Care Insurance in 1996*. Washington: Health Insurance Association of America.

Employee Benefit Research Institute. 1995. *Long-Term Care and the Private Insurance Market*. Washington (July).

Geanakoplos, John, Olivia S. Mitchell, and Stephen P. Zeldes. 1998. "Would a Privatized Social Security System Really Pay a Higher Rate of Return?" In *Framing the Social Security Debate: Values, Politics, and Economics*, edited by R. Douglas Arnold, Michael J. Graetz, and Alicia Munnell, 137–57. Washington: National Academy of Social Insurance.

Gramm, Phil, Andrew J. Rettenmaier, and Thomas R. Saving. 1998. "Medicare Policy for Future Generations—A Search for a Permanent Solution." *New England Journal of Medicine* 338 (April 30): 307–10.

Health Care Financing Administration. 1999. *National Health Expenditures Projections 1998–2008.* Washington.

Kemper, Peter, and Christopher M. Murtaugh. 1991. "Lifetime Use of Nursing Home Care." *New England Journal of Medicine* 324 (February 28): 595–600.

Komisar, Harriet L., Jeanne M. Lambrew, and Judith Feder. 1996. *Long-Term Care for the Elderly: A Chart Book.* New York: Commonwealth Fund (December).

Lewin-VHI and Brookings Institution. 1996. "Key Issues for Long-Term Care Insurance: Ensuring Quality Products, Increasing Access to Coverage, and Enabling Consumer Choice." Draft Final Report, Contract 500-89-0047 (February).

Liska, David, and others. 1996. *Medicaid Expenditures and Beneficiaries: National and State Profiles and Trends, 1988–94,* 2d ed. Washington: Kaiser Commission on the Future of Medicaid (November).

Murthi, Mamta, J. Michael Orszag, and Peter R. Orszag. 1999. "The Change Ratio on Individual Accounts: Lessons from the U.K. Experience." Discussion Paper. University of London, Birbeck College, Department of Economics (March).

National Economic Council. 1999. *The President's Plan to Modernize and Strengthen Medicare for the 21st Century,* detailed description. Washington.

O'Brien, Ellen, Diane Rowland, and Patricia Keenan. 1999. "Medicare and Medicaid for the Elderly and Disabled Poor." Washington: Kaiser Commission on Medicaid and the Uninsured (May).

U.S. Department of Health and Human Services. Office of the Assistant Secretary for Planning and Evaluation, Administration on Aging, 1998. *Informal Caregiving: Compassion in Action* (June).

U.S. House of Representatives. Committee on Ways and Means. *1998 Green Book.* Government Printing Office (May).

Weiner, Joshua M., and David G. Stevenson. 1998. "State Policy on Long-Term Care for the Elderly." *Health Affairs* 17 (May–June): 81–100.

Wiener, Joshua M., Catherine M. Sullivan, and Jason Skaggs. 1996. "Spending Down to Medicaid: New Data on the Role of Medicaid in Paying for Nursing Home Care." Washington: AARP Public Policy Institute (June).

HENRY J. AARON
WILLIAM GALE
JAMES SLY

7

The Rocky Road
to Tax Reform

FROM THE BOSTON Tea Party through recent revelations of Internal Revenue Service abuses, paying taxes has aroused public passions in the United States. Every president in the past four decades has proposed significant tax changes, and successive Congresses have enacted many tax bills, major and minor. Seemingly endless tinkering has not, alas, bred satisfaction. Almost everyone concurs that the tax system could be improved. But agreement on the nature and severity of the problems and how to resolve them remains elusive.

The basic goals of tax reform seem clear. Taxes should be simple and fair. They should be conducive to economic prosperity and market efficiency. And, not least, they should raise sufficient revenue to cover the "appropriate" level of government spending without unduly compromising freedom and privacy.[1]

We thank Eric Engen, Janet Holtzblatt, John Karl Scholz, and David Weiner for very helpful comments, and Ben Harris for outstanding research assistance.

1. Taking exception to these statements is a group of economists who believe that an inefficient, unfair, or complex tax system makes it more difficult politically to raise revenues, which helps hold down the size of government. They argue that, on balance, a smaller government with a more cumbersome tax system is better for the economy than a larger government with a more efficient tax system. Friedman (1993); and Becker and Mulligan (1998).

211

Despite the motherhood and apple pie quality of these goals, tax policy remains controversial. First, the goals are imprecise: views of what
constitutes a fair tax, for example, vary widely. Second, controversy
arises over how to achieve each goal. Supporters of increased growth
may disagree over whether across-the-board income tax cuts, targeted
tax cuts for saving and investment, or paying down public debt will do
most for the economy. The most important source of controversy, however, is differing value judgments concerning the relative importance
of the goals coupled with the fact that the goals sometimes conflict with
one another. Research and data may answer technical questions, but
they cannot resolve disagreements based on divergent values and
preferences.

This chapter first summarizes the main features of federal taxes and
explains the sources of tax complexity, distribution of tax burdens, and
effects of taxes on economic growth. It then describes and evaluates
proposals to reduce the level of tax revenues via across-the-board cuts
in income tax rates and other options. Subsequent sections examine
strategies and specific options for modifying the structure of the current system, including the general tax base, rates, and special provisions. Finally, the chapter examines proposals for fundamental tax
reform—replacing existing taxes with a whole new system.

Federal Taxes: An Overview

One of the most fundamental decisions in any tax system is what to
tax—wages, income, wealth, or consumption?[2] The federal government taxes all four but taxes consumption lightly compared with other
countries. About half of federal tax revenue comes from personal
income taxes and another third from payroll taxes (table 7-1). The corporation income tax, estate and gift taxes, and excise taxes supply most
of the rest. The composition of revenues has changed dramatically over
the past fifty years. In 1952 about 10 percent of revenues came from
payroll taxes and one-third from corporate taxes. By 1998 those pro-

---

2. Throughout this section numbers have been calculated by the authors using
data from various sources, including Bureau of Economic Analysis, Internal Revenue Service, Office of Management and Budget, Joint Committee on Taxation, and
Commerce Clearing House.

Table 7-1. *Federal Tax Revenues, 1999*

Type of Tax	Billions of dollars	Percent of GDP	Percent of revenues
Individual income tax	887	10.0	48.7
Corporate income tax	178	2.0	9.8
Social insurance taxes	607	6.9	33.3
Estate and gift taxes	28	0.3	1.5
Other	121	1.4	6.6
Total	1,821	20.6	100.0

Source: Authors' calculations based on data from Congressional Budget Office (1999a).

portions had reversed. The overall level of revenues hovered between 16 and 19 percent of GDP from 1951 to 1995 but has risen in recent years to 20.5 percent of GDP in 1998, the largest share since 1944.

Personal Income Tax

The modern personal income tax was established in 1913 after ratification of the Sixteenth Amendment to the Constitution eliminated the requirement that taxes be apportioned across the states solely on the basis of population. Until 1940 the tax fell only on the relatively wealthy and never yielded more than 1.5 percent of GDP in revenue. The revenue demands for World War II, however, led to the transformation of the income tax from a "class" tax to a "mass" tax. By 1952 the tax collected 8 percent of GDP in revenues. After remaining relatively flat through 1995, revenues rose to 9.9 percent of GDP by 1999.

TAX BASE. In principle an income tax should fall on *all* net additions to individual spending power during the tax period and *only* on these net additions. In practice the combination of personal and corporate income taxes varies significantly from this norm: some income is taxed once—either when it is earned or consumed—some income is taxed more than once, some not at all, and some flows that are not income are taxed.[3]

---

3. The justification for taxing income as opposed to, say, consumption, is examined later in the chapter in the section on fundamental tax reform.

The personal income tax is levied annually on the worldwide nominal income of U.S. residents, including wages and salaries, interest, dividends, rents, royalties, net business income, unemployment insurance and part of social security benefits, pension and annuity income, and realized capital gains. Wages account for most of adjusted gross income, but the composition of income varies dramatically at different income levels. Capital gains, dividends, interest, and business incomes account for more of the incomes of high-income households than those of low-income households (table 7-2).

Some forms of income are excluded from federal taxation, including noncash income (such as employer-financed health insurance premiums and imputed rent from housing), part of social security benefits, and interest from state or local government bonds. Taxes on deposits and investment earnings in pensions, Individual Retirement Accounts, and 401(k) plans are deferred until the income is realized. Taxes on capital gains—the increase in value of assets over time—are deferred until the asset is sold and are not levied at all if the asset is held until the owner dies.[4] Up to $500,000 in capital gains from the sale of owner-occupied housing by couples ($250,000 by single persons) are also excluded from income tax.[5]

EXEMPTIONS AND DEDUCTIONS. After determining their gross income, tax filers may subtract personal exemptions; in 1999 the exemption is $2,750 for the filer, spouse, and each dependent. Filers may also claim a standard deduction: $7,200 for couples filing joint returns and $4,300 for single filers in 1999. The combination of exemptions and the standard deductions relieves almost all households with income below the poverty line from paying federal income tax. Personal exemptions are phased out for high-income taxpayers.[6]

---

4. There are some important exceptions to this rule. The accruing value on zero-coupon bonds is imputed and taxed annually. Futures contracts are "marked to market," and the change in value is subject to taxation each year.

5. This exemption is available every two years provided that the filer has resided in the house for two of the preceding five years.

6. Joint Committee on Taxation (1999). The phaseout of personal exemptions begins for single filers, heads of household, and couples filing jointly at $126,600, $158,300, and $189,950, respectively. The reduction is 2 percent for each $2,500 or

Table 7-2. *Composition of Income by Income Level, 1996*
Percent

Type of income	Adjusted gross income		
	All filers	$10,000–$20,000	$200,000 or more
Wages	74.4	75.2	45.5
Interest and dividends	7.0	7.3	12.0
Realized capital gains	5.6	1.0	21.1
Business and partnership income	7.1	4.7	19.4
Pension and social security income	11.5	19.2	4.3
Other	−5.6	−7.4	−2.3

Source: Authors' calculations based on data from Internal Revenue Service (Fall 1998).

Instead of using the standard deduction, households may itemize deductions for expenditures on state and local taxes, mortgage interest, business or personal investment expenses, charitable contributions, some medical expenses, and other items. Mortgage interest, charity, and state and local taxes account for more than 90 percent of all itemized deductions. In recent years, about 29 percent of tax filers have taken itemized deductions, but the proportion varied in 1996 from less than 9 percent among filers with adjusted gross incomes below $30,000 to 88 percent among filers with incomes of $75,000 or more. Itemized deductions are reduced by formula for high-income tax filers.[7]

TAX RATES. Income is subject to six statutory tax rates. The rate is zero if exemptions and deductions exceed adjusted gross income. Taxable income—the excess of adjusted gross income over exemptions and deductions—is subject to rates of 15, 28, 31, 36, or 39.6 percent that rise

---

fraction thereof above the beginning of the phaseout. The phaseout is complete at incomes of more than $249,100, $280,800, and $312,450, respectively.

7. For single taxpayers and couples filing jointly; itemized deductions other than those for medical expenses, gambling losses, investment interest, and nonbusiness casualty or theft losses are reduced by 3 percent of income over $126,600 but never by more than 80 percent of their original amount.

with income.[8] The brackets to which these rates apply, as well as personal exemptions and the standard deduction, are adjusted annually to offset the effects of inflation. Most filing units are in low tax brackets. In 1998 some 30 percent had no taxable income and therefore were in the zero bracket, 46 percent were in the 15 percent bracket, and 20 percent were in the 28 percent bracket. Only 3.5 percent faced rates higher than 28 percent, and only 0.5 percent faced the highest rate of 39.6 percent. Tax legislation in 1981 and 1986 sharply lowered statutory marginal tax rates for all income groups. Legislation in 1990 and 1993 raised marginal rates for high-income taxpayers, but even so, marginal rates on high incomes are substantially lower than they were twenty years ago.[9] Capital gains on assets held more than one year are taxed at lower rates than other income with the rate depending on the type of property, when it was purchased, how long it is held, and the taxpayer's income.

TAX CREDITS. Tax credits directly reduce tax liability. A $100 credit reduces taxes by $100 (or the taxpayer's liability, whichever is less). In contrast, a $100 exemption or deduction reduces taxable income and thereby reduces tax liabilities by $0 to $39.60 depending on the taxpayer's marginal tax rate. Credits are provided for families with children, for low earned income, and for expenses relating to child and dependent care, higher education, and adoption. All credits are phased out as income rises, except for the child care credit, which is phased down. The earned income credit is refundable and thus can reduce tax payments below zero, generating net payments from the government to the filer. Most other credits are not refundable and therefore are of no value to filers with no taxable income.

---

8. For example, a couple filing jointly in 1999 would pay a rate of 15 percent on taxable income up to $43,050, 28 percent on income from $43,050 up to $104,050, 31 percent on income from $104,050 up to $158,550, 36 percent income from $158,550 up to $283,150, and 39.6 percent on income above $283,150. Different income ranges apply to single persons, heads of households, and married persons filing separately. Approximately 25 percent of tax payers face effective marginal tax rates that differ, sometimes considerably, from their statutory tax rates because of the phaseouts of tax credits, personal exemptions, and itemized deductions.

9. Burman, Gale, and Weiner (1998a).

ALTERNATIVE MINIMUM TAX. Besides the regular income tax, there is also a personal alternative minimum tax (AMT), a parallel tax system that applies to gross income less an exemption ($45,000 for married couples) and a very restricted menu of deductions. Taxpayers whose AMT liability exceeds their regular income tax liability must pay the AMT. The AMT is one of several methods Congress has used to limit tax avoidance, but it is very complex. In recent years about 0.4 percent of households paid the personal AMT. By 2009, about 6.3 percent of filers are projected to have to pay minimum tax because the AMT exemption is not indexed for inflation or rising incomes.

ADMINISTRATION AND EVASION. The overall rate of evasion of income tax is estimated to be about 20 percent of actual tax revenues, but the evasion rate varies dramatically by type of income. The compliance rate is about 99 percent for income and payroll taxes that employers withhold and remit to the government. Withholding not only minimizes evasion but also reduces compliance costs. The compliance rate for taxes on interest, dividends, pensions, and social security, which are reported to the government by the payer but for which no taxes are withheld, is 92–98 percent. The compliance rate by sole proprietors (small businesses) and farms, whose income is neither withheld nor reported by a third party, is about 70 percent.[10]

SUMMING UP. The two most notable features of the personal income tax are graduated tax rates and a narrow tax base. Graduated tax rates are a primary means of collecting proportionately more tax from high- than from middle- and low-income filers. The narrow tax base, created by the exclusions, deferrals, deductions, exemptions, and credits already noted, reduces taxable income. In 1996, taxable income was 68 percent of adjusted gross income and 48 percent of personal income in the national income accounts. The narrow tax base generates complexity and equity problems explained later and raises the tax rates needed to generate a given amount of revenue.

10. All data in the paragraph are based on U.S. Department of the Treasury (1996); and Gale and Holtzblatt (1999, p. 20 and table 3).

Corporation Income Tax

All income, whether earned by individuals or businesses, eventually accrues to people. Income from sole proprietorships and partnerships is taxed under the personal income tax, but corporations face a separate tax.[11] Corporations are legal entities that limit the liabilities of their owners to the amounts they have invested. The primary reason to place a tax on corporate income is to discourage people from using corporations to avoid taxes.

The corporation income tax base includes receipts from sales of goods and services and from investments, less deductions for costs used to produce revenue, including wages and fringe benefit payments, the cost of purchased goods and services used as inputs, interest payments, and the depreciation—loss of value—of plant, equipment, and other capital. Depreciation deductions are typically set by formula based on the estimated economic life of the asset. Additional corporate deductions and credits target exports, foreign investment, research and development, charitable contributions, and small businesses in general. A variety of industry-specific provisions, often derided as "corporate welfare," favor insurance, energy, natural resources, agriculture, shipping, and finance. In recent years, increased attention has also been given to corporate shelters. Generally, these are complex tax arrangements, designed primarily to avoid taxes, that often depend on aggressive interpretation of existing law and, when discovered by the Internal Revenue Service, are often disallowed.[12]

The personal and corporation income taxes are not integrated. As explained later, some—but certainly not all—corporate source income is taxed twice: once at the corporate level through the corporation tax and again at the personal level, through taxes on dividends and capital gains. The legitimate reasons for taxing corporations once do not justify taxing corporate income twice.

The basic corporate tax rate is 35 percent on profits exceeding $18,333,333, but corporations with lower profits pay marginal rates as

11. Corporations with fewer than seventy-five shareholders are an exception. They may organize as "S corporations" and be taxed as partnerships, imputing the business income to the individual shareholders.
12. U.S. Department of Treasury (1999).

low as 15 percent. Low rates on low profits are rationalized as a spur to small business, but the rationale is weak because large businesses may earn few profits and small businesses may earn large ones. As with the personal income tax, there exists a parallel corporate alternative minimum tax, levied at a 20 percent rate on a complex and broader tax base than that of the regular corporation income tax. Companies that pay the AMT receive a credit applicable against ordinary corporation tax they may owe in later years.

Estate and Gift Taxes

The estate, gift, and generation-skipping transfer taxes form an integrated tax on transfers of assets from one person to another. Transfer taxes have several aims: to tax previously untaxed income, such as unrealized capital gains; reduce the concentration of wealth; and increase the progressivity of the overall tax and transfer system.

The estate tax is levied on taxable estates above a floor, which will rise from $650,000 in 1999 to $1 million after 2005. Owners of family businesses and farms enjoy additional exclusions that effectively exempt estates worth up to $1.3 million. The taxable estate consists of net assets less charitable contributions and transfers to one's spouse. Every person may also give up to $10,000 a year each to as many other people as he or she wishes without paying gift tax or affecting subsequent estate tax liability. Because of these provisions, the estate tax applies only to about 2.1 percent of decedents.[13]

Marginal rates rise from 37 percent on the smallest taxable estate to 55 percent for taxable estates in excess of $3 million. For estates valued between $10 million and $21.04 million, an additional 5 percent tax is effectively added, boosting the average rate on large estates to 55 percent. Credits are provided for state-level estate tax payments. As a result of high marginal tax rates, a significant number of loopholes, and plenty of time to anticipate the tax, estate taxes engender a large amount of tax avoidance and planning activity, and estate tax revenues have made up only about 10 percent of gross estates in recent years.

Between 1988 and 1998 estate tax revenues grew much faster than other revenue sources because of the rapid appreciation of the asset val-

13. Davenport and Soled (1999, p. 594).

ues of the 1990s, because limits on transfers between spouses removed in 1981 had led to the deferral of taxes that began to come due as the second spouses died, and because provisions to limit avoidance, such as a tax on generation-skipping trusts, were beginning to have a major effect on revenues. The graduated increases in the estate tax credit will retard revenue growth through 2006, but unless Congress raises the threshold at which it takes effect, the estate tax will continue to grow as a share of federal revenues.

Payroll Taxes

Unlike income and estate taxes, which flow into general revenues, payroll taxes are earmarked to pay for social insurance benefits — social security, medicare, and unemployment insurance. The social security tax is 12.4 percent of earnings up to a wage ceiling, $72,600 in 1999, divided equally between levies on employees and employers and imposed fully on the self-employed. The medicare tax is 2.9 percent of all earnings, again divided equally between employees and employers. The unemployment insurance tax, 6.2 percent of earnings up to $7,000, is levied only on employers. The employer taxes are deductible in computing business income subject to corporation or personal income tax but employee contributions are not.

Most analysts believe the employer tax depresses wages and that workers therefore bear most or all of the burden of payroll taxes. If this assumption is correct, 74 percent of taxed households pay more in payroll taxes than in income taxes.[14] The reason is that payroll taxes are due on the first dollar of earnings while income taxes are due only when income exceeds personal exemptions and deductions. Even then, the first positive income tax rate of 15 percent is lower than the combined social security and medicare payroll tax rate of 15.3 percent, and income taxes are further reduced by the earned income credit and other credits.

Effects of Federal Taxes

Three of the primary goals of tax policy arc to make taxes simple, fair, and conducive to economic growth. How does the federal system measure up?

---

14. Congressional Budget Office (1998a, p. 32).

Complexity

Perhaps the most vexing aspect of taxes for many people is actual or perceived complexity. The Internal Revenue Code contains more than 1 million words, and regulations contain 5 million more. Business owners must keep track of inventory and compute depreciation, a particular problem for small companies. Accounting for international income and the alternative minimum tax creates additional problems. Low-income households must deal with child and dependent care credits and the earned income credit. Itemized deductions, the treatment of capital income (particularly capital gains, interest deductions, and passive losses), and the alternative minimum tax bedevil higher-income filers. Just over half of individual filers hire tax professionals to prepare their tax returns.

Yet compliance costs can easily be overblown or distorted. Many people go to preparers to expedite refunds or because they would rather pay a professional to complete their returns than spend their own time on this chore. For many people, the tax system is not complicated. In recent years about 38 percent of filers have used the simplified 1040A or 1040EZ forms and another 18 percent have filed the standard 1040 but did not have itemized deductions or business income. According to one study, 45 percent of taxpayers spent fewer than ten hours preparing their income tax returns, and 30 percent spent fewer than five hours. About half had no out-of-pocket expenses for tax preparation, and another 17 percent paid less than $50. But for some households, taxes can be quite complex. The same study showed that about 11 percent of filers spent fifty to one hundred hours on taxes and 5 percent spent more than one hundred hours. Expenditures of time and money were highest among high-income and self-employed taxpayers.[15]

Some tax complexity is an unavoidable by-product of trying to achieve other policy goals. For example, basing tax liabilities on individuals' characteristics—marital status, number of dependents, and income and expenditures—may be fair, but it requires reporting and documentation. Giving tax breaks to meritorious activities—home ownership, charitable gifts, the purchase of health insurance, post-

15. Blumenthal and Slemrod (1992, p. 189).

secondary education, child care, retirement saving, or entrepreneurial activity—may be worthwhile, but it adds paperwork, reporting, and auditing requirements. Preventing abusive use of deductions and credits also increases complexity. If the child care credit, for example, is not intended to subsidize children's ski lessons in Aspen, rules are necessary to specify which expenditures are acceptable and which are not. Simply preventing evasion—the illegal failure to pay taxes—may necessitate complex rules.[16]

The political process is another wellspring of complexity. Private groups lobby for targeted tax-reducing provisions, which inevitably complicate taxes. There is no organized lobby for simplicity.[17] So long as complex provisions reduce their taxes, filers tend not to object to them. But such provisions do not lower the cost of government. As special provisions proliferate, the population is ultimately left with the same tax bill collected through an increasingly burdensome system.

Reasonable estimates of the costs of complying with and running the individual and corporation income taxes, based on 1995 data, range between $75 billion and $130 billion, or 10–17 percent of income tax revenue. Even at $75 billion, or $634 per income tax return per year, the administrative costs of compliance are significant.[18]

The real question is not the size of compliance costs, but whether the United States gets good value for tax complexity. Generally, it does not. The many base-narrowing special provisions raise the tax rates on other activities necessary to meet any given revenue target, and incentives to avoid or evade taxes increase as rates rise. Many complicating tax provisions embody social policy that would be difficult to defend if cast as a direct expenditure. A government expenditure program that gave each wealthy donor a 39.6 cent rebate for every dollar given to qualifying charities, but gave middle-class donors only a 15 cent rebate for each dollar given by the middle class, and gave nothing at all to low-

---

16. The choice to tax income rather than consumption also has implications for tax complexity, but as shown in the section on fundamental tax reform, it is probably not the central determinant of the complexity of a tax system.

17. A well-designed campaign finance reform might reduce these problems but is difficult to achieve (see chapter 14).

18. Calculations based on data from Gale and Holtzblatt (1999, p. 11).

income donors would be regarded as outrageous. Yet the charitable contributions deduction has just such an effect and is widely supported.

The Distribution of Tax Burdens

Tax policy affects the distribution of income among living members of the population and across generations. Intergenerational effects arise, for example, from tax policies that affect economic growth, the budget surplus, or future tax revenues. In this section we focus on the distribution of tax burdens among living households. Several factors complicate this task. First, those who remit taxes to the government may not be made worse off by the tax. For example, taxes on business eventually burden some person—customers, owners, workers, or suppliers. To estimate total tax burdens, these taxes must be assigned to particular people.

The second problem is how to classify households. Annual income is a standard measure of a household's well-being, and we use it in this chapter. But many analysts prefer to classify households by annual consumption or lifetime income. This choice bears on whether income or consumption is the better base for a personal tax, an issue we examine later.

The typical household paid about 18.9 percent of its income in all federal taxes in 1999 (table 7-3 and figure 7-1).[19] Average tax burdens increase with income, which means that taxes are progressive. Most of the progressivity comes from the personal income tax with its gradu-

19. The Congressional Budget Office (1998a, p. 32) reports estimates of effective federal taxes as a percentage of adjusted family income for selected years. It assumes that income and payroll taxes are borne by the households on whose income and earnings they are levied. Excise taxes are borne by those who purchase the taxed commodities. Corporate income taxes are assigned to capital income recipients. Adjusted family income equals total cash income plus the employer share of social security and federal unemployment insurance payroll taxes and the corporation income tax, adjusted for differences in family size by the equivalence scale implicit in the official federal poverty thresholds. The income measure excludes all income received in kind, such as health insurance, and unrealized capital gains.

Some tax cut advocates claim that the typical household pays almost 40 percent of its income in federal, state, and local taxes. This claim, however, is flawed. It misrepresents a study by the Tax Foundation, and the study itself is dated, overstates taxes, and understates income (see Auerbach and Gale, 1999).

Table 7-3. *Average Effective Federal Tax Rates,*
by Tax and Income Group, 1999[a]

All families	Individual income taxes	Social insurance taxes	Corporate income taxes	Excise taxes	All federal taxes
Lowest quintile	−6.8	7.9	0.5	2.9	4.6
Second quintile	0.9	10.0	1.0	1.8	13.7
Middle quintile	5.4	10.8	1.3	1.3	18.9
Fourth quintile	8.4	11.4	1.3	1.1	22.2
Highest quintile	16.1	7.7	4.6	0.6	29.1
Overall	11.1	9.2	3.0	1.0	24.2
Top 10 percent	18.0	6.4	5.7	0.5	30.6
Top 5 percent	19.6	5.0	6.8	0.4	31.8
Top 1 percent	22.2	2.7	9.2	0.3	34.4

Source: Congressional Budget Office (1998a).

a. The average tax rate is defined as the ratio of the taxes listed divided by adjusted family income.

ated statutory tax rates and exemptions, deductions, and credits. Because of personal exemptions, standard deductions, the earned income credit, and the child credit, in 1999 a family of four with all income from earnings owed no income tax unless it earned more than $28,200. The family would, however, owe payroll taxes on the first dollar of earnings.

Official statistics show that federal tax revenues as a share of GDP are near all-time highs. Paradoxically, the 1999 average tax rates of families at most points of the income distribution are light relative to what they have been over the past twenty to thirty years. Overall tax payments have risen because the incomes of high-income households have risen sharply and because Congress raised taxes in 1990 and 1993 on high-income taxpayers.

Federal taxes are a lower portion of income in 1999 than at any time since at least 1977 for households in the bottom 40 percent of the income distribution because 1981 legislation lowered marginal tax rates, 1986 legislation increased personal exemptions, the earned income credit was expanded several times, and a child credit was introduced in 1997 (figure 7-1).

Figure 7-1. *Average Effective Federal Tax Burdens,*
by Income Percentile, 1977–99

Tax rate (percent)

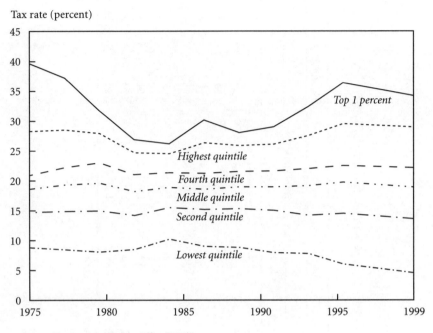

Source: Congressional Budget Office (1999b).

For households in the middle 20 percent, taxes in 1999 are at their average level over the past twenty years, while families in the 60th to 80th percentiles are facing tax burdens slightly greater—by less than 0.5 percentage point—than average. Only among the top 20 percent of households have tax burdens increased significantly since the 1980s, and even for these families, the burdens are smaller now than in the 1970s. Moreover, real growth of pretax and after-tax income for the top 20 percent of households far outpaced growth in other quintiles (table 7-4). Among the top 1 percent of filers, real after-tax incomes rose 120 percent.[20]

20. Congressional Budget Office (1999b). Furthermore, the CBO data understate income growth among high-income households in recent years by omitting unrealized capital gains, which have been enormous (Gale and Sabelhaus, 1999).

Table 7-4. *Average Real Income Levels and Growth, by Income Group, Selected Periods, 1977–99*[a]
Percent unless otherwise specified

Income groups	Pretax income				After-tax income			
	Income level	Growth			Income level	Growth		
	1999	1977–99	1985–99	1995–99	1999	1977–99	1985–99	1995–99
Lowest quintile	8,400	–16	–3	4	8,014	–12	3	5
Second quintile	21,200	–11	0	5	18,296	–9	2	7
Middle quintile	35,400	–3	4	6	28,709	–3	3	7
Fourth quintile	53,000	8	7	7	41,234	6	6	7
Highest quintile	132,000	40	21	10	93,588	38	14	11
Overall	49,500	15	11	8	37,521	13	8	9
Top 10 percent	188,000	50	27	12	130,472	51	18	13
Top 5 percent	276,000	66	33	13	188,232	70	22	15
Top 1 percent	719,000	102	37	9	471,664	120	22	13

Sources: Authors' calculations based on data from Congressional Budget Office (1999b).
a. All incomes are in 1995 dollars.

Americans also pay a smaller share of their incomes in taxes than do citizens of any other developed nation except Japan. Of the twenty-nine countries in the Organization for Economic Cooperation and Development (OECD) in 1996, the United States had the twenty-fifth lowest ratio of taxes to GDP, almost tied with Japan and higher only than Mexico, Turkey, and Korea.[21]

Whether the level and distribution of taxes among income classes is satisfactory is a matter of judgment. Certainly, it would be hard to claim that the haphazard and politically motivated tax reforms of the past twenty years have led to the ideal distribution of tax burdens. But two facts are clear. First, the distribution of income, before or after taxes, has become dramatically less equal in the United States than it was as recently as two decades ago. Second, tax burdens vary widely *within* income brackets because not all taxpayers are equally able to avail themselves of itemized deductions, credits, and allowances and because taxpayers derive varying fractions of their income from capital gains, which are taxed at much lower rates than apply to other income. Many of the provisions that cause tax rates to vary were introduced to recognize tax-relevant variations in ability to pay that are not well measured by ordinary income. But there is no doubt that tax burdens vary even among similarly situated filers, a situation known as "horizontal inequity."

Economic Growth

Critics charge that the income tax reduces economic growth because rates are too high and too uneven. High rates, it is alleged, discourage work, saving, investment, and entrepreneurship. Uneven rates encourage investors to choose activities with relatively low economic returns but favorable tax treatment instead of projects with superior economic returns but less favorable tax treatment. The overall effects of taxation on economic growth, however, are far from clear. Estimates from a symposium sponsored by the Joint Committee on Taxation in 1997 suggest that the combined effects of integrating the corporate and individual income taxes, broadening the tax base to smooth out the variation in tax rates across uses, and flattening income tax rates would

21. Organization for Economic Cooperation and Development (1998).

change the size of the economy between −3 and 4 percent in the long run. If the taxation of all capital income were eliminated, including transition relief for income from existing assets, the economy would expand in the long run by 1–5 percent.[22]

WORK. Evidence suggests that taxes depress the labor supply of men and single women only slightly but have a larger impact on the labor supply of married women. Taxes on work can be surprisingly high. If workers bear the full 15.3 percent payroll tax for social security and medicare, the combined federal marginal tax rate on a worker in the 15 or 28 percent income tax bracket is 28.1 or 40.2 percent.[23] This calculation wholly ignores the increased social security benefits that higher earnings will generate later on. Taking these benefits into account lowers the tax rate. For similar reasons, pension contributions are not considered a tax because they are correlated with future pension benefits. Because the social security payroll tax does not apply to earnings higher than the payroll tax ceiling, the effective marginal tax rate on labor income may decline when earnings rise above the ceiling.

PERSONAL SAVING. Most of the evidence indicates that taxes have small effects on the level of saving. The taxation of returns to personal saving is enormously varied. Deposits in ordinary bank accounts generate no deductions, and income earned on such accounts is taxed when earned. But most personal saving occurs in tax-sheltered accounts such as ordinary or Roth Individual Retirement Accounts, Keogh plans, and 401(k) plans and employer contributions to pension plans.[24] Personal income

22. Joint Committee on Taxation (1997, table 1). Mroz (1987), Hausman (1985), Eissa (1996), Eissa and Liebman (1996), and Bosworth and Burtless (1992) examine the impact of taxes on labor supply. For the impact of taxes on saving, see Bernheim (1999). Cummins, Hassett, and Hubbard (1994) and Clark (1993) examine taxes and investment.

23. The money wage cost to the employer of hiring the worker is 1.0765 times stated pay because the employer must pay 7.65 percent of the wage in payroll tax. The effective tax rate is the sum of the income tax (15 percent) and the payroll tax (15.3 percent) divided by the total money wage: $(0.15 + 0.153)/1.0765 = 0.281$. This calculation ignores the earned income tax credit, which lowers rates over the income range in which it is increasing and raises rates in the range over which it is being phased out.

24. Gale and Sabelhaus (1999).

taxes on deposits and all investment earnings in most such accounts are deferred until the funds are withdrawn. Deferral conveys large tax benefits. Saving faces a zero net tax rate when the tax rate applicable to deductions of contributions is the same as that applied to withdrawals. When the rate on withdrawals is lower than that on contributions, the overall tax rate on saving is negative in the sense that the return to the saver is higher than it would be if the tax system disregarded the deposits, investment income, and withdrawals.[25]

As noted earlier, capital gains on assets held outside of tax-preferred accounts receive many tax benefits: deferral of taxes until realization, exclusion of taxes if held until death, application of lower tax rates than would apply to other forms of income, and a large exclusion if earned on owner-occupied housing. The effective tax rates on capital gains are much lower than those on earnings or other forms of capital income.[26]

BUSINESS INVESTMENTS. Taxes discourage investment, but how much is subject to controversy. Taxes inhibit growth if they treat different forms of income differently. For example, investors would choose a project yielding 15 percent that is taxed at an average rate of 40 percent over an alternative project that yields 20 percent but is taxed at a 60 percent rate. And they would jettison both projects in favor of one that generates

25. See Burman, Gale, and Weiner (1998b). The tax treatment of ordinary and Roth IRAs is equivalent if people face the same marginal tax rate throughout their lives. Under ordinary IRAs, people earn Y, save it, receive investment returns of rY, and pay tax at the rate, t, on withdrawals. At the end of the day, they have $Y(1+r)(1\ t)$. Under Roth IRAs, people earn Y, pay tax at the rate, t, on the income and then pay no further tax on investment earnings and withdrawals. At the end of the day, they also have $Y(1+r)(1\ t)$.

26. A simple example illustrates the size of this differential. Suppose that a person in the 28 percent bracket invests $1,000 in a thirty-year bond yielding 10 percent annually in taxable interest and invests the interest earnings in bonds also yielding 10 percent. At the end of thirty years the investment will have grown to $8,051. Suppose instead that the investor buys an appreciating asset that grows at an annual rate of 10 percent, sells the asset after thirty years, and pays the capital gains tax of 20 percent on the appreciation. The investor will realize $14,160 after paying tax, a value 76 percent larger than on the bond. The annual tax rate equivalent of the capital gains tax is only 7.6 percent.

economywide returns of only 8 percent but had a 25 percent subsidy attached to it.

In practice, tax rates on investments differ widely, depending on the type of investment, the form of income generated, the form of the financing, and the identity of the investor. Special rules favor certain investments—for example, those promoting historic preservation or research and development. Small businesses receive significant tax benefits. Some investments can be structured so that tax rates levied on the project as a whole are negative. This situation can occur when the project generates fully deductible expenses (interest payments, for example) and lightly taxed capital gains in roughly equal amounts. Effective tax rates are negative because the tax reduction from the expenses will exceed the tax payments from the capital gains income. The effect is magnified when deductions can be packaged and sold to high-bracket filers while income flows to low-bracket filers.

The fact that corporate source income may be taxed twice can raise tax burdens and increase disparities in taxes across assets. But it is unclear how much corporate income is doubly taxed. Rather than paying dividends, some corporations distribute profits to shareholders by repurchasing shares, which does not generate individual-level taxes. A significant portion of all dividends accrues either to tax-exempt shareholders—foundations, universities, churches, or hospitals—or to pension funds, IRAs, or 401(k) plans, which typically face zero or negative effective tax rates. None of these dividends faces double tax burdens. A significant portion of capital gains on corporate stock accrues either to individuals who hold the gains until they die, to tax-exempt shareholders, or to pension funds broadly defined, and so also escapes the burden of double taxation. Finally, shareholders escape the burden of the corporation tax if the market price they pay for the shares is reduced by the value of future corporation taxes.[27] To the extent that taxes are capitalized into profits, only the person who holds the stock at the time

27. Suppose an investor would be willing to pay $1,000 to own stock that promises annual earnings of $100, a price/earnings ratio of ten. If a tax of 35 percent is now imposed on the company, the after-tax earnings will become $65. The investor who insists on a ratio of price to *net* earnings of ten would now pay only $650 for the stock.

the tax is announced (or, for new issues, when the stock is issued) bears a burden from the tax.

Economists and tax lawyers have produced a small library of proposals to eliminate double taxation by integrating the personal and corporation income taxes, typically by imputing to shareholders part or all of corporate profits and permitting individuals to claim credits for part or all of corporate tax payments.[28] Despite extensive academic analysis, integration plans that did not invite massive tax avoidance would be complex and expensive, and generate little political support.

Another reason tax rates vary across investments and over time is that neither the personal nor corporate income tax adjusts the tax base for inflation. Depreciation deductions are based on historical cost, not replacement cost. Parts of interest income and deductions represent inflationary erosion of fixed nominal obligations. And part of capital gains during inflationary periods represents a general increase in price, not an increase in the relative value of the asset. The failure to adjust these items for inflation leads to an overstatement of income and taxes for recipients of interest, realized capital gains, and those claiming depreciation deductions, and an understatement of income and taxes for people taking deductions for interest payments, including homeowners.

Indexing all capital income and expenses for inflation would be administratively complex, expensive, and politically difficult. But making only some of these adjustments—for example, indexing only capital gains for inflation—would widen opportunities for tax avoidance. Fortunately, the waning of inflation has reduced the importance of the failure to index the tax base.

These myriad provisions produce widely varying effective tax rates. The largest practical issues arise with respect to the relative treatment of owner-occupied housing versus business investment, and within business categories between corporate and noncorporate entities. Taxes on housing are low or even negative because homeowners may deduct mortgage interest and property tax payments but need not report as income the imputed rent on the house that generates those deductions. Homeowners also escape tax on almost all capital gains on their resi-

---

28. U.S. Department of Treasury (1992).

dences. One study reports marginal effective tax rates of 26–31 percent on new corporate investment, 18 percent on noncorporate, nonresidential investment, and 5 percent or less on owner-occupied housing. The economywide effective marginal tax rate on new investment income was about 16 percent.[29]

Does the Budget Surplus Justify Large Tax Cuts?

Projections of large future budget surpluses burst upon the economic scene in 1998 and promise to influence debate for the next several years, just as large and stubborn deficits dominated economic debate during the 1980s. Do the projected surpluses justify tax cuts? And if so, what form should the cuts take?

At least four reasons have been advanced for tax cuts. The first is that government is taking in more revenue than it needs to pay for current obligations. This argument is invalid. To be sure, the Congressional Budget Office in July 1999 estimated that the ten-year unified budget surplus will total about $2.9 trillion. But $1.9 trillion of that amount comes from the social security trust fund.[30] Leaders of both parties agree that the trust fund should be preserved for social security, which has significant unfunded liabilities. More than $500 billion of the remaining $1 trillion consists of surpluses in the military and civilian pensions and medicare (part A) programs that will be needed to meet future benefit commitments. Thus the same logic that establishes the imprudence of basing tax cuts on social security surpluses applies equally to accumulations in these trust funds. The remaining projected surplus exists only because of highly restrictive and unrealistic assumptions regarding cuts in real discretionary spending for national defense and domestic programs (see chapter 1). Under more plausible assump-

---

29. Auerbach (1996, p. 42 and table 2-1). Gravelle (1994, p. 294) finds higher rates: 33 percent for all capital income, 22 percent for noncorporate investment, and 43 percent for corporate investment. The differences stem from different treatment of pensions and differences in the modeling of the burden of the corporate tax. Two other studies concluded that average rates of tax on capital income in the 1980s were negative (Gordon and Slemrod, 1988; and Shoven, 1991), but this result is controversial (Gravelle, 1994).

30. Congressional Budget Office (1999a).

tions about discretionary spending and the preservation of pension and health reserves, there would be no surplus available for tax cuts.

The second possible justification for cutting taxes is that burdens are too great. While nobody likes high taxes, we have shown that current burdens for most filers are actually as small as or smaller than they have been in two decades.

The third reason advanced in support of tax cuts is to promote economic growth. Advocates claim an across-the-board tax cut would boost personal saving and labor supply enough to raise national output by about 0.3 percent after ten years.[31] But reducing taxes could actually lower growth by lowering national saving. A tax cut would reduce budget surpluses nearly dollar for dollar, but almost all of the increase in household disposable income that is the counterpart to lower government revenues would be consumed, not saved. And, with the economy booming, if consumer spending rises, the Federal Reserve would probably feel compelled to tighten monetary policy.

The final argument for tax cuts is that they will help reduce the size of government. There is ample room for political disagreement over the proper role of government. Recent history suggests that cutting taxes is a poor instrument for reducing the size of government, but a very effective device for producing large government budget deficits. In the decade after the massive tax cuts of 1981 took effect, federal government spending actually rose from 22.3 percent to 22.6 percent of GDP. During this period the national debt in the hands of the public skyrocketed from $785 billion (25.8 percent of GDP) to $2.7 trillion (45.9 percent of GDP). Government spending as a share of GDP has come down since 1991. The prospects for major additional cuts seem poor because of the need to maintain national defense and the imminent onset of pension and health care costs for retiring baby boomers.

Although the economic case for tax cuts is weak, both houses of Congress passed tax cut bills that would reduce revenues by $800 billion in the next ten years and by triple the amount in the succeeding ten.[32]

---

31. Beach and others (1999, p. 1864).

32. The conference agreement contained the odd provision that the entire tax cut would be abolished after ten years to conform with Senate budgetary rules, but no one expects this provision to be sustained.

The conference agreement, which the president had not signed as this book went to press, would reduce all income tax rates by 1 percentage point, reduce capital gains tax rates, index capital gains for inflation, expand Individual Retirement Accounts, abolish the estate tax, provide dozens of tax breaks for corporations, and subsidize education and health care. The agreement would also reduce the marriage penalty by expanding the standard deductions for couples to double that for singles and by extending the 15 percent tax bracket for couples.

Whatever the political appeal of such proposals, both would significantly reduce national saving, which is the sum of private and government saving. Furthermore, the income tax cuts would go mostly to the well-to-do. When fully phased in, they would deliver an average of $31,768 a year to each of the top 1 percent of households, but an average of only $353 a year to each household in the middle 20 percent of the income distribution, and a paltry $22 a year to the average household in the bottom 20 percent. Cuts in capital gains taxes and estate taxes, which are not included in these distributional estimates, are even more heavily skewed toward the nation's wealthiest households. In view of the sharp recent increase in income inequality, such tax cuts seem poorly targeted.

If tax cuts prove irresistible despite long-term revenue needs, better designs exist than were embodied in either the House or the Senate bills in 1999. A refundable income tax credit for payroll tax payments would distribute benefits more equally than would an across-the-board proportional tax cut. It would be even more desirable to use tax reductions to help ease the way to tax reforms that would simplify the system and reduce distortions. Tax cuts can compensate the losers from reforms that withdraw provisions that complicate the code or inhibit growth.

However, now is not the time for large tax cuts. The economy is strong, and most households already face tax burdens that are low relative to burdens in the past twenty years. Although the budget is in surplus, these surpluses are mostly needed to meet pension and health care obligations. After these problems are resolved, it would be appropriate to debate whether any remaining surpluses should be used for tax cuts, spending increases, or debt repayment.

Strategies for Modifying the Current Tax System

Proposals to modify the current tax system abound. Most fall into one of three categories: proposals to create additional incentives for promoting specific activities, such as saving, investment, education, charity, or child care; proposals to simplify taxes by curbing or eliminating special tax provisions and reducing rates; and proposals to place limits on taxes.

Additional Targeted Provisions

Whether they are trying to help low-income households, improve education or health, or encourage saving and investment, elected officials often turn to the tax code rather than to direct government spending. As noted, provisions that would be derided if described as expenditures often seem sensible to lawmakers as tax provisions. In addition, most tax provisions do not expire, while most expenditure programs require periodic reauthorization and appropriations. Furthermore, tax provisions sometimes have genuine administrative advantages over government expenditures. The earned income credit, for example, is probably less costly to administer than an equivalent expenditure program to subsidize low earners because most who claim the credit would file tax returns anyway and are spared the need to fill out additional forms in the office of some agency charged with administering identically distributed direct subsidies.

Despite their political appeal, targeted tax provisions are usually poor public policy. Many are unfair. Congress has generally been unwilling to make tax deductions or credits refundable. Households with incomes too low to generate positive tax liability receive no benefit from nonrefundable credits, and households whose liability is smaller than the credits, receive only partial benefit from them. For example, about two-fifths of children live in families with income too low to benefit from the child credit enacted in 1997.[33]

---

33. Greenstein and Shapiro (1997). Nonrefundable credits designed to achieve social objectives include the credit for child and dependent care expenses, the credit for the elderly or for the permanently and totally disabled, the child tax credit, education credits, and the adoption credit.

Targeted provisions add complexity to the tax return. They also reduce revenues, thereby requiring higher tax rates on income that is not favored. These two problems are related. A credit available to all is very costly. But limiting eligibility requires rules or phaseouts, which increase effective marginal tax rates. The reduction in the child tax credit by $50 for every $1,000 of income is equivalent to adding 5 percentage points to the filer's marginal tax rate. Without a phaseout, however, the credit would be available to high-income households, necessitating higher tax rates on other income to raise the same revenue. Because tax-induced distortions in economic behavior increase with the marginal tax rate, legislators face a dilemma: they must either impose significantly higher marginal tax rates on households affected by the phaseout or slightly higher tax rates on everyone. Tax preferences also typically make the economy less efficient by diverting investment and economic activity from their best economic uses toward their best tax-motivated uses.

Furthermore, tax incentives breed more tax incentives. For example, President Clinton proposed and Congress enacted tax credits to encourage the first two years of postsecondary education. But why not also give credits for kindergarten through twelfth-grade schooling costs, home schooling, and adult education? Where and by what criteria should future Congresses draw the line? Lawmakers who have just persuaded their colleagues of the merits of one particular targeted provision may find it hard to oppose the next similar provision. But as the number of tax-favored activities grows, complexity increases and the special advantage of each tax-favored activity gradually diminishes. In the end the nation is stuck with the same tax liability raised through an ever more complicated tax system.

Targeted tax provisions also provide opportunities to game the tax system. The clearest example is the preferential treatment of capital gains, which lies behind many tax avoidance schemes. To prevent avoidance from getting out of hand, Congress is driven to further complicate the tax system with such provisions as the alternative minimum taxes.

Despite these drawbacks, targeted tax provisions might be worthwhile if they worked well. Usually, they do not. Current proposals to use tax credits to reduce the number of people who are without health insurance illustrate some of the problems. Most of the tax relief would go to people whose behavior is unaffected by the provision. Providing tax credits across the board to make certain that the 16 percent of nonelderly adults who currently lack health insurance receive the credit means that 84 percent of the credit is "wasted." Large credits would entail lengthy or steep phaseout ranges. Small or nonrefundable credits would do little to help make health insurance affordable for low-income households, many of whom have no tax liability. Limiting the credit to households with low incomes would improve the efficiency of the credit, but even among households with incomes below $25,000, three-quarters already have health insurance. Furthermore, the credits might cause some employers to stop offering health insurance as a fringe benefit.

The increasing use of targeted tax provisions is deceptive and dangerous. It fools people into thinking that they are the beneficiaries of reduced taxes, it complicates taxes for everyone, and the net impact is usually tiny compared with the overall costs. It would usually be far better to run subsidies the old-fashioned way—as spending programs. The tax base would be broader. The tax form would be shorter. And tax rates would be lower and clearer, permitting taxpayers and their representatives to understand better the costs and benefits of policy choices.

Fewer Targeted Tax Provisions

The second approach to the reform of the current system would curtail special incentive provisions and lower statutory tax rates. The 1986 Tax Reform Act embodied this approach. It eliminated enough special deductions and loopholes to reduce the top individual income tax rate from 50 percent to 28 percent and to reduce the top corporation rate from 46 percent to 34 percent without lowering revenues or significantly changing the distribution of tax burdens across income classes. It simplified taxes and contributed to growth by reducing and equalizing rates.[34]

The 1986 act was the high-water mark for base broadening, however. Since then targeted tax provisions have proliferated. To broaden the tax base more than was done in 1986 will prove difficult, not only

---

34. Mark Hankerson, "History of Recent Tax Bills," *Congressional Quarterly*, July 17, 1999.

because successive Congresses and presidents have displayed a penchant for tax incentives, but also because the deductions remaining after the 1986 act involve core social policies relating to owner-occupied housing, retirement saving, charitable contributions, health insurance premiums, state and local taxes, education, and children.[35] Nonetheless, we believe that some progress can be made through a limited reduction in the value of these tax incentives in one or both of two ways.

The first would convert some major itemized deductions to 15 percent tax credits.[36] The change would reduce the number of households that itemize, which would simplify taxes. It would not affect any of the three-quarters of tax filers in the zero or 15 percent tax bracket but, holding tax rates constant, would raise an estimated $60 billion a year from taxpayers in the 28 percent and higher tax brackets.[37] The revenue could be used to reduce tax rates in those brackets significantly. The result would be a simpler tax system with the same revenue. This reform could be structured to maintain the distribution of taxes by income bracket with reduced marginal rates. However, the proposal would inflict some economic harm on the sectors that generate the current deductions.

A related policy would be to greatly increase the standard deduction. Unlike the conversion of deductions into credits, raising the

35. Congressman Richard Gephardt introduced a proposal in 1996 that would have eliminated deductions for state and local taxes, charity, and pension contributions and eliminated exemptions of municipal bond income. Income tax rates would have been reduced 10 to 34 percent.

36. Whether taxpayers should receive a deduction or a credit for what are now itemized deductions depends on whether one sees the deduction as an incentive for particular kinds of expenditures or as a way of computing the filer's properly taxable income. Some current deductions—charitable contributions, for example—are seen most naturally as pure incentives because people may choose whether to consume their incomes directly or donate them to others. If the charitable contributions deduction is seen as a tax incentive to encourage people to give to meritorious organizations, it is hard to see why some people should receive an incentive of 39.6 cents in reduced taxes for each dollar they give while others receive only 15 cents. From this perspective a credit seems fairer than a deduction. Other deductions—for state and local taxes, large medical expenses, or casualty losses, for example—may be seen as involuntary payments that reduce the filer's ability to pay taxes. In those instances a deduction rather than a credit seems fairer.

37. Congressional Budget Office (1997a, p. 344).

standard deduction would reduce revenues. For this reason it would have most appeal as part of a tax reduction package. Increases in the standard deduction would raise the income level at which filers first owe taxes, reduce the number of filers who need to itemize deductions, and lower the total net value of deductions for those who continue to itemize. For example, raising the standard deduction by $1,000 would simplify taxes by reducing the number of itemizers by about 6.5 percent and would provide progressive tax cuts of $50 billion. If instead the number of personal exemptions each tax return was granted was reduced by one, and the standard deduction was raised by $4,000, the number of itemizers would decline by more than one-third, revenues would be maintained, and progressivity would be increased.[38]

Tax Limits

Rather than reforming the tax system, some analysts have advocated establishing a parallel system with no deductions and flat rates, while others have proposed limits on the maximum share of each filer's income that taxes could claim. The idea of a parallel tax system dates back to at least 1964, when Senator Russell Long suggested that taxpayers be permitted to file under an alternative tax system with fewer deductions and a tax rate well below the maximum rate under the regular personal income tax. In 1998 Stephen Moore of the Cato Institute proposed to allow people to pay a flat 25 percent of their gross income in tax instead of the current personal income tax and employer and employee payroll taxes. This idea—The Freedom to Choose Flat Tax—is embodied in bills introduced by Senator Spencer Abraham and Representative Vince Snowbarger.[39]

This approach suffers from critical flaws. Creating a parallel system does nothing to simplify the measurement of income, the major

38. Calculations based on data from Treasury tax file.

39. A striking indicator of how much personal income tax rates have been reduced is that the capped rate under Senator Long's alternative tax was 50 percent, well below the maximum personal rate then in effect of 77 percent but well above current rates. Pechman (1966); Congressional Record—Senate, vol. 110, pt. 18, September 29–October 3, 1964, p. 23653; and Stephen Moore, "The Freedom to Choose Flat Tax" (http://www.cato.org/dailys/6-09-98.html [August 11, 1999]).

source of complexity. And many taxpayers would have to compute tax under both the current system and the new one to determine which generates the lower tax. Even in the absence of changes in taxpayer behavior, the plan would reduce revenues dramatically—by an estimated $108 billion had it been enacted in 1996—with tax cuts averaging more than $30,000 for taxpayers in the top 1 percent of the distribution and $80 for taxpayers with incomes of $30,000 or less. The parallel tax would also create major opportunities for tax avoidance.[40]

Others have proposed legislated or even constitutional limits on the proportion of individual or aggregate income that can be collected in taxes. Such limits carry significant dangers, particularly if embedded in the Constitution, because revenue requirements may rise suddenly to meet national emergencies. Furthermore, neither "tax" nor "income" have clear definitions. Were such limits in effect, one could anticipate the creative use of "user charges" instead of "taxes" and other efforts to skirt the rules.

Specific Reforms

Many specific issues persistently appear on the tax reform agenda. We examine five here: simplification, the marriage penalty, saving incentives, capital gains, and reform of the Internal Revenue Service.

---

40. For example, an individual on January 1 could "invest" $1 million in a corporation. Proceeds from sale of stock are not taxable income to the corporation. The corporation on January 2 could pay the individual $1.5 million in wages, which is a deductible expense and therefore costs a corporation subject to a 35 percent tax rate only $975,000. The individual pays 25 percent tax on the $1.5 million in wage income and keeps $1,125,000. At the end of the day the corporation has made $25,000 and the individual has made $125,000. And there are 363 more days in the year. Such chicanery could be avoided under the new system if the corporation income tax were also reduced to 25 percent, but that step would reduce revenues by about $50 billion. It is probably possible to prohibit such obvious manipulations in other ways, but as long as the tax rate differential existed, clever accountants, attorneys, and tax planners would be able to invent very complex, hidden schemes that would go undetected. Gale (1999a).

Simplification

Several reforms could simplify the tax system without materially changing the level or distribution of taxes.

THE AMT EXEMPTION. The personal AMT currently raises little revenue but threatens to become a major nuisance for millions of filers because the exemption above which the AMT applies is not indexed for inflation. Significantly raising the personal AMT exemption and indexing it for inflation would simplify the tax system and prevent the imposition of this parallel tax on millions of filers, but would still prevent people from making so-called excessive use of otherwise legal provisions. In addition, not allowing items such as personal exemptions, state and local tax deductions, or tax credits to affect a taxpayer's AMT status would make the AMT simpler and better targeted at those who exploit tax shelters.

ELIMINATE PHASEOUTS OF PERSONAL EXEMPTIONS AND ITEMIZED DEDUCTIONS. The phaseouts of itemized deductions and personal exemptions for high-income filers raise effective marginal tax rates, add complexity, and yield little revenue. These phaseouts should be repealed and marginal tax rates should be increased (very slightly) to maintain tax burdens by income class. This change would make effective tax rates more transparent and simplify tax filing. Phaseouts for the various nonrefundable credits occur at different income levels and create a panoply of effective taxes. It would cost little to unify the phaseouts and save taxpayers from having to fill out several worksheets.

CONSOLIDATE SAVING INCENTIVES. The tax code contains many saving incentives, which we examine in more detail in the next section. The rules are varied and confusing. Replacing all with one set of simple rules would simplify record keeping and investment and withdrawal decisions.

CAPITAL GAINS. Currently, capital gains are taxed at twelve different rates, depending on the asset, the owner's income, when the asset was purchased, and how long it was held. If capital gains are to be taxed at reduced rates, excluding a fixed proportion of capital gains from taxation would achieve this objective more simply. A distinction for long-term and short-term gains could be retained, if desired. It would be easy to design a revenue-neutral reform of this sort.

DEPRECIATION DEDUCTIONS. Calculating depreciation is one of the most complex features of the tax code, especially for small and medium-sized businesses. Permitting businesses to deduct the present value of all depreciation deductions for an asset in the year of purchase could dramatically simplify this element of the tax code without reducing revenues in the long run.[41]

SIMPLIFIED FILING. Filing burdens could be reduced in two ways. The Internal Revenue Service could accelerate the conversion from paper returns to electronic filing, a procedure that encourages filers to use computer software and thereby reduces error rates. The IRS Restructuring and Reform Act of 1998 established a goal that 80 percent of all tax returns should be filed electronically by 2007.

Some simplification could also be achieved by instituting a "return-free" system for filers with simple returns under which the taxpayer or the taxpayer's employer supplies a few information items to the Internal Revenue Service, which calculates the tax due and bills the taxpayer. Up to 52 million taxpayers (more if the standard deduction were significantly increased) could be placed on a return-free system with relatively minor changes in the structure of the income tax. These include filers with income only from wages, pensions, IRA distributions, interest, dividends, and unemployment compensation who do not take itemized deductions or credits other than the EITC and are in the zero or 15 percent tax bracket. A return-free system would spare these taxpayers, most of whom already file the relatively simple 1040EZ or 1040A forms, much or all of the costs of preparing the final return and the fear or aggravation of filing. They would still have to grapple with state income taxes, however.[42]

---

41. Auerbach and Jorgenson (1980) originated this proposal.
42. Gale and Holtzblatt (1997, p. 750).

The Marriage Penalty

The idea that two people should be taxed more heavily just because they are married seems absurd. Yet many married couples do face a tax penalty, not because tax legislators oppose marriage, but because tax penalties for being married or for being single are inescapable unless one is prepared to abandon either of two other principles: that families with the same income should pay the same taxes or that tax rates should rise with income. Consider two couples facing hypothetical tax rates of 10 percent on the first $30,000 of income and 20 percent on all income above $30,000. In couple A one spouse earns $60,000 and the other earns nothing. In couple B, both spouses earn $30,000. If couples are taxed as a unit, both pay $9,000 in tax, 10 percent on the first $30,000 and 20 percent on the next $30,000. Couple B, who faces this marriage penalty of $3,000, could reduce its tax to $6,000 by getting a divorce, so that each (former) spouse would face a 10 percent rate. Couple A would not reduce its taxes by divorcing and so faces no marriage penalty. Giving these couples tax brackets twice as wide as those of single persons—10 percent on the first $60,000 of income and 20 percent on all higher income—would end the marriage tax on couple B, which would pay $6,000 in taxes whether married or not. But it would create a marriage bonus for couple A: if married, their taxes would be $6,000; if divorced, their taxes would rise to $9,000.

Many provisions of the personal income tax cause marriage penalties and bonuses, including tax brackets and the standard deduction (which are about 1.66 times as large for couples as for single filers), the earned income tax credit, phaseouts of personal exemptions and itemized deductions (which affect high-income filers), and floors on certain deductions expressed as a percentage of income. Marriage penalties under medicaid, food stamps, and income-tested cash assistance affect low-income households. They are not currently politically active issues.

The personal income tax system in 1996 provided 42 percent of married couples with a marriage penalty and 51 percent with a marriage bonus. Among filers with incomes greater than $50,000, penalties outnumbered bonuses. The value of bonuses exceeded the value of penalties by $4 billion overall and by $2 billion for filers with incomes higher than $50,000.[43]

Marriage penalties or bonuses have little effect on whether people marry, but may influence when.[44] Joint filing, which produces both marriage penalties and rewards, affects marginal tax rates, and tax rates do affect labor supply. When two people get married, the higher earner (usually the man) ordinarily faces marginal tax rates equal to or lower than when single, because the tax brackets are wider for couples, while the lower earner (usually the woman) often gets pushed into a higher tax bracket by the additional earnings of the spouse. Because the labor supply decisions of married women tend to be more sensitive to marginal tax rates, the higher tax rates on the lower earner have a larger effect than the lower tax rates on the higher earner.[45] One simulation estimated that this feature of the tax system reduces the labor supply of married couples by about 1 percent relative to a system under which marriage did not affect tax rates.[46]

Because the sources of marriage penalties are several, the proposed reforms are many and diverse. These include increasing the width of tax brackets and the size of the standard deduction for couples to twice those of single people, various changes in the earned income tax credit to make it more generous for couples, tax credits for second earners, and providing couples the choice of filing jointly or as two single people. The plans differ in costs, the proportion of tax reduction that flows to low-income filers, and the extent to which they raise marriage bonuses instead of just eliminating marriage penalties.

Several countries avoid marriage penalties by requiring individual filing. Under this approach, each spouse would be taxed on his or her own earnings. Capital income would be taxed to the person who owns

43. Congressional Budget Office (1997b, p. xiv).

44. Alm and Whittington (1995); and Sjoquist and Walker (1995).

45. Mroz (1987); Hausman (1985); Eissa (1996); and Bosworth and Burtless (1992).

46. Congressional Budget Office (1997b, p. 12). This section ignores the separate category "head of household," which receives treatment intermediate between the treatments of singles and couples filing jointly. Marriage penalties can be calculated in many ways, depending on how children or deductions are assumed to be distributed between couples when computing their taxes as singles.

the asset. This reform could create large marriage bonuses for couples with substantial capital income if they were able to arrange their affairs so that capital income could be allocated to the spouse facing the lower marginal tax rates, and deductions could be allocated to the spouse facing higher tax rates.[47]

Saving Incentives

Congress has adopted many tax provisions over the years to encourage saving. The incentive comes through the exemption from current tax of investment income as it accumulates in the sheltered account. Roth IRAs also exempt withdrawals. Individual Retirement Accounts, 401(k) plans, Keogh plans, Savings Incentive Match Plan for Employees (SIMPLE plans), simplified employee pensions (SEPs), and defined contribution and defined benefit pensions allow tax-deductible ontributions.

A critical flaw in these saving incentives is that taxpayers do not need to save—that is, reduce their consumption—to benefit from them. Taxpayers can shift funds from ordinary saving accounts, run up credit card balances, increase home loans, or borrow to finance the contributions that generate the tax benefits. Limits on current tax sheltered savings vehicles curtail, even if they do not prevent, such avoidance. Relaxing contribution limits would be unwise. The success of these incentives in promoting saving is in considerable doubt; personal saving rates have fallen since most of these provisions were introduced.[48] Furthermore, they create new opportunities for tax avoidance, especially by the wealthy, who can shift assets or exploit borrowing strategies.

Raising deposit limits on Roth IRAs would be particularly imprudent. Deposits in Roth IRAs do not reduce current taxes, but withdrawals are wholly tax free. As a result, deposits reduce revenues little in the first few years but massively later on. Offering such incentives may

47. In some of the countries that tax on an individual basis, capital income is taxed at a separate rate, independent of the taxpayer's total income.

48. Econometric analysis of saving incentives has focused on microeconomic evidence. See Engen, Gale, and Scholz (1996) and Poterba, Venti, and Wise (1996) for opposing viewpoints.

appear costless to elected officials whose terms in office will have ended long before the bill comes due.

The Clinton administration recently proposed a new saving incentive, Universal Savings Accounts, which could be described as progressive, government-sponsored 401(k) accounts. This plan is described in detail in chapter 6.

Tinkering with tax-based saving incentives diverts attention from potentially more effective ways to increase saving. The surest way to raise national saving is to maintain budget surpluses. In addition, several options to expand private saving are worth exploring. The most obvious is financial education. The households that do not use currently available saving incentives tend to be the ones with few other assets, and thus the ones who are least able to manage the accounts. Improved education would also help prepare American households for the move from private, defined-benefit pension plans to defined-contribution plans, which place more responsibility on workers to manage their own funds.

Capital Gains

Lower capital gains tax rates, advocates claim, would stimulate economic growth, raise tax revenues, and give a big boost to middle-income households. The data suggest that these claims are false. Capital gains already receive highly preferential treatment under the income tax: they are taxed on a deferred basis, they are not taxed at all if held until death, and they face lower rates than apply to other income if and when they are taxed. Cutting capital gains taxes further would widen the tax differential between capital gains and other income, encourage additional costly and complicated sheltering arrangements, and reduce revenue. Even if a cut in capital gains led to higher revenues from the capital gains tax itself, which is doubtful, it would lead to larger cuts in revenues from other sources as other forms of income were converted into capital gains. Furthermore, capital gains tax cuts provide large windfalls for the wealthy and little for anyone else. The 8 percent of taxpayers with income above $100,000 account for 88 percent of all long-term gains.

Capital gains tax cuts might stimulate private saving and investment, but they would lower national saving by reducing federal revenues more than they increase private saving.[49] Nor would a cut in capital gain taxes increase venture capital very much. Capital gains on small new ventures are already taxed at half the rate of other capital gains. In addition, a significant portion of funds for venture capital comes from sources that do not pay capital gains taxes and so would not be affected by cuts. Taxing realized capital gains at the same rate as other income has significant appeal: it would simplify taxes and increase national saving and investment.

The Internal Revenue Service: Freddy Krueger or Mr. Rogers?

Popularity may be impossible for an organization such as the Internal Revenue Service that is charged with making sure that people regularly surrender a sizable fraction of their incomes. But at least grudging acceptance of the IRS's legitimacy is essential because effective tax collection is possible only if the vast majority of citizens voluntarily comply with the laws. To achieve and sustain such compliance, filers must feel they are paying taxes for a government they fundamentally support under a tax system that is reasonably fair and is perceived as basically efficient. That sense of efficiency and justice requires that the IRS have the capacity to identify and come down hard on cheaters without needlessly harassing honest filers.

An external commission and congressional investigations have revealed serious shortcomings in IRS administration that call efficiency and justice into question. Because of these revelations, legislation and internal management reforms are now under way that address such problems as a lack of long-term planning (arising in part from the brief tenure of successive IRS commissioners), poor customer service (arising from inadequate internal training and supervision and insufficient use of computer technology), and abuse of taxpayers by IRS officials.

On July 22, 1998, the president signed into law the IRS Reform and Restructuring Act of 1998 that institutes various corrective measures. The law gives the commissioner of the IRS, its chief executive, a fixed

49. Even the effect on private saving is estimated to be minuscule. The Congressional Budget Office estimated that reducing the capital gains rate from 20 percent to 15 percent would raise the return to private saving by only 0.03 percentage point, which would have a negligible effect on private saving. Congressional Budget Office (1998b, pp. iv, 4).

five-year term and broadened the commissioner's powers to replace top management. It established an external supervisory board, consisting of private and public members, to oversee the work of the IRS. It extended a Taxpayer Bill of Rights that proscribes revenue quotas for auditors, limits the authority of the IRS to seize property, and protects people from being held responsible for the tax liabilities of former spouses.

The reform of the IRS raises fundamental and difficult questions about the proper managerial stance for the nation's revenue agency. Abusive practices create public anger and can erode voluntary compliance. But so too can administrative laxity that permits people to cheat with impunity. If the IRS is unduly draconian, it courts the first risk. Procedural hurdles that prevent it from aggressively pursuing evaders raise the second risk. Although there can be no doubt that the IRS needed administrative modernization and that some overly zealous revenue agents abused their power, recent legislation will need careful monitoring to make sure that the agency retains the power to do an inherently unpopular job.

Fundamental Tax Reform

Rather than modify the existing tax system, another option would be to junk it and start over. Although fundamental reform has been the subject of academic analysis for years, it achieved a politically higher profile after Republicans became the majority party in Congress in 1995 and during the presidential primaries in 1996. The furor has since died down, but fundamental tax reform merits careful attention because it continues to resonate among many experts and laypersons and because it raises important issues for tax policy. Advocates have claimed that fundamental tax reform could boost growth, slash burdens, simplify tax compliance, and eliminate the IRS. Unfortunately, a new tax system would not be exempt from the nagging trade-offs or the political constraints that plague less radical tax policies.

Options for Reform

Four different taxes have been put forth as alternatives to the existing system: a national retail sales tax (NRST), value-added tax (VAT), flat tax, and an "unlimited saving account" (or USA) tax. Under an NRST, a single tax rate would apply to all sales by businesses to households. Sales between business and between households would be untaxed. Government would pay sales tax to itself on all government purchases of labor, materials, services, and capital, thereby taxing personal consumption of government-produced goods and services.

Under a VAT, each business would pay tax on the difference between its total sales to consumers and other businesses less its purchases from other businesses, including investment. Thus, the increment in value of a product at each stage of production is subject to tax. Cumulated over all stages of production, the tax base just equals the value of final sales by businesses to consumers—that is, the same as in an NRST.

The flat tax, originally developed by Hoover Institution scholars Robert Hall and Alvin Rabushka, is simply a two-part VAT: the business tax base would be exactly like the VAT except that businesses would be allowed deductions not only for purchases from other businesses but also for cash wage and salary payments and employer pension contributions.[50] Individuals would pay tax on wages, salaries, and pension income that exceeded personal and dependent exemptions. Businesses and individuals would be taxed at a single flat rate.

The USA tax would combine a VAT on businesses with a personal consumption tax. Under the personal tax, people would report all income from earnings and investments, but they would be allowed a new deduction for all net saving. Thus, the personal tax falls on the difference between income and saving, which is consumption. In addition, the USA tax would retain some of the deductions and credits allowed under the current personal income tax and would have progressive rates.

Our analysis focuses on the NRST and the flat tax. We exclude the USA tax because tax lawyers and economists have argued that it would be unduly complex and difficult to administer.[51] We exclude the value-added tax because it exists now in many countries and would pose few novel issues for the United States.

In their pure forms the NRST and the flat tax would replace the current tax base—a convoluted concept of income—with consumption,

50. Hall and Rabushka (1985).
51. Ginsburg (1995); Slemrod (1996); and Graetz (1997).

replace the current graduated rate structure with a single tax rate, and eliminate all tax credits and deductions.[52]

Tax Rates

To make sensible comparisons across tax systems, it is important to distinguish between two ways to express tax rates. Suppose a good has a sticker price of $100, excluding taxes, and that a $30 sales tax is placed on the good. The "tax-exclusive" sales tax rate is 30 percent, calculated as T/P, where T is the tax payment and P is the pretax price of the good. The "tax-inclusive" sales tax rate is about 23 percent, calculated as $T/(P+T)$. The tax-inclusive rate is always lower than the tax-exclusive rate. At low rates there is little difference. But a 100 percent tax-exclusive rate corresponds to a 50 percent tax-inclusive rate. Sales taxes are usually quoted in tax-exclusive terms. Income taxes are usually quoted in tax-inclusive terms. Neither method is superior, but they must be distinguished to avoid confusion.

NATIONAL RETAIL SALES TAX. Representatives Dan Schaefer and Billy Tauzin have proposed to replace the $1,174 billion raised by individual and corporation income taxes, the estate tax, and federal excise taxes in 2000 with a 15 percent tax-inclusive (17.6 percent tax-exclusive) retail sales tax. Americans for Fair Taxation (AFT), a private lobbying group, proposes a 23 percent tax-inclusive (30 percent tax-exclusive) retail sales tax to replace the estimated $1,748 billion that the individual and corporation income taxes, the estate tax and the payroll tax will yield in 2000. The AFT plan would include a cash payment or *demogrant* calculated to offset taxes for low-income families. Each family—rich and poor alike—would receive a cash payment equal to the sales tax rate multiplied by the official poverty threshold. For a four-person family, the payment in 1999 would equal an estimated $3,841.

---

52. The distinction between pure income and pure consumption taxes is often exaggerated. Under the typical consumption tax—a VAT or a flat tax, for example—businesses are allowed immediate deductions for investments. If businesses were permitted only to deduct depreciation over the life of the investment, the VAT would be levied on income rather than consumption. See Bradford (1996). Slemrod (1997) describes the changes needed to convert the current income tax into a flat-rate consumption tax.

The actual rates in both proposals would be far higher than acknowledged by their supporters. First, the plans fail to allow for the increase in the cost of maintaining government services. The problem is easiest to see if it is assumed that producer prices (not including sales taxes) stay constant after conversion to a sales tax. In that event, consumer prices—producer prices *plus the new tax*—would rise by the full amount of the sales tax. The plans stipulate that government will pay sales taxes on its own purchases, but the revenue estimates do not recognize this added cost. Furthermore, to maintain their real value, federal transfer payments would have to be increased by the amount of the new tax, but the proposals make no allowance for this cost, either.[53]

Second, the rate estimates for the NRST assume no tax avoidance or evasion, although the higher rates under a national sales tax would produce larger incentives to avoid or evade tax than do current state sales taxes, which taxpayers do avoid and evade to some degree.[54] Third, the estimated rates presume that a very broad base of personal consumption would be taxed with virtually no exclusions, despite the fact that states now exclude about half of consumption, including health insurance premiums and hospital bills, rents, and most other services. At the rates under an NRST required to sustain revenues, political pressure to exempt or subsidize additional consumption would intensify.

Under relatively optimistic assumptions about these factors, the rates needed to maintain government skyrocket. If the evasion rate under a NRST were 15 percent, tax avoidance reduced the effective sales tax base by 5 percent, and political and administrative concerns reduced the starting tax base by only 10 percent—not the 50 percent typical of current retail sales taxes—the Schaefer-Tauzin proposal would require a tax-exclusive rate of 60 percent and the AFT proposal would require a tax-exclusive rate of 101 percent (table 7-5). Higher rates could easily be

---

53. Gale and others (1998). Alternatively, if producer prices (not including sales tax) fall after switching to a sales tax, the problem still arises but in another guise. In this case the government does not need to raise its nominal revenue target. But the nominal sales tax base (producer prices times quantities of goods sold) would shrink, so that the sales tax would raise less revenue than the proposals assume it would.

54. Gale and Holtzblatt (1999, p. 481).

Table 7-5. *Required National Sales Tax Rates*
Percent

Plan	Tax inclusive	Tax exclusive
To replace income, payroll, and estate taxes		
AFT proposal	22.8	29.6
Plus adjusted to hold government constant	34.9	53.6
Plus allowing for 5 percent avoidance rate, 15 percent		
evasion rate, and 10 percent statutory base erosion	50.4	101.4
To replace income, estate, and excise taxes		
Schaefer-Tauzin proposal	14.9	17.5
Plus adjusted to hold government constant	24.0	31.6
Plus allowing for 5 percent avoidance rate, 15 percent		
evasion rate, and 10 percent statutory base erosion	37.4	59.8

Sources: Gale (1999a).

required to maintain revenues if avoidance and evasion rates are higher or if Congress spared more than 10 percent of the potential base from tax.

THE FLAT TAX. The Treasury Department has estimated that a pure flat tax with a 20.8 percent rate would have generated as much revenue as the personal and corporation income taxes and the estate tax in 1996.[55] Unlike the advocates' estimates for the sales tax, the flat tax estimates include tax evasion and are based on logically consistent assumptions about price level changes. Nevertheless, in practice, rates would likely be higher for several reasons.

Congress would face intense pressure to offer transition relief to businesses that would be treated less generously under the new rules than under current rules. Repeal of the income tax would destroy remaining depreciation deductions for businesses that own capital at the time of transition. Owners of such "old capital" would be at a disadvantage in competition with owners of "new capital" purchased after the implementation of the new tax, which could be expensed. Similarly,

55. U.S. Department of Treasury (1996, p. 451). This includes personal exemptions of $10,700 (single), $21,400 (married), and $14,000 (head of household), and child exemptions of $5,000.

companies that have borrowed funds would lose deductions for interest payments and would have a disadvantage in competition with companies that have not borrowed. The flat tax would also eliminate carry-forwards relating to net operating losses, alternative minimum tax payments, and other items that business can currently use to reduce future taxes. Business owners would doubtless seek relief.[56]

More generally, taxes are deeply embedded in the structure of existing contracts and other transactions. Moving to a flat tax could upset these arrangements. For example, the flat tax would change the substance of every alimony agreement, because alimony payments are currently deductible and alimony receipts are taxable, but under the flat tax, those treatments would reverse. Likewise, the flat tax would alter every loan repayment plan because interest payments are currently deductible and interest receipts are taxable, but neither activity would affect tax liabilities under the flat tax.

These problems would create a dilemma. Most of the gains in economic efficiency and much of the political appeal of the flat tax derive from low rates made possible by a broad tax base. But providing transition relief would raise rates and would reduce gains in economic efficiency. Transition rules would also erode gains in simplicity.

Beyond transitional concerns, the permanent elimination of existing deductions and credits would prove difficult. Removing deductions for mortgage interest and property taxes would raise tax burdens for about 29 million homeowners who itemize, reduce the real value of homes, and possibly increase mortgage defaults.[57] Terminating deductions for charitable donations under the personal, corporation, and

56. Perlman (1996).
57. The impact on housing prices is controversial. Capozza, Green, and Hender-shott (1996, p. 201) estimated that the flat tax would reduce the price of owner-occupied housing (the structure plus the land) by an average of 29 percent if interest rates were constant. If the flat tax led to a fall in interest rates of 2 percentage points, the estimated average fall in housing prices would be 9 percent (p. 190). Bruce and Holtz-Eakin (1998) estimate that nominal house structure prices would rise by 10 percent in the short run and 17 percent in the long run. However, Gale (1999b, pp. 6–7) shows that under consistent assumptions about price-level effects, and including land in the analysis, the Bruce and Holtz-Eakin model suggests that real housing prices would fall by 7–10 percent in the short run and by 2–6 percent in the long run, depending on how interest rates adjust.

estate and gift taxes would reduce contributions by about 11–23 percent.[58] Eliminating deductions for health insurance premiums employers pay for workers would have increased the number of uninsured in 1994 by between 5.5 million and 14.3 million, about 14 to 36 percent.[59] Removing the deduction for state and local taxes would increase the effective burden of subfederal government on taxpayers who currently itemize. Deductions for casualty losses would end, meaning that a victim whose earnings were stolen would still have to pay taxes on them. Businesses would lose more than $300 billion in deductions for payroll taxes. The flat tax would also eliminate the earned income credit, which raises the labor supply of, and redistributes income to, low earners.[60]

If Congress provided limited transition relief; retained individual deductions for mortgage interest, charitable contributions, and state and local income and property taxes; continued business deductions for health insurance premiums and payroll taxes; and kept the earned income tax credit the revenue-neutral rate would rise from 20.8 percent to 31.9 percent (table 7-6).[61]

Regardless of the economic wisdom of retaining these aspects of the current income tax under a flat tax, political support for them will be powerful. Even flat-tax designers now acknowledge that transition relief will be inescapable in practice.[62] And some recent proposals, termed

58. Clotfelter and Schmalbeck (1996, pp. 229, 232, 234) estimate that the end of the charitable contributions deduction would reduce individual giving by 10 percent to 22 percent, corporate giving by 15 percent to 21 percent, and testamentary gifts by 24 percent to 44 percent.

59. Gruber and Poterba (1996, p. 142).

60. Dickert, Houser, and Scholz (1995); and Eissa and Liebman (1995).

61. This estimate understates the increase in rates that would be necessary because it is based on itemized deductions claimed under the personal income tax. But many taxpayers who use the standard deduction and therefore do not explicitly list such outlays as mortgage interest or charitable contributions also incur these expenses and would claim them under a flat tax if such itemized deductions were retained. Furthermore, if political pressure or policy consideration led Congress to retain itemized deductions, similar considerations might lead to the retention of such provisions as child care or education credits.

62. Representative Richard Armey and Professors Robert Hall and Alvin Rabushka, for example, have already acknowledged the need for transition relief. A commission studying tax reform chaired by former Representative Jack Kemp blandly remarked that "policymakers must take care to protect the existing savings, invest-

Table 7-6. *Required Tax Rates under the Flat Tax*
Percent

Adjustment	Flat rate if only one adjustment is made	Flat rate if all adjustments up to this point are made
Armey-Shelby flat tax (no adjustments)	20.8	20.8
Allow transition relief	23.1	23.1
Retain mortgage interest, health insurance, charitable contribution, state and local income, and property tax deductions	25.0	28.4
Retain earned income tax credit	21.1	27.5
Retain payroll tax deduction (businesses)	22.3	31.9

Sources: Authors' calculations.

"McFlat" taxes, would allow the flat tax to include deductions for mortgage interest and charitable contributions.[63] These cracks in the armor, which have appeared long before any serious legislative consideration has occurred, suggest that more would open in the political horse-trading surrounding actual legislation.

Simplicity, Compliance, and Administration

The appeal of fundamental tax reform stems in no small measure from claims that it would greatly simplify taxes, reducing compliance costs for households and businesses and defanging or even eliminating the IRS. However, while the NRST and flat tax clearly have some advantages over the existing system, they also create new problems. And responsible observers on all sides agree that an IRS-like agency is here to stay.

ment, and other assets" during a transition to a new tax system. Although the Kemp Commission did not elaborate on this seemingly innocuous statement, it has far-reaching implications for tax reform. Kemp Commission Report; http://www. flattax.house.gov/reptoc.htm [August 13, 1999].

63. See Specter (S. 488, 1995); and the Kemp Commission Report.

THE RETAIL SALES TAX. The fact that state sales taxes are generally thought to be simple casts an aura of simplicity over the NRST. Under a sales tax, few households would need to keep federal tax records, know federal tax law, or file federal returns. Filing the NRST for businesses would generally be relatively easy.

Few savings in compliance costs would be achieved, however, unless states also abandoned their personal and corporation income taxes. And if they replaced their income taxes with sales taxes, the combined rates would be astronomical, compounding the administrative difficulties that high federal rates would cause. Furthermore, experience with the state sales taxes provides no guidance on how to administer a demogrant to over 270 million people. Payments would be based on family size, a design feature that necessitates filing by all families and raises problems of enforcement because two separate one-person families would receive larger grants than would one two-person family.[64]

In addition, almost all states collect a significant share of their sales tax revenue from business-to-business sales. Inputs may pass through many stages before reaching consumers, and taxes can accumulate. This situation is tolerable when rates are low, but not when rates are high. Distinguishing sales to businesses from sales to consumers will require detailed audits of retailers and other businesses, because incentives for households to masquerade as businesses to evade the tax will increase with the increases in the tax rate.

Almost all states exempt a large number of difficult-to-tax consumer goods or services. At low rates these gaps in coverage matter little, but when rates are high, distortions and inefficiencies would become serious. No state, for example, taxes financial services, and only a handful tax services generally, yet the NRST proposals would tax all services.

A threshold administrative question regarding a national retail sales tax is whether it could be enforced at rates necessary to sustain revenues.[65] Retail sales tax rates in foreign countries are typically in the range of 4–6 percent, although a few countries have had higher rates.

---

64. For the same reason, the sales tax would create a sizable marriage penalty for all couples. See Gale (1998); and Gale and Holtzblatt (1999).

65. For a detailed analysis, see Gale and Hotlzblatt (1999). Mastromarco (1998) presents an opposing view.

No country has run a sales tax at anywhere near the rates that would be required to sustain revenues in the United States.[66] Although implementation of the sales tax at the rates shown in table 7-5 might not prove impossible, extreme caution would be appropriate.

THE FLAT TAX. The alleged simplicity of the flat tax, symbolized by a post-card-sized return, is one of its great selling points. A pure flat tax would be simpler than the current income tax, but some problems would carry over to the new system. These include distinguishing independent contractors from employees, determining who are qualified dependents, enforcing tax withholding for domestic help, limiting home office deductions, determining and collecting taxes from the self-employed, reconciling state and federal taxes, and distinguishing travel and food expenses incurred while doing business, which should be deductible, from other travel and food expenses, which should not be deductible.[67]

Several problems for tax administration could actually intensify, including the sheltering of personal consumption as a business expense, the tax treatment of mixed business and personal use property, rules regarding how taxes or losses may be allocated among different taxpayers, and distinctions between financial and real transactions.

The flat tax would also create new opportunities for avoidance and evasion. For example, wages and salaries would be deductible business expenses but fringe benefits would not. Businesses might find it desirable to hire physicians and nurses directly rather than purchase health

---

66. The OECD has stated that "Governments have gone on record as saying that a retail sales tax of more than 10 to 12 percent is too fragile to tax evasion possibilities." Vito Tanzi, director of Fiscal Studies at the International Monetary Fund has said, "The general view among experts, a view obviously shared by most governments, is that 10 percent may well be the maximum rate feasible under an RST" (Tanzi, 1995, pp. 50–51). British fiscal expert Alan Tait expressed a similar view: "At 5 percent, the incentive to evade [the retail sales tax] is probably not worth the penalties of prosecution; at 10 percent, evasion is more attractive, and at 15–20 percent, becomes extremely tempting" (quoted in Tanzi, 1995, p. 51). Slemrod (1996) and others have expressed similar sentiments.

67. Graetz (1997) describes numerous problems in the current system that will not disappear with the flat tax.

insurance for their employees. Because sales proceeds are taxable to businesses but interest income is not, businesses would find it profitable to discount prices for installment purchasers who accepted high interest rates. One author concluded that the flat tax would create a dilemma—either a complicated tax law would be necessary to reduce the evasion possibilities or complicated business transactions would arise to game the law or both.[68] After a careful review of estimates of the costs of administering the income tax, another study concluded that administrative costs for a pure flat tax would be about half those of the corporation and individual income taxes.[69] If Congress retained some itemized deductions and the earned income tax credit and granted transition relief, however, these savings would shrink.

Fairness and the Distribution of Tax Burdens

The debate over whether consumption or income is a better measure of ability to pay taxes has been going on for centuries. Proponents of consumption taxes argue that consumption usually approximates lifetime income because few people inherit or bequeath more than a small fraction of their lifetime earnings. For that reason, taxing consumption is equivalent to taxing households on the basis of their ability to pay taxes over long periods of time. However, advocates of the income tax counter that current income may be a better measure of ability to pay because few households can borrow much against future income and the prospect of having a large future income may not prove much help.

Fundamental tax reform would redistribute tax burdens. The shift from an income base to the consumption base of the NRST or the flat tax would tend to reduce the burden on high-income filers because they consume a smaller than average share of their income. The shift from graduated rates to a flat rate would also tend to reduce their burden. Ending double taxation of corporate income and the estate tax and providing transition relief would have similar effects.

As a simple matter of arithmetic, if wealthy households pay less in taxes, others have to pay more, assuming revenues are held constant.

68. Feld (1995, p. 615).
69. Slemrod (1996, p. 375).

Both the NRST and the flat tax would eliminate the earned income credit and thus make poor working households worse off. And middle-class households would have to bear a higher burden of taxation.

Figure 7-2 shows the estimated distributional effects of moving to the flat tax. Households in the top 1 percent of the income distribution would receive average tax cuts of $38,000.[70] These tax cuts would be financed by tax increases of $350 per household in the bottom 50 percent of the income distribution, and about $700 per household in the 75th–99th percentiles of the distribution. Taxes on households in the 50th–75th percentiles would be largely unaffected.

In examining the distributional effects of fundamental tax reform, it is important to keep in mind that people eventually bear the burden of business taxes. For this reason the practices of some advocates of fundamental tax reform of comparing individual tax liabilities under the flat tax with those under the current income tax are extremely misleading. The reason is that most flat taxes would sharply increase the proportion of taxes collected directly from business. Furthermore, even if one limits one's attention to personal liabilities, the likely curtailment of health insurance fringe benefits that would result from repeal of business deductions for health insurance and the effects on house prices of repeal of deductions for mortgage interest and property taxes could easily swamp changes in direct personal tax liabilities.

A second claim, that fundamental tax reform would be profamily because of the demogrant in the sales tax and the large personal and child exemptions in the flat tax, is also misleading. Families with children would be hurt by the elimination of current deductions for health insurance, mortgage interest, state and local income and property taxes (which finance schools and other services), the earned income credit, child care credits, education credits, and child credits. Switching to a consumption tax would put families with children at a disadvantage because at each income level they tend to have higher consumption requirements than do couples without children. One recent study found that a broad-based, flat-rate consumption tax would have hurt low-income families with children and helped families with incomes

---

70. This estimate does not include the effects of eliminating the estate tax or of providing transition relief.

Figure 7-2. *Effective Tax Rates under Current Law and Flat Tax*

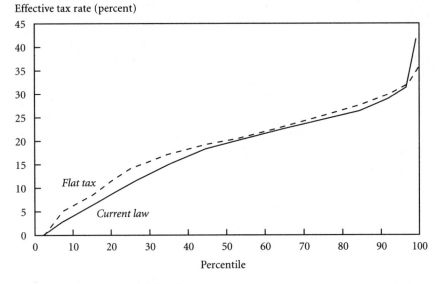

Effective tax rate (percent)

Source: Gale, Houser, and Scholz (1996).

over $200,000.[71] This analysis was based on pre-1997 tax law. Including the child and education credits enacted in 1997 would imply even larger losses for families with incomes below $200,000.

Effects on Economic Growth

Many of the problems and trade-offs created by fundamental tax reform could be reduced if reform boosted growth dramatically. Fundamental tax reform could increase growth by reducing marginal tax rates on capital and labor income, reducing the disparity in taxation of different types of capital and labor income, and imposing a lump-sum tax on old capital by not providing transition relief. But the impact on growth depends critically on the "purity" of the reform.[72]

71. McIntyre and Steuerle (1996, p. 15).
72. Estimates of the effects on growth also depend on how the current system is characterized. Engen and Gale (1996) document that most private saving and growth now occurs in tax sheltered forms. If one recognizes this fact, the impact on saving and growth of switching to a consumption tax will be smaller than it would be if one assumes that the current system is a pure income tax.

A pure consumption tax with no personal exemptions or product exemptions and no deductions, credits, or transition relief could increase the size of the economy by 9 percent in the ninth year after reform and would require a tax-inclusive rate of 14 percent (table 7-7). Compared with the estimated impacts of other policies, these are enormous. Unfortunately, the growth effect shrinks rapidly as the pure reform is made more realistic. Adding modest personal exemptions (smaller than in the flat tax proposed by Representatives Richard Armey and Richard Shelby)[73] and providing transition relief for existing depreciation deductions (but not interest deductions) reduces the growth impact by 80 percent, leaving increased growth of only 1.8 percent in the ninth year, and requires a tax-inclusive rate of 24 percent. Allowing for additional deductions, credits, and child exemptions or other forms of transition relief would raise the tax rate considerably, as shown in table 7-6. There are no estimates of the growth impacts of these changes, but the data in table 7-7 suggest that at the required rates shown in table 7-6, the growth effect would likely be near or below zero.[74]

Conclusion

The U.S. tax system collects nearly $2 trillion from a public that dislikes taxes but for the most part complies voluntarily. However, taxes have become encrusted with provisions that confuse filers, distort economic decisions, and necessitate higher marginal tax rates than would be required if the provisions were curbed or eliminated. Impatience with this system has led some to call for its complete replacement. At first glance, starting afresh may sound attractive, but the idea raises formidable problems of redistribution and transition and would create major uncertainties. Incremental reform is more promising, if less dramatic. Specific steps could make taxes easier to comply with and to

73. H.R. 2060 and S. 1050, The Freedom and Fairness Restoration Act of 1995.
74. Other models, reported in Joint Committee on Taxation (1997) generate a range of results that, dropping the high and low estimates, are fairly close to the results reported in the text. See also Auerbach (1996); Engen and Gale (1996); and Fullerton and Rogers (1996).

Table 7-7. *Economic Growth, Alternative Versions of the Flat Tax*
Percent

Alternative	Increase in the size of the economy in			Revenue-neutral tax rate in		
	2 years	9 years	Steady-state	2 years	9 years	Steady-state
Pure consumption base	6.9	9.0	10.9	14.7	13.9	12.5
Add limited personal exemptions[a]	2.5	4.0	6.1	22.1	21.2	19.4
Add limited transition relief[a,b]	0.6	1.8	3.6	24.4	23.5	22.0

Source: Altig and others (1997).
a. In these simulations, personal exemptions are set at $9,000, and child exemptions are set at zero. In the Armey-Shelby flat tax, these exemptions are set at $10,700 and $5,000 respectively.
b. Transition relief is provided only for existing depreciation deductions, not for interest payments.

enforce, permit rates to be cut, and promote economic growth. In taking these steps, selective tax reductions would help smooth the way to achieving these goals because every tax reform creates losers as well as winners. For that reason as well as for reasons of fiscal prudence, massive tax cuts now would be massively unwise. The nation should instead husband its resources, not only to meet looming problems of an aging population, but also to accumulate a down payment on tax reform.

References

Alm, James, and Leslie A. Whittington. 1995. "Does the Income Tax Affect Marital Decisions?" *National Tax Journal* 48 (December): 565–72.

Altig, David, and others. 1997. "Stimulating U.S. Tax Reform." NBER Working Paper W6248. Cambridge, Mass.: National Bureau of Economic Research.

Auerbach, Alan J. 1996. "Tax Reform, Capital Allocation, Efficiency, and Growth." In Henry J. Aaron and William G. Gale, eds., *Economic Effects of Fundamental Tax Reform*. Brookings.

Auerbach, Alan J., and William G. Gale. 1999. "Does the Budget Surplus Justify a Large-Scale Tax Cut?" *Tax Notes* (March 22): 1827–50.

Auerbach, Alan, and Dale Jorgenson. 1980. "Inflation Proof Depreciation of Assets." *Harvard Business Review* (September–October): 113–18.

Beach, William W., and others. 1999. "The Economic and Revenue Effects of Reducing Tax Rates by 10%." *Tax Notes* (March 22): 1851–65.

Becker, Gary Stanley, and Casey B. Mulligan. 1998. "Deadweight Costs and the Size of Government." NBER Working Paper 6789. Cambridge, Mass.: National Bureau of Economic Research.

Bernheim, B. Douglas. 1999. "Taxation and Saving." NBER Working Paper 7061. Cambridge, Mass.: National Bureau of Economic Research.

Blumenthal, Marsha, and Joel Slemrod. 1992. "The Compliance Cost of the U.S. Individual Income Tax System: A Second Look after Tax Reform." *National Tax Journal* 45 (June): 185–202.

Bosworth, Barry, and Gary Burtless. 1992. "Effects of Tax Reform on Labor Supply, Investment, and Saving." *Journal of Economic Perspectives* 6 (Winter): 3–25.

Bradford, David F. 1996. "Consumption Taxes: Some Fundamental Transition Issues." In Michael J. Boskin, ed., *Frontiers of Tax Reform*, 123–50.

Burman, Leonard E., William G. Gale, and David Weiner. 1998a. "Six Tax Laws Later: How Individuals' Marginal Federal Income Tax Rates Changed between 1980 and 1995." *National Tax Journal* 51 (September): 637–52.

———. 1998b. "The Taxation of Individual Retirement Accounts" (August).

Capozza, Dennis R., Richard K. Green, and Patrick H. Hendershott. 1996. "Taxes, Mortgage Borrowing, and Residential Land Prices." In Aaron and Gale, eds., *Economic Effects of Fundamental Tax Reform*, 171–210.

Clark, Peter K. 1993. "Tax Incentives and Equipment Investment." *Brookings Papers on Economic Activity* 1: 317–39.

Clotfelter, Charles T., and Richard L. Schmalbeck. 1996. "The Impact of Fundamental Tax Reform on Nonprofit Organizations." In Aaron and Gale, eds., *Economic Effects of Fundamental Tax Reform*, 211–46.

Commerce Clearing House. 1999. *US Master Tax Guide 1999*. Chicago.

Congressional Budget Office. 1997a. *Reducing the Deficit: Spending and Revenue Options*.

———. 1997b. *For Better or for Worse: Marriage and the Federal Income Tax*.

———. 1998a. *Estimates of Federal Tax liabilities for Individuals and Families by Income Category and Family Type for 1995 and 1999*.

———. 1998b. *An Analysis of the Potential Macroeconomic Effects of the Economic Growth Act of 1998*.

———. 1999a. *The Economic and Budget Outlook: An Update*. http://www.cbo.gov [August 5, 1999].

———. 1999b. "Memorandum: Preliminary Estimates of Effective Tax Rates." July 15.

Cummins, Jason G., Kevin A. Hassett, and R. Glenn Hubbard. 1994. "A Reconsideration of Investment Behavior Using Tax Reforms as Natural Experiments." *Brookings Papers on Economic Activity*, 1, 1–59.

Davenport, Charles, and Jay A. Soled. 1999. "Enlivening the Death-Tax Death-Talk." *Tax Notes* (July 26): 591–631.

Dickert, Stacy, Scott Houser, and John Karl Scholz. 1995. "The Earned Income Tax Credit and Transfer Programs: A Study of Labor Market and Program Participation." In James M. Poterba, ed., *Tax Policy and the Economy*, 1–50. MIT Press.

Engen, Eric M., and William G. Gale. 1996. "The Effects of Fundamental Tax Reform on Saving." In Aaron and Gale, eds., *Economic Effects of Fundamental Tax Reform*, 83–112.

Engen, Eric M., William G. Gale, and John Karl Scholz. 1996. "The Illusory Effects of Saving Incentives on Saving." *Journal of Economic Perspectives* 10 (Fall): 113–38.

Eissa, Nada. 1996. "Tax Reforms and Labor Supply." In James M. Poterba, ed., *Tax Policy and the Economy*, 119–51. MIT Press.

Eissa, Nada, and Jeffrey B. Liebman. 1995. "Labor Supply Response to the Earned Income Tax Credit." *Quarterly Journal of Economics* 111 (May): 605–37.

Feld, Alan L. 1995. "Living with the Flat Tax." *National Tax Journal* 48 (December): 603–17.

Friedman, Milton. 1993. "Why Government Is the Problem." Working Paper, Essays in Public Policy, 39. Stanford, Calif.: Hoover Institution on War, Revolution, and Peace.

Fullerton, Don, and Diane Lim Rogers. 1996. "Lifetime Effects of Fundamental Tax Reform." In Aaron and Gale, eds., *Economic Effects of Fundamental Tax Reform*, 321–52.

Gale, William G. 1998. "Don't Buy the Sales Tax." Brookings Policy Brief. March.

———. 1999a. "The Required Tax Rate in a National Retail Sales Tax." Paper prepared for the National Tax Association Spring Symposium.

———. 1999b. "Comments on 'Will Consumption Tax Reform Kill the Housing Market' by Donald Bruce and Douglas Holtz-Eakin." June.

Gale, William G., and Janet Holtzblatt. 1997. "On the Possibility of a No-Return Tax System." *National Tax Journal* 50 (September): 475–85.

———. 1999. "The Role of the Administrative Factors in Tax Reform: Simplicity, Compliance, and Enforcement."

Gale, William G., and John Sabelhaus. 1999. "Perspectives on the Household Saving Rate." *Brookings Papers on Economic Activity* 1: 181–224.

Gale, William, and others. 1998. "Taxing Government in a National Retail Sales Tax." *Tax Notes* (October 5, 1998): 97–109.

Gale, William G., Scott Houser, and John Karl Scholz. 1996. "Distributional Effects of Fundamental Tax Reform." In Henry J. Aaron and William G. Gale, eds., *Economic Effects of Fundamental Tax Reform*, 281–320.

Ginsburg, Martin D. 1995. "Life under a Personal Consumption Tax: Some Thoughts on Working, Saving, and Consuming in Nunn-Domenici's Tax World." *National Tax Journal* 48 (December): 585–602.

Gordon, Roger H., and Joel Slemrod. 1988. "Do We Collect Any Revenue from Taxing Capital Income?" In Lawrence Summers, ed., *Tax Policy and the Economy*, vol. 2, 89–103. MIT Press.

Graetz, Michael J. 1997. *The Decline (and Fall?) of the Income Tax*. Norton.

Gravelle, Jane. 1994. *The Economic Effects of Taxing Capital Income*. MIT Press.

Greenstein, Robert, and Isaac Shapiro. 1997. "Families Denied Child Tax Credit by Ways and Means Proposal." Washington: Center on Budget and Policy Priorities (July).

Gruber, Jonathan, and James Poterba. 1996. "Fundamental Tax Reform and Employer-Provided Health Insurance." In Aaron and Gale, eds., *Economic Effects of Fundamental Tax Reform*, 125–70.

Hall, Robert E. and Alvin Rabushka. 1985. *The Flat Tax*. Hoover Institution Press.

Hausman, Jerry. 1985. "Taxes and Labor Supply." In Alan Auerbach and Martin Feldstein, eds., *Handbook of Public Economics*, vol. 1, 213–63. Amesterdam: North-Holland.

Internal Revenue Service. 1996. *Federal Tax Compliance Research: Individual Income Tax Gap Estimates for 1985, 1988, and 1992.* Internal Revenue Service Publication 1415, Revision 4-96. U.S. Department of the Treasury.
———. 1998. *Statistics of Income Bulletin* 18 (Fall).
Joint Committee on Taxation. 1997. *Joint Committee on Taxation Tax Modeling Project and 1997 Tax Symposium Papers.* Government Printing Office.
———. 1999. *Overview of Present Law and Issues Relating to Individual Income Taxes,* JCX-18-99.
Mastromarco, Dan. 1998. "The 'Fair Tax' and Tax Compliance: An Analytical Perspective." *Tax Notes* (April 20): 379–87.
McIntyre, Michael J., and C. Eugene Steuerle. 1996. "Federal Tax Reform: A Family Perspective." Washington: Finance Project.
Mroz, Thomas A. 1987. "The Sensitivity of an Empirical Model of Married Women's Hours of Work to Economic and Statistical Assumptions." *Econometrica* 55 (July): 765–99.
Organization for Economic Cooperation and Development. 1998. *Revenue Statistice, 1965–1997.* Paris.
Pechman, Joseph A. 1966. *Federal Tax Policy.* Washington: Brookings.
Perlman, Ronald A. 1996. "Transition Issues in Moving to a Consumption Tax: A Tax Lawyer's Perspective." In Aaron and Gale, eds., *The Economic Effects of Fundamental Tax Reform,* 393–434.
Poterba, James M., Steven F. Venti, and David A. Wise. 1996. "How Retirement Saving Programs Increase Saving." *Journal of Economic Perspectives* 10 (Fall): 91–112.
Shoven, John. 1991. "Using the Corporate Cash Flow Tax to Integrate Corporate and Personal Taxes." In *National Tax Association—Tax Institute of America Proceedings,* pp. 19–27. Columbus: National Tax Association.
Sjoquist, David L., and Mary Beth Walker. 1995. "The Marriage Tax and the Rate and Timing of Marriage." *National Tax Journal* 48 (December): 547–58.
Slemrod, Joel. 1996. "Which Is the Simplest Tax System of Them All? In Aaron and Gale, eds., *Economic Effects of Fundamental Tax Reform,* 355–91.
———. 1997. "Deconstructing the Income Tax." *American Economic Review* 87 (May): 151–55.
Tanzi, Vito. 1995. *Taxation in an Integrating World.* Washington: Brookings.
U.S. Department of Treasury. 1992. "Integration of Individual and Corporate Tax Systems."
———. 1999. *The Problem of Corporate Tax Shelters: Discussion Analysis and Legislative Proposals.*
U.S. Department of Treasury, Office of Tax Analysis. 1996. "'New' Armey-Shelby Flat Tax Would Still Lose Money, Treasury Finds." *Tax Notes* (January 22, 1996): 451–61.

PART III

Domestic Priorities

DIANE RAVITCH   8

The National Agenda in Elementary and Secondary Education

SINCE THE MID-1960s the primary goal of federal policy has been to ensure equality of opportunity in elementary and secondary education. Title I, Head Start, bilingual education, and other programs enacted in the 1960s, and special education for handicapped children, enacted in the 1970s, directed resources and established legal rights for children who had previously been poorly served by the education system.

Measured by the goal of removing legal barriers based on race, poverty, ethnic origin, and handicap, these policies have achieved much. The continued pursuit of equality of educational opportunity now requires that federal education policies seek to improve student achievement for all groups. U.S. students are not performing adequately for various reasons, including lack of incentives, inadequate preparation of many teachers, and unduly rigid, bureaucratic school governance. Federal policy can address many of these issues directly and can streamline its own programs to reduce regulatory burdens on schools and increase incentives for better student performance. The federal Head Start program should be made far more effective for poor children, and the biggest program—Title I—should be turned into a portable entitlement for all needy children.

Although the federal role in elementary and secondary education is important, it is necessarily limited; total federal spending is less than

10 percent of the nation's total budget for elementary and secondary education (about $300 billion). The federal role is limited not only by dollars spent but by the principle of federalism that reserves significant powers to states and localities to manage public schools. The leverage exercised by the federal government should be used not only to ensure equality of opportunity but to promote greater student achievement, better information about the condition and progress of education, and improved teacher preparation.

Student Performance

In 1983 the report of the National Commission on Excellence in Education encouraged most states to increase their graduation requirements. In *A Nation at Risk* the commission recommended that all high school students study four years of English and three years of social studies, mathematics, and science. In 1982 only 14 percent of high school graduates met these enrollment standards. By 1994 the proportion had grown to 50 percent. The commission also recommended that the college bound take two years of a foreign language, an enrollment standard only 9 percent of graduates met in 1982 (even though 50 percent of high school graduates enrolled in college immediately after high school); 39 percent met the standard in 1994 (60 percent were college bound).[1]

Academic Performance

Although students are taking more courses, their achievement has not kept pace. The only measure of academic achievement that tests representative national samples is the federally funded National Assessment of Educational Progress (NAEP). The results, shown in table 8-1, are mildly encouraging for the achievement of younger pupils but discouraging for those at the end of their precollege education.

The NAEP also reports student performance in relation to standards or "achievement levels" identified as "basic," "proficient," or "advanced" that describe what students in grades four, eight, and twelve should

1. National Commission on Excellence in Education (1983); National Center for Education Statistics (NCES) (1998).

Table 8-1. *Age Group and Trends in Performance*

Subject area and year	Nine-Year-Olds	Thirteen-Year-Olds	Seventeen-Year-Olds
Science 1969–96	↑	↔	↓
Mathematics 1973–96	↑	↑	↔
Reading 1971–86	↑	↑	↔
Writing 1984–96	↔	↔	↓

Source: National Assessment of Educational Progress, various years.
a. Up (↑), down (↓), unchanged (↔).

know and be able to do. The results indicate that large numbers of students are not learning much (table 8-2). Evidence on gaps between racial and ethnic groups is particularly disturbing. Despite significant improvement in scores of black and Hispanic students in the 1970s and 1980s, the NAEP scores of these groups at age 17 are equivalent to scores of white students at age 13 in every academic subject. For example, 76 percent of black students and 64 percent of Hispanic students were "below basic" in science in 1996, compared with 27 percent of white students.[2]

International assessments offer an additional perspective on overall student performance. The only international assessment on which American students did well was a test of basic reading skills, in which American nine-year-olds ranked second to those in Finland.[3] American students perform better in science than in mathematics but poorly on both on international tests. The Third International Mathematics and Science Study (TIMSS), released in 1997 and 1998, provides the most up-to-date comparisons. The test assessed the performance of more than one-half million students at grades four, eight, and twelve in forty-one countries. The findings are sobering. U.S. students do well in the primary grades but fall behind as they advance in school. In the fourth grade U.S. students were above the international average in both mathematics and science. Only one country, Korea, performed significantly better than U.S. students did in science. By eighth grade U.S. performance in mathematics had dropped below the international mean but

2. NCES (1997c, 1997d, 1996a, 1999a).
3. For a description of American participation in the international assessments, see Ravitch (1995, pp. 83–89).

Table 8-2. *Students in Various Competence Levels, Selected Subjects, Grades 4, 8, and 12*

Subject and grade	Below basic	Basic	Proficient or advanced
Reading			
4	38	62	31
8	26	74	33
12	23	77	40
Mathematics			
8	38	62	28
12	31	69	18
History			
8	39	61	14
12	57	43	11
Science			
8	39	61	32
12	43	57	24

Sources: National Center for Education Statistics (1999a, 1997c, 1996a, 1997d).

remained above the international mean in science. By the last year of secondary school, American students ranked poorly in both mathematics and science.

In twelfth grade, TIMSS tested two populations: a representative sample of students in twenty countries and a sample of elite students in sixteen who were studying advanced science and advanced mathematics. (The usually high-performing Asian nations—Japan, Korea, and Singapore—did not participate in the twelfth-grade TIMSS.) American students performed poorly across the board. The tests of general knowledge asked the kinds of questions that a high school senior or a well-informed citizen should be able to answer; the mathematics test represented seventh-grade content for most nations (but ninth grade in the United States), and the science test represented ninth-grade level comprehension in other nations (but tested what is usually taught in eleventh grade in the United States). On the test of general knowledge of mathematics, U.S. seniors outperformed only those from Cyprus and South Africa, lagging far behind the top-scoring students in the Netherlands, Sweden, Denmark, and Switzerland. On the test of general knowledge in science, U.S. students ranked below the international mean, behind eleven countries, similar to seven, and ahead of only two (again, Cyprus and South Africa).[4]

Reactions to Low Test Scores

The response to TIMSS results in the news media was nearly as worrisome as the unexpectedly poor showing of American high school seniors. Articles in the *New York Times, Washington Post, Los Angeles Times, Newsweek,* and *New Republic* dismissed the TIMSS results. A front-page article in the *New York Times* quoted academics who believed that low scores were actually evidence of freedom and creativity, though none suggested how students who lacked fundamental knowledge and skills would be able to exercise their creativity or advance the frontiers of technology. Another common theme among TIMSS critics was that low test scores did not matter because the nation's economy was booming. If the United States should need additional engineers, scientists, or mathematicians, it could presumably import them from high-scoring countries. Some complained that average students in the United States had been compared with academic elites in Europe. This was untrue; TIMSS included representative samples from most countries, including students in vocational and technical programs.

Much of the criticism of TIMSS reflects a long-standing debate between those who have urged higher standards and those who argue that our schools are better than ever.[5] The critics claim that American students lack adequate incentives for achievement and that American schools tolerate mediocre performance. The more optimistic observers hold that allegations of low academic performance are the result of a manufactured crisis, one invented to damage the reputation of public education and pave the way for vouchers and privatization.[6] These competing views proceed from different assumptions: the standards constituency insists that the new economy demands higher performance by virtually all students, and the no-crisis constituency discounts the need or even the possibility of higher standards for all. At least one

4. Mullis and others (1998).
5. Stedman (1998).
6. Berliner and Biddle (1995).

commentator has alleged that a poorly educated underclass serves the national interest by providing a pool of unskilled workers willing to perform distasteful work, a position that few others embrace.[7]

Fortunately, support for higher standards is notably bipartisan. Both conservatives and liberals have long supported higher educational standards. Secretary of Education Richard W. Riley identified "low expectations and low standards," as well as the failure of students to take challenging courses, as causes of the drop in scores between the fourth and twelfth grades. And Commissioner of Education Statistics Pascal D. Forgione Jr. has pointed out that the range of student scores in other countries was equally broad but that U.S. scores start lower and end lower on the scale.[8]

The need for higher standards in school is indicated by the high proportion of students who require remediation in reading, writing, or mathematics in the first year of college. Nearly one-third of first-time freshmen enrolled in at least one remedial course in 1995, including 41 percent of freshmen in public two-year colleges, 26 percent of freshmen in private two-year colleges, 22 percent in public four-year colleges, and 13 percent in private four-year colleges. It has been estimated that the likely cost of remediation is "only" about $1 billion. Some consider this outlay a solid investment in upgrading the skills of students who would otherwise have little opportunity for advancement. Others suggest that remediation represents a failure of elementary and secondary education and that colleges understate the actual cost.[9] Both may be right.

Recent debates about student performance have relied almost completely on data collected by the National Center for Education Statistics. Without the testing program of the National Assessment of Educational Progress, there would be no valid way to gauge the performance of American students. Without the surveys conducted by NCES, information about trends in the condition and progress of education would be minimal. The value of this information in shaping policy underscores the critical role of the federal government in research, statistics, and assessment.

7. Bracey (1991, pp. 111–12).
8. U.S. Department of Education (1998); Forgione (n.d.).
9. Breneman (1998); Abraham (1998); Hoxby (1998); NCES (1996b, p. 10).

The Problem of Teacher Quality

Improving teacher quality is critical to better student achievement. At a minimum, teachers should be knowledgeable in the subject they are teaching. Yet many, particularly in mathematics and science, have neither a major nor a minor in their main teaching assignment. Although some excellent teachers may be self-educated, training helps. Studies have repeatedly shown that the teacher's knowledge of mathematics and science, as measured by having a bachelor's or master's degree in the subject, has a significant positive influence on student achievement.[10]

It should be axiomatic that teachers must know their subject, but as one analyst noted, "There is an alarming level of underqualified teaching in American high schools."[11] The Department of Education has issued contradictory data about the extent of out-of-field teaching, which is defined as lacking even a minor in the subject one teaches. In 1997 the department reported that in 1993–94, 27.7 percent of public school teachers were teaching out of field, including 39.5 percent of science teachers, 34 percent of mathematics teachers, 17.4 percent of social studies teachers, and 25 percent of English teachers. In 1999 the department used different measures that produced far lower numbers: 12 percent in science, 18 percent in mathematics, 11 percent in social studies, and 14 percent in English. The numbers reported vary according to which teachers are counted (full-time teachers versus part-time teachers) and how the subject is defined (general science versus specific subfields such as chemistry or physics).

A more reliable and alarming indicator of the significance of out-of-field teaching is the proportion of students whose teachers have neither a major nor minor in the subject—20.8 percent of students taking English, 26.6 percent of those in mathematics, 38.5 percent in life science, 56.2 percent in physical science, and 53.9 percent in history in grades seven to twelve.[12]

The number of instructors who are teaching out of field in advanced mathematics and science may partially explain the poor performance of U.S. high school seniors on the TIMSS. In schools enrolling high pro-

10. Goldhaber and Brewer (1997).
11. Ingersoll (1999, p. 27); NCES (1997a, p. 26; 1999b, p. 12).
12. Ingersoll (1999, p. 30).

portions of low-income students, the proportion of teachers who are teaching out of field is especially high. Where more than 40 percent of the students are low income, 40 percent of the teachers are out of field. But even affluent schools have large numbers of teachers who are out of field. The Department of Education reported in 1999 that only 38 percent of the nation's full-time public school teachers have an undergraduate or graduate major in an academic field (including 66 percent of high school teachers, 44 percent of middle school teachers, and 22 percent of elementary teachers).[13]

Throughout the twentieth century, teaching standards have been lax in most states. Certification requirements vary widely and frequently consist of little more than a minimal test of basic skills or evidence that the candidate has taken certain prescribed courses in pedagogy. The unwillingness of many states to set high standards for entry to teaching has created the problem of out-of-field teachers. According to the National Commission on Teaching and America's Future,

> No state will allow a person to fix plumbing, guard swimming pools, style hair, write wills, design a building, or practice medicine without completing training and passing an examination, [but] more than forty states allow school districts to hire teachers on emergency licenses who have not met these basic requirements. States pay more attention to the qualifications of veterinarians treating the nation's cats and dogs than to those of teachers educating the nation's children and youth.[14]

What can the federal government do to alleviate this serious problem? Current federal programs should focus on helping future teachers acquire preparation in the major academic fields that are taught in school: English, history, mathematics, science, foreign languages, and the advanced subfields in mathematics and science. Federal teacher education programs could encourage prospective teachers to earn a bachelor's degree in an academic field, even if they plan to teach in elementary or middle school. In addition, Congress could spur states and local districts to offer differential pay to highly qualified teachers in

13. NCES (1997a, p. 26; 1999b, p. 12); Ingersoll (1999, p. 30).
14. National Commission on Teaching and America's Future (1996, pp. 14–15).

fields with persistent shortages, such as advanced mathematics and physical science, as well as to those who teach in inner-city schools with concentrations of low-income students. States that require future teachers to pass examinations on the subject matter they intend to teach could receive incentive awards. The National Science Foundation could develop model examinations for states to use to assess teachers' subject matter knowledge in mathematics and science at different levels. The National Endowment for the Humanities could assist states that want to develop tests of teachers' knowledge of English and history. It is hard to think of any reform that is more fundamental than making certain that every classroom has a well-educated teacher.

Reforming the Governance of Education

To improve student performance, many states and school districts are trying to reform the management of education. The goal is to get greater accountability for student performance by replacing bureaucratic, top-down management by local school boards with other formats, such as charter schools, contract management, and vouchers. None of these initiatives has been tried long enough to permit a definitive judgment about its effect on student achievement.

Charter Schools

The father of the charter school movement was the late Albert Shanker, who served for many years as president of the American Federation of Teachers. In 1988 he wrote that "the poor results of education are a function of a bureaucratic, hierarchical, and factory-like structure of schooling that has remained virtually the same for 150 years." He asked, "Why not devise a district policy mechanism to enable any school or any group of teachers, say, six to twelve, within a school to develop a proposal for how they could better educate youngsters and then give them a 'charter' to implement that proposal?" He suggested that charter schools should be free of the usual regulations and should receive "their share of the per pupil budget spent in other schools, as well as the space and resources they might ordinarily have."[15]

---

15. Shanker (1988, pp. 91–92, 98).

Charter schools are public schools that agree to meet certain performance standards in exchange for waivers from most regulations other than those governing health, safety, and civil rights. Charter schools are supposed to accept accountability for results in exchange for autonomy on how those results are produced. State legislation determines such issues as how charters are granted, whether there is an appeals process if a charter is refused or revoked, what standards must be met, how many charters will be awarded, whether teachers must be certified, and whether existing public schools may convert to charter status. If a charter school fails to meet its educational and fiscal commitments, it may lose its charter. This accountability for performance sets these schools apart from regular public schools, which may produce poor educational results for many years without any penalty.

Minnesota passed the first charter school legislation in 1991. Since then about thirty-five states and the District of Columbia have followed suit. In the 1998–99 school year, more than 1,200 charter schools were in operation in twenty-seven states and the District of Columbia, with large numbers located in Arizona, California, Colorado, Texas, and Michigan.

Charter schools are popular, in part, because they promise to reduce bureaucratic micromanagement, trim overhead costs, and dedicate a greater proportion of funds for actual instruction. Educational administration has become top-heavy and excessively costly as administrators, support staff, and other personnel have proliferated. According to surveys by the Organization for Economic Cooperation and Development, less than half of employees in U.S. schools are teachers; the National Commission on Teaching and America's Future reports that the proportion of classroom teachers has declined from more than 70 percent of all staff in 1950 to about 45 percent in 1995.[16]

The primary opposition to charter schools has come from local school boards, which see charter schools as unwelcome competition for students and public dollars, and from teachers' unions, which want to protect collective bargaining agreements. Some charter laws are considered strong because they allow applicants to be chartered either by a

16. Organization for Economic Cooperation and Development (OECD) (1992, pp. 66–67); National Commission on Teaching and America's Future (1996, pp. 48–49).

local school board, a state agency, or a public university. Other state laws are intentionally weak because only a local school board may issue a charter and may reject applicants without a right of appeal. States with weak charter laws, like Arkansas and Kansas, have few or no charter schools.

Contract Management

Some education scholars have argued that public schools should be managed by contract, with the local school board selecting the managers and then leaving them free to meet agreed-upon standards. Paul T. Hill, Lawrence C. Pierce, and James W. Guthrie maintain that contracting "promises to do better than the current system and any competing strategy on support for initiative-taking in schools, creation of strong pressures for high performance in schools, stabilizing the funding schools receive and the rules under which they must work, and protecting children from failing schools."[17] In recent years, private companies have assumed the management of some charter schools and have also contracted with school districts to manage one or more regular public schools. In 1998–99 the Edison Project was managing fifty-one public schools in twelve states. Most Edison Project schools, which have a longer school day and year than regular public schools, are showing significant achievement gains and have long waiting lists. Additional contract management companies are competing to manage charter schools as well as regular public schools. Some states prohibit contract management of instructional services, in part because members of public employee unions fear that outsourcing threatens their jobs.[18]

Vouchers

Providing poor parents with vouchers that they can use to defray the costs of education at schools they select for their children is a third important innovation. Programs in Milwaukee (since 1990) and in Cleveland (since 1996) have provided publicly funded vouchers to low-

17. Hill, Pierce, and Guthrie (1997, p. 124).
18. Edison Project (1999). In its January–February 1998 issue, the cover of *Public Employee*, the magazine of the American Federation of State, County and Municipal Employees, was titled "Raiders of the Lost Jobs: The Corporate Pirates Taking over Public Services."

income students. It would be more accurate to call them income-tested government scholarships, rather than vouchers, whose purpose is to provide additional education options to poor children at risk of educational failure.

The concept of vouchers, even when limited only to poor children in low-performing schools, also arouses intense opposition from public employee unions who fear job loss, from those who are concerned about backdoor subsidies to religious education, and from others who fear the decline of the public school. The Wisconsin legislature established a voucher program that allowed low-income children to enroll in either secular or religious private schools. After a prolonged legal battle, the program was upheld by the Wisconsin Supreme Court in 1998, and the U.S. Supreme Court declined to hear a challenge to the ruling later the same year. In Cleveland, students in the program are also permitted to attend both secular and religious schools. The courts barred religious schools, but the program remains in effect while the case is on appeal.

A heated debate among researchers has produced conflicting interpretations of evidence on educational outcomes of voucher programs. The state-appointed monitor in Milwaukee found no real improvement, but independent analysts have reported academic gains. Studies of the Cleveland program have led to similar disagreements. More studies, better data, and more experience will be required before it is possible to reach firm conclusions about the effects of vouchers on student achievement.

Support for Educational Choice

Despite the lack of solid evidence for the academic benefits of vouchers (that is, income-tested government scholarships), the issue has become more salient, both as a strategy to help poor kids in low-performing schools and to spur public school reform through the force of competition. In the spring of 1999, the Florida legislature passed a statewide voucher program allowing children in low-performing schools to attend other public or private schools (the plan will surely be challenged in the courts). Opposition to government subsidies for children to attend nonpublic schools, once solid, has been eroding. The Phi Delta Kappa-Gallup Poll reported in 1997 that opposition had fallen from 74 percent to 52 percent in the previous five years. More recent polls show that the public is almost evenly divided on whether government funds should be used for students in nonpublic schools. Even though the Republican Party supports vouchers and the Democrats oppose them, the Gallup Poll reported in 1998 that 51 percent of Democrats but only 47 percent of Republicans favor them. The Joint Center for Political and Economic Studies found in 1998 that 53 percent of blacks support income-tested vouchers, as do 60 percent of blacks between 26 and 35 years old. One point seems clear: the only program for vouchers that has survived legislative and judicial scrutiny is explicitly income-tested and designed as a scholarship rather than as aid for the "haves."[19]

The federal government should remove impediments created by federal programs to the successful operation of charter schools, contracting, and voucher experiments in those states and localities that authorize them. An important way to support reform without predetermining any particular result would be to reform funding formulas for such major federal programs as Title I, special education, and bilingual education so that the money follows the student, as it does in higher education, to whatever accredited institution they enroll in. If a state or district prohibits charter schools, contracting, and vouchers, federal dollars would follow students to their regular public school. If, however, a state or district establishes any of these approaches, the federal dollars would follow students to the school of their choice instead of going to the school district.

The federal government appropriated $100 million for a Public School Charter Program in 1999, and President Clinton has requested an increase to $130 million for 2000. With bipartisan support, appropriations for this program have grown from $6 million when it was initiated in 1995. These funds are targeted to encourage the start-up of new charter schools. Once a charter school is launched, the flow of regular public funding should be adequate to its needs. This program would be improved by refusing funds to states that have created no charter schools (Oregon has received millions of dol-

19. Joint Center for Political and Economic Studies (1997, 1998); Rose and Gallup (1998).

lars from the charter program without even passing a charter school law).[20]

As for vouchers, the federal government should support a significant demonstration program for low-income students in not less than ten hard-pressed urban school districts for five to ten years.[21] Too many big-city school systems have failed to use resources wisely, set clear academic standards, improve teacher recruitment and compensation, and most important, increase achievement. The situation for many students in the nation's inner cities is so desperate that government at all levels must take bold steps to alter the status quo. Such a demonstration voucher program should be limited to children who are currently enrolled in public schools and poor enough to be eligible for the federal free lunch program. The scholarship should be equal to the average per pupil expenditure of the district plus whatever additional funds—Title I or special education—the student is entitled to receive. Any school accredited by the state should be eligible to receive scholarship students, and these schools should be expected to comply with federal civil rights laws and to administer the same tests as the public schools. With carefully designed monitoring and evaluation, significant questions could be answered about the power of incentives, competition, and choice. A large federal demonstration program, carefully targeted to children with the greatest needs, would resolve debates that have been deadlocked by politics and ideology.

The Need to Reform Categorical Programs

The largest categorical federal programs were created to promote equality of educational opportunity. When these programs were established—Head Start as part of the War on Poverty in 1964, Title I as part of the Elementary and Secondary Education Act of 1965, bilingual education in 1968, and special education in 1975—hopes were high for what they might accomplish. For different reasons, each has failed to

20. Schroeder (1997).
21. This approach was suggested by William A. Galston and Diane Ravitch, "Scholarships for Inner-City School Kids," *Washington Post,* December 17, 1996, p. A23.

meet the expectations of its sponsors, though all have developed ardent constituencies and are politically popular.

Title I

The Title I program distributes about $8 billion annually to districts with large numbers of disadvantaged students. It was intended to narrow the substantial gap in achievement between poor children and their more advantaged peers. Two major congressionally mandated evaluations, one in the late 1970s and the other in 1993, concluded that Title I had not closed the test score gap. Unfortunately, neither the program nor the evaluations were designed to identify which factors were most successful in improving the academic performance of poor children.[22]

After its disappointing 1993 evaluation, Title I was reoriented to emphasize schoolwide reforms rather than remediation for individual children. Whether whole-school reform will prove more effective than the practice of removing individual children from their regular classrooms for additional instruction remains to be determined. In 1999 in preparation for the reauthorization of Title I, the Department of Education reported that children in high-poverty schools had made large gains since 1994 but acknowledged that their reading scores had rebounded only to where they had been in 1990. In addition, 70 percent of children in high-poverty schools were reading "even below the basic level."[23] One unfortunate consequence of the 1994 reauthorization is that Title I funds are now spent in all grades, even high school, instead of focusing assistance on needy children in the early elementary grades, when they first begin to fall behind their peers.

The unwieldy bureaucratic structure of Title I should be reformed because of what Florida Commissioner of Education Frank Brogan has called "the crushing burden caused by too many federal regulations, procedures and mandates. Florida spends millions of dollars every year to administer inflexible, categorical federal programs that divert precious dollars away from raising student achievement." Brogan complained that in Florida, "because of federal requirements, there are 297 state employees to oversee and administer approximately $1 billion in

22. Carter (1984, pp. 5, 11).
23. U.S. Department of Education (1999).

federal funds. By contrast, we have 374 state-funded positions to over-see and administer approximately \$7 billion in state funds."[24] In Arizona, State Superintendent Lisa Graham Keegan noted that 165 members of her department's staff manage federal programs, which is "roughly 45 percent of my staff working to oversee about 6 percent of Arizona's total spending on education."[25] In some state education departments, a majority of staff members are assigned to monitor federal programs.[26]

Currently, the federal funding for Title I goes to school districts, and many qualified poor students who are not in Title I schools do not receive any benefits from the program. In some urban districts, poor children in public schools that are "only 60 percent poor" get no Title I services. Title I should serve all eligible poor children, wherever they reside, which would require increased appropriations. The program should be converted to a portable entitlement, which would allow the money to follow eligible students to any accredited school in which they enroll, consistent with state laws, just as federal scholarships follow eligible college students to the institutions they choose. Schools would still be able to adopt schoolwide reforms or design their own strategies for children who need extra help. But the fundamental principle should be that the federal money is allocated to benefit needy children, not to sustain administrative overhead. States and school districts would continue to monitor school performance and to exercise the ultimate form of accountability: the power to close or deny accreditation to schools that do not perform adequately.

Special Education

If Title I has fostered an insulated bureaucracy, the Individuals with Disabilities Education Act (IDEA) has created an empire controlled by lawyers, bureaucrats, and interest groups. When the legislation was enacted in 1975, more than 1 million children were excluded from free public education because of their disabilities. Today, nearly 6 million children are enrolled in special education.

24. Brogan (1998).
25. Keegan (1999, p. 125).
26. Hill (1999, p. 156).

Total national spending for special education was approximately $32.6 billion in 1995–96 (the last estimate available), and it is certainly larger now; the federal budget for special education (grants to states) in 1999 was $4.3 billion.[27] For states and districts, special education is a huge unfunded mandate. Although the federal government pays for only a small portion of the state and local costs (usually about 10 percent), it imposes extensive, minutely detailed, and very expensive mandates. It requires that all children receive a "free and appropriate public education" provided in the "least restrictive" environment, which means that most disabled students receive their education in regular classrooms, not in separate classes with other similarly disabled students. The law also provides legal remedies for parents who do not approve of the placement or treatment of their children. Parents of disabled children regard such recourse as a valuable protection against school boards that may be more interested in saving money than in providing full service.

But some costs seem to be excessive. The National School Boards Association has described special education as a "lawyers' playground" because so many decisions at the state and local level are driven by litigation and fear of litigation. Local school boards complain about out-of-control costs, such as lawyers' fees, tuition at expensive private schools, technological devices, eyeglasses, wheel chairs, expenditures that should be considered health services, even "first class travel for parents of children in special education." The school boards allege that the legal protection accorded special education students makes it difficult to remove them even when they are disruptive or violent.[28] Some of the local boards' fears of spiraling costs in a zero-sum budget situation were realized by a Supreme Court decision in March 1999, which held that the IDEA law required the Cedar Rapids school district to pay for a full-time nursing aide for a paralyzed boy; the district had unsuccessfully claimed that such care was a "medical service," which was not covered by the law.[29]

27. Chambers and others (1998).
28. National School Boards Association (1995, pp. 2–3).
29. Walsh (1999, p.1).

Originally, IDEA was enacted to protect children with physical and
mental handicaps who had been excluded from educational opportunity. In the past twenty years, children with such disabilities have composed a stable or shrinking proportion of those covered. The greatest
growth in special education has been in the number and proportion of
children described as "learning disabled," who now constitute about half
of all children in the program. The category frequently lacks any precise
or objective definition, and the incidence of learning disabled children
varies widely, from 11 percent of pupils in Massachusetts to only 2 percent in Georgia. Researchers at the National Institute of Child Health
and Human Development have found that most children who are classified as learning disabled have difficulty learning to read, and that with
well-trained teachers, their conditions can be reduced or corrected.[30]

The importance of guaranteeing equal educational opportunity to
students with disabilities is indisputable. But concern is growing about
the constantly increasing cost of special education, the overidentifica-
tion of children as learning disabled, the inflexibility of federal regulations, the growth of an unaccountable bureaucracy, and the failure of
Congress or the administration to overhaul the program. According to
estimates by Richard Rothstein of the Economic Policy Institute, an
estimated forty cents of every new educational dollar annually was
spent for special education between 1967 and 1996. Rothstein cautioned that "this growth may be occurring at the expense of regular
education. The fact that a program that consumes 19 percent of total
funds is consuming 40 percent of new funds should attract the attention of policy makers."[31] John Merrow of National Public Radio spent
nearly a year interviewing students, teachers, parents, and others and
concluded that special education ill serves the children it is supposed
to benefit; that it focuses on process and paperwork, rather than outcomes for students; that only 44 percent graduated from high school;
and that most children with learning disabilities in special education

---

30. Research released by the National Institute of Child Health and Human Development suggests that the recent whole language movement in reading instruction
may have contributed to the rising number of "learning disabled" children. Lyon
(1996, pp. 63, 71); Merrow (1996).

31. Rothstein (1997).

show "no signs of improvement." Merrow continued, "Process turns out to be the system's strong point . . . process requires people, and special education has plenty of them." He found that during the past twenty years enrollment in special education had increased by 40 percent, but special education staff had grown by 80 percent, many of whom were not working in the classroom.[32]

Politicians' fear of offending the groups representing disabled children and of being perceived as critical of a program that aims to protect children who are deaf, blind, autistic, retarded, or otherwise deserving of special help stands as a major obstacle to reforms that might curb the programs' current excesses and allow it to serve the children better. During the 1997 reauthorization, only the National School Boards Association raised serious questions about the program's pernicious effects. Despite the many problems that the law causes, despite the limited progress of the children in the program, it is politically unpalatable to challenge a law that serves such vulnerable clients.

Reform may require a political device similar to that used to close supposedly sacrosanct military bases at the end of the cold war. The administration and Congress should create a commission removed to the greatest extent possible from the political pressures of advocacy groups. The commission would propose legislative changes whose purpose would be to restore the capacity of teachers and other school officials to exercise their best judgment in providing a free and appropriate public education to disabled children. The commission should also make recommendations for cost containment, reducing excessive litigation, shrinking the administrative bureaucracy, removing incentives to label children as requiring special education when what they need is more intensive instruction, and allowing schools to use common sense when dealing with disruptive or violent children, even if they are disabled. The goal should be to restore flexibility to schools to respond appropriately to individual children while fully protecting their rights.

Bilingual Education

The Bilingual Education Act of 1968 was intended to help Hispanic children learn English. All of the witnesses at congressional hearings

32. Merrow (1996, pp. 48–49).

and the bill's principal sponsor concurred in this goal.[33] Some witnesses at the original hearings also held that because their native tongue was not the language of instruction, Hispanic children had a poor self-image, which contributed to their poor school performance. Several educators asserted that Hispanic children would learn English better and faster if they first learned Spanish. This theory eventually led to federal regulations and court orders requiring instruction not in English but in the child's presumed native language.

Bilingual education is now concentrated in the Southwest, New York, and Florida. The program appears in different forms. In the traditional version students take most of their academic courses in their native language. In English as a Second Language (ESL), students receive intensive instruction in English. Sometimes districts combine these approaches.

Although the program is supposed to teach children from many different language groups, most participants are Hispanic, in part because it is hard to find enough bilingual teachers in languages other than Spanish and in part because running a program with dozens of different language groups is administratively difficult. Consequently, children from Asia and eastern Europe tend to move quickly out of bilingual programs and into the regular English language curriculum, but Hispanic children do not.

Unfortunately, bilingual education appears to have done little to improve the educational outcomes of Hispanic children. Their academic performance, as measured by NAEP, remains poor. Their dropout rate is far higher than for any other group. In 1995 it was 17.9 percent for Hispanic youth, 16 to 24 years old, born in the United States, and 23.7 percent for Hispanics who were foreign born but attended school in the United States. By comparison, the dropout rate was 8.6 percent for whites and 12.1 percent for blacks. Hispanic stu-

---

33. The sponsor, Senator Ralph Yarborough of Texas, said that he had proposed the legislation because "unless a child becomes very fluent in English he will rarely reach the top in American cultural life. He might as a baseball player, but he could not as a performer on radio; he could not in law; he could not in medicine; he could not in any of the professions or in business." Senate Committee on Labor and Public Welfare (1967, pp. 4–6, 21, 35, 37, 43, 424); Ravitch (1983, pp. 272–73).

dents who speak English well are less likely to drop out than those who do not.[34]

In 1994 the New York City Board of Education released a longitudinal study of bilingual education. Of those children who entered a bilingual program where most instruction was not in English in the third grade, 78 percent had not learned enough English to leave the program after three years. Of those who started bilingual instruction in the sixth grade, 93 percent were unable to pass an English test after three years. The majority of those who failed to learn enough English to leave native language bilingual classes were Hispanic.[35]

Despite doubts about the methods and efficacy of bilingual education, the federal appropriation expanded from $178 million to $380 million between 1996 and 1999. Richard Rothstein calculated that spending on bilingual education rose from an estimated 1.9 percent of total education spending in 1991 to 2.5 percent in 1996.[36] If the program worked to give non-English-speaking children the English-language skills they need, this large outlay would be a good investment. Unfortunately, it seems to have failed.

The purpose of bilingual education should be to teach English to children who have limited English proficiency. For American students it is certainly valuable to know two or more languages, but one of them must be English. Competency in English is a prerequisite for success in U.S. education and in the modern economy. The rationale for the program is to provide equal educational opportunity. Therefore, the federal program should help children rapidly achieve full English proficiency, not mastery of their (or their parents') native tongue. The program should be rechristened the English-language Literacy Program to express this goal, and federal grants to states and school districts should emphasize that the primary goal of the program is to help children gain English proficiency. Congress should require that no child may be assigned to a predominantly non-English instructional program without prior, explicit parental consent.

34. NCES (1997b, pp. 31, 36).
35. New York City Board of Education (1994).
36. Rothstein (1997).

Head Start

Created in 1965 as part of President Lyndon Johnson's War on Poverty, Head Start was launched as a summer program for half a million disadvantaged preschoolers. When President Nixon terminated the Office of Economic Opportunity, Head Start was relocated to what is now the Department of Health and Human Services. Head Start was gradually transformed into a year-round program in the early 1970s. Enrollments declined, reaching a low of about 333,000 in 1977. Between 1983 and 1993, enrollments increased from 415,000 to 714,000, and by 1998 it served 830,000, about one-third of those eligible. President Clinton wants to increase enrollment to 1 million by 2002. In 1999 Head Start received appropriations of $4.66 billion.

In its early years, proponents of the program claimed unrealistically that a year or two in Head Start would wipe out the cognitive gap between poor children and their middle-class peers. A 1969 study reported that the program produced small and only temporary cognitive gains, and enthusiasm among educators waned.[37] Nonetheless, the program became immensely popular with the general public and with Congress because it provides crucially important health, nutrition, social, and psychological services to poor children, whatever its cognitive effects may be. The placement of Head Start in the Department of Health and Human Services, not in the Department of Education, symbolizes the program's focus on social services rather than cognitive development. Head Start also employs many poor parents as teachers and aides.

Because early evaluations cast doubt on the capacity of Head Start to produce lasting intellectual growth, advocates for the program appear to have accepted that its chief purpose is to provide a nurturing environment where poor children are fed and receive medical attention and social services and where some of their parents are employed. Minimal expectations for cognitive development have been institutionalized. For example, Head Start pays very low salaries to its teachers; the average in 1996–97 was $17,800. The average salary for a senior Head Start teacher with a graduate degree was about $30,000, roughly the same as the starting salary for a New York City public school teacher

37. Vinovskis (1997, pp. 182–84).

with no experience and no graduate degree. As a result, Head Start has difficulty hiring teachers, especially ones with good credentials. In 1997, of 155,000 paid staff, only 36,000 were teachers, approximately one-third of whom had a bachelor's degree, and about 50,000 were parents of current or former Head Start children.[38]

The possibility that Head Start might produce significant cognitive growth should not have been abandoned. The cumulative evidence from the Perry Preschool Program in Ypsilanti, Michigan, suggests that a high-quality program can make a long-term difference in "achievement, grade retention, special education, high school graduation, and socialization."[39] French preschools, designed as schools, not day care centers, also report positive results. These preschools may well be the best in the world. They serve nearly all children between the ages of three and five. Teachers and directors are highly qualified. A well-planned curriculum provides active experiences with language and mathematics, as well as games, arts, and crafts.[40] One need not go to France to find a high-quality preschool curriculum, however. The Core Knowledge Foundation, which has a network of more than 700 elementary schools, has recently developed one based on the best practices in France and the United States.[41]

At present, Head Start has only vague performance standards and no curriculum to stimulate the growth of literacy and numeracy. It is ironic that the federal government is urging states to adopt academic standards, yet has failed to put them in place in a vitally important federal program. A curriculum that established clear standards for what teachers and students should know and be able to do would help prepare disadvantaged children for success in school. Such standards should not be controversial for Head Start, as they are for public elementary and secondary education, because it is a federal program.

To expand Head Start as it is currently designed to larger numbers of children would be a mistake. Only if redesigned and vastly improved can the program honor its promise to give poor children a head start

38. Data provided by Tom Schultz, Administration for Children and Families, March 1998. See also Whitebook (1995).
39. Barnett (1995, p. 43).
40. Richardson and Marx (1989).
41. Core Knowledge Foundation (1998).

in school. Such a course will require a well-planned educational curriculum for literacy and numeracy, higher salaries, and a better-trained staff—and that means larger appropriations. The short-term goal should be improved effectiveness. The long-term goal should be expansion. A Head Start program that significantly boosted academic performance and graduation rates and reduced referrals to special education would increase the program's political support. More important, it would improve the lives of poor children, and it just might save some money later on for the American taxpayer.

In all of the major federal education programs—Title I, special education, bilingual education, and Head Start—the stakeholders have shown that they will preserve the status quo even when the status quo is not working for children. If Americans are serious about equal educational opportunity—the stated goal of all of these initiatives—public officials must be willing to make whatever changes will enable the programs to achieve the purpose for which they were created.

Standards and Assessments

Clear academic standards and good tests of student performance in relation to those standards are vital if federal policy is to succeed in improving academic performance and reducing the gaps among different groups of students. Through the Goals 2000 program, the federal government encouraged the states to develop academic standards and tests based on those standards. The quality of the states' standards and tests varies widely.

Current federal law prohibits the federal government from exercising "any direction, supervision, or control over the curriculum, program of instruction [or] administration . . . of any educational institution."[42] Although this law is regularly circumvented, the federal government cannot create a national curriculum and must carefully respect the role of the states even as it encourages higher standards of performance. The Bush administration funded the development of voluntary national standards in the major academic subjects by leading organizations of teachers and scholars. Unfortunately, the process was rushed and lacked any mechanism for trial and evaluation. As a result, proposals for

42. Ravitch (1995, p. 158; 1998).

national standards were based on views of dominant professional groups rather than on careful assessment of successful applications.[43]

Compared with those used by NAEP, the states' proficiency standards are not especially rigorous.

	Proportion of students scored as proficient in mathematics	
State	State standards (seventh and eighth grades, 1994–95)	NAEP (eighth grade, 1992)
Georgia	83	16
Louisiana	80	10
North Carolina	68	15

Only in Delaware and Kentucky were state proficiency standards as challenging as NAEP's.[44] Because of their interest in creating common benchmarks, the National Governors Association and business leaders established an organization called Project Achieve specifically to help the states improve their standards and tests. This is a private sector activity that requires no federal direction. Its purpose is to improve the rigor and comparability of state standards and assessments.

The federal government can do a great deal to advance the cause of rigorous standards without interfering with the states' right to set education policy. President Clinton proposed the establishment of voluntary national tests of fourth grade reading and eighth grade mathematics. In 1997 Congress directed that this activity should be aligned to the maximum extent possible with NAEP and turned control of the test over to the National Assessment Governing Board (NAGB), which sets policy for NAEP. Congress also prohibited any deployment of the national test unless the legislature specifically authorized it. If Congress lifts the prohibition and permits testing in 2001, it will supply valuable information to parents, students, and teachers.

NAEP has achieved unusual credibility because its standards (or "achievement levels") make test results understandable to noneducators

43. Musick (1996).
44. Musick (1996).

and provide more rigorous benchmarks than the commercial tests that report "norms." Congress should permit school districts and schools to administer NAEP on a voluntary districtwide or schoolwide basis for those that wish to compare their performance to NAEP standards. States should be encouraged to embed NAEP test items in their own tests. This step would allow them to see whether their standards are as rigorous as NAEP's and would enable them to maintain control over the nature and content of their own tests while calibrating them if they choose to do so to NAEP standards.

The importance of test score information for measuring performance underlines the value of NAEP. Keeping NAEP and the National Assessment Governing Board independent of political control should be an important national priority. The 1994 reauthorization undercut the independence of NAGB and tied it too closely to the Department of Education. The validity and credibility of NAEP data would be best served if Congress made NAGB, NAEP, and the National Center for Education Statistics part of an independent statistical and research agency. Both political parties should seek this goal to feel assured that national test results and national statistics are insulated from any partisan or political influence.

Tests not only provide information but may also provide incentives to test takers. As Albert Shanker used to say, students want to know: Does it count? Will it be on the test? Does it matter whether I try hard or not? The usual answer is, "No, it doesn't count, even if it is on the test. You will be promoted, you will graduate, you will go to college no matter what the quality of your work in school." Can the federal government do anything to create incentives for stronger performance? The most effective way to do that has been suggested by columnist Robert Samuelson, who proposed that the federal government require applicants for federal college aid to pass a test of reading, writing, and mathematics to demonstrate their readiness to go to college. Such a qualifying test would have wide reach since more than half of all college students now receive some form of federal aid. It would also have the immediate benefits of signaling to students that schoolwork is important and to teachers that their work is crucial to their students' future. It would also eliminate the need for most remedial college courses. As Samuelson wrote, "Even a modestly rigorous exam would cause students to work harder. Those who passed would be better pre-pared. Those who didn't would receive a clear message: Students must earn college aid through achievement. It's not an automatic entitlement."[45] Even a test pegged to only the tenth-grade level for four-year colleges and the ninth-grade level for two-year colleges, Samuelson held, "would compel more students to work harder, foster a climate of learning in classrooms, and create popular pressure for school systems to do better." Those who cannot pass the test could retake it until they do. Only then would they be certified as ready for college studies. Those who can never pass are unlikely to benefit from going to college.[46]

Federalism in Education

The federal role in assisting elementary and secondary education has been changing quickly since the election of President Clinton. Educa-tion has always been primarily a state and local responsibility, and the federal government's financial contribution has always been much smaller than that of states and localities. In 1867 Congress passed a law creating "a department of education" to collect statistics to show "the condition and progress of education" and to diffuse whatever infor-mation would help to improve it. Over the years Congress added voca-tional education, aid to higher education, the G.I. Bill, support for science and engineering, and other programs. When general federal aid to education finally became a reality in 1965, it was targeted specif-ically to promote equality of educational opportunity for disadvantaged students. In the succeeding thirty-five years federal policy has remained focused on that goal.

The active interest of President Clinton in education has made the public aware of the crucial role of education in securing individual opportunity, economic growth, and social progress. Clinton has force-fully advocated increased funding for almost all federal education pro-grams but specifically for Title I, bilingual education, Head Start,

45. Robert J. Samuelson, "The Hypocrisy Scholarship," *Washington Post*, February 12, 1997, p. A3.
46. Robert Samuelson, "The Height of Hypocrisy," *Newsweek*, September 22, 1997, p. 53.

special education, and financial aid to college students, while urging the creation of new federal programs. He has strongly promoted national standards, national tests, and charter schools. In addition, he has proposed federal tax credits of nearly $22 billion in bonds for school construction, a $12 billion program to hire 100,000 teachers to reduce class size in grades one through three; and a grant program of $200 million a year to pay for before and after-school programs. He has called on schools to forgo social promotion and promote the use of school uniforms. He has also vigorously supported community service for college students, tax credits for college tuition, access to the Internet for every school, technology education, mentors for middle school students, character education, public school choice, national board certification for 100,000 teachers, and many other initiatives.

These proposals are almost all popular, especially if they come with new federal funding. States, school districts, teachers, and parents react happily to the idea that the federal government will pay for a new school or more teachers or more programs; it is "found money."

But fundamental issues concerning the federal role in education should be addressed. Is there a difference among the federal, state, and local governments in setting education policy? Where does the president's role end and that of the governor, mayor, or school superintendent begin?

Take the matter of reducing class size. This proposal is very popular among parents and teachers, but it is also very expensive. Are decisions about class size best made at the federal, state, or local level, or even in schools themselves? Perhaps the federal government could do more to enable districts to hire more teachers if its categorical programs did not require the hiring of so many program administrators. Reducing class size has some unwanted consequences; it worsens teacher shortages and makes it more difficult to raise standards for entry to teaching or to increase salaries, both of which are important for long-term improvement of the profession. In California, which mandated smaller class sizes, severe problems ensued, including "desperation hiring" of teachers who were "less experienced, less qualified, and less skilled" than in previous years; the exodus of inner-city teachers to the suburbs, leaving some urban districts worse off than before; and a shortage of facilities, leading to the conversion of art rooms, computer rooms, auditoriums, and other spaces into classrooms.[47] Although issues of principle should be distinguished from issues of implementation, both matters demand careful consideration before the federal government adopts a popular initiative that will have enormous financial consequences far into the future and may subvert other necessary improvements of the status of teachers.

As education becomes increasingly important in American society, stresses and strains on our complicated federal system are inevitable. That there should be equality of educational opportunity is settled in principle. Implementing that principle is more complicated. How should we establish the conditions that create equality of opportunity? What programs will encourage excellence? Which level of government should do what? How should we balance entitlements and incentives? How should we change programs that are ineffective but whose termination will be strongly resisted by current beneficiaries?

The federal government has and will continue to have a large role in ensuring equality of educational opportunity as well as in encouraging higher student achievement. It has a well-established responsibility to provide additional funds for the education of poor and handicapped children, ensure an adequate supply of well-educated teachers, support excellent preschools for poor children, help non-English-speaking children succeed in school, collect and disseminate accurate information about the condition and progress of education, and engage in research about teaching and learning.

However, the federal government cannot manage the daily life of the nation's schools and classrooms. Its large and enduring responsibilities will be best served if it does not attempt to tell teachers and principals how to do their jobs. Micromanagement of education is beyond the capacity of the Department of Education and Congress. Furthermore, the proliferation of federal programs, program administrators, regulations, mandates, and auditing requirements itself hampers teachers and principals, who should devote their full attention to the children in their care.

47. McRobbie (1997); Mosteller, Light, and Sachs (1996); Hanushek (1998); Michael Kirst, "Smaller Classes Aren't a Cure-All," *New York Times*, August 18, 1997, p. A19.

At present, American education is marked by low productivity, uncertain standards, and lack of accountability. The most important national priority now must be to redesign federal policies and programs so that education funding is used to educate all children to their highest potential, not to preserve the status quo.

References

Abraham, Ansley A. Jr. 1998. "Comment." In *Brookings Papers on Education Policy, 1998,* edited by Diane Ravitch, 371–76. Brookings.

Berliner, David C., and Bruce J. Biddle. 1995. *The Manufactured Crisis: Myths, Frauds, and the Attack on America's Public Schools.* Addison-Wesley.

Barnett, W. Stephen. 1995. "Long-Term Effects of Early Childhood Programs on Cognitive and School Outcomes." *Future of Children* 5 (Winter): 25–50.

Bracey, Gerald W. 1991. "Why Can't They Be Like We Were?" *Phi Delta Kappan* 73 (October): 104–17.

Brogan, Frank T. 1998. "Statement to Senate Budget Committee's Task Force on Education." Government Printing Office (January 28).

Breneman, David W. 1998. "Remediation in Higher Education: Its Extent and Cost." In *Brookings Papers on Education Policy,* edited by Diane Ravitch, 359–71. Brookings.

Carter, Launor F. 1984. "The Sustaining Effects Study of Compensatory and Elementary Education." *Educational Researcher* 13 (August–September): 4–13.

Chambers, Jay G., and others 1998. "What Are We Spending on Special Education in the United States?" Brief 8. Palo Alto: Center for Special Education Finance (February).

Core Knowledge Foundation. 1998. *Core Knowledge Preschool Sequence: Content and Skill Guidelines for Children Ages Three–Five.* Charlottesville, Va.

Edison Project. 1999. "Second Annual Report on School Performance." New York (March).

Forgione, Pascal D. Jr. n.d. "New Benchmarks for Mathematics and Science: Implications of the Third International Math and Science Study." U.S. Department of Education, National Center for Education Statistics.

Goldhaber, Dan D., and Dominic J. Brewer. 1997. "Evaluating the Effect of Teacher Degree Level on Educational Performance." *Developments in School Finance 1996,* 197–210, edited by William J. Fowler, Jr. NCES 97-535. U.S. Department of Education.

Hanushek, Eric A. 1998. "Improving Student Achievement: Is Reducing Class Size the Answer?" Policy Briefing. Washington: Progressive Policy Institute (June).

Hill, Paul. 1999. "Getting It Right the Eighth Time: Reinventing the Federal Role." In *New Directions: Federal Education Policy in the Twenty-First Century*, edited by Marci Kanstoroom and Chester E. Finn Jr., 147–70. Washington: Thomas B. Fordham Foundation.

Hill, Paul T., Lawrence C. Pierce, and James W. Guthrie. 1997. *Reinventing Public Education: How Contracting Can Transform America's Schools*. University of Chicago Press.

Hoxby, Caroline M. 1998. "Comment." In *Brookings Papers on Education Policy, 1998*, edited by Diane Ravitch, 376–83. Brookings.

Ingersoll, Richard M. 1999. "The Problem of Underqualified Teachers in American Secondary Schools." *Educational Researcher* 28 (March): 26–37.

Joint Center for Political and Economic Studies. 1997. "1997 National Opinion Poll: Education." Washington.

———. "1998 National Opinion Poll: Education." Washington.

Keegan, Lisa Graham. 1999. "Arizona: Back Off, Washington." In *New Directions: Federal Education Policy in the Twenty-First Century*, edited by Marci Kanstoroom and Chester E. Finn Jr., 121–26. Washington: Thomas B. Fordham Foundation.

Lyon, G. Reid. 1996. "Learning Disabilities." *Future of Children* 6 (Spring): 54–76.

McRobbie, Joan. 1997. "Class Size Reduction: A One-Year Status Check." San Francisco: West Ed (http://www.wested.org/policy/pubs/leadership.htm [May 5, 1999]).

Merrow, John. 1996. "What's So Special about Special Education?" *Education Week* 15 (May 8): 48–49.

Mosteller, Frederick, Richard J. Light, and Jason A. Sachs. 1996. "Sustained Inquiry in Education: Lessons from Skill Grouping and Class Size." *Harvard Educational Review* 66 (Winter): 797–842.

Mullis, Ina V.S., and others. 1998. *Mathematics and Science Achievement in the Final Year of Secondary School: IEA's Third International Mathematics and Science Study (TIMSS)*. Chestnut Hill, Mass.: TIMSS International Study Center (February).

Musick, Mark D. 1996. "Setting Education Standards High Enough." Atlanta: Southern Regional Education Board.

National Center for Education Statistics (NCES) 1996a. *NAEP 1994 U.S. History Report Card: Findings from the National Assessment of Educational Progress*. NCES 96-085. U.S. Department of Education.

———. 1996b. *Remedial Education at Higher Education Institutions in Fall 1995*. NCES 97-584. U.S. Department of Education.

———. 1997a. *America's Teachers: Profile of a Profession, 1993–94*. NCES 97-460. U.S. Department of Education.

———. 1997b. *Dropout Rates in the United States: 1995*. NCES 97-473. U.S. Department of Education.

————. 1997c. *NAEP 1996 Mathematics Report Card for the Nation and the States: Findings from the National Assessment of Educational Progress.* NCES 97-488. U.S. Department of Education.

————. 1997d. *NAEP 1996 Science: Report Card for the Nation and the States.* NCES 97-497. U.S. Department of Education.

————. 1998. *The 1994 High School Transcript Study Tabulations: Comparative Data on Credits Earned and Demographics for 1994, 1990, 1987, and 1982 High School Graduates.* Rev. NCES 98-532. U.S. Department of Education.

————. 1999a. *NAEP 1998 Reading Report Card for the Nation.* NCES 1999-459. U.S. Department of Education.

————. 1999b. *Teacher Quality: A Report on the Preparation and Qualifications of Public School Teachers.* NCES 1999-080. U.S. Department of Education.

National Commission on Excellence in Education. 1983. *A Nation at Risk: The Imperative of Educational Reform.*

National Commission on Teaching and America's Future. 1996. *What Matters Most: Teaching for America's Future.* New York (September).

National School Boards Association. 1995. "Recommendations to Improve the Individuals with Disabilities Education Act." Washington.

New York City Board of Education. 1994. "Educational Progress of Students in Bilingual and ESL Programs: A Longitudinal Study, 1990–1994."

Organization for Economic Cooperation and Development. 1992. *Education at a Glance: OECD Indicators: 1992.* Paris.

Ravitch, Diane. 1983. *The Troubled Crusade: American Education, 1945–1980.* Basic Books.

————. 1995. *National Standards in American Education: A Citizen's Guide.* Brookings.

————. 1998. "The Controversy over the National History Standards." Cambridge, Mass.: American Academy of Arts and Sciences.

Richardson, Gail, and Elisabeth Marx. 1989. *A Welcome for Every Child: How France Achieves Quality in Child Care: Practical Ideas for the United States.* New York: French-American Foundation.

Rose, Lowell, and Alec M. Gallup. 1998. "The 30th Annual Phi Delta Kappa/Gallup Poll of the Public's Attitudes toward the Public Schools." *Phi Delta Kappan* 80 (September): 41–56.

Rothstein, Richard. 1997. "Where's the Money Going?: Changes in the Level and Composition of Education Spending, 1991–96." Economic Policy Institute. Washington.

Schroeder, Jon. 1997. "Defining a Proper Federal Role in Support of Charter Schools," Policy Briefing. Progressive Policy Institute. Washington (October).

Senate Committee on Labor and Public Welfare, Special Subcommittee on Bilingual Education. 1967. *Bilingual Education,* 90th Cong. 1 sess. Government Printing Office.

Shanker, Albert. 1988. "Restructuring Our Schools." *Peabody Journal of Education* 65 (Spring): 88–100.

Stedman, Lawrence C. 1998. "An Assessment of the Contemporary Debate over U.S. Achievement." In *Brookings Papers on Education Policy, 1998,* edited by Diane Ravitch, 53–85. Brookings.

U.S. Department of Education. 1998. "Remarks as Prepared for Delivery by U.S. Secretary of Education Richard W. Riley, Press Conference on 12th Grade TIMSS Results" (February 24).

———. 1999. "Promising Results, Continuing Challenges: The Final Report of the National Assessment of Title I: Executive Summary." Prepublication copy. U.S. Department of Education.

Vinovskis, Maris A. 1997. "The Development and Effectiveness of Compensatory Education Programs: A Brief Historical Analysis of Title I and Head Start." In *Giving Better, Giving Smarter,* edited by John W. Barry and Bruno V. Manno, 169–92. Washington: National Commission on Philanthropy and Civic Renewal.

Walsh, Mark. "Educators Say Ruling Could Drain Budgets." 1999. *Education Week* (March 10): 1, 22.

Whitebook, Marcy. 1995. *Salary Improvements in Head Start: Lessons for the Early Care and Education Field.* Washington: National Center for the Early Childhood Work Force.

BRUCE KATZ 9

Beyond City Limits:
A New Metropolitan Agenda

A FTER DECADES OF ACADEMIC INTEREST but practical neglect, America's cities and suburbs are turning to metropolitan policy solutions for their joint problems. The political renascence of "metropolitanism" reflects the recognition that metropolitan areas are the true competitive units in the new economy, the realization that such complex issues as traffic congestion and air quality cross political boundaries and are immune to parochial fixes, and the coexistence of labor shortages in the suburbs and persistent unemployment in the central cities.

The primary force behind the new wave of metropolitan solutions is the relentless decentralization of economic and residential life in the United States. Every day, housing subdivisions, shopping malls, industrial clusters, and corporate offices spring up at the metropolitan fringe. As a result, rapidly developing suburbs are a major locus of population, employment growth, and wealth creation. The benefits of this economic prosperity are not shared equitably. Left behind are older communities—central cities and inner suburbs—that harbor growing

The author thanks his Brookings colleagues Kate Allen, Jennifer Bradley, Matthew Lambert, Amy Liu, Dao Nguyen, Janet Pack, and Stephan Rodiger for their assistance and input.

concentrations of the poor—particularly the minority poor. These older communities lack the fiscal capacity to grapple effectively with the consequences of these concentrations of poverty—joblessness, family fragmentation, and failing schools. The costs of sprawl, however, extend beyond fiscal disparities and racial and social separation. All families living in a region are affected as traffic congestion worsens, open space and farmland vanish, and a sense of community disappears.

Politicians, policymakers, community activists, and others are beginning to recognize that individual local governments cannot by themselves solve the problems that sprawling development creates. And, just as important, they are also coming to understand that governments are partly responsible for these problematic patterns. This realization is causing governments at all levels to change the rules governing development and to create what I call a metropolitan agenda, which brings disparate jurisdictions together to curb sprawl and promote reinvestment in urbanized areas.

The Patterns of Metropolitan Growth

American metropolitan areas are getting larger, and less dense, as people and businesses move to once open land that was used for orchards, farms, and pasture. Between 1970 and 1990, for example, the populations of the Los Angeles and Chicago metropolitan areas grew 45 percent and 4 percent, respectively, but paved or developed land expanded by 300 percent and 46 percent, respectively.[1] Although Pittsburgh's metropolitan area population fell 9 percent, land used for urban purposes grew by 30 percent.

Suburban growth causes this decline in density. In 1990 suburbs accounted for almost 70 percent of the national metropolitan population, and they are gaining population twice as fast as central cities (9.6 percent versus 4.2 percent between 1990 and 1997).[2] Census data reveal that from 1980 to 1997, twenty-three of the largest twenty-five central cities in 1980 either declined while their surrounding metro-

1. Diamond and Noonan (1996, p. 4, fig. 3).
2. Rusk (1998, p. 14); U.S. Department of Housing and Urban Development (1998, p. 8).

politan areas grew or grew more slowly than did their surrounding metropolitan areas.[3]

In principle, rapid suburban growth could be good news for central cities. In practice, central cities have lost disproportionate numbers of middle- and upper-income households that form the backbone of economically strong communities. From 1989 to 1996, 7.4 million upper- and middle-income households left cities for suburbs while only 3.5 million moved from suburb to city.[4] Central cities have increasingly become home to those who made disproportionate use of welfare, subsidized medical assistance, and other social services. The proportion of central city population with incomes below official poverty thresholds has risen from 14.2 percent in 1970 to 19.6 percent in 1996.[5] And, as explained more fully below, the concentration of the *very* poor in cities has increased even further.

Jobs, too, are moving from city to suburb and often to the outer suburbs. As University of North Carolina Professor John Kasarda has concluded:

> Examination of overall national trends in the suburbanization of employment since 1970 shows that metropolitan employment balance for combined industries shifted to the suburbs during the mid-1970s and has been deconcentrating at a rate of approximately 1 percent per year. Manufacturing employment is now over 70 percent suburban; that of wholesaling and retailing is just under 70 percent. Even the last bastion of central-city employment dominance—business services— succumbed to the powerful suburban pull, with suburban office employment surpassing the central cities during the mid-1980s.[6]

A study of seven Ohio metropolitan areas illustrates this trend. From 1994 to 1997, the state's seven major central business districts experienced a net increase of only 636 jobs. The net increase in their suburbs, by contrast, was 186,410 jobs.[7] The city of Atlanta had 40 percent

---

3. Based on analysis by the Brookings Institution Center on Urban and Metropolitan Policy.

4. Kasarda and others (1997, pp. 341–42).

5. U.S. Department of Housing and Urban Development (1997, p. 5; 1998, p. 8).

6. Kasarda (1995, p. 235).

7. Hill and Brennan (1998, table 3).

of all metropolitan area jobs in 1980 but only 24 percent in 1996.[8] Similarly, in the Washington, D.C., metropolitan area, the District of Columbia went from having 33.1 percent of the region's jobs in 1990 to 24.3 percent in 1998, while the share of area jobs in the outer suburbs grew from 38.7 percent to 50.1 percent.[9] This shift would not be a problem if fiscal obligations moved along with business, population, and jobs. Unfortunately, the tax base has moved, but the fiscal obligations have not. Central cities have become disproportionately responsible for dependent populations and for large obligations to support schools, police, welfare, and social services in excess of their capacity to pay for them.

The Dark Side of Metropolitan Growth

Suburbs grow because people like them. Residents like the large houses, spacious lawns and yards, comparatively good schools, and sense of personal safety. Businesses benefit from proximity to the suburban labor pool and from cheaper land and lower taxes and construction costs than cities offer. In the process of enjoying these benefits, however, suburban households and businesses generate costs or escape obligations that others have to pay. The result is more sprawl and dispersion and higher social costs than would occur if the costs of sprawl were correctly assigned. Even suburbanites are finding that sprawl adversely affects the quality of their own lives, as traffic congestion worsens, infrastructure costs rise, and the environment deteriorates. The growing recognition of these costs, which are borne by both urban and suburban households and businesses, explains an emerging interest in changing the policies that facilitate these growth patterns.

Central Cities

Urban poverty has worsened over the past three decades. The urban poverty rate rose from 14.2 percent to 19.6 percent between 1970 and 1996. To make matters worse, the geographical concentration

8. Sawicki (1998, p. 3).
9. Rubin and Turner (1998).

and social isolation of poor people—especially poor minorities—also worsened. Between 1970 and 1990, the population of neighborhoods where 40 percent or more of residents are poor nearly doubled from 4.1 million to 8 million. Seventy-seven percent of the residents of high-poverty neighborhoods are either African-American or Hispanic.[10]

High-poverty neighborhoods in the 1990s differ from those of the 1950s and 1960s. In Chicago's Bronzeville neighborhoods, for example, 69 percent of males 14 and over worked in a typical week in 1950. By 1990, only 37 percent of males 16 and over—a slightly older group that should have a somewhat higher employment rate—held jobs in a typical week. William Julius Wilson has described poor urban neighborhoods as places "in which a substantial majority of individual adults are either unemployed or have dropped out of the labor force altogether."[11]

Many scholars believe that the movement to the suburbs of simple service and retail jobs has placed central city residents with little education and few skills at a disadvantage. The idea that there is a mismatch between the homes of low-skilled workers and the sites of entry level jobs—the "spatial-mismatch hypothesis"—has been the subject of scholarly debate for thirty years. Most recent inquiries into the hypothesis support it. One overview of the literature concluded, "There seems to be more consensus on the validity of this idea than there was in the past. The evidence is particularly compelling in the case of welfare recipients, who often live in high-poverty neighborhoods of central cities and older suburbs."[12] The inability of residents to gain access to jobs—which certainly depends on many factors besides transportation—undermines many central city neighborhoods.[13]

10. Jargowsky (1997, pp. 30, 38).

11. Wilson (1996, pp. 19–20). For a full discussion of the so-called neighborhood effects of concentrated poverty, see Ellen and Turner (1997) and Brooks-Gunn, Duncan, and Aber (1997).

12. Pugh (1998). Pugh's review of the spatial mismatch literature addressed the controversy and noted that most of the studies that argued that spatial mismatch was a myth relied on data from the 1970s or earlier. See also Colton, Verma, and Guo (1996); Colton, Leete, and Bania (1997); Leete and Bania (1995a , 1995b); Rich and Coughlin (1998); Weir (1998).

13. For more discussion see Wilson (1996).

With so many of the low-skilled, low-paying entry level jobs being created in suburban airport complexes, shopping malls, and office facilities, many government and community leaders are emphasizing "access to jobs" initiatives to help people move from welfare to work. The reasons are simple: "Only one in 20 welfare recipients owns a car and mass transit does not provide adequate or timely connections for those living in the city and traveling out to suburban jobs. The public transit system currently does not well serve those with nontraditional work hours or parents who require day care in order to work."[14]

Finally, the high concentration of poverty in cities means that people and businesses that remain in cities face higher tax rates than do suburbanites. As taxes rise, those who are most vulnerable to high taxes— businesses and relatively well-paid individuals—face incentives to escape these burdens by leaving the city. Thus, the growing spatial isolation of the urban poor and the continued exodus of middle-class families and low-skilled jobs to the outer fringes of metropolitan areas cause a cycle of urban decline.[15]

The Challenges Facing Metropolitan Communities

Complaints about urban life are as old as the cities. But suburbanites are also becoming upset about the conditions they face—congested roads, overcrowded schools, deteriorating air and water quality, and the

14. U.S. Department of Housing and Urban Development (1997, p. 53).

15. Suburbs that were built just after World War II and that have the bad luck to be poorly located face the same challenges as cities do—an aging housing inventory, high levels of poverty, poor schools, and deteriorating commercial districts. Phillips and Lucy's study of twenty-four urbanized areas found that in twenty of these metropolitan areas median family income in older suburbs fell relative to the metropolitanwide median between 1960 and 1990 (Phillips and Lucy, 1996, p. 16). For more data on inner suburban changes and stresses, see *Suburban Racial Change*, papers from a conference sponsored by the Civil Rights Project at Harvard University and the Taubman Center on State and Local Government at Kennedy School of Government, 1998. See also Orfield (1997).

loss of open space. Suburbanites seem to feel, "This is not what we moved out here for."

New empirical research confirms the popular perception. Evidence is accumulating that traffic congestion is worsening as minor suburban roadways have become conduits for thousands of people commuting to and from new office complexes, malls, and factories. Sprawl increases such congestion by raising the number and length of automobile trips.[16] Between 1982 and 1994 urban roadway congestion rose more than 22 percent. Traffic congestion worsened in forty-eight major metropolitan areas between 1982 and 1994. The resultant travel delay and excess fuel consumption imposed excess costs of $53 billion in 1994 in the fifty largest metropolitan areas, a 4 percent increase from 1993.[17]

Sprawl-style development also raises the costs of building new and maintaining existing infrastructure. Roads and utilities for compact developments cost 75 and 80 percent, respectively, of what sprawl development costs. Estimates show that over a twenty-year period sprawl would cost the state of New Jersey $1.4 billion more than compact growth would have cost.[18]

Sprawl also jeopardizes environmentally sensitive lands, such as wetlands, estuaries, and flood plains. One study estimated that sprawl-style development in New Jersey, Kentucky, and Michigan would consume almost one-fifth more sensitive environmental land than more compact types of development. Other studies of Orlando, San Diego, the San Francisco Bay area, and the Chesapeake Bay region of Maryland have reached similar conclusions.[19] In Western states, sprawl is overtaxing the region's water supply.[20]

16. Burchell and others (1998, pp. 62–63).

17. Schrank and Lomax (1997, pp. 31, 38). Congestion levels are determined using an index that "combines daily vehicle-kilometers of travel per lane-kilometer for freeways and principal arterial street systems in a ratio comparing the existing value to values identified with congested conditions."

18. Burchell and others (1998, p. 136).

19. Burchell and others (1998, pp. 78–79).

20. Jonathan Weil and Patrick Barta, "Water War May Affect City's Spread," *Wall Street Journal*, May 6, 1998, p. T1; "Phoenix: Have Water, Will Grow." *Economist*, September 2, 1995, pp. 25–26.

In short, sprawl imposes unnecessary costs not only on the residents and governments of central cities and inner suburbs but also on those of outer suburbs.

The Impact of Federal and State Policies on Patterns of Metropolitan Growth

While market forces and individual preferences have contributed to urban decline and suburban growth, government subsidies and policies have reinforced these tendencies. The economic forces include falling transportation and information costs and a decline in the weight of typical industrial and consumer goods. As a result, location close to rivers and railroad hubs is of diminishing economic significance. Businesses and individuals have also fled the failing schools, street crime, bloated bureaucracies, and inadequate services that characterize too many cities.

Government in the Service of Sprawl

Government policies have reinforced the economic trends that initiated suburban growth. Major federal and state spending programs, tax incentives, and regulations have also worked to the disadvantage of cities, facilitating the migration of people and jobs to the outer metropolitan fringe and reinforcing the concentration of poverty in the older core.

TRANSPORTATION POLICIES. Construction of the interstate highway system encouraged suburban development by enabling people and businesses to locate miles from urban centers but still benefit from metropolitan life. Even within metropolitan areas, transportation spending, especially highway spending, has favored suburbs in general and suburbs with large employment concentrations in particular. For example, between 1986 and 1995, per capita expenditures on highways and mass transit in the Greater Philadelphia region from state and federal sources were 47 percent higher in the suburbs than in the central

21. Voith (1998, pp. 4–5).

city.[21] One study reports that this difference in transportation expenditures reduced city employment by 40,000 jobs and was likely to have increased the concentration of higher-income families in the suburbs and lower-income families in the city.[22]

The Intermodal Surface Transportation Efficiency Act (ISTEA)—the 1991 legislation reauthorizing the nation's basic transportation law—first permitted state and local authorities to use available funds not only for road expansion but also for mass transit, other efforts to reduce congestion, and measures to improve air quality. In addition, ISTEA gave metropolitan planning organizations the responsibility to devise regional transportation strategies and some ability to carry them out. Since 1991, however, few states have taken much advantage of their new flexibility and powers. Of flexible funds spent on highways, states in 1996–97 spent 41 percent on reconstruction and repair of existing roads and 59 percent on new construction.[23] From 1992 through 1997, they used only 5 percent ($3.6 billion) of total flexible funds, a $71.3 billion pool, for transit purposes.[24]

Many factors may explain the failure of state and local authorities to use the flexibility granted to them, but inconsistent federal regulations and state laws impede transit projects and other alternative transportation strategies. Federal law, for example, requires a 20 percent local match for most transportation projects. Yet constitutions in nineteen states—including high-growth states like California, Florida, Georgia, and Texas—have restrictions on the use of the state gasoline tax. For example, Georgia requires that the gasoline tax be spent exclusively on roads and bridges.[25] Transit and alternative projects, therefore, must compete for state general revenues with other local nontransportation programs, while highways can tap into gasoline taxes. In addition, a crazy quilt of small, overlapping highway, transit, and planning agencies in many metropolitan areas makes intergovernmental

22. Voith (1998, pp. 19–20).

23. See table 5 in Surface Transportation Policy Project, "Potholes and Politics 1998: The Money's There but the Roads Are a Mess: What's Going On?" Washington (November) (www.transact.org [May 14, 1999]).

24. U.S. Department of Transportation (1998, p. 57).

25. Edward Walsh, "Highway Bill Could Help, Hurt Atlanta," *Washington Post*, April 12, 1998, p. A4.

coordination almost impossible; in many metropolitan areas, central cities and inner suburbs are underrepresented in metropolitan transportation decisionmaking.[26]

Recent events promise more suburban road construction that will continue to help drain population and business from core cities and do little to relieve metropolitan traffic congestion. Congress in 1998 reauthorized the nation's basic transportation legislation, renaming it the Transportation Equity Act for the 21st Century (TEA-21), and raised authorized spending by 41 percent. While TEA-21 supporters justified the higher funding by citing the need to rebuild America's "crumbling infrastructure," many states and metropolitan areas are embarking on expensive road-building projects in the outer suburbs — a $1.8 billion fourth beltway around Houston; a multistage beltway project in Austin, Texas, the first stage of which will cost $1 billion; and the Route 202 Corridor project, which will function as an outer ring road in suburban Philadelphia. These projects are likely to further undermine older, established urban economies and accelerate the decline of inner suburbs.

HOMEOWNERSHIP POLICIES. Federal and state tax laws powerfully influence where people live and businesses locate. The deductibility under state and federal income taxes for mortgage interest and property taxes and various other tax provisions that promote homeownership encourage increased housing consumption. These provisions, which lowered federal revenues $58 billion in 1998, appear spatially neutral, as high-rise condominiums in central cities are just as eligible for these tax breaks as suburban single-family houses. In practice, however, they favor suburban communities, particularly those with higher-income residents, for three reasons.

First, tax breaks matter most to those who are in upper tax brackets and matter least to those whose income is so low that they owe no tax at all. The value of tax deductions is greatest to people who face the highest tax rates and who itemize deductions. One hundred dollars of deductions lowers taxes $39.60 for someone in the 39.6 percent bracket, only $15 for someone in the 15 percent bracket, and not at all for some-

26. Benjamin, Kincaid, and McDowell (1994); Lewis and Sprague (1997).

one who owes no tax or who takes the standard deduction. The approximately 10 percent of taxpayers with annual incomes greater than $100,000 receive 44 percent of the benefits of the mortgage interest deduction; 90 percent of the benefits of the deduction go to homeowners with incomes above $40,000 a year.[27] Second, upper-income households consume more and newer goods of all kinds than do low-income households, and this pattern extends to housing. But new housing is scarce in older cities and abundant in suburbs. Third, tax incentives apply to the combination of buildings and land that constitute the owner-occupied house. Suburbs, with their unbuilt lots, are a far better place than cities, with their dense housing, to consume the services of land. The interaction of these three factors means that tax incentives have favored the movement of upper-income households to the suburbs. As Joseph Gyourko and Richard Voith point out, "(1) higher-income households purchase more expensive houses; (2) higher-income households have higher marginal tax rates; and (3) lower-income households seldom find it advantageous to use itemized deductions, which eliminates the possibility of receiving the subsidy."[28] Thus, one study put forth a preliminary estimate that about three-quarters of the benefits of the mortgage interest and property tax deductions accrue to suburban land markets.[29]

In theory, these homeowner tax benefits do more than just reflect the metropolitan growth patterns described in this chapter. These subsidies may fundamentally shape the decentralization of residential life in the United States. By lowering housing costs, they encourage people to "over consume" housing, which means buying larger homes on larger lots—and, as noted, the size of the tax breaks rises with income.[30] Gyourko and Voith summarize these effects: "The decentralized, stratified urban form of America's cities could be the result of people reacting to a price system profoundly affected by tax policy as opposed to a reflection of intrinsic American preferences for low density, stratified communities."[31]

27. Green and Reschovsky (1997, p. 1, table 2, p. 16); see also Joint Center for Housing Studies of Harvard University (1999); Green and Vandell (1996).
28. Gyourko and Voith (1997, p. 7).
29. Gyourko and Voith (1997, table 6).
30. U.S. Office of Technology Assessment (1995, p. 201).
31. Gyourko and Voith (1997, p. 10).

LAND USE POLICIES. Land use policies also facilitate migration of people and jobs to the suburbs. Most states delegate planning, zoning, subdivision, and other decisions to counties, municipalities, and other local jurisdictions, where dozens of local governmental entities independently regulate growth and development. Although admittedly extreme, the situation in the Chicago metropolitan area is revealing. Serving almost 7.7 million people are 1,300 units of government, including 558 single-purpose governments, 306 school districts, 270 municipalities, and 113 townships.[32] With the exception of Portland, Oregon, and Minneapolis/St. Paul, Minnesota, American metro areas have no coordinated planning or regulation of land use.

In general, local governments are free to make growth decisions—for example, on whether to build a new retail mall or office complex—without any consideration of how those decisions affect other jurisdictions in the metropolitan area and without having to offer compensation for any costs these developments impose on other jurisdictions. Each local government reaps the exclusive revenue benefit of development within its boundaries and has sole responsibility for many public services for its citizens. In the contest to attract new businesses and real estate developments, those governments with heavy obligations, such as cities and inner suburbs, are not as well positioned as new suburbs to offer tax abatements and discounted services.

Other Policies

The policies identified above—transportation spending, homeownership tax expenditures, state land use and governance—do not reflect the total federal and state government influence on metropolitan growth patterns. At the federal level, for example, major environmental policies have made the redevelopment of urban land prohibitively expensive and cumbersome.[33] The Small Business Administration's development program loans have gone more often to higher-income, farther-out areas than to low-income, urban core neighborhoods.[34]

32. Johnson (1999, pp. 3, 46).
33. See *Cityscape* 2 (September 1996) for a collection of articles on environmental policy and urban redevelopment.
34. Immergluck and Mullen (1998). For a discussion of other policies that have shaped urban form, see Nivola (1999).

Fueling the Rise in Concentrated Poverty

Many federal programs—cash assistance, food stamps, and medical assistance, for example—alleviate the privations of poverty. However, federal housing policies have contributed to the geographical concentration of poverty within particular neighborhoods in city cores, which frequently has detrimental effects on poor families. Until recently, federal public housing policies catered almost exclusively to the very poor by housing them in special units concentrated in isolated neighborhoods. From the late 1970s until 1995, for example, the rules governing admission to public and assisted housing gave first priority to the poorest households, who jumped ahead of less poor households who may have been on the waiting list for vacant units for months or years. The unsurprising result was that the average income of households in public housing fell sharply—from 35 percent of area median income in 1980 to less than 17 percent in the mid-1990s.[35] Projects that once were home to families of varying economic status and many full-time earners turned into pits of poverty, crime, and unemployment.

The U.S. Department of Housing and Urban Development (HUD) recently concluded that the combination of federal admission rules and the physical siting of public housing developments has been disastrous for residents and neighborhoods, leading to "the physical, social and racial isolation of public housing in many cities, cutting off residents from jobs, basic services, and a wide range of social contacts."[36] More than half (close to 54 percent) of public housing residents live in high-poverty neighborhoods—defined by HUD as greater than 30 percent poor. Only 7.5 percent live in low-poverty neighborhoods, where fewer than 10 percent of residents are poor.[37]

Even the federal housing voucher program has failed to offset other forces leading to residential segregation. Nonwhite recipients of vouchers are much more likely than whites to live in high-poverty, mostly nonwhite neighborhoods.[38] While personal preferences of aided households and racism on the part of potential landlords and neighbors play a large part in these patterns, fragmented governance hinders the ability

35. U.S. Department of Housing and Urban Development (1996a, p. 5).
36. U.S. Department of Housing and Urban Development (1996a, p. 5).
37. Turner (1998, p. 378).
38. Turner (1998, p. 381).

of central city residents to exercise choice in the metropolitan market-place because voucher recipients cannot easily learn about housing opportunities in other jurisdictions. In the Detroit metropolitan area, for example, thirty-one public housing agencies administer separate Section 8 programs.[39]

Policies of state and local governments contribute directly to sustaining racially segregated living patterns. Many suburban communities, under the aegis of state law, establish zoning regulations, such as large lot requirements for single-family houses or tight limits on land zoned for multifamily housing, that have the practical effect of barring low-income households. In addition, building codes often raise the price of new housing well beyond the reach of low-income families.[40] Though not explicitly discriminatory, such policies have the effect of confining low- and moderate-income families to decaying inner-city and inner suburban neighborhoods and denying them access to the same good schools, good services, and good jobs that financially comfortable suburban families enjoy.

The Rise of Metropolitan Politics

An emerging awareness of the costs of sprawl—and the role of government policies in facilitating sprawl—is transforming metropolitan area politics around the country. Elected officials from cities and inner suburbs; downtown corporate, philanthropic, and civic interests; minority and low-income community representatives; environmentalists; slow-growth advocates in the new suburbs; farmers and rural activists; and religious leaders all are realizing that uncoordinated suburban expansion brings needless costs. In Chicago the Commercial Club, an organization of top regional business leaders, has released the Chicago Metropolis 2020 report, an ambitious plan for meeting that area's myriad challenges in the coming decades. In Ohio elected officials from inner suburbs around Cleveland are joining forces with farm preservation constituencies to push state growth management reforms. In Maryland a coalition of environmentalists (the Chesapeake Bay Foundation), busi-

39. Hughes (1997, p.11).
40. Downs (1998, p. 9).

ness leaders (the Greater Baltimore Committee) and inner-city advocates (the Enterprise Foundation and the Citizens Housing and Planning Association) are leading statewide efforts to curb suburban sprawl and promote reinvestment in older established communities. In Missouri a coalition of eighty Protestant and Catholic churches is leading the fight to promote smarter growth in the St. Louis area.

These nascent coalitions reach past city limits and cross traditional constituency lines. The motivations behind these coalitions differ. Groups that are driven by a concern for equity and the burden of concentrated poverty that cities and inner suburbs must bear push for tax reforms that would reduce fiscal disparities among jurisdictions. Coalitions concerned about runaway growth advocate curbs on sprawl and try to direct infrastructure investment to older established areas. Both kinds of coalitions seek metropolitan collaboration to solve such cross-jurisdictional problems as transportation, environmental quality, water treatment, and work force and economic development. These reforms are mutually reinforcing. Mayors who care about tax-base equity may find common cause with no-growth advocates in the outer suburbs. Environmentalists and rural constituencies pushing to conserve open space and farmland understand that a stronger urban core is in their interest. As one would expect, the various coalitions encompass diverse interests that reflect the nature of their metropolitan areas.

The new metropolitan coalitions are making a difference on transportation and land use issues. Leaders in Chattanooga, Portland, and St. Louis are choosing to repair existing infrastructure, invest in mass transit, and preserve open space rather than to build more roads. In virtual revolt over congested roads, overcrowded schools, and loss of open space, citizens of outer suburban communities of such fast-growing metropolitan areas as northern Virginia and Seattle have pushed county governments to increase developer fees, scale back existing plans for residential growth, and buy land to preserve open space.[41] Often, how-

41. Dan Eggen, "In Outer Suburbs, Homeowners Pay the Price of Overbuilding," *Washington Post*, January 25, 1998, p.A1; Dan Eggen and Justin Blum, "Va. Counties Look to Fees to Ease Growing Pains," *Washington Post*, March 15, 1998, p. B1; Eric Pryne, "Counting the Costs of New Development," *Seattle Times*, June 7, 1998, p. A5; Cohen (1998).

ever, these coalitions find that power over land use, welfare, housing, tax policy, and local governance is exercised in state capitals and Washington, D.C.

Several states have recognized the power of a new "metropolitics" and are pursuing a variety of policies to support it. They have embraced land use reforms to manage growth at the metropolitan fringe. They have spent state funds to buy tracts of undeveloped land, thereby establishing a "no-sprawl zone." They have begun to steer infrastructure investment and other resources to older established areas. They have restructured taxes to pool resources among jurisdictions. And they have authorized new forms of metropolitan governance to handle such crossjurisdictional issues as transportation, environmental protection, waste management, cultural amenities, and economic development.

Growth Management

Since the early 1970s, eleven states—Delaware, Florida, Georgia, Maine, Maryland, New Jersey, Oregon, Rhode Island, Tennessee, Vermont, and Washington—have enacted state land use laws to direct local governments in the management of growth. Oregon has the most comprehensive growth management effort in the United States. In 1973 the state enacted the Land Conservation and Development Act to contain urban sprawl and preserve forests and farmland. The act has four main provisions: a requirement that urban growth boundaries be drawn around all cities throughout the state; a mandate for comprehensive land use planning at both the local and metropolitan level; a requirement that all city, county, and metropolitan plans be consistent with state planning goals; and authorization for a state agency, the Land Conservation and Development Commission, to enforce compliance with the consistency requirement.

Oregon's growth management framework—coupled with enlightened local leadership—has helped to steer development and investment to the central core of the Portland metropolitan region.[42] Jobs

42. In the 1960s, for example, the expressway along the Willamette River was torn down, making way for the revitalization of the downtown and waterfront. In the 1970s and 1980s, the metropolitan area scrapped road expansion projects in favor of an extensive light rail system.

in downtown Portland increased from 89,000 to 104,000 between 1980 and 1994.[43] From 1980 to 1995, 8.2 percent of the building permits issued in the Portland metropolitan area were for housing located inside the city, compared with 6.0 percent for Seattle, 3.5 percent for Chicago, 2.0 percent for Cleveland, and 0.6 percent for Detroit.[44]

Other states have followed the Oregon model to some extent. In a series of laws, starting in 1972 and most forcefully in 1985, Florida has required all cities, counties, and regions to devise land use plans consistent with a state comprehensive plan and empowered the State Department of Community Affairs to withhold state funds from local jurisdictions that are not in compliance. Unlike Oregon, Florida has not mandated the adoption of urban growth boundaries. Rather, Florida requires local jurisdictions to demonstrate that the public infrastructure and facilities, such as roads, water, and sewers are in place and adequate at the time they are needed. While these measures may have been intended to curb sprawl, these provisions "have proven difficult to implement" and, one observer believes, may have "propelled development to rural areas where road and school capacities were not a problem."[45]

Growth management will probably expand in the next few years. In 1998 Tennessee passed a law requiring counties to adopt land-use plans that designate growth boundaries for existing municipalities and set aside rural preservation and "planned growth areas." If a county does not have a land use plan in place in eighteen months, it will lose access to some state infrastructure funds, including federal highway grants.[46] Land use reforms are picking up steam in Pennsylvania, Ohio, and

---

43. Abbott (1997, p. 15). Debates continue in Portland and elsewhere over how far to extend urban growth boundaries, given rapid population growth and rapid economic expansion. Portland recently extended its growth boundary slightly and is using zoning policy to contain housing costs. Some, however, have raised serious questions about the impact of the urban growth boundary on housing affordability, and it is not clear whether Portland's efforts to date adequately address this issue.

44. Author's calculations based on data from Bureau of the Census, Manufacturing and Construction division.

45. Porter (1998, p. 4).

46. Rusk (1998, p. 14).

Michigan. Maryland and New Jersey, where growth management laws are already on the books, are expanding state intervention.

Open Space Conservation

Recently, an increasing number of local and state governments have been spending money to conserve open space. In 1998 ballot initiatives asked voters to approve bond measures or tax increases to preserve open space or acquire parks and wildlife habitats in Alabama, Arizona, Florida, Georgia, Michigan, Minnesota, New Jersey, New Mexico, Oregon, and Rhode Island. All passed except Georgia's and New Mexico's. New Jersey amended its constitution so that $98 million a year will go to open space conservation efforts. Arizona's plan will devote $20 million a year over eleven years to protect open space — although the measure also forbids statewide antisprawl measures and for that reason was opposed by many environmentalists.[47]

In the 1998 elections, voters approved 72 percent of ballot measures to preserve open space and promote conservation, entailing a commitment to spend $7.5 billion, directly or indirectly, to implement these measures. Cities and counties are also acting. In 1998, voters in Austin, Texas, approved use of a $65 million increase in water rates to buy 15,000 acres of environmentally fragile land. Dade County, Florida; Baltimore County, Maryland; Medina, Ohio; and Albany, California, are among the places where voters have agreed to bonds or higher taxes to keep some land out of the path of development.[48]

Smart Growth

Maryland and New Jersey are in the vanguard of the "smart growth" movement, which refers to state efforts to target direct spending and tax incentives to communities where infrastructure is already in place. In 1997 Maryland enacted laws to steer state road, sewer, and school monies away from farms and open spaces to "priority funding areas." Some are designated in the law — Baltimore and certain areas within

47. Myers (1999, pp. 2, 3, 9).
48. Myers (1999, pp. 1, 2). See Phyllis Myers, "Greensense Bulletin Elections 1996." (http://www.igc. apc.org/tpl/elect1996.htm [May 13,1997]). See also Jennifer Preston, "Some States Tackling Urban Sprawl with New Taxes, *New York Times*, June 9, 1998, p. A1.

the Baltimore and Washington beltways, for example. Counties may designate other areas if they meet certain guidelines. In 1998 New Jersey expanded on Maryland's approach; Governor Christine Todd Whitman ordered state agencies to give preference to projects in areas where infrastructure was already in place.

Smart growth policies do not stop development or repeal the operation of market forces; they simply control where the government chooses to spend its resources. According to Maryland's state planning director, smart growth policies repeal an "insidious form of entitlement—the idea that state government has an open-ended obligation, regardless of where you choose to build a house or open a business, to be there to build roads, schools, sewers."[49]

In the state debates over sprawl, smart growth policies may ultimately prove to be smarter politics than efforts to manage growth through regulatory restrictions. They appeal to the natural desire of state legislators to maximize the resources their jurisdictions receive while avoiding the enactment of regulatory prohibitions on the use of property. They therefore blunt the "property rights" attacks on growth management legislation, which are generally waged by real estate interests and their allies.

Metropolitan Resource Pooling

Some communities have taken steps to reduce fiscal disparities arising from the uneven distribution of taxable real property among jurisdictions. Such disparities result from fragmented governance and would not exist if a single government served an entire metropolitan area. The nation's most advanced example of resource pooling exists in the Minneapolis/St. Paul metropolitan area. Since the 1970s, Minnesota's fiscal disparities law has allocated 40 percent of the increment to property tax revenues arising from the area's commercial and industrial development to a metropolitan tax-base pool. Funds in the pool— more than $367 million in 1996—are then redistributed to communi-

49. Neil Pierce, "Maryland's 'Smart Growth' Law: A National Model?" National Academy of Public Administration (http://www.alliance.napawash.org/[May 24, 1999]).

50. Orfield (1997, pp. 143–44, 65). Net commercial tax capacity is defined as the revenue-producing power, at a metropolitan average tax rate, of the commercial property tax value in a given area.

ties in inverse proportion to net commercial tax capacity.[50] Such redistribution makes economic sense since neighboring jurisdictions generally have to deal with such negative spillover effects of development as increased congestion but receive no tax benefit.

The Minnesota approach narrows, but does not eliminate, fiscal disparities, and it does not guarantee that jurisdictions with the highest expenditure needs (and highest poverty burden) receive funds from the regional pool. Growing suburbs continue to have 25-30 percent more tax base per household than do central cities and inner suburbs.[51] Despite such difficulties, interest in metropolitan resource pooling has increased markedly over the past few years. In Baltimore, for example, various corporate, civic, and community organizations are now exploring how resource pooling would apply.[52]

Metropolitan Governance

States are extending metropolitan governance over government activities that naturally cross jurisdictional lines and benefit residents of an entire region, including transportation, land use planning, and economic development. The most ambitious efforts are under way in Oregon and Minnesota.[53] These states have created multipurpose regional entities in Portland and the Twin Cities to carry out certain operational and planning functions. In 1978 Oregon created the Greater Portland Metropolitan Service District, an elected body that oversees regional transportation and land use planning, including the development and preservation of the urban growth boundary. It also operates the mass transit system, various parks, and cultural facilities. In the early 1990s, Minnesota placed all regional sewer, transit, and land use planning in the Twin Cities area under a single entity, the Metropolitan Council. The state's action transformed a planning

51. Orfield (1997, p. 65); see also Luce (Forthcoming).

52. Much of the credit for interest in tax-base sharing goes to Minnesota State Rep. Myron Orfield, who has mapped demographic, market, and fiscal disparity trends in fourteen metropolitan areas. See also "Regionalism That Works: Tax-Sharing Makes Sense," *Baltimore Sun*, January 8, 1998, p. 20A.

53. The current state efforts are more modest than the consolidation of city and county governments that took place in the 1960s and 1970s.

agency with a $40 million budget into a regional authority with a $600 million annual budget. Legislation making the Metropolitan Council an independent, accountable elected group passed the state legislature in 1997 but was vetoed by the governor.[54]

In other states, the new wave of metropolitan governance involves various activities: the creation of special entities to administer such services as transportation, solid waste disposal, and water treatment that operate on a regional level; regional funding of such services as arts and culture; and regional coordination of such activities as attracting businesses that benefit residents of the entire area.[55] The federal government has mandated metropolitan governance on transportation and clean air policies.

Three lessons emerge from these state-level metropolitan efforts. First, the composition of metropolitan coalitions and the nature of policies vary from state to state. States with a single major metropolitan area might choose to fashion a special solution for that place, while a state with several metropolitan areas may have the more difficult task of designing statewide laws. Motivations also differ. Voters and legislators in Maryland and Oregon are concerned about environmental health; in Michigan about loss of farmland and open space; in Ohio about farm preservation, inner suburban decline, and traditional urban concerns. Future metropolitan coalitions are likely also to be designed to deal with local problems, not simply to mirror solutions developed and implemented elsewhere.

Second, various policies should be mutually consistent and reinforcing. The successes in New Jersey and Maryland were logical extensions of existing state growth management laws. Similarly, growth management and tax-base sharing are alternative means to achieving greater equity between central city and inner suburban jurisdictions and booming outer suburbs.

54. Orfield (1998, p. 34).
55. In 1993, for example, Pennsylvania authorized the creation of a regional asset district in Allegheny County (the home of Pittsburgh). The district uses funds raised from a countywide sales tax to support cultural assets in the region (for example, parks, libraries, and the zoo). Other metropolitan areas have long had mechanisms for metropolitan collaboration, although their efficacy has varied greatly. See Hollis (1998); Summers (1997).

Third, metropolitan coalitions everywhere confront powerful political forces. The successes in Oregon and Minnesota did not come easily and face continual challenges and scrutiny because policies to shape growth create winners and losers, even where the overall gain to the metropolitan area is demonstrable. Furthermore, the politics of metropolitan initiatives do not conform to traditional partisan or ideological lines. Governor Parris Glendening, a Democrat, pushed through Maryland's efforts, and Republican Governor Whitman is spearheading New Jersey's. These leaders recognize the common ground between the cities and a good portion of the suburbs on growth and development issues.

The Federal Metropolitan Agenda

States have the primary responsibility in efforts to rejuvenate metropolitan areas and reduce the costs of sprawl because they set the rules for land use, state and municipal taxes, transportation, and governance. But the federal government will also play a major part in determining the success or failure of efforts to advance the metropolitan agenda described in this chapter because many federal policies facilitate sprawl and concentrate poverty, and new policies can promote metropolitanwide coordination by states and localities.

Transportation

The federal Department of Transportation (DOT) can help curb sprawl through its administration of the Transportation Equity Act for the 21st Century (TEA-21). Without guidance from DOT, most state and metropolitan transportation bureaucracies will continue to do what they always have done—support more building beyond metropolitan areas—and are unlikely to use the authority in TEA-21 to reallocate funds to other modes of transportation and other means of dealing with congestion. The department will have an opportunity over the next few years to influence state transportation policies, as it will have to recertify every metropolitan planning organization in the country. It can use this opportunity to encourage states to balance new road building projects with infrastructure repair; to ensure that states comply with civil rights laws in their operations and investments; and to provide the public with information about state investment decisions. Recertification should be more than a rubber stamp.

The department can also assist state policymakers by providing them with assessments of the effects on a metropolitan area of large road expansion projects, including the effects on older communities. For example, if a second, or even third, metropolitan beltway—or even a large connector road to a new retail or office complex—is going to be built, the public, particularly the residents of older communities, should know what the full impact of such projects will be.

Overhaul Affordable Housing Policies

The Clinton administration has initiated efforts to overhaul federal policies, such as low-rent public housing, that have encouraged the concentration of the poor in particular urban neighborhoods. With congressional approval, the administration will demolish some 100,000 public housing units, about one-twelfth of the entire public housing stock, by 2003. These units will be replaced with smaller housing developments integrated into the larger community—and with housing vouchers that provide eligible families greater choice in the private rental market.

In 1998 Congress also enacted measures, sought by the administration, to bring more working families into public housing, deconcentrate poverty, encourage and reward work, and improve public housing management. Congress also approved the Clinton administration's request for an increase in voucher housing assistance, a reversal of appropriations policy since 1995. Congress specifically appropriated $283 million in fiscal year 1999 for 50,000 new vouchers and authorized funding for another 100,000 vouchers a year for the next two years.

Additional changes in the housing voucher program could further the goals of deconcentrating poverty and assisting low-income people in choosing where to live. The current system is administered by 3,400 local bureaucracies and makes it difficult for low-income recipients to understand, let alone exercise, their choices in a metropolitan housing market. Placing administrative responsibility for housing vouchers with public, quasi-public, or nonprofit metropolitan entities or requiring, at a minimum, all housing agencies in a metropolitan area to have the same rules would reduce duplicative administrative over-head and enhance housing choices of voucher recipients.

Other Metropolitan Policies

The federal government could take a number of actions to provide support for greater metropolitan governance. First, the federal government could require metropolitan level administration as it is doing in TEA-21. Metropolitanwide administration makes sense in areas like housing—particularly vouchers—and work force and economic development. The parochial administration of housing and labor programs hinders low-income families from connecting to economic opportunities in the larger metropolitan marketplace.[56] The fragmented governance of economic development programs does not conform to or leverage the metropolitan supplier and labor networks of the new economy.

Where metropolitan governance is impractical, the federal government could encourage crossjurisdictional collaboration. Recently, the federal government has authorized and appropriated funding for supports—transportation, job training, housing—for people moving from welfare to work. As local governments compete for scarce federal resources, the federal government could give preference to applicants that demonstrate crossjurisdictional collaboration. Preferences of this sort could also apply to block grant programs.

Furthermore, the federal government can promote cross-system, as well as crossjurisdictional, collaboration. Making welfare reform work, for example, requires close coordination among transportation, work force, and child care bureaucracies and the private and nonprofit intermediaries through which they operate at the neighborhood level. Some collaboration is happening, but, as ISTEA demonstrated, a strong push (with funding incentives) from the federal government can break down the barriers between separate bureaucracies.

But metropolitan governance efforts will not be sufficient if other federal inducements to sprawl are left in place. The federal government should, as a matter of course, provide metropolitan areas with a clear spatial analysis of how federal resources are allocated. The federal

56. Hughes (1997).

government should as a matter of course systematically examine the spatial impacts of major spending programs, tax expenditures, and regulations. Are central cities and inner suburbs treated fairly in the allocation of federal resources, particularly resources that leverage private sector investments and create wealth? If not, why not? Do federal and state regulations tilt the playing field against the redevelopment of urban land or investment in urban neighborhoods? If so, why? Answering these questions and correcting the policies that are found to have distorting effects will go far toward promoting fairer metropolitan growth patterns in the future.

National lawmakers increasingly recognize the political strength behind and substantive rationale for a federal metropolitan agenda. The administration, for example, recently proposed a range of initiatives to promote Vice President Al Gore's version of "livable communities": a land acquisition tax initiative designed to leverage $9.5 billion in state and local bonds for open space and brownfields remediation (modeled on some of the state ballot referenda that passed in 1998): a combined $90 million to support cross-jurisdictional information sharing on growth planning and crime prevention; and a $50 million request to encourage crossjurisdictional partnerships for metropolitan smart growth, reinvestment, and work force development efforts.[57] The House and Senate have also formed bipartisan task forces on metropolitan and smart growth issues and have begun to hold hearings and informal briefings on the subject. Whether these efforts will result in substantive metropolitan policies, or answers to the questions above, remains to be seen.

The Promise and the Challenge

Curbing the needless costs of sprawl and helping restore the vitality of older cities will not happen easily. Some people and businesses benefit from sprawl and enjoy the lifestyle that it allows. Deficient city schools, crime, and bad services impede urban restoration. A metropolitan approach is not an urban panacea, but it can help mayors, community

57. "Clinton-Gore Livability Agenda: Building Livable Communities for the Twenty-First Century," press release, Office of the Vice President, January 11, 1999.

groups, and civic and corporate leaders reverse decades of core city decline.

The obstacles to effective metropolitan coalitions are formidable. Governance in most metropolitan areas remains highly fragmented, which means that forums in which metropolitan conversations can easily occur are rare. The divisions of race, ethnicity, and class remain sharp. It is no accident that the early metropolitan discussions have revolved around environmental protection and infrastructure investment. Issues like helping low-income families actually live near suburban employment opportunities are still too hot to handle.

But the metropolitan agenda is the first effort in years that offers an alternative vision to development patterns that undermine cities and inner suburbs and cause serious fiscal stress and possibly environmental and social harms in outlying new suburbs. Even better, it offers a concrete plan of action for people who want to reshape American growth. It recognizes that the suburbs are not monolithic and that there is true common ground between the cities and a good portion of the suburbs on issues as diverse as transportation spending, environmental protection, and fiscal equity. It taps into a widespread feeling that our current growth patterns are just not sustainable. It holds the promise of a true urban revival, improved equity, and a sustained improvement in living standards for residents of both cities and suburbs.

References

Abbott, Carl. 1997. "The Portland Region: Where City and Suburbs Talk to Each Other—And Often Agree." *Housing Policy Debate* 8 (1): 11–51.Washington: Fannie Mae Foundation.

Benjamin, Seth B., John Kincaid, and Bruce D. McDowell. 1994. "MPOs and Weighted Voting." *Intergovernmental Perspective* 20 (Spring): 31–35.

Brooks-Gunn, Jeanne, Greg J. Duncan, and J. Lawrence Aber, eds. 1997. *Neighborhood Poverty,* vols. 1 and 2. New York: Russell Sage Foundation.

Burchell, Robert W., and others. 1998. *The Costs of Sprawl Revisited.* Report 39. Transit Cooperative Research Program. Washington: National Academy Press.

Cohen, Natalie. 1998. "Paying for Growth: Impact Fees Heat Up." *Fiscal Stress Monitor* (May) 5–7. New York: National Municipal Research.

Colton, Claudia, Nandita Verma, and Shenyang Guo. 1996. "Time Limited Welfare and the Employment Prospects of AFDC Recipients in Cuyahoga County." Baseline Technical Report. Case Western Reserve University, Center on Urban Poverty and Social Change (December).

Colton, Claudia, Laura Leete, and Neil Bania. 1997. "Housing, Transportation and Access to Suburban Jobs by Welfare Recipients in the Cleveland Area." Paper presented at the Fannie Mae Foundation Policy Research Roundtable (July).

Diamond, Henry L., and Patrick F. Noonan. 1996. "Healthy Land Makes Healthy Communities." In *Land Use in America*, edited by Henry L. Diamond and Patrick F. Noonan, 1–11. Washington: Island Press.

Downs, Anthony. 1998. "The Big Picture: How America's Cities Are Growing." *Brookings Review* 16 (Fall): 8–11.

Ellen, Ingrid Gould, and Margery Austin Turner. 1997. "Does Neighborhood Matter? Assessing Recent Evidence." *Housing Policy Debate* 8: 833–66. Washington: Fannie Mae Foundation.

Green, Richard K., and Andrew Reschovsky. 1997. "The Design of a Mortgage Interest Tax Credit," Report to the National Housing Institute (July). Orange, N.J.: National Housing Institute.

Green, Richard K., and Kerry D. Vandell. 1996. "Giving Households Credit: How Changes in the Tax Code Could Promote Homeownership." University of Wisconsin-Madison School of Business, Center for Urban Land Economics Research (August).

Gyourko, Joseph, and Anita A. Summers. 1997. "A New Strategy for Helping Cities Pay for the Poor." Policy Brief 18. Brookings (June).

Gyourko, Joseph, and Richard Voith. 1997. "Does the U.S. Tax Treatment of Housing Promote Suburbanization and Central City Decline?" Working Paper 97-13. Federal Reserve Bank of Philadelphia (September).

Hill, Edward W., and John Brennan. 1998. "Where Is the Renaissance? Employment Specialization within Ohio's Metropolitan Areas." Paper prepared for the Conference on Interdependence of Central Cities and Suburbs (September).

Hollis, Linda E. 1998. "Regionalism Today: Background, Timeliness, and Current Practice." Working Paper 658. Washington: Urban Land Institute (January).

Hughes, Mark Alan. 1997. "The Administrative Geography of Devolving Social Welfare Programs." Joint Occasional Paper 97-1. Brookings Institution Center for Public Management and the Center on Urban and Metropolitan Policy.

Immergluck, Daniel, and Erin Mullen. 1998. "The Intrametropolitan Distribution of Economic Development Financing." *Economic Development Quarterly* 12 (November): 372–84.

Jargowsky, Paul A. 1997. *Poverty and Place: Ghettos, Barrios, and the American City*. New York: Russell Sage Foundation.

Johnson, Elmer W. 1999. "Chicago Metropolis 2020: Preparing Metropolitan Chicago for the 21st Century." A project of the Commercial Club of Chicago (January).

Joint Center for Housing Studies of Harvard University. 1999. "Towards a Targeted Homeownership Tax Credit." Discussion paper prepared for the Brookings Institution Center on Urban and Metropolitan Policy (January).

Kasarda, John D. 1995. "Industrial Restructuring and the Changing Location of Jobs." In *State of the Union: America in the 1990s*, vol. 1, edited by Reynolds Farley, 215–67. New York: Russell Sage Foundation.

Kasarda, John, and others. 1997. "Central-City and Suburban Migration Patterns: Is a Turnaround on the Horizon?" *Housing Policy Debate* 8 (2): 307–58. Washington: Fannie Mae Foundation.

Leete, Laura B., and Neil Bania. 1995a. "Assessment of the Geographic Distribution and Skill Requirements of Jobs in the Cleveland-Akron Metropolitan Area." Case Western Reserve University, Center for Urban Poverty and Social Change (July).

———. 1995b. "The Impact of Welfare Reform on Local Labor Markets." Case Western Reserve University, Center for Urban Poverty and Social Change (August).

Lewis, Paul G., and Mary Sprague. 1997. "Federal Transportation Policy and the Role of Metropolitan Planning Organizations in California." San Francisco: Public Policy Institute of California (April).

Luce, Thomas. Forthcoming. "Regional Tax Base Sharing: The Twin Cities Experience." In *Local Government Tax and Land Use Policy*, edited by Helen Ladd. Washington: Edward Elgar Publishing.

———. 1999. "Liability at the Ballot Box: State and Local Referenda on Parks, Conservation, and Smarter Growth, Election Day 1998." Discussion Paper. Brookings Institution Center on Urban and Metropolitan Policy (January).

Nivola, Pietro S. 1999. *Laws of the Landscape: How Policies Shape Urban Cities in Europe and America*. Brookings.

Orfield, Myron. 1997. *Metropolitics: A Regional Agenda for Community and Stability*. Brookings.

———. "Conflict or Consensus?" *Brookings Review* 16 (Fall): 31–35.

Pack, Janet Rothenberg. 1998. "Poverty and Urban Public Expenditures." *Urban Studies* 35 (11):1995–2019.

Phillips, David L., and William H. Lucy. 1996. Report to the Center on Urban Development. "Suburban Decline Described and Interpreted, 1960 to 1990: 554 Suburbs in 24 Large Urbanized Areas." Virginia Commonwealth University, Virginia Center for Urban Development.

Porter, Douglas R. 1998. "States Managing Growth: A Status Report." Draft. Chevy Chase, Md.: Growth Management Institute.

Pugh, Margaret. 1998. "Barriers to Work: The Spatial Divide between Jobs and Welfare Recipients in Metropolitan Areas." Discussion Paper. Brookings Institution Center on Urban and Metropolitan Policy (September).

Rich, Michael, and Joseph Coughlin. 1998. "The Spatial Distribution of Economic Opportunities: Access and Accessibility Issues for Welfare in Metropolitan Atlanta." Paper presented at the ninety-fourth annual meeting of the Association of American Geographers. Boston (March).

Rubin, Mark, and Margery Austin Turner. 1998. "Patterns of Employment Growth in the Washington Metropolitan Area." Draft. Washington: Urban Institute and Brookings (September).

Rusk, David. 1998. "The Exploding Metropolis: Why Growth Management Makes Sense." *Brookings Review* 16 (Fall):13–16.

Sawicki, David, director, and graduate students. 1998. "Jobs — Housing Imbalance in Atlanta: Regional Consequences and Solutions. Research Paper. Georgia Institute of Technology (Winter).

Schrank, David L., and Timothy J. Lomax. 1997. *Urban Roadway Congestion — 1982 to 1994*. College Station, Tex.: Texas Transportation Institute.

Summers, Anita A. 1997. "Major Regionalization Efforts between Cities and Suburbs in the United States." Paper prepared for the Wharton Regionalization Project. University of Pennsylvania, Wharton School.

Turner, Margery Austin. 1998. "Moving Out of Poverty: Expanding Mobility and Choice through Tenant-Based Housing Assistance." *Housing Policy Debate* 9 (2):373–94. Washington: Fannie Mae Foundation.

U.S. Department of Housing and Urban Development. 1996a. "Public Housing That Works." (May).

———. 1996b. *Cityscape: A Journal of Policy Development and Research, Issues in Urban Environmental Policy* 2 (September).

———. 1997. "State of the Cities 1997."

———. 1998. "State of the Cities 1998."

U.S. Department of Transportation. Federal Transit Administration. 1998. "1997 Statistical Summaries, FTA Grant Assistance Programs." (March).

U.S. Office of Technology Assessment. 1995. *The Technological Reshaping of Metropolitan America*. Government Printing Office (September).

Voith, Richard. 1998. "Transportation Investments in the Philadelphia Metropolitan Area: Who Benefits? Who Pays? And What Are the Consequences?" Working Paper 98-7. Federal Reserve Bank of Philadelphia.

Weir, Margaret. 1998. "Big Cities Confront the New Federalism." *In Big Cities in the Welfare Transition*, edited by Alfred J. Kahn and Sheila B. Kamerman, 8–35. Columbia University School of Social Work, Cross-National Studies Research Program.

Wilson, William Julius. 1996. *When Work Disappears: The World of the New Urban Poor*. Knopf.

JOHN J. DiIULIO JR. # 10

Federal Crime Policy: Declare a Moratorium

BEFORE THE LATE 1960S, crime was rarely on the federal government's agenda. Most legal experts and judges thought that the national government had no constitutional role in crime control. The public had no expectation that Washington would, should, or could do much to combat crime. Most members of Congress behaved accordingly. Finally, many in the South feared that if the federal government started passing criminal laws, it might make a violation of civil rights a federal crime.

Over the past three decades, these barriers to an expansive federal role in crime control have fallen. Washington's role in crime grew after the late 1960s as the U. S. Supreme Court expanded its interpretation of the power to regulate interstate commerce. For example, the Consumer Credit Protection Act of 1968 made lending money at exorbitant interest rates and enforcing repayment by the threat of force a federal crime. The Supreme Court ruled that even if loan sharking was a purely local activity, it might affect interstate commerce. Congress was therefore free to regulate it. In 1993 the U.S. Advisory Commission on Intergovernmental Relations estimated that more than 3,000 activities had become federal crimes, and federal judges had hundreds of state and local criminal justice agencies, especially state prisons and local jails, responding to their orders on matters of policy, administration, and finance.[1]

Since the late 1960s crime has consistently been a top public concern, and elected leaders at both ends of Pennsylvania Avenue and in both parties have campaigned and governed accordingly. During the Johnson administration, the President's Commission on Law Enforcement and Administration of Justice declared, "Warring on poverty, inadequate housing, and unemployment, is warring on crime,"[2] and recommended more than half a dozen new federal law enforcement and prevention efforts. After defeating Hubert Humphrey in a campaign that made "law and order" a key issue, Richard Nixon appointed "law-and-order" attorneys to the Justice Department and increased federal spending on antidrug law enforcement and drug prevention. During the 1980s Congress passed at least one new crime or drug control bill every two years. For example, the sweeping Anti-Drug Abuse Act of 1988 created the Office of National Drug Control Policy (commonly known as the "drug czar"). The Crime Control Act of 1990 created new federal anticrime responsibilities or beefed up old ones against scores of criminal activities, ranging from international money laundering to selling drugs in or near local schools. The Violent Crime Control and Law Enforcement Act of 1994 expanded the list of offenses for which federal courts could prescribe the death penalty, mandated life imprisonment for federal criminals convicted of three violent offenses, and banned certain assault weapons. It also authorized $8 billion to hire 100,000 more police officers, $8 billion to build prisons for state offenders, and $9 billion for crime prevention.

Since the late 1960s state and local leaders and members of Congress from the solidly Republican South, the nation's most conservative region on crime and many social issues, have evolved from being brakes to being bulldozers on federal crime policy. Bill Clinton, the pro–death penalty governor from Arkansas who came to Washington in 1992 with a domestic policy blueprint that pronounced crime a policy domain in which "no federal role is justified," pushed hard for the Brady Handgun Violence

1. Advisory Commission on Intergovernmental Relations (1993, p. 207); and DiIulio (1990).
2. President's Commission on Law Enforcement and Administration of Justice (1967, p. 6).

Prevention Act of 1993 and the Violent Crime Control and Law Enforcement Act of 1994.[3] Speaker of the House of Representatives Newt Gingrich (Republican of Georgia) and other key members of the Southern-led 104th Congress talked devolution, but the "Taking Back Our Streets" provision of their Contract with America represented a $20 billion widening of the federal role in crime control. The crime block grants they eventually adopted expanded Washington's reach in making, administering, and financing crime policy.

In the 104th and 105th Congresses, the crime policy debate in Washington took shape largely around four Republican proposals. Three of these became law—restricting the role of federal judges in directing state prisons and local jails; increasing funding for states that adopt and enforce toughened sentencing practices in cases involving adult felons convicted of multiple violent crimes; and continuing the thirty-year-old war on drugs. A fourth—giving the federal government a major role in assisting state and local governments in responding to violent and repeat juvenile offenders—provoked three years of ideologically charged and highly partisan debate, but it failed to become law.

Public Concern Keeps the Focus on Crime

Crime is sure to stay on the federal agenda. Even as crime rates fall nationally, crime and drugs remain a top public worry. In a mid-1997 CNN–Time Magazine poll, 14 percent of respondents cited crime as "the main problem facing the country today," tied with "lack of morals, values" and ahead of those who ranked the budget deficit (10 percent), drugs (9 percent), or education (6 percent) as the main problem. "Taxes, high taxes" (3 percent) and health care (2 percent) were well behind. A mid-1998 survey by Roper Starch Worldwide reported that 30 percent of respondents in 1974 had listed "crime and lawlessness" as one of the issues that they were "personally most concerned about today." In August 1998, despite a post-1993 drop nationally of approximately 21 percent in violent criminal victimization, "crime and lawlessness" was respondents' number

---

3. Marshall and Schram (1993, pp. 250–51).

one concern (46 percent), followed by such concerns as "breakdown of the family" (36 percent) and "the quality of public education" (30 percent).[4]

Some argue that the public's continued concern about crime at a time of falling crime rates mirrors misunderstanding bred by a steady diet of journalism and media hype whose theme is "if it bleeds, it leads." Others point out that, despite the drop in crime rates, most Americans, especially minority citizens and their children living in central city neighborhoods, remain more likely to be victimized by crime today than they were decades ago when crime first became a national issue. Still others stress that whatever crime rates do, the contemporary public's concerns about crime combine two elements: doubts about how committed criminal courts really are to protecting the public; and deep discontents about being the first generation of Americans to routinely condition everyday decisions on (and to devote ever-increasing shares of disposable income to) making the places where they live, work, play, shop, or attend school relatively impervious to crime.

Theories abound about why crime has decreased. Some cite changes in policing strategies and tactics (for example, New York's quality-of-life policing initiative and the subsequent dramatic citywide drops in murder and other crime). Others highlight shifts in drug markets, especially the demise of crack cocaine on inner-city streets. Still others cite the drop in the number of young males, or improved economic conditions, or carrot-and-stick antiviolence efforts undertaken through police-probation partnerships with community and church leaders (as in Boston), or packed prisons, or even such federal crime policies as the Brady bill or "100,000 cops."

Strictly speaking, the explanation cannot be "all of the above." For example, New York–style policing is one story, but murders have also plummeted in several other big-city jurisdictions—Los Angeles, to name one—where no such policing innovations have been made, as well as in communities, such as Boston, that have followed a targeted community–based approach focused on gun-related youth violence in a few high-crime neighborhoods rather than citywide, saturation policing. Neither crack cocaine nor drug-selling, gun-toting street gangs have

---

4. *American Enterprise*, January/February 1999, p. 93, reporting data from surveys by Roper Starch Worldwide; Rand (1998).

disappeared. Such data as we now have give only highly variable and highly state-specific answers to the question of what fraction of the decrease in crime rates has been due to increased imprisonment.

Whether the public's continuing concern with crime is justified has little political significance, and what criminologists conclude about the causes of changing crime rates matters almost not at all. Federal officials will continue to respond to the public's fear of crime—real and perceived—and to the public's moral outrage against adults or juveniles who murder, rape, rob, assault, steal, and deal deadly drugs, as well as to episodes of violence that are well publicized nationally.

Anyone who doubts the public's continuing identification with this issue need only trace the federal crime policy–mongering that followed the seven well-publicized school shootings between October 1997 and April 1999. The incidents differed widely with respect to everything from the motivations of the killers to their relationships with parents. Police charged a Fayetteville, Tennessee, high school student with fatally firing on a boy who dated his ex-girlfriend. An Edinboro, Pennsylvania, eighth-grader was charged with killing his science teacher at a graduation party. A Pearl, Mississippi, sixteen-year-old was convicted of murdering his mother before shooting nine classmates, assisted, police believe, by two other boys. And so on, to the bloodbath in Littleton, Colorado, which, as of this writing, local police have only just begun to investigate, but in response to which Washington has already begun to legislate.

Whatever its origins, crime control now comprises a diverse and complex set of intergovernmental programs that would be administratively difficult for federal, state, and local justice system practitioners to curtail and politically difficult for elected leaders at all levels of government to kill, no matter how effective the programs might be in preventing or controlling crime.[5] It would be unrealistic, therefore, to call on federal lawmakers to turn back the crime policy clock and get out of the crime-fighting business. It is appropriate, however, to encourage federal lawmakers to resist, and in some areas to begin to reverse, the trend toward federalizing crime prevention and control. Congress should declare a moratorium on federal crime policy, and the White House should comply. Thirty years have passed since the first omnibus federal crime pack-

5. For an overview, see DiIulio, Smith, and Saiger (1995, chap. 19).

age. Members of the next several Congresses would be well advised to ponder the areas where, if anywhere, the federal government has a real advantage over local government in crime prevention and control. But most of all, they should stop getting out ahead and start getting back behind state and local crime policy initiatives and cease questioning the motives and morality of those whose views on crime and punishment differ from their own.

In some areas—for example, developing national data-gathering and information systems that enable federal agencies to measure criminal victimization and assist state and local justice officials—the federal government has made tremendous strides since the late 1960s but needs to do far more and far better. In other areas—for example, helping to stiffen state sentencing policies against adult violent offenders—the federal government has done some good, but it is enough. In still other areas—for example, antidrug enforcement—it initially did some good but needs to reverse field and cut back toward treatment. And in a few important areas—for example, handling juvenile criminals—the federal government, while focusing public attention on a serious crime threat, has in recent years often gone beyond promoting reasonable changes in how states keep and use juvenile crime records to mandating questionable changes in how states process and punish juvenile offenders.

Counting Crime Victims

Thanks to federal policy initiatives and the work of Justice Department survey researchers and statisticians, information on crime rates, patterns, and trends is far better than it was three decades ago. Even today, however, the federal government definitely and seriously undercounts the incidence of criminal victimization.

There are two main measures of crime in America. The Federal Bureau of Investigation compiles the "Uniform Crime Reports" (UCR) on eight crimes based on voluntary reports by local police departments. The UCR includes four violent crimes (murders and nonnegligent manslaughters, forcible rapes, robberies, and aggravated assaults) and four property crimes (burglaries, larceny thefts, motor vehicle thefts, and arson). The UCR takes no notice of drug crimes. Nor does it include any but the most serious crimes committed during a single incident. For example, if a woman is raped by someone who then steals her car, the UCR counts the rape but not the car theft. Likewise, if a criminal steals two cars and burglarizes two houses on the same night, the UCR includes only the crime deemed to be the most serious of the four-crime spree.

This procedure guarantees that even complete and accurate UCR data would undercount crime. But UCR data are neither complete nor accurate. Some of the more than 16,000 state and local law enforcement agencies have neither compiled nor reported UCR data. For example, California does not include in its UCR tally reports on the 40–60 percent of reported felony crimes that do not have fingerprint cards attached. Oakland, California, has not submitted crime data to the FBI for several years.[6] In 1998, Philadelphia's new police commissioner, John Timoney, uncovered and publicized evidence that his department had been deleting or downgrading UCR crimes for years by classifying beatings and stabbings as "hospital cases," gunpoint holdups as "threats," burglaries as "missing property," robberies as "larcenies," aggravated assaults as "simple assaults," and attempted rapes as "miscellaneous incidents."[7] Philadelphia's UCR data were so unreliable that the FBI dropped the city from the program. According to the *Philadelphia Inquirer*, however, Philadelphia was hardly the lone suspect. Incidents of deleting or downgrading of UCR data have also occurred in Atlanta, Baltimore, and New York City. And, in Boca Raton, Florida, a police "captain systematically downgraded property crimes like burglaries to vandalism and other felonies to minor infractions," single-handedly reducing Boca's UCR—calculated felony rate "by almost 11 percent in 1997."[8]

6. Alan W. Bock, "There Are Reasons to Mistrust Crime Statistics," *Orange County Register*, August 10, 1998, p. G5.

7. Michael Matza, Craig R. McCoy, and Mark Fazlollah, "Panel to Overhaul Crime Reporting: A Criminologist Will Head a Philadelphia Effort to Ensure Accuracy by Police," *Philadelphia Inquirer*, December 9, 1998, p. A1; Lawrence W. Sherman, "Needed: Better Ways to Count Crooks," *Wall Street Journal*, December 3, 1998, p. A22; John J. DiIulio Jr. and Anne Morrison Piehl, "What the Crime Statistics Don't Tell You," *Wall Street Journal*, January 8, 1997; Fox Butterfield, "As Crime Falls, Pressure Rises to Alter Data." *New York Times*, August 3, 1998, p. A1.

8. "A National Scandal" (editorial), *Philadelphia Inquirer*, November 25, 1998, p. A18.

Several efforts to improve the FBI's UCR data have been made, but none has been wholly successful. For example, several states and cities have experimented with the FBI's National Incident-Based Reporting System, or NIBRS. Under NIBRS, data are collected on forty-six specific crimes. For each crime, there are a half-dozen categories of reporting, including details about the incident, the victim, and the offender. NIBRS includes a multiple-offense option. But software bugs and administrative problems plagued NIBRS from its inception, and there is as yet no publicly announced plan for addressing the UCR's undercount of crimes reported to the police.

The other main measure of crime in America is the National Crime Victimization Survey (NCVS) of the Bureau of Justice Statistics (BJS). It is based on an annual household survey of both reported and unreported crimes, excluding murders and drug crimes. The NCVS counts four types of violent crimes (rape, robbery, aggravated assault, simple assault) and several types of property crimes (burglaries, motor vehicle thefts, thefts of other property, and vandalism). Over the years the NCVS has changed its survey methods. For example, in the early 1990s it began to use computer-assisted telephone interviewing and "short cues"—examples of specific people, places, objects, or actions that may have been associated with a victimization—to jog respondents' memories of events. In May 1995 a redesigned NCVS reported new data on criminal victimization for 1992. The old NCVS method had found that about 34 million Americans suffered criminal victimization in 1992. The new method put the crime count at 43 million, more than 25 percent higher. The new method also resulted in a 55 percent increase in the count of violent crimes in 1992—from 6.6 million violent crimes to 10.3 million.[9]

Even the redesigned NCVS, however, undercounts crime in at least three ways. It does not count crimes against children aged twelve or younger, although separate analyses by the same agency that administers the NCVS suggest that young children suffer lots of serious crime. For example, an estimated one of every six rape victims is a young child.[10]

---

9. Compare Bureau of Justice Statistics (1995, 1994).
10. Langan and Harlow (1994).

Nor does the NCVS count crimes against people in jails, hospitals, shelters, or other institutional settings that are often full of persons recently victimized by crime. Finally, the NCVS does not count serial victimization; for example, if a woman cannot recall precisely the number of times her boyfriend beat her, the survey counts just one crime. A separate but serious limitation of the NCVS is that the data cannot be disaggregated on a city-by-city basis.

The flaws of federal crime data information systems offer federal crime policymakers one way to make their mark. Given greater fiscal support, public recognition, and political backing, the chronically short-changed but highly professional BJS and the FBI crime-counters could administer more complete, timely, and jurisdiction-specific measures of crime rates, trends, and patterns and provide better assistance to state and local criminal justice agencies. A bipartisan presidential commission should examine the costs and consequences of the federal government's crime undercounts and propose methods to improve national crime measurements.

Sentencing Violent Felons

Federal efforts to strengthen state initiatives dealing with violent adult offenders and career criminals have made a demonstrable difference, but further expansion in federal fiscal support for state prisons would be hard to justify.

In 1984 Washington State adopted the nation's first truth-in-sentencing (TIS) law. It requires persons imprisoned for murder, rape, robbery, or aggravated assault to serve a substantial portion of their sentence before being released. In 1993 only five states required persons imprisoned for murder, rape, robbery, or aggravated assault to serve at least 85 percent of their sentences before being released. Provisions of the Violent Crime Control and Law Enforcement Act of 1994 (amended in 1996) offered incentive grants to states that adopted TIS laws requiring persons imprisoned for the worst violent crimes to serve at least 85 percent of their imposed sentences. In 1998 federal TIS grants were awarded to twenty-seven states and the District of Columbia. Eleven states adopted TIS laws in 1995, the year after the federal TIS incentive grant program was enacted.

According to the BJS, the average time served in prison by people imprisoned for murder, rape, robbery, or aggravated assault rose from forty-three months in 1993 (representing 47 percent of sentence) to forty-nine months in 1997 (representing 54 percent of sentence). Time served by these categories of released violent felons rose in at least thirty-eight states during that period. Nationally, at the start of 1999, nearly seven persons in ten imprisoned for murder, rape, robbery, or aggravated assault were in a state that required 85 percent of the sentence to be served. The BJS estimates that violent felons committed to prison in 1996 will serve an average of seventy-three months and that continued implementation of TIS laws will increase the average minimum prison term for murder, rape, robbery, or aggravated assault to eighty-eight months, or roughly double the average time served by persons released from prison for these violent crimes (forty-three months) in 1993.[11]

According to the NCVS, violent crime fell more than 21 percent between 1993 and 1997.[12] It is impossible to specify precisely what fraction of this decrease in violent crime is due either to increased rates of imprisonment in general or to truth in sentencing or kindred laws in particular. But two facts are inescapable: most of those in prison for violent crimes have committed multiple crimes, and imprisoning violent felons helps to cut violent crime. Incarceration of known, adjudicated, violent felons, not petty drug offenders or other categories of nonviolent convicted criminals, accounts for most of the increase in the state prison population since 1980. The BJS has documented that 62 percent of state prisoners in 1991 had been convicted of one or more violent crimes.[13] Between 1980 and 1993, the number of violent offenders behind bars in the states grew by 221,200, representing 42 percent of the total growth in state prison populations during that period.[14] State prison populations totaled 1.1 million in 1997, up from 690,000 in 1990. Violent offenders accounted for 50 percent of the total increase in state prison populations during this seven-year period, drug offenders for 19 percent, and property offenders for 16 percent.[15] From 1990 to 1996,

11. Ditton and Wilson (1999).
12. Rand (1998).
13. Beck and others (1993, p. 12).
14. Beck and Gilliard (1995, p. 11).
15. Ditton and Wilson (1999, p. 4).

new state prison commitments for violent crimes rose by about 11 percent, while new state prison commitments for drug offenses fell by nearly 4 percent.[16] In 1996 the rate of new state prison commitments per 1,000 arrests was 613 for murder, 277 for robbery, 219 for rape, and 77 for drug offenses.[17]

Even on its most aggressive day, America's criminal justice system functions like a sorting machine that routinely diverts most criminals, including violent felons, away from prison and releases even some of the most serious adjudicated violent felons to freedom. For each convicted offender in a prison or jail, approximately three convicted offenders are under probation or parole supervision.[18] More convicted felons are released than are imprisoned. In 1996, 96,300 convicted violent felons were sentenced to state prisons, but 115,300 convicted violent felons were released from state prisons.[19] Not even close to all convicted violent felons go to prison. In 1994, 43 percent of all adjudicated violent offenders with one felony conviction, 31 percent with two felony convictions, and 21 percent with three or more felony convictions were not sentenced to prison. The comparable nonimprisonment percentages for convicted violent offenders in 1992 were 47, 31, and 23, respectively.[20]

Next to murderers, rapists are more likely than any other category of convicted violent felons to be sentenced to prison. In 1994, 68 percent of adjudicated rapists with one felony conviction, 71 percent with two, and 82 percent with three or more were sentenced to prison.[21] Nevertheless, in 1994 there were 167,550 rapes (plus another 148,610 attempted rapes and 116,590 other sexual assaults) in the United States, but only 20,068 state felony convictions for rape, about 14,248 of which resulted in prison sentences—or one imprisonment for every eleven rapes.[22] From 1984 to 1993, the NCVS recorded several million rapes/sexual assaults in the United States, but on any given day in 1994, only about 234,000 convicted sex offenders remained under any form of criminal custody in the nation, 134,300 (60 percent) of them on pro-

16. Ditton and Wilson (1999, table 3).
17. Ditton and Wilson (1999, table 4).
18. Brown and others (1996).
19. Ditton and Wilson (1999, tables 3, 13).
20. Langan and Brown (1997, table 7); Langan and Graziadei (1995, table 7).
21. Langan and Brown (1997, table 7).
22. U.S. Bureau of Justice Statistics (1997, table 1); Langan and Brown (1997, table 1).

bation or parole.[23] On average, offenders released from prison for rape in 1996 served sixty-six months (52.6 percent of their sentence), up from sixty-two months (45.5 percent of their sentence) for those released from prison in 1990.[24]

Rapists sentenced to probation or discharged from prison have a lower rate of rearrest than other violent offenders, but they are about 7.5 times as likely as those convicted of other crimes to be rearrested for a new sexual assault.[25] Although rapists thus tend to specialize in sexual assault, some commit other crimes, and even household burglars sometimes behave like sexual predators. As James Q. Wilson has observed, most of the relevant research suggests that there is "not a great deal of specialization among criminals—a person arrested today for robbery might be arrested next time for burglary."[26] Nor is there a great deal of specialization among the small fraction of all felons who go to prison. Both academic studies and first-hand accounts attest that many persons imprisoned for nonviolent felony crimes have either committed one or more violent crimes in the past or plea-bargained their way to a lesser sentence for a violent or nonviolent felony—about 90 percent of all felony convictions are plea-bargained.[27]

Imprisonment has at least four potential social benefits. The first is retribution: imprisoning Peter punishes him and expresses society's desire to do justice. Second is deterrence: imprisoning Peter may deter either him or Paul or both from committing crimes in the future. Third is rehabilitation: while behind bars, Peter may participate in drug treatment or other programs that reduce the chances that he will return to crime when free. Fourth is incapacitation: from his cell, Peter cannot commit crimes against anyone save other prisoners, staff, or visitors.

As Ben Wattenberg has quipped, "A thug in prison cannot mug your sister."[28] Using a variety of measures, various researchers have estimated

23. Greenfeld (1997).
24. Ditton and Wilson (1999, table 7).
25. Greenfeld (1997, p. 27).
26. Wilson (1983, p. 149)
27. See DiIulio and Piehl (1991); Piehl and DiIulio (1995); DiIulio and Mitchell (1996); Rothwax (1996, chapter 7).
28. Ben Wattenberg, "Circling Crime Hawk," *Washington Times*, June 10, 1999, p. A19.

that prisoners commit an average of at least a dozen crimes (excluding all drug crimes) in the year before their incarceration.[29] Whatever its deterrent effect, imprisonment at least reduces crime when one or more of three conditions are met: the incarcerated offenders commit multiple crimes if they are free; when the incarcerated offenders are not replaced on the streets immediately and completely by new recruits; and when the prison experience either does not increase the incarcerated offenders' post-release criminal activity or does not increase it by enough to offset the crimes averted during their time in prison.[30]

With one important exception, which I will examine presently, the best available evidence indicates that most categories of imprisoned felons, especially those being sentenced for violent crimes, meet the aforementioned conditions. Patrick A. Langan has estimated that had the number of violent, repeat, and violent repeat offenders behind bars not tripled from 1975 to 1989, violent crime would have been 10 to 15 percent higher during that period than it was. In fact, in 1989 alone there would have been 390,000 more murders, rapes, robberies, and aggravated assaults.[31] Steven D. Levitt has estimated that "the impact of prison populations on crime is two to three times greater than previous estimates would imply." Into the early 1990s, each additional incarceration averted about fifteen crimes a year, including two or three violent crimes.[32] Charles Murray has estimated that, had the incarceration rate remained unchanged from 1980 to 1997, 869,600 people who were incarcerated on any given day in 1997 would have been on the streets, and the crime rate for that year would have been considerably higher than at any time in the 1990s. Murray invites those who would quibble with this specific numerical claim to undertake this imaginative exercise: What do you think would happen to the crime rate if 869,600 prisoners—or a million, if you prefer—were released tomorrow?[33] BJS data leave little to the imagination: persons released early from prison on parole who were back in prison for a parole violation or a new crime in 1991 had committed

29. For example, see DiIulio and Piehl (1991); Piehl and DiIulio (1995); Levitt (1996); Marvell and Moody (1994).
30. Wilson (1983, p. 146).
31. Langan (1994, 1991).
32. Levitt (1996, pp. 323–24, 345).
33. Murray (1999, pp. 7–9).

at least 6,800 murders, 5,500 rapes, 8,800 assaults, and 22,500 robberies while under community-based parole supervision.[34]

As James Q. Wilson has explained, during the 1960s, while crime rates were soaring, there was "an actual decline in the number of prisoners, state and federal, from about 213,000 in 1960 to 196,000 in 1970."[35] Taking all crimes together, "the amount of time served in state prison has been declining more or less steadily since the 1940s. . . . Only for rape [were] prisoners serving as much time [in 1994] as they did in the 1940s."[36] Wilson and Richard J. Herrnstein concluded in 1985 that the evidence on imprisonment is "consistent with the view that states (or other jurisdictions) in which the probability of going to prison is high have, other things being equal, lower crime rates than states in which that probability is low."[37] Correcting the pundits who proclaim that "prisons have failed," Steven D. Levitt pointed out in 1996 that to the "extent that the underlying determinants of crime . . . have worsened over time, the increased use of prisons may simply be masking what would have been a far greater rise in criminal activity."[38]

The longest prison sentences tend to fall on adult felons who are well into their criminal careers. As Wilson has noted, the "peak ages of criminality are between sixteen and eighteen; the average age of prison inmates is ten years older."[39] It would, therefore, not be terribly surprising if, as the number of teenagers in the population rose to 21,000,000 by the year 2006, a level not seen since 1980, prison populations began to drop even as crime rates stabilized or turned back up.[40] It is also worth noting that growth of the state and federal prison population declined from 90,881 during the twelve-month period ending June 30, 1995, to 58,090 in the twelve-month period ending June 30, 1998, and has for the past three years been below the 1990–98 average annual increase of 63,992. About 45 percent of the growth in prison populations during the 1997–98 period occurred in four states—Texas (6,700 additional

34. Cohen (1995).
35. Wilson (1977, p. 194).
36. Wilson (1994, p. 30).
37. Wilson and Herrnstein (1985, p. 390).
38. Levitt (1996, p. 321).
39. Wilson (1994, p. 28).
40. Bureau of the Census (1994, 1996, and 1998).

prisoners), California (5,732), Louisiana (2,525), and Ohio (2,041)—plus the federal system (8,748).[41]

Since 1993 Truth in Sentencing laws have gradually increased the incarceration time for people convicted of murder, rape, robbery, or aggravated assault. Even the much-debated "three-strikes-and-you're-out" laws, targeted on repeat violent felons and adopted by twenty-three states and the federal government since 1993, have produced neither the prison crowding crisis nor the dire fiscal consequences that many experts predicted. As Walter Dickey has acknowledged, in the federal system as in every three-strikes state except California, the laws have been little used—fewer than five times in Tennessee, once in Wisconsin, New Mexico, and North Carolina, and not at all in Colorado or Indiana.[42]

Still, with nearly 2 million people in prisons and jails on any given day, there is a case to be made for zero prison growth.[43] Even where repeat violent felons are concerned, imprisonment is neither the primary nor the most cost-effective or compassionate way to cut crime. No one can say with scientific certitude what fraction of the post-1993 decrease in crime is due to imprisonment. By the same token, however, no one can make empirically precise estimates of the effect of crime prevention programs for at-risk youth, improved policing, private spending on personal security, demographic trends, or the myriad other factors that, if the best scientific evidence is to be believed, probably affect crime rates.

Of one thing, however, we can be sure: no policy measure is immune to the law of diminishing returns. The criminologists and commentators who insisted that America was imprisoning too many in 1970, 1980, or 1990 may finally be right in 2000, at least for certain categories of imprisoned drug offenders. Putting violent and habitual offenders behind bars is one thing; insisting that every convicted felon spend every sentenced minute behind bars is quite another.

On balance, Washington's role in encouraging the states to sentence violent felons to prison for definite terms has been not only good elec-

---

41. Gilliard (1999, table 2, p. 3).

42. Dickey (1997, p. 56).

43. John J. DiIulio Jr., "Two Million Prisoners Are Enough," *Wall Street Journal*, March 12, 1999, p. A14.

toral politics but good public policy. But federal dollars should not be used to defray the costs of administering justice in states that go so far as to choose to abolish parole for all convicted felons, whether de jure—as fourteen states had done legislatively as of January 1999—or de facto— as most states have done administratively by returning ever more parole violators to prison on drug charges or the like. In 1995 just 5.8 percent of all state and local government spending was for all corrections functions—prisons, jails, probation, and parole—and in 1999 many states were running big dollar budget surpluses.[44] The states are now doing a sensible job of sentencing violent felons, but they could still use federal help in treating drug offenders and rethinking mandatory-minimum drug laws.

Treating Drug-Only Offenders

The 1989 report of William Bennett, the first director of the Office of National Drug Control Policy (sometimes called the drug czar), advised that regardless of the success of federal antidrug efforts, "There will remain millions of individuals who need help to stop using drugs. . . . For these reasons and more, the effective treatment of drug dependent individuals must be an important element in our overall strategy for reducing drug use in America." The report stressed the urgent need to get "more users into treatment."[45] A decade and several federal drug czars later, however, nothing much has happened. The 1999 drug czar's report adopted the same urgent tone on drug treatment and called for "closing the public treatment system gap."[46]

"Drug treatment programs for all prisoners" was the chief recommendation for federal policy in my chapter on crime for the 1992 Brookings publication *Setting Domestic Priorities*.[47] The crux of the problem, as was noted in the 1989 drug czar's report, was and remains that "the treatment system remains largely voluntary."[48] Research since 1992 supports the value of "coerced treatment" substance abuse programs of various types.

44. Nelson A. Rockefeller Institute (1999, table 3, graph 1).
45. White House (1989, pp. 35, 41).
46. White House (1999, p. 59).
47. DiIulio (1992, chapter 4).
48. White House (1989, p. 41).

Despite convincing surveys by the BJS and other research organizations showing that fully half of all adult probationers and state prisoners committed their offenses while under the influence of alcohol or drugs, the federal government has not widely funded such programs for convicted offenders in prison, in jail, on probation, or on parole.[49]

I also suggested in 1992 that "no firm evidence shows that stepped-up drug enforcement reduces crime rates" and that one of the three aforementioned conditions under which imprisonment can be expected to result in fewer crimes "may not apply: namely, drug offenders taken off the streets seem to be immediately and completely replaced by other drug offenders."[50] In 1994 James Q. Wilson likewise observed that sentencing drug felons to prison does not have "the same incapacitative effect as sentences for robbery. A robber taken off the street is not replaced by a new robber who has suddenly found a market niche, but a drug dealer sent away is replaced by a new one because an opportunity has opened up."[51] Anne Morrison Piehl and I speculated in 1995 that perhaps 15 percent or more of New Jersey's incoming prison population consisted of offenders whose only crimes were nonviolent, small-scale drug sales, and we termed these felons "drug-only offenders."[52] In research completed in 1999 Piehl, Bert Useem, and I estimated that in 1997, 28 percent of incoming male prisoners in New York State, 18 percent in Arizona, and 15 percent in New Mexico were drug-only offenders, most of them with criminal histories linked to substance abuse.[53]

In the late 1990s in New York State and other states, mandatory-minimum drug laws have netted ever more nondangerous drug-dependent drug-only criminals.[54] Federal lawmakers should encourage state and local lawmakers to require drug treatment for prisoners and probationers, to rethink mandatory-minimum drug laws, and to manage the continued increase in the number of violent offenders behind bars by not incarcerating drug-only felons rather than by continually constructing new prisons.

49. Mumola with Bonczar (1998); Mumola (1999).
50. DiIulio (1992, p. 126).
51. Wilson (1994, p. 31).
52. Piehl and DiIulio (1995).
53. Piehl, Useem, and DiIulio (1999).
54. DiIulio (1999, pp. 46–51).

The best way for the federal government to lead is by example. Most drug-dependent felons who recidivate do so within a year after being released from prison. A 1998 study indicates that, six months after leaving prison, federal prisoners who participated in the Bureau of Prisons (BOP) prerelease drug treatment program were 73 percent less likely to be rearrested, and 44 percent less likely to use drugs, than otherwise comparable federal prisoners who did not participate in the program.[55] My 1992 recommendation bears repeating: "Mandate that drug treatment programs of the type being offered to prisoners in the federal system be extended to prisoners in every state correctional system in the country and be fully funded with federal dollars."[56]

In 1990 the BOP held 48,000 prisoners, 52 percent of them sentenced for drug crimes. By mid-1998, the BOP held 95,500 prisoners, 59 percent of them sentenced for drug crimes. Even if the BOP held no offenders sentenced for drug crimes, it would still hold 50,000 convicted federal felons—twice as many as in 1980 and the same number it held in 1990.[57] The increase in the number of drug offenders behind federal prison bars has been driven since 1980 by successive waves of federal antidrug laws and the federal sentencing guidelines enacted in 1987.

At a minimum, Congress and the White House should stop enacting new federal antidrug laws. Even better would be to replace the federal sentencing grid with antidrug policies and guidelines that restore some judicial discretion to the sentencing of federal drug offenders and to provide federal support for intensive, coerced, community-based abstinence programs for all probationers, state and federal, with a history of substance abuse.

Handling Juvenile Offenders

In 1967 the President's Commission on Law Enforcement and the Administration of Justice noted with alarm that "enormous numbers of young people appear to be involved" in "juvenile delinquency and youth crime,"

---

55. Federal Bureau of Prisons (1998).
56. DiIulio (1992, p. 132).
57. Federal Bureau of Prisons (1999, p. 4).

a problem reflected in statistics such as the 1965 rate of juvenile violent crime arrests: 223 per 100,000 persons aged fifteen to seventeen.[58] Black youth, "who live in disproportionate numbers in slum neighborhoods, account for a disproportionate number of arrests," and there is "no reason to doubt that delinquency, and especially the most serious delinquency, is committed disproportionately by slum and lower class youth."[59]

By 1994 violent crime arrests per 100,000 persons aged ten to seventeen exceeded 500.[60] In 1994 black males aged fourteen to twenty-four were 1 percent of the population but 17 percent of the homicide victims and 30 percent of the homicide perpetrators.[61] In the nation's seventy-five largest counties, black males accounted for seven in ten violent juvenile defendants in criminal courts and about 65 percent of juvenile murder defendants in criminal courts.[62]

As former New Jersey Superior Court judge Daniel R. Coburn has stated, whatever their socioeconomic status or demographic description, most of today's juvenile offenders "are neither sharks nor minnows."[63] On the one hand, the vast majority of crimes committed by and against juveniles are nonviolent. In the nation's seventy-five largest counties, 55 percent of all juvenile defendants formally processed in juvenile courts are adjudicated as "delinquents," and most receive probation.[64] Since 1994 juvenile crime rates have been falling.

On the other hand, juveniles perpetrated 137,000 more violent crimes in 1994 than they did in 1985 and were responsible for 26 percent of the growth in violent crime during that period, including 50 percent of the increase in robberies, 48 percent of the increase in rapes, and 35 percent of the increase in murders.[65] In 1995 a fifth of the country's 1.7 million "delinquency" cases were for "person offenses," mainly robberies and

---

58. President's Commission on Law Enforcement and Administration of Justice (1967, p. 55 and table 1, p. 56).

59. President's Commission on Law Enforcement and Administration of Justice (1967, p. 57).

60. Snyder, Sickmund and Poe-Yamagata (1996, p. 14).

61. Fox (1996, p. 2).

62. Strom and Smith (1998, p. 3).

63. Council on Crime in America (1997, p. 6).

64. Strom and Smith (1998, p. 1).

65. Snyder, Sickmund and Poe-Yamagata (1996, pp. 10, 12, 13, 20).

aggravated assaults.[66] In 1996, 2,172 juveniles were arrested for murder, up from 1,860 in 1980, but down from the frightening 1993 peak of 3,790.[67]

Some cities have witnessed remarkable declines in youth crime and violence. In Boston, for example, between January 1, 1995, and September 30, 1998, the total number of homicides among persons aged twenty-four and younger fell from forty to fourteen, and the city enjoyed one period of nearly two and a half years during which not a single homicide was committed with a gun by persons aged sixteen and younger.[68] Other cities, however, have experienced no such steep declines in juvenile crime and murder. In Philadelphia, for example, the number of homicide victims aged twenty-four and younger fell insignificantly, from 164 in 1995 to 157 in 1998, and in both years more than 80 percent of the city's homicides were committed with guns (137 in 1995, 136 in 1998).[69]

Levitt has argued that since 1978, "the punitiveness of the juvenile justice system has declined substantially relative to the adult courts." He has estimated that, had juvenile and adult incarceration rates risen at the same rates between 1978 and 1993, about a third of the violent and property crime committed by juveniles in these years would have been averted.[70]

In the late 1980s and early 1990s, most states toughened their juvenile justice sentencing policies. Still, from 1990 to 1994, in the nation's seventy-five largest counties, barely 2 percent of the juveniles aged fifteen or older who were formally handled in adult court were transferred to criminal (adult) courts by judicial waiver.[71] In mid-1998 there were 592,462 persons in local jails, only 8,090 (1.3 percent) of them aged eighteen or younger.[72]

In the 105th Congress, proposals were made to relax federal restrictions on incarcerating juveniles with adults and to mandate that states try violent juveniles in criminal courts ("as adults"). Only a few jail-short

66. Sickmund and others (1998).
67. FBI, UCR (1980, 1993, 1996, available at http://www.fbi.gov/ucr.htm [8/27/99]).
68. Data supplied by Boston Police Department, October 2, 1998.
69. Tierney and Loizillon (1999, p. 4).
70. Levitt (1997, p. 1).
71. Strom and Smith (1998).
72. Gilliard (1999, p. 9).

rural jurisdictions, however, had any immediate public safety rationale for being permitted to house juvenile offenders with adult felons. No persuasive public safety or other rationale was offered to explain why an otherwise increasingly devolution-minded Washington should tell state and local lawmakers how best to prosecute and sentence violent juvenile offenders.

The 105th Congress also considered various proposals to strengthen the federal role in maintaining complete and accurate state and local juvenile crime records and to expand the federal role in promoting interjurisdictional record-sharing. Washington should broker the institutionalization of a better national crime information system for use by state and local criminal justice officials. Even here, however, Washington should follow, not lead, leaving it to the states and localities to decide, for example, whether the time has truly come to reverse the near-universal practice of expunging a young offender's record of delinquency when he or she reaches a certain age (usually between seventeen and twenty-one).[73]

Philip J. Cook and John H. Laub have attributed the "epidemic in youth violence" that ebbed in 1994 to "more and more violence-involved youths" who "turned to guns during this period."[74] Following each of the aforementioned school shootings, Congress was flooded by new gun-control proposals. But there is as yet no evidence that the post-1994 reduction in juvenile violence was occasioned by a post-1994 contraction in the availability of firearms. The federal government has a sorry record when it comes to prosecuting violations of existing federal antigun laws. U.S. attorneys and other federal officials, however, have played an important role in several successful state and local efforts to curb youth violence and restrict the availability of illegal firearms. More of the same on an as-requested basis would be desirable.

As Eric C. Schneider has cautioned, we should not "take too much hope from the recent downturn in homicide and other violent crime" among juveniles because each cycle of youth crime "ends at a higher point than the previous one and then recedes to a higher plateau.[75] By the year

73. Funk (1996).
74. Cook and Laub (1996, p. 29).
75. Schneider (1999, p. 258).

2006, America will be home to 21 million teenagers, the largest teen cohort since 1980. This coming demographic boomlet is likely to exert upward pressure on juvenile crime rates. Despite all the good post-1993 news about crime and other social trends, several factors that research has strongly and consistently linked with crime and delinquency have abated little if at all. To cite just one example, independent of other factors, boys raised in mother-only homes are about twice as likely as otherwise comparable boys to commit crimes that lead to imprisonment.[76] In 1990, 28 percent of all births in America were to unwed mothers. In 1998, 32.4 percent of all births in America were to unwed mothers. About 70 percent of black children born in 1996 were born to unwed mothers.[77]

But, as I have argued elsewhere, that pressure probably can be countered if not conquered through prevention, intervention, and enforcement programs that intensively monitor and mentor at-risk children, especially programs that get inner-city ministers and religious volunteers involved in the lives of high-risk urban youth.[78]

What, if anything, can and should the federal government do to foster community-based or church-anchored anticrime efforts? What, if anything, can Washington do to alter social policy or civic life in ways that cut crime? These questions remain unanswered, but do not be surprised if the answer turns out to be "very little."

References

Advisory Commission on Intergovernmental Relations. 1993. *The Role of General Government Elected Officials in Criminal Justice.* Washington (May).

76. Harper and McLanahan (1998); Horn (1998, p. 54–61).
77. Morehouse Research Institute, (1999, p. 10).
78. John J. DiIulio Jr., "Stop Crime Where It Starts," *New York Times*, July 31, 1996, p. A15; "Jail Alone Won't Stop Juvenile Super-Predators," *Wall Street Journal*, June 11, 1997, p. A23; "The Coming of the Super-Preachers," *Weekly Standard*, June 23, 1997, pp. 23–26; "How Philadelphia Salvages Teen Criminals" (with Beth Palubinsky), *City Journal*, Summer 1997, pp. 29–40; "The Lord's Work: The Church and the 'Civil Society Sector,'" *Brookings Review*, Fall 1997, pp. 27–31; "Police Alone Won't Solve the Crime Problem," *Philadelphia Inquirer*, September 19, 1997, p. A27; "Preventing Crime, Saving Children: Sticking to the Basics," *Prosecutor*, November/December 1997, pp. 14–20.

Beck, Allen J., and Darrell K. Gilliard. 1995. *Prisoners in 1994*. Washington: U.S. Bureau of Justice Statistics.

Beck, Allen J., and others. 1993. *Survey of State Prison Inmates, 1991*. Washington: U.S. Bureau of Justice Statistics.

Brown, Jodi M., and others. 1996. *Correctional Populations in the United States, 1994*. Washington: U.S. Bureau of Justice Statistics.

Bureau of the Census. 1994. *Statistical Abstract of the United States: 1994*. GPO. 114th ed.

———. 1996. *Resident Population of the United States: Middle Series Projections, 2006–2010, by Age and Sex*. GPO (March).

———. 1998. *Population Estimates of the U.S. by Age and Sex*. GPO (December).

Bureau of Justice Statistics. 1994. *Criminal Victimization in the United States, 1973–92 Trends*. Washington.

———. 1995. *Criminal Victimization, 1993: National Crime Victimization Survey*. Washington.

———. 1997. *Criminal Victimization in the United States, 1994: A National Crime Victimization Survey Report*. Washington.

Cohen, Robyn L. 1995. *Probation and Parole Violators in State Prison, 1991*. Washington: U.S. Bureau of Justice Statistics.

Cook, Philip J., and John H. Laub. 1996. "The Unprecedented Epidemic in Youth Violence." Draft of article for *Crime and Justice*, Michael Tonry and Mark H. Moore, eds. (December 3).

Council on Crime in America. 1997. *Preventing Crime, Saving Children: Monitoring, Mentoring, and Ministering*. New York: Manhattan Institute.

Dickey, Walter J. 1997. "The Impact of 'Three Strikes and You're Out' Laws: What Have We Learned?" *Corrections Management Quarterly* 1(4): 55–64.

DiIulio, John J. Jr., ed. 1990. *Courts, Corrections and the Constitution: The Impact of Judicial Intervention on Prisons and Jails*. Oxford University Press.

———. 1992. "Crime": In *Setting Domestic Priorities: What Can Government Do?*, edited by Henry J. Aaron and Charles L. Schultze, chapter 4. Brookings.

———. 1999. "Against Mandatory Minimums." *National Review* (May 17): 46–51.

DiIulio, John J. Jr., and George Mitchell. 1996. *Who Really Goes to Prison in Wisconsin?* Wisconsin Policy Research Institute.

DiIulio, John J. Jr., and Anne Morrison Piehl. 1991. "Does Prison Pay?" *Brookings Review* 9 (Fall): 28–35.

DiIulio, John J. Jr., Steven K. Smith, and Aaron J. Saiger. 1995. "The Federal Role in Crime Control." In *Crime*, edited by James Q. Wilson and Joan Petersilia. San Francisco: Institute for Contemporary Studies.

Ditton, Paula M., and Doris James Wilson. 1999. *Truth in Sentencing in State Prisons*. Washington: U.S. Bureau of Justice Statistics.

Federal Bureau of Prisons, Office of Research and Evaluation. 1998. *TRIAD Drug Treatment Evaluation Project: Six-Month Interim Report.* January 31.
———. 1999. *Quick Facts*, June 30.
Fox, James Alan. 1996. *Trends in Juvenile Violence.* U.S. Bureau of Justice Statistics. March.
Funk, T. Markus. 1996. "A Mere Youthful Indiscretion? Reexamining the Policy of Expunging Juvenile Delinquency Records." *University of Michigan Journal of Law Reform* 29 (Summer): 885–938.
Gilliard, Darrell K. 1999. *Prison and Jail Inmates at Midyear 1998.* Washington: U.S. Bureau of Justice Statistics.
Greenfeld, Lawrence A. 1997. *Sex Offenses and Offenders: An Analysis of Data on Rape and Sexual Assault.* Washington: U.S. Bureau of Justice Statistics.
Harper, Cynthia C., and Sara S. McLanahan. 1998. "Father Absence and Youth Incarceration." Paper presented at the annual meeting of the American Sociological Association, San Francisco, August.
Horn, Wade F. 1998. *Father Facts.* 3d ed. Gaithersburg, Md.: National Fatherhood Initiative.
Langan, Patrick A. 1991. "America's Soaring Prison Population." *Science* (251): 1568–73.
———. 1994. "Between Prison and Probation: Intermediate Sanctions." *Science* (264): 791–93
Langan, Patrick A., and Jodi M. Brown. 1997. *Felony Sentences in State Courts, 1994.* Washington: U.S. Bureau of Justice Statistics.
Langan, Patrick A., and Helen A. Graziadei. 1995. *Felony Sentences in State Courts, 1992.* Washington: U.S. Bureau of Justice Statistics.
Langan, Patrick A., and Caroline Wolf Harlow. 1994. *Child Rape Victims, 1992.* Washington: U.S. Bureau of Justice Statistics.
Levitt, Steven D. 1996. "The Effect of Prison Population Size on Crime Rates: Evidence from Prison Overcrowding Litigation." *Quarterly Journal of Economics* 3 (May): 319–52.
———. 1997. "Juvenile Crime and Punishment." Harvard University, Society of Fellows (March).
Marshall, Will, and Martin Schram, eds. 1993. *Mandate for Change.* Berkeley Books.
Marvell, Thomas B., and Carlisle E. Moody. 1994. "Prison Population Growth and Crime Reduction." *Journal of Quantitative Criminology* 10 (2): 109–40.
Morehouse Research Institute. 1999. *Turning the Corner on Father Absence in Black America.* Atlanta.
Mumola, Christopher J. 1999. *Substance Abuse and Treatment, State and Federal Prisoners, 1997.* Washington: U.S. Bureau of Justice Statistics.
Mumola, Christopher J., with Thomas P. Bonczar. 1998. *Substance Abuse and Treatment of Adults on Probation, 1995.* Washington: U.S. Bureau of Justice Statistics.

Murray, Charles. 1999. "The Underclass Revisited." Washington: American Enterprise Institute.

Nelson A. Rockefeller Institute. 1999. *State Fiscal Brief: State and Local Criminal Justice Spending: Recent Trends and Outlook for the Future* (February).

Sickmund, Melissa, and others. 1998. *Juvenile Court Statistics, 1995.* Office of Juvenile Justice and Delinquency Prevention, U.S. Department of Justice (May).

Snyder, Howard N., Melissa Sickmund, and Eileen Poe-Yamagata 1996. *Juvenile Offenders and Victims: 1996 Update on Violence.* Office of Juvenile Justice and Delinquency Prevention, U.S. Department of Justice (February).

Piehl, Anne Morrison, and John J. DiIulio Jr. 1995. "Does Prison Pay? Revisited." *Brookings Review* 13 (Winter): 20–25.

Piehl, Anne Morrison, Bert Useem, and John J. DiIulio Jr. 1999. *Right-Sizing Justice.* Manhattan Institute, Center for Civic Innovation (May).

President's Commission on Law Enforcement and Administration of Justice. 1967. *The Challenge of Crime in a Free Society.* GPO (February).

Rand, Michael. 1998. *Criminal Victimization 1997: Changes 1996–97 with Trends, 1993–97.* Washington: U.S. Bureau of Justice Statistics.

Rothwax, Judge Harold J. 1996. *Guilty: The Collapse of Criminal Justice.* Random House.

Schneider, Eric C. 1999. *Vampires, Dragons, and Egyptian Kings: Youth Gangs in Postwar New York.* Princeton University Press.

Strom, Kevin J., and Steven K. Smith. 1998. *Juvenile Felony Defendants in Criminal Courts.* Washington: U.S. Bureau of Justice Statistics.

Tierney, Joseph, and Anais Loizillon. 1999. *Violence Reduction A Report of the Community Policy Research Center at Public/Private Ventures.* Philadelphia (May).

White House Office of National Drug Control Policy. 1989. *National Drug Control Strategy.* GPO (September).

———. 1999. *The National Drug Control Strategy, 1999.* Washington.

Wilson, James Q. 1977. *Thinking about Crime.* Vintage Books.

———. 1983. *Thinking about Crime,* rev. ed. Basic Books.

———. 1994. "What to Do about Crime." *Commentary* 98 (September): 25–34.

Wilson, James Q., and Richard J. Herrnstein. 1985. *Crime and Human Nature.* Simon & Schuster.

PAUL R. PORTNEY

11

Environmental Policy in the Next Century

T HE TURN OF THE CENTURY offers a fitting moment in which to take stock of the progress that has been made and problems that remain in environmental policy. The year 2000 marks the thirtieth anniversaries of three separate but significant events in the development of U.S. environmental policy. The first and most important anniversary belongs to the Environmental Protection Agency (EPA), created in 1970 as part of President Richard Nixon's reorganization of the executive branch. One dimension of this reorganization involved combining in a new agency the air pollution authority then residing in the Department of Health, Education, and Welfare, the water pollution control responsibilities from the Department of the Interior, the pesticide regulatory authority of the Department of Agriculture, and other environment-related authorities scattered throughout the federal government. The EPA is now the largest and arguably most powerful of all federal regulatory agencies, revered in some quarters, reviled in others.[1]

The Council on Environmental Quality (CEQ) was also created in 1970 as an advisory body within the executive office of the president. Modeled after the Council of Economic Advisers, the CEQ was never

1. See Graham (1999) for an elegant description of the origins of the EPA and federal environmental legislation.

359

intended to be as powerful as the EPA. Indeed, at times, it has teetered perilously close to extinction. Nevertheless, its importance in ensuring that government agencies took seriously the requirement in the National Environmental Policy Act of 1970 that all agencies produce environmental impact statements for all of their significant actions was unquestioned in its early years. The CEQ still actively strives to coordinate the environmental policy actions of the cabinet departments and other parts of the executive branch.

Finally, in 1970 Congress amended the Clean Air Act of 1963 in ways that significantly expanded the authority of the federal government in air pollution control. More than any other action, this one marked the dawning of the federalization of environmental policy—and the advent, as well, of the last great expansion of federal regulatory authority. To say that this enlarged federal role has engendered controversy is an understatement.

This chapter provides an overview of environmental regulation as the year 2000 approaches. Given the size and complexity of environmental policy, the chapter must be less than exhaustive. The focus is on the EPA and issues related to pollution policy—air and water pollution control, solid and hazardous waste management, and climate policy. Missing is a discussion of other important environmental policy issues, such as forest and fisheries management; endangered species policy; the management of national parks, wilderness areas, and other public lands; and the preservation of biodiversity. These concerns are sometimes referred to as natural resource policy matters to distinguish them from the pollution issues addressed in this chapter.[2]

Trends in Environmental Quality and Public Opinion

By almost any standard, environmental quality has improved significantly throughout the United States (and in most of the Western industrial democracies). The most obvious example—and perhaps the most important considering the human health and aesthetic values at

2. For an even-handed and thorough evaluation of pollution policy in the United States, see Davies and Mazurek (1998). For a much broader and thoughtful treatment of environmental policy, see Easterbrook (1995).

stake—is air quality in metropolitan areas, where close to 80 percent of the nation's population lives. Data are not available to easily compare air quality today with that of 1970—when the federal role in air pollution was significantly expanded through amendments to the Clean Air Act. Nevertheless, starting in the mid-1970s the EPA has routinely compiled trend data that can be used to illustrate progress. For instance, between 1978 and 1997, ambient (or airborne) concentrations of five of the six common air pollutants on which the EPA focuses much of its attention fell significantly around the United States. As measured by thousands of air pollution monitors located in hundreds of metropolitan areas, concentrations of carbon monoxide fell by an average of 60 percent, nitrogen dioxide by 25 percent, ozone (smog) by 30 percent, and sulfur dioxide by 55 percent.[3]

The picture is brightest of all for airborne concentrations of lead—arguably the most harmful of these pollutants—which fell by a whopping 97 percent between 1978 and 1997. Concentrations of fine particles, air pollutants of great concern because of their possible effect in hastening mortality, were not monitored routinely on a national basis until 1988. Between that year and 1997, concentrations of fine particles in the air averaged over major metropolitan areas fell by more than a quarter. It is hard to find a metropolitan area today where air quality is not significantly better in nearly every respect than it was twenty or thirty years ago.[4]

These great improvements in U.S. air quality are all the more impressive when one considers that since 1977, real gross domestic product has increased 64 percent and the number of vehicle miles traveled has increased by nearly 160 percent. Vehicle miles are especially important because fuel combustion by cars, trucks, and buses is the principal source of several of the air pollutants and an important contributor to others. Some analysts have pointed to the improvements in air quality in the United States before 1970 as evidence that the Clean Air Act was

3. See Environmental Protection Agency (1998, p. 9).
4. Despite this impressive record, in many metropolitan areas the national air quality standards are violated more often than the EPA allows. But this number is falling steadily, and how frequently these areas violate the standards is also dropping. See Environmental Protection Agency (1998, pp. 38, 65–67).

perhaps limited in its effectiveness—that is, that air quality was already on the mend.[5] Although favorable changes were under way, it is very unlikely that the improvements in air quality since 1970 would have been as significant without the federal controls imposed under the 1970 amendments to the Clean Air Act.

It is more difficult to speak confidently about nationwide trends in other dimensions of environmental quality because good data on the quality of the nation's rivers, lakes, bays, and coastal waters are notoriously hard to come by. Satisfactory indicators of drinking water quality are also few and far between, as are measures of the adequacy of the landfills and other facilities at which solid and hazardous wastes are disposed. This lack of data is troubling. Indeed, one would think that a country that spends $180 billion or so each year on environmental protection would be intensely interested in knowing whether these expenditures are generating year-to-year improvements in what really matters—the quality of the ambient environment.

Despite the lack of good data on environmental conditions and trends apart from air quality, it is hard to avoid the conclusion that much progress is being made. For instance, rivers that twenty years ago could no longer support certain forms of fish life—the Detroit, Cuyahoga, Hudson, Potomac, and Monongahela Rivers, to pick but a few—now do. In fact, they are occasionally venues for water skiing and even swimming, something that would have been unheard of ten or fifteen years ago. The Great Lakes have enjoyed improvements in water quality; and ocean beaches are, overall, closed less frequently because of bacterial contamination or unsanitary material washing up on them.[6]

Undoubtedly, the nation is disposing of solid and liquid wastes much more carefully than in the past. Open dumps or quarries into which garbage is carelessly tossed are the rare exception now rather than the rule. Indeed, most garbage from metropolitan areas is now shipped—often long distances—to state-of-the-art landfills where clay and plastic liners protect underlying ground water and where waste gases are sometimes collected and used to power electricity generation. Paradox-

5. See Goklany (forthcoming).
6. For a review of the statistical evidence that does exist, see Davies and Mazurek (1998, pp. 68–77).

ically, this "export" of solid waste from one state to another now appears to stir up more concern than did the unregulated disposal of earlier years. Finally, hazardous wastes are being generated in ever-smaller quantities, typically are stored under carefully regulated conditions, and often are disposed of under the kind of scrutiny once accorded only radioactive waste.

Despite these accomplishments, environmental concerns should not be thought of as a thing of the past. Some problems remain resistant to improvement. For instance, the nation has never done a very satisfactory job of regulating the water pollution that washes off farmers' fields or city streets—in contrast to that emanating from the outfall pipes of factories or sewage treatment plants. Such runoff—referred to as "nonpoint" source pollution—has gone largely unregulated for two reasons. First, it is difficult to monitor and control because there is no pipe or smokestack onto the end of which a pollution control device might be attached. This is not a good excuse for failing to limit pollution, however. In fact, one of the most compelling criticisms of the way the factories, sewage treatment plants, and other "point" sources have been regulated since 1970 is that Congress and the EPA have relied far too heavily on technological requirements.[7] This bias has frozen into place the pollution control technologies that prevailed in the early- to mid-1970s and blunted incentives that firms may have had to search for cheaper and better ways of removing pollution. Some measures can be taken to reduce runoff—for instance, requiring farmers to maintain natural buffers between their fields and stream banks.

There is a second reason why the nation's legislators and regulators have turned their heads when pollution originates in the agricultural sector or in municipal settings. Farms and cities are seen by many as more "benign" than profitmaking companies and therefore less fitting targets for fines or other civil or criminal penalties. Why is a bit baffling, because agricultural operations, sewage treatment plants, or municipal storm drains discharge at least some of the same types of pollutants as privately owned factories, and because, in general, publicly owned facilities have much worse compliance records than do indus-

---

7. For an early warning against this approach, see Kneese and Schultze (1975).

trial sources. The recent spate of unfavorable publicity directed toward privately owned large animal feedlots may mark the beginning of a new effort to control agricultural and perhaps even municipal water pollution; but the policy landscape is littered with remains of other such new beginnings related to nonpoint sources of water pollution.

Public Opinion

One reason environmental quality has improved markedly in the United States during the past thirty years has been the support it has received from the American public. Beginning in the mid-1970s, pollsters began asking the public about the possible trade-off between environmental quality and economic growth. Although respondents' answers can be very sensitive to the way pollsters frame their questions, some questions have been asked in essentially the same form for years, making for interesting comparisons.

For instance, respondents have been asked rather consistently whether they were prepared to sacrifice economic growth for environmental quality or vice versa. In 1976, 38 percent of those polled by Cambridge Reports-Research International opted for environmental quality when this choice was posed, and 21 percent opted for economic growth (41 percent responded "don't know"). The same poll, conducted annually over the period 1976–94, showed that those choosing to sacrifice economic growth for environmental quality always outnumbered those making the opposite choice. The greatest difference came in 1991 when the margin was 63 percent to 18 percent.[8] A 1997 Roper Starch Worldwide poll, which asked nearly the same question, found that 69 percent expressed the view that environmental quality ought to be protected at the expense of economic growth if a choice had to be made. Only 15 percent expressed the opposite opinion.[9]

Though broad, however, public support for environmental protection is not especially deep. For example, relatively few people express the view that pollution is a very important problem to them. Even in the early 1970s when the EPA was launching its first major regulations, only 12 percent of the public identified pollution as one of the top three

8. See Ladd and Bowman (1995, p. 26).
9. National Environmental Education and Training Foundation (1997, pp. 15–16).

problems that concerned them. Paradoxically, during the next twenty years, a period in which environmental conditions improved substantially, the share of the public who identified the environment as an important issue more than doubled, reaching a high of 23 percent in 1991. By 1994, however, the figure had fallen back to 12 percent.[10] Recently, the Gallup Organization, in a poll for CNN and *USA Today*, asked one thousand adults to identify the nation's most important problem.[11] Only 2 percent volunteered the environment in response.

Of course, these relatively low numbers reflect at least partly the significant improvements in environmental quality that have occurred during in the past three decades. Twice during these thirty years major efforts were launched to scale back the growth of new regulations and even to revisit some rules already on the books, with an eye to reducing regulatory burdens on business. The first attempt began in 1981 when Ronald Reagan became president and the second in 1995 when new Republican majorities took control of the House and Senate. In both instances adverse public reaction to these perceived assaults on regulation short-circuited the "reform" efforts.

The past twenty years, however, have seen an almost unprecedented and uninterrupted expansion in the U.S. economy that has given many Americans a sense that they can afford to attend to the environment. It is no accident that in 1979, during a period of double-digit inflation and interest rates, nearly a third of those polled by Cambridge Reports-Research International were willing to sacrifice environmental quality for economic growth—the highest fraction ever recorded.[12]

The Environmental Protection Agency and Environmental Regulation

Although the EPA was created through a presidential executive order, all of its regulatory authority derives from laws passed by Congress. This seemingly obvious point is worth mention if for no other reason than the not infrequent spectacle of legislators complaining vigorously when

---

10. Ladd and Bowman (1995, pp. 18–19).
11. As reported by Marlin (1999).
12. See Ladd and Bowman (1995, p. 26).

the EPA goes about doing exactly what previous Congresses have directed it to do. It seems not to dawn on some lawmakers that they and they alone have the power to give the EPA new marching orders, should they so desire.

The EPA does almost all of its regulating under eight major statutes. These are the Clean Air Act; the Clean Water Act; the Federal Insecticide, Fungicide and Rodenticide Act; the Safe Drinking Water Act; the Resource Conservation and Recovery Act; the Toxic Substances Control Act; the Comprehensive Environmental Response, Compensation, and Liability Act (also known as the Superfund); and the Emergency Planning and Community Right-to-Know Act. Under each one, Congress has spelled out (sometimes in great detail) the problems it wants the EPA to address, the approaches it wants the agency to take, and the powers it has delegated to the EPA to enforce the regulations the agency issues. In this sense, the EPA acts as an extension of the legislative branch, translating the usually general expressions of congressional intent on the environment into specific rules that proscribe the actions of individuals, other parts of government, and businesses.

Because Congress has been in the habit of giving the EPA more and more to do each year, the agency has grown significantly over time. At its creation in 1970, the EPA had 4,100 employees and spent about $205 million. By 1990 the agency had grown to nearly 15,600 employees and spent about $3.6 billion. By 1999 staffing exceeded 18,000, and spending is estimated in excess of $5.2 billion.[13] As such, the EPA is by far the largest of the federal regulatory agencies—in staffing, nearly twice as large as the Food Safety and Inspection Service, its closest competitor.

Although some would surely consider it heretical to ask, the obvious question raised by the agency's growth is: why does the EPA spend more and have a larger staff than at any time in its history, when the United States has conquered many of its most pressing environmental problems, and the force of public opinion makes backsliding highly unlikely? Several answers suggest themselves. First, not every serious problem has been addressed. As already noted, for instance, the nation needs to make much better headway dealing with the water pollution

---

13. See Warren and Lauber (1998, pp. 11, 14, 17).

that originates from nonpoint sources. Furthermore, guarding the progress that has been made will require a continued significant commitment of people and money. In at least several areas Congress would do well to increase the resources available to the EPA—most notably for a significantly stepped-up program of environmental monitoring and reporting, for improved analysis of the economic impacts of regulation (favorable and unfavorable), and for an enlarged and improved program of research and development. Yet one can acknowledge all this and still wonder whether it might be possible to trim the size of the EPA and refocus its efforts on the most pressing problems.

The Broader Costs of Regulation

The previous discussion on staff size and the annual expenditures required to operate the EPA should not divert attention from a fundamental and most important fact about environmental and other regulation: the vast majority of the resources devoted to regulation each year do not pass through the federal budget but rather are expended by those who must comply with the rules and regulations issued by the federal agencies. Estimates of these compliance costs, as they are often called, are made by federal agencies, independent researchers, and interest groups and are often controversial.

According to a 1990 report issued by the EPA, the nation is expected to spend $180 billion in current dollars in 1999 on environmental compliance.[14] About three-fifths of that sum will fall at least initially on the private sector. Another quarter of these costs (or about $45 billion annually) is borne initially by state and local governments, principally for the construction, operation, and maintenance of sewage treatment plants and for compliance with federal drinking water and also solid waste disposal (or landfill) standards. Even other parts of the federal government incur costs necessitated by EPA regulations. To take one example, each year the Department of Energy spends more than $6 billion on environmental management (principally at the sites where nuclear weapons are or were manufactured), a significant portion of

14. Environmental Protection Agency (1990, p. 8–51). The producer price index for capital equipment was used to convert 1986 dollars to current dollars.

which is in response to EPA rules governing the generation, treatment, or storage of nuclear and other hazardous wastes.[15]

In considering compliance costs, however, one should not attach too much confidence to any particular estimate of their overall magnitude. Unlike expenditures by the Social Security Administration or the Department of Defense, where the government in effect can review its "canceled checks" annually, there is no neat way to tote up at the year's end how much money was spent by the hundreds of thousands of businesses and governmental bodies affected by environmental regulation, not to mention the millions of individuals who incur such costs. As a result, even estimates made by different government agencies may differ significantly. For example, the Commerce Department's Bureau of Economic Analysis, which until recently conducted its own annual survey of compliance expenditures, routinely produced estimates that were far below those of the EPA, often differing by tens of billions of dollars during the 1990s.[16]

Recently, a group of researchers scrutinized more than twenty significant environmental and safety regulations. Most of them had been issued by the EPA, but some had been promulgated by other agencies.[17] The researchers identified some cases in which agency estimates overlooked costs likely to result from the regulations they were proposing. On the whole, however, they found that the EPA and other regulatory agencies tended rather systematically to overestimate how much it would cost to comply with the regulations they had proposed, in part because they were unable to foresee how technological change would bring down the costs of controlling the pollutants in question. Suffice it to say that regulatory cost estimation, while greatly improved over the past twenty years, is still far from precise.

---

15. No matter where the *initial* burden of compliance costs falls, the ultimate burden always rests on individuals in one of three ways. First, compliance costs may be passed on to consumers in the form of higher product prices or higher taxes. Second, under certain circumstances these costs may manifest themselves in the form of reduced payouts to shareholders of regulated firms. Finally, in some cases regulatory burdens may depress wages or even result in the loss of jobs. In all three instances, individuals bear the costs.

16. Vogan (1996).

17. Harrington, Morgenstern, and Nelson (1999).

Another important observation about the cost of complying with environmental regulations is that these costs are not subject to fiscal restraints. Many critics believe that federal environmental (and indeed other forms of) regulation has gotten out of control because the costs that are incurred pursuant to regulation do not pass through the federal budget.[18] When Congress passes a new law or amends an existing statute expanding the EPA's regulatory authority, and once the EPA issues the resultant regulations, costs are incurred by someone. These regulated groups or individuals may be electric utilities that have to reduce power plant emissions, farmers who must switch to a less potent (and often less effective) pesticide, or local governments that must upgrade their drinking water treatment facilities or strengthen the environmental safeguards at the landfills they operate. But the groups also include individual citizens who must, for example, pay more than they did in the past to dispose of the paint thinners, used motor oil, or other household hazardous wastes that they used to throw out with the rest of the garbage or even pour down the drain.

These costs imposed by regulation are a kind of "tax," one whose burden is difficult to discern and trace back to the EPA or to the legislation passed by Congress. Critics argue that this lack of accountability leads to much more regulation than can be justified on the basis of the benefits that it provides. They believe that the absence of any limit on the compliance costs that the EPA can impose on the economy each year through its regulations facilitates this tendency.[19]

This situation has prompted some thoughtful observers to propose changes in the way regulation is conducted. One proposal, for example, envisions Congress enacting an annual "regulatory budget" for the EPA (and other agencies) that would limit the amount of new compliance expenditures the EPA could impose on the economy each year.[20] That idea has some appealing features. For one, it would provide some certainty about the timing of regulatory burdens, since agencies could

---

18. Crews (1999).

19. To be sure, like every other part of the federal government, the EPA has an operating budget within which it must live, specifying how much it can spend on personnel, rent, travel, research support, and other expenses.

20. For the most thoughtful presentation of this case, see Demuth (1980a, 1980b).

only issue new regulations up to their annual "cap." The EPA or other regulatory agencies would also have every incentive under such a system to address the most serious problems first if they were limited in the amount of compliance costs they could impose. In other words, they would not want to exhaust their compliance cost budget on trivial problems. Third, a regulatory budget would give the EPA a stronger incentive to make use of least-cost approaches to regulation. By doing so, the agency would "stretch" its compliance cost budget and could thus address more problems.

However, a regulatory budget approach also raises some conspicuous problems. Most important, it would be difficult if not impossible to know how much of an agency's regulatory budget had been spent at any point in time, largely because environmental compliance costs are often hard to disentangle from the other expenditures made by regulated parties. For instance, if a chemical company subject to EPA regulation built a new plant, how much of the cost of that plant ought to be allocated to environmental compliance (and therefore ought to count against the EPA's regulatory budget) and how much to other productivity-enhancing purposes? If a semiconductor manufacturer realigned its manufacturing process because it wanted to improve the quality of its microprocessors, but the new process also reduced emissions of a regulated substance, how much if any of its expenditure should be counted against the EPA's regulatory budget for that year? Another problem with a regulatory budget is that it ignores the benefits of regulation. That is, would we really want the EPA to stop regulating in a given year when it reached its compliance cost limit if additional regulations would generate benefits clearly in excess of costs?

These and other problems with a "hard" regulatory budget have led those who would more closely monitor and restrain regulatory initiatives to suggest less stringent measures. For example, economists Robert Litan and William Nordhaus have suggested that Congress review annually the regulatory agendas of each federal agency and then negotiate informal guidance on the amount of new regulatory authority each should exercise.[21] Overall, the debate about a regulatory budget has had a healthy impact; it has heightened the appreciation of the eco-

21. See Litan and Nordhaus (1983).

nomic implications of environmental regulation. When Congress considers new legislation, it now pays at least some attention to the overall impacts of regulation. Under the Unfunded Mandates Reform Act of 1995, the Congressional Budget Office must prepare for Congress an estimate of the costs imposed on businesses and state and local governments by new legislation when these costs exceed certain thresholds.

The Benefits of Regulation

The costs of environmental regulation must be weighed against their benefits, which manifest themselves in many ways. Most notable are improvements in human health from reduced exposure to air and water pollutants, contaminants in drinking water, and exposures to pesticides, radiation, and hazardous wastes. Environmental benefits also take the form of increased agricultural and forest yields; reduced damage to buildings, houses, statues, other structures, and materials exposed to air pollution; enhanced commercial and recreational fishing; increased productivity of aquatic and terrestrial ecosystems (which can result in cost savings too); and a host of aesthetic benefits such as clearer air in urban and wilderness settings, reduced odors from landfills, and brighter, bluer waters.

It would be ideal, of course, if estimates of the total annual benefits of all environmental regulation were readily available to match up against the costs. They are not. This deficiency is explained not only by the relative difficulty of estimating benefits—a task that involves the skills of economists, epidemiologists, terrestrial and aquatic ecologists, toxicologists, and experts from other disciplines. Less is known about benefits also because Congress has not required the EPA to produce periodic estimates of annual benefits corresponding to the ones it has required the agency to make for compliance costs.

It is possible to provide information on annual benefits for at least one important regulatory program, however. When Congress amended the Clean Air Act in 1990, it directed the EPA to conduct a comprehensive analysis of the costs and benefits of all air pollution control regulation from 1970 to 1990. In 1997, after more than five years of air quality modeling, economic analysis, and other investigations, the EPA finished its analysis and had it reviewed by an independent, expert panel that Congress created expressly for that purpose.

According to the EPA report, there were 206,000 fewer premature deaths, 674,000 fewer cases of chronic bronchitis, 22,000 fewer cases of coronary heart disease, and many fewer cases of other acute and chronic illnesses as a result of the improvements in air quality attributable to regulations made between 1970 and 1990.[22] Improved air quality during this period also resulted in other types of benefits, such as improved visibility, reduced damage to materials, and increased agricultural output. Translating these results into dollar terms, the EPA concluded that the annual benefits of air quality regulation were on the order of $1.1 trillion annually, as contrasted with annual costs that the EPA pegged at approximately $25 billion.

Although a side-by-side comparison of aggregate environmental regulatory benefits and costs would be interesting to have, other bits of missing information would be much more valuable to lawmakers. For instance, to make informed judgments about individual regulatory programs, policymakers need to know the costs and benefits connected with specific rules and regulations.[23] More important still would be an understanding of the incremental benefits and costs associated with the possible tightening or relaxation of individual regulations. For instance, how might the health and other benefits arising from a slightly more stringent air quality standard compare with the added costs entailed? Such information is of much greater use than aggregate comparisons of benefits and costs because no one would ever think of eliminating the entire corpus of environmental regulations currently on the books; yet that is all the aggregate comparison is useful for.[24]

Valuable as information on incremental costs and benefits might be to policymakers in theory, in practice its use would be limited. This is because of one key feature of the major environmental laws—they often prohibit the administrator of the EPA from taking potential compliance costs into account when setting certain types of standards. For instance, under the Clean Air Act the EPA administrator is directed to set national air quality standards on the basis of health evidence alone.

22. Environmental Protection Agency (1997).

23. See Hahn and Hird (1991); Office of Management and Budget (1998).

24. On March 25, 1999, Senators Fred Thompson (R-Tenn.) and Carl Levin (D-Mich.) introduced legislation, S. 746, that would require regulatory agencies to provide information on incremental benefits and costs.

In effect, the law says that if tightening a particular air quality standard can be shown to provide protection against adverse health effects, that action must be taken regardless of how much it might cost to do so. Several challenges to this approach have gone all the way to the Supreme Court. Like lower courts, the Supreme Court has ruled that had Congress intended for health gains to be balanced against costs, it would have said so in the Clean Air Act.[25]

The problem this poses for priority setting is clear. In order to ensure that the resources being devoted to any set of problems—environmental or otherwise—are doing the most good, one must know the magnitudes of the various problems, how amenable each is to possible solutions, and what the costs of the several solutions are. Statutes that prohibit costs from being considered when regulating make it very difficult, if not impossible, to concentrate on those problems for which regulation would do the most good per dollar spent.

New Directions in Environmental Policy

Environmental policy has evolved during the three decades since the EPA was created in ways too numerous to mention. These range from large manufacturing firms such as Monsanto virtually remaking itself in the name of sustainable development to previously unheard of alliances between corporations and environmental advocacy groups.

Several interesting developments bear mention. The first is the move away from prescriptive, technology-based regulation to market-oriented approaches to environmental protection. In the early years of environmental regulation and policy, Congress regularly directed the EPA to issue what are called technology-based standards to limit pollutant discharges from factories, sewage treatment plants, and other easily identifiable facilities. In other words, at the direction of Congress, the EPA regularly told polluters not only how much their emissions had

25. On May 14, 1999, the U.S. Court of Appeals for the D.C. Circuit overturned the EPA's 1997 standards for ozone and fine particles. Importantly, however, the court did not question—indeed, reaffirmed—that the agency could not take costs into account in setting ambient air quality standards. Joby Warrick and Bill McAllister, "New Air Pollution Limits Blocked; Appeal Judges' Ruling May Curb Agencies' Powers," *Washington Post*, May 15, 1999, p. A1.

to be reduced but also in effect what specific types of pollution control equipment they had to install. As already mentioned, while helping to account for some of the early success of the environmental protection efforts, this approach had the effect of slowing the pace of technological advance in the pollution control industry.

For many years, economists and other policy analysts had been urging a different approach to environmental regulation. Under their preferred approach, the government would—through regulation—create a new set of economic signals that would steer polluters in the direction of cleanup. This approach would do so without necessarily specifying how much each polluter had to cut back on emissions and certainly not by mandating exactly how pollution was to be reduced. These so-called incentive-based programs include fees or taxes paid per unit of pollution discharged, deposit-refund systems, and permits initially limiting the pollution that any source could discharge—permits that also could be bought and sold freely. Although these approaches were roundly condemned in the early years of environmental regulation as unworkable and perhaps unwise, they began to be viewed more charitably as the increasing costs and diminished effectiveness of the technology-based approach started to receive wide attention. Moreover, experiments with incentive-based approaches, in the United States and elsewhere, produced convincing evidence that they could accomplish all that had been claimed for them.

When Congress amended the Clean Air Act in 1990, it enacted the first large-scale program making use of this approach. In an effort to limit sulfur dioxide emissions from 110 large coal-fired powerplants in the eastern and midwestern United States, Congress directed the EPA to write regulations that first capped emissions from each of these plants at a level about 50 percent below then-current levels. However, the EPA was also directed to create a program through which each plant could reduce emissions in whatever it considered to be the best way. This freedom included allowing a plant to exceed its emissions limit if it paid another plant or plants to reduce emissions by an equivalent amount below their permitted levels. The appeal of this approach was that it would reduce pollution but ensure that the emissions reductions that did take place would happen at those plants where the costs of abatement were the lowest.

Early evidence suggests that the United States would have done well to turn to this approach much earlier. Not only have sulfur dioxide emissions been reduced faster and by a greater amount than required in the 1990 amendments, but this progress has come at a much lower cost than would have been required under the technology-based approach. Although estimates of these costs savings vary (again, because of the difficulty of estimating compliance costs accurately), the flexibility permitted under the 1990 change is saving electricity consumers at least $1 billion annually. Once the program is fully implemented, these cost savings could amount to between $3 billion and $4 billion a year.[26]

As a result of this success and earlier experimental programs, regulators in the United States and abroad are looking with much greater favor on incentive-based approaches. An active market for air pollution permits is now in place in southern California, a federal tax is levied on annual emissions of chlorofluorocarbons, and deposit-refund programs are being implemented to ensure that car batteries are recycled. Some local governments are even charging households for waste collection based on the number or weight of the garbage bags they put out for curbside collection (these are sometimes referred to as "pay as you throw" systems). Although incentive-based approaches will never completely replace technology-based or other inflexible forms of regulation, they are fast becoming the first thing the EPA or other regulatory agencies think of when they approach a new regulatory problem.

A second important trend in environmental regulation in the United States is the rapidly increasing use of what might be called environmental reporting or information provision. In 1986 Congress amended the Superfund law to require certain industries to report annually to the EPA their emissions of a large number of chemical compounds, whether discharged into the air, into water bodies, or disposed of in landfills or other places. The clear understanding was that the EPA would make this information public as soon as possible.

It is fair to say that both proponents and opponents of this legislation have been surprised by the effect that it has had on pollutant emissions. As a result of mandatory environmental reporting, members of the public have access to this information (admittedly often quite tech-

26. Carlson and others (1999).

nical) about emissions in the communities in which they live. While the law required no emissions reductions, almost every company that files an annual report feels pressure to show that its emissions are declining in absolute terms or at least declining relative to its output.[27] The law has spurred firms to engage in environmental cleanup without the expense and frequent litigation associated with conventional regulatory approaches. Since 1986, moreover, the number of sources that must report under the law has expanded greatly, as has the number of compounds for which annual emissions reports must be filed. It would be most surprising if both do not grow more.

The benefits of information provisions are obvious: who could object to informing the public about the substances to which it is exposed? The challenges are more subtle. For instance, even proponents of environmental reporting acknowledge that few members of the public are able to make sense of the information reported. It might be wise before requiring additional reporting to invest time and money in helping people make better use of existing data. This effort could entail giving them information on the risks posed by the discharged substances *at the concentrations likely to be encountered*. The EPA must also strive to balance the public's right to know against the importance of protecting manufacturers' trade secrets, although this does not seem to have become a problem yet.

A third interesting trend in environmental regulation may prove every bit as important. It involves a gradual but perceptible shift in the locus of environmental power away from the EPA—in two opposing directions. First, with the growing recognition of the international and interdepartmental nature of some environmental problems, it is more and more common to see that not only the EPA but also the Departments of State, Energy, Agriculture, Commerce, and other government agencies are involved with other countries in negotiations and policy-making related to environmental issues. The EPA played the lead role for the U.S. government in 1987 in negotiating an international protocol to limit emissions of chlorofluorocarbons and other substances

---

27. A company could be working very hard and succeeding at making its manufacturing operation cleaner but still show emissions increasing if its output is increasing faster than the ratio of emissions per unit of output is falling.

that were contributing to the depletion of the stratospheric ozone layer; but it did not act alone. This trend continued in negotiations over the environmental provisions in the North American Free Trade Agreement. And the State Department rather than the EPA is the lead agency for the U.S. government in international negotiations on climate change. One should not make too much of these examples, since many environmental problems do not spill over in any major way to other countries; but a number of important ones do.

The internationalization of some important environmental problems has several implications for the EPA. First and most important, the EPA needs to broaden its efforts to help other countries—especially those in the developing world— to develop efficient and effective regulatory programs. They can learn much from the successes of U.S. environmental policy and even more from our failures, and our environmental quality is often affected by their decisions. Second, it would behoove the top officials of the EPA to focus more attention on educating the American public, not to mention its elected representatives, about the advantages of a coordinated international approach to problem solving.

Even for environmental problems that are contained within the boundaries of the United States, it is not necessarily true that a federal approach is always the best one, although that is the approach taken in the United States since 1970. The issue is one of environmental federalism.

Almost all air pollution problems and many related to water pollution require a federal or at the very least a regional approach. In the absence of such an approach, a state that set very weak air pollution standards, for instance, would "air mail" at least part of the pollution discharged within its borders to other nearby or even far away states. Similarly, a state that allowed unregulated discharges of pollution into its rivers, lakes, or the ocean could easily adversely affect water quality in other states.[28] For this reason beginning in 1970 Congress gradually began to shift to the federal level the regulatory authority for environmental protection that had previously been vested in the states. Although experts

28. In economic parlance, this is often referred to as creating a "negative externality," that is, imposing a cost on an innocent third party who does not participate in the decision to set weak standards.

debate the wisdom of this federalization,[29] it seems highly likely that this change accelerated considerably the pace of air and water quality improvements in the 1970s.

However, because many environmental problems are best dealt with through regional or federal approaches does not necessarily mean that *all* problems are most effectively handled at these levels. Nevertheless, the federal role in environmental policymaking was consistently enlarged through legislation during the 1970s and 1980s. Only during the 1990s has a willingness arisen to question the wisdom of this enlargement.[30]

Under federal statutes like the Clean Air and Clean Water Acts, as well as under other major environmental laws, an important role has been reserved for the states. For example, states have always issued nearly all of the pollutant discharge and other environmental permits required by the EPA. They have always done most of the monitoring required to determine whether ambient environmental standards are being met; and they have generally been the first to initiate enforcement actions when permit violations were detected. Often they carried out these responsibilities with extensive financial support from EPA grants and technical assistance.

For several reasons, some environmental policy experts have begun to suggest that the state role in environmental policymaking should be expanded still more.[31] One reason for this thinking is the increased capabilities of the states. When the federalization of environmental protection began in 1970, most states lacked the capacity—both budgetary and staff—to deal effectively with the serious environmental problems of the day. Today, however, the fifty states combined employ about 60,000 people in their environmental protection agencies, more than three times the employment of the federal EPA. They also raise three dollars of their own support for every dollar in grant monies they receive from EPA.[32] And several states—California is mentioned most

29. For instance, see Goklany (1998).
30. Oates (1998).
31. See Schoenbrod (1996), for example.
32. Information supplied by the Environmental Council of the States.

frequently—are acknowledged to be every bit as sophisticated in their legal, scientific, and economic expertise as the EPA.

Another reason for the renewed interest in the possibility of devolving complete authority for certain regulatory programs to the states has to do with the nature of the environmental problems that remain. Just as the transboundary nature of most air and water pollution problems make them ideal candidates for regional or federal controls, so, too, do the nature of other environmental problems suggest that they might be better handled by the states. For instance, if one state decided that it was willing to relax the current federal standards for solid waste landfills, both the added risks and the costs savings would be borne by the residents of that state alone in all but the rarest of circumstances. In other words, little or none of the environmental risks would "spill over" into adjacent states. In contrast to the current situation, in which the EPA sets uniform national standards that landfills everywhere must meet, why not allow the individual states to decide whether more secure landfills are worth the added costs?

Similarly, for all but a few biological contaminants in drinking water, the risks linked with higher concentrations of most contaminants would be borne only by those who consume the affected water for a lifetime. Why, then, not allow the states, or perhaps even individual communities, to decide how stringently they wish to regulate their drinking water? One community or state might choose to spend more of its money on vaccinations or schools and elect less strict standards for its drinking water than another; its actions would pose no risks to those living elsewhere or even to those consuming the water while passing through.[33] Under the current Safe Drinking Water Act, however, the EPA is required to set uniform national standards that every community must meet—unless it gets a special exemption. Even if standard-setting authority for drinking water were devolved to lower levels of government, the EPA would still have an important role to play. Since it

33. Certain biological contaminants can occur in drinking water—cryptosporidium, for one—that can cause illness or even death from one exposure. Because the decisions of one jurisdiction on the level of control for these types of pollutants could affect the residents of other jurisdictions, it would be appropriate for the EPA to establish national standards for them.

would make no sense for each and every jurisdiction to conduct its own research on treatment technologies, health effects, and control costs, the EPA could be responsible for such analyses and make its findings available to the states for use in their standard setting.

A final reason for renewed interest in returning to the states at least some federal environmental powers relates to one of the original rationales for federal control. It was argued in the early 1970s, most loudly by environmental advocates, that states would engage in what was called a "race to the bottom" if they, rather than the federal government, had regulatory authority. That is, in an effort to attract new industrial and other economic development, states would compete with one another by lowering environmental standards until they had degraded air and water quality considerably. Thus, the environmentalist argument ran, the federal government should set uniform discharge standards for all industrial sources so that companies could not play one state off against another. Even today it is often argued that the states must be "saved from themselves."

This argument cannot be dismissed lightly. Each time a company announces its intention to build a new plant or office building, mayors and governors rush to offer tax concessions, infrastructural improvements, and other inducements in the hopes that such sweeteners might make the firm choose their location. Possibly, the stringency of environmental standards would become an added bargaining chip in this game.

However, experts who have begun to reconsider the case for federalization have noted that a rather glaring inconsistency arises between the race-to-the-bottom argument on the one hand and the public opinion data that environmentalists often trumpet on the other.[34] Since significant majorities of those polled consistently say that, if forced to do so, they would choose environmental quality over economic growth, why would mayors or governors risk being turned out of office for engaging in a race to the bottom by relaxing pollution controls? With information on pollutant emissions more readily available, the degradation of the environment could not be hidden from the public or political opponents. In the absence of significant interstate spillovers, who better

34. See Revesz (1992) and Schoenbrod (1996), for instance.

to set the priorities—that is, determine the appropriate trade-off between economic growth and environmental quality in a region—than the elected officials closest to the affected parties? To put the matter somewhat differently, while many environmental problems belong squarely in a discussion of national priority setting, we should not assume that is true for all such problems. A thoughtful reappraisal of "who should do what" in the environmental arena would be most welcome.

This last point brings us back to the size of the EPA. Nearly half of the EPA's 18,000 employees are stationed in regional offices around the country, where their principal function is overseeing the activities of state and local environmental officials. This level of "supervision" may have been appropriate in the early years of the EPA, but it is arguable at best whether most states need the EPA to review permits they may have taken years to write. Although one might wish to redeploy elsewhere in the EPA these regional employees, that so many be engaged in their current activities is no longer necessary.

Global Climate Change

No discussion of environmental policy at the turn of the century would be complete without making some mention of global climate change. Although much is complex and controversial about this issue, at least the nature of the problem can be easily explained. Many scientists have become increasingly concerned that the combustion of fossil fuels (coal, oil, and natural gas), the deforestation of large areas, and the release of methane and other gases from both natural sources and human activities are adding to atmospheric concentrations of carbon dioxide and other so-called greenhouses gases, and that this will eventually result in a much warmer planet. Concern is justified because the extent of possible warming, and particularly the speed with which it might occur, could result in serious (some would say catastrophic) consequences for plant and animal life on earth. These consequences might include the spread of disease, the large-scale disruption of agriculture, forestry, fishing, and other economic activities, the loss of countless plant and animal species, an increased frequency of severe weather events (hurricanes and droughts, for instance), and—most calamitously—an increase in sea level that could completely cover small, low-lying island nations and inundate coastal areas that are now the sites of some of the of the world's greatest cities and home to hundreds of millions of people.

Notice the number of "mights" and "coulds" sprinkled throughout the foregoing description of the problem. The defining characteristic of global climate change is the tremendous uncertainty attached to nearly every aspect of it. Some things, however, are not matters of huge controversy. There is broad agreement that the atmospheric concentration of carbon dioxide, the most plentiful greenhouse gas, has increased significantly during the past 150 years, by about 30 percent, and that—at least recently—concentrations of some of the other gases that can trap heat in the earth's atmosphere have also increased. Agreement is also broad (although apparently not unanimous) that the average surface temperature of the earth has increased, especially during the past decade.

Beyond these points, however, disagreement is the rule rather than the exception. For instance, some scientists believe that the warming observed is a consequence of the increased atmospheric concentrations of greenhouse gases. Others, including some who believe the problem is potentially serious, are not prepared to conclude that a causal relationship has been proved. Huge admitted gaps exist in the information necessary for diagnosing the consequences of climate change or combating it in an effective way. For instance, almost no one believes that analysts have the ability now to confidently predict what the effects of a warmer planet might be in a certain geographic area, even if they could predict what the change would be in global average temperature. Furthermore, no one knows with confidence how expensive it might be to reduce the risk posed by global warming.

From a policy perspective, other complications exist. First, the United States is just one of many countries whose emissions of greenhouse gases contribute to atmospheric concentrations, with the United States producing about 20 percent of annual global emissions of carbon dioxide. Even if the United States were to curtail emissions sharply, which at present seems a most unlikely prospect, it would make very little difference in the long run unless other countries also took actions to reduce significantly their contributions to the atmospheric burden of these gases. Second, because carbon dioxide and other greenhouse gases do not dissipate quickly, some time would elapse before even significant actions had perceptible effects.

Third and finally, although no doubt some relatively inexpensive actions could be taken to reduce carbon dioxide emissions, most analyses suggest that even reducing the *rate of growth* of emissions in the United States by an appreciable amount would be expensive. In the short term few alternatives exist for reducing emissions other than increasing the price of energy—coal, gasoline, heating oil, and natural gas—through explicit or implicit taxes on the carbon content of these fuels. Sharp disagreements occur about how much of a burden such measures would impose on the economy. The Clinton administration, using a very optimistic set of assumptions, estimated that it might be possible to reduce absolute annual amounts of emissions—not just their rate of growth—for as little as $10 billion a year.[35] Under a more sober set of assumptions, other experts have estimated that the costs might be as high as $50 billion annually.[36] Those at the most pessimistic end of the spectrum have concluded that the nation may have to spend as much as it spends to comply with all other environmental regulations today to significantly reduce carbon dioxide emissions. In other words, they believe the annual price tag would be in the hundreds of billions of dollars.[37]

Given all the uncertainties involved, as well as the possibility that doing something significant about this problem could be quite costly, why contemplate such measures? The answer is obvious: how could responsible policymakers not at least consider taking action if there is even a small risk of contributing significantly to a catastrophic change in the world's climate, even if the full effects of the calamity would not materialize before another century passes?

The United States has done more than consider taking action. In December 1997 the United States and 130 other countries reached an agreement in Kyoto, Japan, to limit emissions of carbon dioxide and other greenhouse gases from the developed countries. Under the pro-

35. Yellen (1998).
36. Manne and Richels (1999, p. 9).
37. Montgomery (1997).

tocol, the United States is required to reduce its emissions 7 percent below its 1990 levels between 2008 and 2012. Other developed countries face less stringent limits, and no limits were placed on emissions from China, India, Brazil, Indonesia, or other developing countries even though their share of global emissions is rising rapidly.[38] Although the United States has signed this agreement, it is not binding because it has not been submitted to, let alone ratified by, the Senate as required by the Constitution. In the present political climate, not only would the agreement fail to receive the two-thirds majority necessary for approval, it is not clear that it would garner more than a handful of votes.

The best way to view this dilemma is as follows. If the United States and other countries spend money now—in the form of higher energy prices and job losses in at least some industries—they can reduce at least somewhat the likelihood of an unacceptable change in the future climate of the earth. The more nations are willing to spend now, the greater will be the reduction in risk. The question is: what is the right amount to spend?

It seems evident that before the United States is willing to make more than a token effort, at least three things must happen. First, those in favor of reducing greenhouse gas emissions must convince the American public, not just policymakers in the administration or Congress, that such measures will bring important benefits. This is necessary because surely the public will react strongly to any policies that increase energy prices. Second, analysts must develop better estimates of the likely price tags associated with various degrees of action. Although some uncertainty will always characterize such matters, its range can be narrowed with additional work. Third, much effort must go into persuading the developing countries that—eventually, if not immediately—they will have to participate in a global effort to reduce the rate of growth of greenhouse gases in the atmosphere. It is hard to imagine that the United States or other developed countries will long bear climate-mitigation costs if the sacrifices they are making are more than

38. Developing countries were exempted because the existing stock of greenhouse gases in the atmosphere now has come overwhelmingly from the combustion of fossil fuels and the other activities of the developed countries.

canceled out by increased greenhouse emissions from the developing countries.

Conclusion

Federal regulation of the environment is here to stay—a direct consequence of past successes and the broad support that it enjoys among the American public. Although sweeping conclusions are difficult (and dangerous) to make, almost everyone in the United States is better off as a result of the environmental legislative and regulatory programs put into place since 1970, even taking into account the significant costs incurred during the past three decades. This does not mean, however, that the nation should rest on its laurels. Environmental policy can and should be improved significantly. The right kinds of changes will make it possible to have an even better environment than we enjoy now while spending no more than we do currently, or to maintain what we now have while freeing up resources for other social problems.

Both major political parties have roles to play if we are to realize these gains. The Republican Party has the most work to do. It is the party of Theodore Roosevelt, inarguably the most environmentally minded president ever, as well as Richard Nixon and George Bush, presidents who took the environment very seriously and signed into law some of the farthest-reaching statutes. Nevertheless, its image among environmentally minded voters is not a good one. In fact, in a recent Gallup/CNN/*USA Today* poll more than one-third of self-identified Republicans expressed the view that the Democratic Party is able to "do a better job of handling the environment."

On each of the last two occasions when the Republicans set out to "reform" environmental policy—once under President Reagan (when Congress was under Democratic control) and once in 1995 when the Republicans regained control of both houses of Congress—they proceeded in such as way as to suggest to many that at least some of their numbers had more than reform in mind. More than anything else, the Republicans need to reassure an anxious public that they share its core belief in the importance of clean air and water and the careful handling of solid and hazardous wastes, even as they seek to repeal those regulations that do not afford protection commensurate with their cost.

The Democratic Party faces challenges of its own. These will be hard to address, however, because there is a prevailing sense among party leaders that "the environment is an issue on which we win." This makes it difficult to countenance new directions. Yet despite the support for environmental protection among the public, it is not an unmitigated love-in. Among owners and managers of small businesses, for example, great consternation prevails about the required paperwork, procedural delays encountered in obtaining permits, the inflexibility of many environmental regulatory programs, and costs of compliance. These concerns are magnified among those who must run large companies, manufacturing and otherwise. The latter are tempted by the often speedier permitting procedures, more flexible environmental rules, and more welcoming attitudes of other countries, and they have the ability to shift the locus of production and the jobs that come with their businesses to foreign shores. Democrats would do well to listen much more carefully to these concerns and to avoid characterizing each effort to address them as an all-out assault on the progress of the past three decades.

To reiterate, changes are under way in U.S. environmental policy that seem unlikely to be reversed. As long as they are managed carefully, it would be unwise to try. First, command-and-control regulation is gradually giving way to the use of incentive-based approaches, and this change will redound to the benefit of the economy and the environment. By making wider use of pollution taxes, marketable discharge permits, and the like, it should be possible to reduce annual spending on environmental protection by perhaps as much as 15 percent while enjoying the same or better environmental conditions as we do today. Also, in the future we will see more and more information about the environment (pertaining to ambient environmental quality and the performance of individual firms and even plants) made available to the public. This, too, will represent a favorable development as long as significant efforts are made to help the public understand this information and put it into proper context ("How much risk does an exposure entail, and how does that compare to the other risks I encounter in everyday life?"). Finally, the pull of certain environmental responsibilities away from Washington can also be healthy, especially if the nation recognizes that only the federal government can address some important environmental problems effectively. We need to let go of the belief, however, that every environmental problem can only be solved by Washington. One possible by-product of selective devolution to lower levels of government, incidentally, might be a gradual restoration of faith in government. This change in perspective is more likely if and when it becomes more common for problems to be handled at government levels closer to the lives of those affected.

It is much harder to speak confidently about what will or even should happen concerning global climate change. As already discussed, and barring some new scientific discovery suggesting that the problem is far more serious than previously believed, it seems highly unlikely that the Kyoto protocol will come into effect in the United States in anything remotely resembling its present form. If the United States begins now to do research on and invest more heavily in new, less carbon-intensive technologies for transportation, electricity generation, and industrial production, and begin a modest program of reductions in greenhouse gas emissions, the nation will be acting wisely. In fact, a program of decarbonization that begins gradually and saves the biggest emissions reductions for future decades (when the cost of reducing emissions ought to be lower) is to be preferred to one requiring large emissions reductions in the next decade. A more gradual approach has one other compelling feature: it would allow for a midcourse correction in policy should we come to regard climate change as a less pressing problem in years to come. That seems unlikely from the current vantage point, but it is not impossible. Perhaps the most vexing aspect of climate change is the huge disparity between the time horizon of the problem itself—hundreds of years, at the least—and the political horizons of those who must legislate about it—six years at most.

References

Carlson, Curtis, and others. 1999. "Sulfur Dioxide Control by Electric Utilities: What Are the Gains from Trade?" Discussion Paper 98-44 rev. Washington: Resources for the Future.

Crews, Clyde Wayne, Jr. 1999. *Ten Thousand Commandments: An Annual Policymaker's Snapshot of the Federal Regulatory State*. Washington: Competitive Enterprise Institute.

Davies, J. Clarence, and Jan Mazurek. 1998. *Pollution Control in the United States: Evaluating the System*. Washington: Resources for the Future.

DeMuth, Christopher C. 1980a. "Constraining Regulatory Costs, Part I: The White House Review Programs." *Regulation* 4 (January–February):13–26.

———. 1980b. "Constraining Regulatory Costs, Part Two: The Regulatory Budget." *Regulation* 4 (March–April): 29–43.

Easterbrook, Gregg. 1995. *A Moment on the Earth: The Coming Age of Environmental Optimism*. Viking.

Environmental Protection Agency. 1990. *Environmental Investments: The Cost of a Clean Environment*. EPA-230-11-90-083. Washington.

———. 1997. *The Benefits and Costs of the Clean Air Act, 1970 to 1990*. Washington.

———. 1998. *National Air Quality and Emissions Trends Report, 1997*. EPA 454/R-98-016. Washington.

Goklany, Indur M. 1998. *Do We Need the Federal Government to Protect Air Quality?* Policy Study Number 150. St. Louis, Mo.: Center for the Study of American Business.

———. Forthcoming. *Clearing the Air: The Real Story of the War on Air Pollution*. Washington: Cato Institute.

Graham, Mary. 1999. *The Morning after Earth Day: Practical Environmental Politics*. Brookings.

Hahn, Robert W., and John A. Hird. 1991. "The Costs and Benefits of Regulation: Review and Synthesis." *Yale Journal on Regulation* 8 (Winter): 233–78.

Harrington, Winston, Richard D. Morgenstern, and Peter Nelson. 1999. *On the Accuracy of Regulatory Cost Estimates*. Discussion Paper 99-18. Washington: Resources for the Future.

Kneese, Allen V., and Charles L. Schultze. 1975. *Pollution, Prices, and Public Policy*. Brookings.

Ladd, Everett Carll, and Karlyn H. Bowman. 1995. *Attitudes toward the Environment: Twenty-five Years after Earth Day*. Washington: AEI Press.

Litan, Robert E., and William D. Nordhaus. 1983. *Reforming Federal Regulation*. Yale University Press.

Manne, Alan S., and Richard G. Richels. 1999. "The Kyoto Protocol: A Cost-Effective Strategy for Meeting Environmental Objectives?" *Energy Journal*, supplement: 1–23.

Marlin, Adam S. 1999. "A Will of Their Own." *CQ Weekly* 57 (January 30): 250.

Montgomery, W. David. 1997. *Prepared Statement of W. David Montgomery, Vice President, Charles River Associates, Washington D.C.* Hearings before the Subcommittee on Energy and Environment of the House Committee on Science (October 9). Government Printing Office.

National Environmental Education and Training Foundation. 1997. *The National Report Card on Environmental Knowledge, Attitudes and Behaviors.* Washington.

Oates, Wallace E. 1998. "Thinking about Environmental Federalism." *Resources* 130 (Winter): 14–16.

Office of Management and Budget. 1998. *Report to Congress on the Costs and Benefits of Federal Regulations.*

Revesz, Richard L. 1992. "Rehabilitating Interstate Competition: Rethinking the 'Race-to-the-Bottom' Rationale for Federal Environmental Regulation." *New York University Law Review.* 67(6): 1210–55.

Shoenbrod, David. 1996. "Why States, Not EPA, Should Set Pollution Standards." *Regulation* 19: 18–25.

Vogan, Christine R. 1996. "Pollution Abatement and Control Expenditures, 1972-1994." *Survey of Current Business* 76(September): 48–67. Washington: Bureau of Economic Analysis.

Warren, Melinda, and William F. Lauber. 1998. *Regulatory Changes and Trends: An Analysis of the 1999 Federal Budget.* St. Louis, Mo.: Center for the Study of American Business.

Yellen, Janet. 1998. "Testimony of Dr. Janet Yellen, Chair, Council of Economic Advisers before the House Commerce Committee on the Economics of the Kyoto Protocol" (March 4). Government Printing Office.

PART IV

Making Government Work

PAUL C. LIGHT 12

Changing the Shape
of Government

THE PAST FIFTEEN YEARS have witnessed the most dramatic, yet least understood, reshaping of the administrative state in the nation's history. In the span of just three administrations, the federal government reduced its total military and civilian work force by one-sixth (300,000 jobs), eliminated a quarter of its middle-level management positions (35,000 jobs), and sliced its Department of Defense contract work force by nearly one-third (1.6 million jobs).

Not all the reshaping meant cuts. Between 1984 and 1996, the non-Defense Department contract and grant work force grew by one-sixth (600,000 jobs), the most senior layers of government thickened with the creation of 22 new management titles, and 700 new career and political executives were added to the 1,700 already in place. By 1996 the number of middle-level federal employees exceeded, for the first time in civil service history, the number of lower-level employees.[1]

At least as measured by the full-time-equivalent civil service headcount, the size of the federal government has changed little since the early 1960s, even though the federal government's budget and mission have grown dramatically. There are 2 percent fewer civil service

---

1. In 1996 there were 638,427 middle-level employees and 594,126 lower-level employees. Light (1999).

393

employees today than there were in 1962 but 17 percent fewer than in 1990. These figures suggest that President Bill Clinton was correct when, in his 1996 State of the Union address, he declared that the era of big government was over. But beneath this stable surface much has changed. In fact, the true size of the federal government, defined as the number of workers who produce goods and services on the federal government's behalf, wherever those jobs are located, has expanded considerably.

Gone are the days when most of the goods and services consumed by government were produced in house. Because the federal government has become increasingly dependent on contractors, grantees, and state and local employees to meet its missions, its true size at the turn of the century dwarfs that of the early 1960s.[2] The true size of government— a work force that encompasses an estimated 5.6 million jobs created under federal contracts, another 2.4 million jobs generated under grants, and 4.6 million jobs covered under mandates to state and local governments, as well as the formal civil service workers and the uniformed military, totals almost 17 million workers. Big government is alive and well, though undeniably smaller than it was just six years ago.

Gone too are the days when the president could command every last person in the organization, as public administration scholar Luther Gulick once described the job of the chief executive. The federal government has become more elliptical. Increasingly, federal employees are supervising and procuring the work of nonfederal employees who are doing the delivering and producing. Part of this shift reflects a natural evolution as new technologies render some front-line jobs obsolete. Furthermore, federal departments and agencies have done what comes naturally in the face of unrelenting political pressure to keep the civil service small; they have pushed, as much as possible, front-line work outward. The federal government, lacking clear guidelines for deciding which jobs should stay inside government and which should go, eliminated the jobs that were the easiest to abolish, namely, those with the highest attrition and the lowest political profile.

2. These estimates come from Light (1999); the estimating process is described in chapters 1 and 2 of the book.

In the increasingly elliptical future, the rest of the pyramid will still exist; it will just be set outside of the official federal worker headcount among the millions working for contractors, grantees, and state and local governments delivering services on the federal government's behalf. As long as the federal mission continues to grow, the faithful execution of the laws will rely more on writing careful contracts, grants, and mandates than on the traditional chain of command between elected representatives and a career work force. That observation reflects neither a liberal nor a conservative political position. It simply describes the way government must operate under pressure to do more with less.

An Inventory of Change

During the past decade and one-half, the girth, height, and shape of the administrative hierarchy of the federal government have undergone remarkable change.

The Girth of Government

After growing from the 1930s through the late 1980s, the girth of government—the size of the work force—has been shrinking ever since. The total Defense Department work force—civil servants, uniformed military personnel, contractors, and grant-sponsored employees— contracted by over 2.6 million employees between 1984 and 1996 while that of the rest of the federal government, including the U.S. Postal Service, expanded by 800,000.

The very top of the federal hierarchy, where presidential appointees and senior career executives perch, saw a more than fivefold increase between 1960 and 1992. To its credit, the Clinton administration held the total number of top executives—those with some variant of the top five departmental titles (secretary, deputy secretary, undersecretary, assistant secretary, and administrator)—in check. Between January 20, 1993, and the summer of 1998, the number of such executives grew by just fifty-four, from 2,408 to 2,462 officials. Subtracting out the seventy-eight such jobs created in the newly independent Social Security Administration, the top administrator ranks actually thinned during the Clinton administration. In contrast, the Reagan administration added 173 posts to the top of government, while the Bush administration added more than 600.[3]

The Clinton administration also reduced the number of middle managers. The federal government employed 126,000 middle managers in 1997, down from 161,000 in 1992 and 149,600 in 1989, but roughly equal to the number of middle managers in 1983. In 1992 there were eight rank-and-file workers for every supervisor; by 1997 the ratio had risen to eleven to one. All but two departments lost midlevel supervisors during this period. Only the Department of Justice (up roughly 2,000 supervisors) and the Department of State (up exactly 18) expanded midlevel management ranks. The Department of Interior and the Department of Treasury each lost roughly one-sixth of their middle managers; the Departments of Agriculture, Commerce, Labor, and Transportation each lost almost one-fifth. The Department of Education and the General Services Administration experienced cuts of more than one-third; the Environmental Protection Agency and the Department of Housing and Urban Development, almost two-fifths; the Department of Energy and the National Aeronautics and Space Administration, more than half; and the Office of Personnel Management, more than two-thirds.

The attack on middle management, which started with military base closures in the late 1980s, accelerated with Clinton's 1993 executive order mandating a 100,000 reduction in total employment. The Workforce Restructuring Act of 1994 raised the downsizing target to 272,900 positions. Although presidential appointees and senior executives accounted for none of the reductions, and middle managers formed just 10 percent of the total cutback, these initiatives clearly slowed the growth rate in both categories.

The Clinton administration's effort to trim the top ranks was eased when Congress approved $25,000 voluntary buyouts to senior and middle-level managers. These buyouts allowed the administration to shrink the number of retirement-eligible executives and managers. Of

---

3. According to a careful coding of the *Winter 1998 Federal Yellow Book* Leadership Directories (1998), there were 2,462 federal executives. That number includes everything from chiefs of staff to associate undersecretaries, assistant inspectors general to principal deputy administrators. See Light (1995, p. 192).

83,000 buyouts accepted between 1993 and the first half of 1995, almost three-quarters involved workers who were eligible for early or regular retirement. Whether those employees would have departed without the buyout is a matter of debate, but the fact remains that they did vacate at least some of the middle-level management positions.

There is no question that the downsizing hit the bottom levels of government—where the pay is lowest and attrition rates the highest—the hardest. The number of employees in the lower grades of the federal general employment schedule dropped by more than 170,000 between 1992 and 1997, and the number of blue-collar jobs fell by more than 100,000. The average grade of the lower-level employees who remained increased by its largest margin in a decade, meaning that jobs were disproportionately eliminated at the bottom-most levels.

It is not exactly clear where the bottom-level jobs went. Some no doubt disappeared forever; others likely ended up in service contracts. Although the Office of Management and Budget (OMB) asked agencies to collect information on any shift of jobs from employees to contractors, it has not monitored these data so one can only speculate about the extent to which work has been outsourced. It is conceivable that many of the 273,000 positions eliminated during the Clinton administration downsizing had become expendable over the previous decades, but until the early 1990s the federal government lacked the will and the means to abolish positions and terminate workers.

Presidential appointees and senior managers were not alone in surviving the downsizing mostly unscathed. The middle levels of government (as distinct from middle managers) remained largely intact. Even as the number of middle-level managers fell by a quarter, the number of middle-level nonmanagers increased from 485,000 to 510,000. Some managers who were reclassified into nonmanagerial positions could have been left at the same grade. Some vacated positions were "backfilled," meaning that the occupant left, and the person next in line took the job and the grade. Neither Clinton's 1993 executive order nor the Workforce Reduction Act required that the more highly graded jobs be abolished upon the incumbent's departure.

Despite the loss of 35,000 middle-management jobs and the separation of thousands of about-to-retire employees, the average middle-level pay grade increased. The hierarchy most certainly lost weight in the total number of employees but actually gained weight as measured in the average grade of the employees who remained.

The Height of Government

Just because the number of senior executives or middle managers has remained steady or declined does not mean that the number of layers they occupy has remained constant or diminished. At the middle levels, for example, many agencies reduced the number of managers merely by assigning different titles. According to the General Accounting Office, 41 percent of the downsizing of supervisors at the NASA Marshall Space Flight Center involved such reclassification, as did 40 percent of the cuts at the Bureau of Land Management and 35 percent at the Federal Aviation Administration. The Social Security Administration cut nearly 2,800 middle-level supervisory positions between 1993 and 1998 but created 1,900 new nonsupervisory positions, including 500 "team leaders" and 1,350 "management support specialists."

The continued layering of government is most apparent at the top. There, the Clinton administration not only failed to stem the proliferation of new titles but presided over the most significant addition of layers in modern executive history. From 1992 to 1998, the fourteen departments of government abolished three senior-level titles and created nineteen new ones, including several new "alter ego" deputy posts, such as deputy to the deputy secretary, principal assistant deputy undersecretary, associate principal deputy assistant secretary, chief of staff to the undersecretary, assistant chief of staff to the administrator, and chief of staff to the assistant administrator. Government's top tier may not have grown wider, but it most certainly grew taller. The Clinton administration created as many new titles during its first six years as the past seven administrations created over the preceding thirty-three years.

Not all of the new layers will survive. Most of the new titles are held by only one person in one department. But if the past is prologue, some of the titles will spread to other departments, largely through a process that Senator Daniel Patrick Moynihan has referred to as the "iron law of emulation." But for the secretary title, which has existed since the first Congress created the first department, each title originated in only one department.

Layering creates impediments to efficient and effective governance. It increases the distance that ideas must travel up to reach the secretary and that guidance must travel down to the front lines of government. More hands must touch the paper, more signatures grace the page, and more eyes read the memos. It is impossible for the top to know what the bottom is doing when the bottom lies thirty or more layers below; it is impossible for the bottom to understand clearly the top when messages go through dozens of interpretations on their journey down. Like the game of "telephone," in which messages become hopelessly distorted as they are relayed from child to child, the layers merely add to the potential confusion and loss of accountability between the top and the bottom.

The Dominance of Defense

Both the body of government (full-time-equivalent civil service workers) and its shadow (contract- and grant-created workers) appear to have narrowed during the past decade and a half with virtually all of the decline occurring since 1990. It would be a mistake, however, to interpret these declines as entirely, or even largely, the result of President Clinton's 1993 executive order or the Workforce Restructuring Act of 1994. The largest decline, some 260,000 jobs, occurred in the Department of Defense, exactly what one would have expected with the end of the cold war. To be sure, some domestic agencies absorbed significant cuts between 1984 and 1996. The Department of the Interior cut nearly 30,000 jobs, the Department of Agriculture 8,000, the General Services Administration almost 10,000, the Tennessee Valley Authority 16,000, and the Social Security Administration almost 14,000. Yet other domestic agencies expanded and, overall, the nondefense federal civil service grew by 6 percent—from 1.06 million to 1.12 million—between 1984 and 1996. At the same time, the contract work force grew 50 percent— from 1.4 to 2.0 million—and the grant work force 7 percent—from 2.2 million to 2.36 million.

Table 12-1 shows the dominant effects that defense downsizing had on the true size of government. While overall a dramatic 1.7 million drop occurred in the true size of government between 1984 and 1996, the nondefense work force increased by almost 1 million jobs between 1984 and 1990 before falling back by 130,000 jobs by 1996.

Table 12-1. *The Dominant Impact of Defense, 1984–96*

	1984	1990	1996
Total federal work force	13,965,000	13,860,000	12,299,000
Total federal work force minus Defense Department shadow work force	8,717,000	9,571,000	8,612,000
Total federal work force minus Defense Department civil service and military	5,498,000	6,459,000	6,326,000

Source: Light (1999, tables 2-2, 2-5, 2-6).

The dominant impact of defense is even more obvious in table 12-2, which covers a longer period. Between 1960, when John F. Kennedy entered office at the beginning of an eight-year expansion in the federal mission, and 1992, when President Clinton and Congress ordered a serious, often painful, downsizing for most domestic agencies, the total end-of-year headcount of nondefense civil servants rose fairly steadily except for a brief interruption during the first few years of the Reagan administration. Since 1992 this headcount has declined by about 9 percent or 110,000 jobs.

Unfortunately, data are not available for the contract, grant, and mandate work force before 1984. However, the level of real federal consumption expenditures recorded in the National Income and Product Accounts can be used as a rough indicator of trends in the size of this work force.[4] Based on the changes in consumption expenditures, one can see that the combined defense and nondefense shadow work force

4. Both military and civil service compensation are included in how the Bureau of Economic Analysis defines consumption expenditures, which also encompass purchases of durable (aircraft, missiles, ships, electronic equipments, and so forth) and nondurable (fuel, ammunition, food, supplies, water bottles, and so forth) goods, as well as all expenditures on services (research and development, weapons support, personnel support, travel) and structures. The conclusions drawn in the text assume that military compensation has declined over time as the armed services have contracted and that real civilian compensation has remained relatively stable. For a summary of how the BEA records government transactions, see U.S. Department of Commerce (1988).

Table 12-2. *The Impact of Defense on the Size of the Federal Government, 1960–96*

Year	Number of employees, end-of-year civilian employment	Number of employees, minus Defense Department civilian employment	Consumption expenditures (in billions of 1992 dollars)	Minus Defense Department consumption expenditures
1960	1,808,000	761,000	$239.5	$31.0
1964	1,884,000	854,000	277.5	66.0
1968	2,289,000	972,000	357.0	72.2
1972	2,117,000	1,009,000	315.2	84.9
1976	2,157,000	1,147,000	305.0	94.8
1980	2,161,000	1,201,000	341.7	109.0
1984	2,171,000	1,127,000	393.0	96.2
1988	2,222,000	1,172,000	452.0	106.7
1992	2,225,000	1,273,000	448.9	130.0
1996	1,934,000	1,166,000	408.9	138.2
1998	1,856,000	1,163,000	399.5[a]	134.8[a]

Sources: *Budget of the United States Government, Historical Tables, Fiscal Year 2000* (tables 17-1, 14-1).

a. Author's estimate.

has grown significantly since 1960, perhaps doubling over the last thirty-nine years. Excluding defense, there might have been close to a fourfold increase in the shadow over this period. Although defense consumption expenditures have certainly declined since the end of the cold war, nondefense consumption expenditures have increased steadily, showing no parallel decline with the civil service downsizing described above.

Instead of returning the true size of government to 1960s levels, the recent downsizing has returned the defense work force (civilian, military, plus shadow) to that of the 1970s, and the nondefense work force to that seen in the mid-1980s. Both may be notable achievements if only because the earlier trend lines were rising. Although the era of big and growing government may be over, or at least taking a pause, only the most circumscribed reading of the federal work force data would lead one to conclude that an era of small government has begun.

Accidents and Confusion

Undoubtedly the federal hierarchy has been reshaped over the past fifteen years. Government is much slimmer at the bottom, slightly wider at the middle, much taller at the top, and far more dependent on service contractors than ever before. Furthermore, this administrative restructuring has, for the most part, been accidental, that is, unguided. Personnel ceilings, hiring freezes, and civil service rules have combined to produce haphazard downsizing. If there was any underlying logic to the cutbacks, it was to make sure the federal government did not engage in commercial activities in areas that were inherently nongovernmental. Nonetheless reality has generally fallen well short of the intent.

The Accidents of Downsizing

Personnel ceilings and hiring freezes, no matter how they are structured, are at best passive and blunt instruments for reshaping government. The downward pressure they exert is largely accidental. Ideally, downsizing should be a deliberate and well-thought-out process. Departments and agencies should determine the appropriate number of employees needed to fulfill each of their missions and then target areas for downsizing in which there are excess workers. To facilitate elimination of workers in unneeded positions, Congress and the president should authorize an array of tools. Were it possible, redundant workers would be reallocated to jobs in the agency's "core competencies." In practice, of course, the downsizing that has occurred over the past fifty years has been anything but a deliberate process. Rather, it has been largely a random procedure that has relied on voluntary exits at the bottom of government to achieve its goals.

Downsizing through attrition is easily the least painful way for organizations to lose weight. No one but the exiting employee has to make a decision about who stays and goes. Organizations can easily convince themselves that attrition is also the fairest and, possibly, the most sensible way to shrink. If the job is not good enough to hold an employee, perhaps it is not important enough to defend. Unfortunately, vacancies do not occur evenly or where downsizing makes the most sense. Because quit rates are much higher at the bottom of most organizations than at the top, the decision to use attrition-based downsizing is essentially a decision to attack the front-line work force.

What may make the federal government different from smaller organizations is its inability to monitor or control the ebb and flow of personnel. No one knows who's coming and who's going. The federal headcount may look relatively stable on the surface, rarely moving more than ten thousand to twenty thousand from year to year. But underneath the surface there is constant change. In fiscal year 1997 alone, nearly 283,000 accessions to the federal work force and 333,000 separations took place, most of them at the bottom of government.[5]

Thus, more than enough attrition occurs to fashion a deliberative downsizing plan. Yet most of the government's downsizing efforts make no attempt to do so. During the early 1980s, for example, the Department of Labor used attrition to cut its work force by 23 percent. While the department was cutting out 6,000 positions overall, it hired 8,000 new employees but not according to any well-thought-out plan. According to the National Academy of Public Administration, "Neither the hiring activity nor the attrition activity was monitored or managed effectively, resulting in an organization that was older, less diverse, with a higher supervisory ratio to employees supervised, and with skill imbalances, professionals doing clerical work, and significant unmet training needs."[6] Thus an opportunity was lost.

The explanation for this behavior is hardly surprising. Departments and agencies would have to define the core competencies needed to perform their tasks. Imagine the difficulties that would involve! Someone would have to establish clear mission priorities, which in turn would have to be linked clearly to organizational capacity. Someone would have to sort through the responsibilities to determine which ones are inherently governmental and which could be contracted, granted, or mandated outward. Someone would also have to assess the relative skills needed to cover the core competencies. Someone would need the power to rearrange those core competencies from one unit to another

5. For figures from the Office of Personnel Management *Fact Book* see OPM's website (opm.gov/feddata/98 factbk.pdf [July 1, 1999]).

6. National Academy of Public Administration (1995, p. 21).

as priorities shift. And someone would have to forecast future needs in time to recruit new capacity and sever the old. Those someones simply do not exist. Nor do the data needed to track the ebb and flow of capacity across units and time.

When combined with this failure to construct strategic downsizing plans, the tools used in federal downsizing other than attrition— namely, buyouts and reductions in force (RIFs)—raise particular concerns. The two are diametrically opposed in important ways. Buyouts are entirely voluntary and tend to entice more senior employees to leave, while RIFs are coercive and tend to push out more junior employees. Buyouts tend to produce more dollar savings. The General Accounting Office estimated that, early in the Workforce Restructuring Act downsizing, the average salaries of federal employees accepting the buyouts as a step into early or already-planned retirement averaged $48,000 a year; the average for those who took the buyout as part of a simple resignation was $35,000. In contrast, salaries of employees who left government under RIFs averaged just under $30,000.

One reason for the difference involves the practice of "bumping and retreating." Under civil service rules, RIFed workers with seniority have the right to displace more junior employees, and they can retain their higher salaries for a certain period. Although buyouts cost money—as much as $25,000—and RIFs do not, buyouts can save as much as $60,000 more than RIFs over a five-year period.[7]

During the first five years of the Workforce Restructuring Act approximately 175,000 departures with buyouts took place. No one knows, however, how many of these workers would have retired in this period absent the buyouts. More important, there is no evidence whatsoever that buyouts succeeded in separating the *right* employees. This is not to suggest that the Clinton administration ignored the issue. The vice president's reinventing government project targeted so-called control employees—those working in personnel, budget, accounting, or acquisition units—for a 50 percent reduction. As part of their assault on bureaucracy and red tape, the reinventors assumed they could cut control systems and reallocate the controllers to more productive work.

---

7. General Accounting Office (1996b).

The theory, best articulated by the Gore task force on streamlining, posited that if the controls were cut, the controllers would go away.

> The federal government spends an estimated $35 billion annually for salaries, benefits, and the administrative costs of its management control functions. Roughly one in three federal employees is involved. The job of many of these people is to create and enforce rules. Without dramatically reducing the influence of these people on line managers and workers, reinvention and culture change cannot succeed. As a result, streamlining headquarters and regional offices where most of these control functions are located is essential, and additionally will save money without cutting services.[8]

The problem with the initiative was that the reinventors had no way of clearly identifying their targets. The best they could do was bomb the headquarters and regional offices in the hope that control jobs would be part of the collateral damage. However, the postbombing survey shows mixed impacts. Control jobs were cut but so were noncontrol jobs. According to the General Accounting Office, the downsizing resulted in little change in the ratio of control to noncontrol personnel.[9]

Ironically, the inability to target control personnel resulted from the failure of previous administrations to build a work force tracking system that could be used to distinguish essential from nonessential jobs. Just as liberating armies need good intelligence and accurate maps to ensure victory, the reinventors needed information systems and a bit of scientific management to find the leverage points within the agencies. Had they had the work force planning system that the General Accounting Office had long recommended, they could have targeted the downsizing more accurately.

That would have meant more pain for the work force, of course, which is something the reinventing campaign foreswore from the beginning. "An aggressive attack on the management control structure must not become an attack on the civil servants employed in these structures," the streamlining task force cautioned.

---

8. National Performance Review (1993, p. 4).
9. General Accounting Office (1996a, p. 26).

They have been doing the jobs they were asked to do. They deserve an opportunity to redirect their careers, to be retrained and perhaps relocated, and to directly provide services rather than controlling the people who do. If an employee whose job is eliminated cannot retire through an early retirement program, and does not elect to take a cash incentive to leave government service, then every effort will be made to find another job offer, either within the government or in the private sector.[10]

No work force planning system meant no precise targeting. Contrary to the rhetoric, the destruction from downsizing was haphazard. Control positions, as a proportion of total department employment, increased as a result of the downsizing at the Department of Defense. Long-standing organizational theory offers a straightforward explanation for this unexpected result. Control personnel can be expected to increase during downsizing, both because more control is needed to manage the transitions and because control personnel are, well, good at controlling their own destiny.

Better work force planning could have produced a much better result. As the General Accounting Office concluded, "The buyout authority gave agencies a powerful tool to manage their downsizing by directing personnel cuts where they were needed most. However, it appears that many agencies used buyouts to meet work force reduction goals without restructuring their agencies' workforces."[11]

Some would argue that RIFs gave the government downsizers an effective tool for reshaping the hierarchy. RIFs are compulsory, cannot be avoided, and require specific target identification. This is why involuntary separation is the primary tool used in nearly three-quarters of all downsizings in the private sector. What makes government different is that RIFs interact with civil service rules to create a toxic poison that affects morale. As already noted, RIFs can create extraordinary disruption as employees spend countless hours trying to figure out their bumping opportunities within their departments. "Retention, removal, and related RIF decisions are based on seniority, employment status, veterans preference, and past performance. As a result, RIF decisions

10. National Performance Review (1993, p. 4).
11. General Accounting Office (1996a, p. 33).

are historically-based rather than based on the ability of employees to meet an agency's current and future needs."[12]

Moreover, it is nearly impossible to use RIFs to target poor performers or weak units. The bumping and retreating rights are simply too powerful. Although several federal agencies did use RIFs to meet the Workforce Restructuring Act targets, the total numbers were small compared with the voluntary and attrition-based separations. In all, only 7,500 federal employees were RIFed in 1994–95. One-third of the separations occurred at the Philadelphia, Portsmouth, and Norfolk naval shipyards.

Although neither buyouts nor RIFs were used to target poor performers, several agencies did use deliberate means to protect their core work force. For example, the Army Material Command did not allow its scientists and engineers to participate in the agency's buyout program. By restricting access to the buyouts, the agency ensured that its core competency remained mostly intact as it dropped from 110,000 to 60,000 employees. Similarly, the Office of Personnel Management (OPM) targeted nonessential activities for an aggressive privatization program. By reducing its headcount through the privatization of its investigations service and training programs, OPM maintained its core competency as its overall work force fell by almost half. Denying buyouts to certain staffs and red-lining specific units for elimination were hardly popular approaches to managing the downsizing. It would have been much easier to let attrition and random retirements take their course. But the U.S. Army Materiel Command and OPM chose to make the hard choices necessary for strategic downsizing.

Confusions of Intent

Together with targeting the downsizing on control personnel, the past three administrations could have decided to target cuts on federal employees engaged in "commercial activities," while protecting those involved in "inherently governmental functions." The distinction, while appearing to offer useful guidance on which employees should stay and which should leave, turns out to be of little practical use because both terms are too vague.

12. National Academy of Public Administration (1997, p. 52).

COMMERCIAL ACTIVITIES. Over the years, the government has had a difficult time providing a clear definition of "commercial activities," arguably the simpler of the two terms. OMB Circular A-76 offers guidance to federal government agencies on the extent to which they can engage in activities that are of a commercial nature, which the circular defines as "the process resulting in a product or service that is or could be obtained from a private sector source."

In 1955 the distinction was important because the Eisenhower administration wanted to prohibit federal departments and agencies from starting or carrying on "any commercial activity to provide a service or product for its own use if such product or service can be procured from private enterprise through ordinary business channels."[13] More than a quarter century later, in 1983, the Reagan administration restated that principle:

> In the process of governing, the Government should not compete with its citizens. The competitive enterprise system, characterized by individual freedom and initiative, is the primary source of national economic strength. In recognition of this principle, it has been and continues to be the general policy of the government to rely on commercial sources to supply the products and services the Government needs.[14]

Thirteen years later still, the Clinton administration shifted the rationale for the A-76 process from being a device to protect the private sector from government to a tool for stimulating greater efficiency inside government.

> Americans want to "get their money's worth" and want a Government that is more businesslike and better managed. . . . Circular A-76 is not designed to simply contract out. Rather, it is designed to: (1) balance the interests of the parties to a make or buy cost comparison, (2) provide a level playing field between public and private offerors to a competition, and (3) encourage competition and choice in the management and

13. Bureau of the Budget, Bulletin 55-4 (1955), cited in Kettl (1993, p. 41); Kettl's book is required reading on the evolution of contracting out as a device for delivering federal services.

14. Office of Management and Budget (1983, p. 1); see Kettl (1993) for the general history of Circular A-76.

performance of commercial activities. It is designed "to empower Federal managers to make sound and justifiable business decisions."[15]

Even if the purpose of comparing the cost of government and private delivery were clear, the actual process for testing the respective strength of the two sectors is cumbersome and confusing. Federal agencies are allowed to engage in commercial activities for an assortment of reasons. Some are primarily objective—including national defense, intelligence security, patient care, temporary emergencies, and functions for which there is no commercial source available or those involving ten or fewer employees—and others are more subjective—including the need to maintain core capability, engage in research and development, or meet or exceed a recognized industry performance or cost standard.

Agencies can use two justifications for rejecting the A-76 requirement that government rely on available private sector sources for commercially available products and services. The first relates to inherently governmental activities, which are exempt from A-76 entirely. The second arises when the agency claims that government can produce the product or service at a lower cost. This assertion must be proven through the following three-step cost comparison study: development of a work statement for a specific commercial activity; completion of a management study laying out the organization, staffing, and operation of the government's most efficient organization (MEO) for producing the good or service; and a request for bids from private sources to assess the relative cost of private sector versus MEO delivery. A private source can only win with a bid that is at least 10 percent lower than the MEO price. Taxpayers should benefit, regardless of who wins the competition.

Taxpayers cannot benefit, of course, unless these A-76 studies are completed. The number of such studies has declined dramatically since the mid-1980s. According to the General Accounting Office, there were no nondefense positions studied in 1997, and at least three departments—Education, Housing and Urban Development, and Justice—had not studied a single position since 1988.[16] Some departments and agencies may be convinced that a decade of downsizing has somehow

---

15. Office of Management and Budget (1996, p. iii).
16. A-76 activity is measured in the total number of positions studied, not dollars.

exempted them from the process; others may not have the staff resources to conduct the studies or may believe that everything they do is inherently governmental.

The general commitment of recent administrations to the A-76 process has varied significantly. The federal government studied an average of more than 16,000 positions a year under Reagan (1983–88), 5,200 a year under Bush (1989–92), and 7,000 under Clinton (1993–97). As was true with downsizing, the Department of Defense dominates the A-76 process.[17] Remove defense from the A-76 totals, and activity tumbles from 4,100 nondefense positions a year under Reagan to less than 1,500 under Bush, and exactly 84 under Clinton.

In sum, recent experience suggests that the A-76 process has limited success as the primary device for allocating headcount constraints systematically. Even with the fullest presidential commitment possible in the mid-1980s, A-76 was applied to barely 2 percent of the full-time-permanent civil service. In abstract discussions, the definition of commercial activity may seem clear, but when attempts are made to apply the concept, definitions blur and confusion reigns.

INHERENTLY GOVERNMENTAL FUNCTIONS. Departments and agencies can exempt themselves from A-76 by declaring a given commercial activity an "inherently governmental function," but that term is not easy to define. According to the Office of Federal Procurement Policy (OFPP), which was created in 1974 to strengthen federal oversight of an increasingly complicated procurement system, the term encompasses "a function that is so intimately related to the public interest as to mandate performance by Government employees." That means activities that "require either the exercise of discretion" or "the casting of value judgments in casting decisions for the Government."[18] Inherently governmental

---

17. These figures come from General Accounting Office (1998, p. 4) in testimony before the Subcommittee on Oversight of Government Management, Restructuring, and the District of Columbia given by J. Christopher Mihm, associate director, Federal Management and Workforce Issues, General Government Division. He provided a remarkably concise statement on why the A-76 process has not worked as effectively as possible in the past and how it might be improved in the future.

18. Office of Federal Procurement Policy, "Inherently Government Functions," Policy Letter 92-1 to the Heads of Executive Agencies and Departments (1992, p. 1).

functions seem, therefore, to encompass the faithful execution of the laws, which OFPP defines as any action to:

(a) bind the United States to take or not take some action by contract, policy, regulation, authorization, order, or otherwise; (b) determine, protect, and advance its economic, political, territorial, property, or other interests by military or diplomatic action, civil or criminal judicial proceedings, contract management, or otherwise; (c) significantly affect the life, liberty, or property of private persons; (d) commission, appoint, direct, or control officers or employees of the United States; or (e) exert ultimate control over the acquisition, use, or disposition of the property, real or personal, tangible or intangible, of the United States, including the collection, control, or disbursement of appropriated and other Federal funds.

Much as one can admire the office's effort to draw a bright line, its guidance is replete with exemptions, ambiguities, and caveat-filled illustrations. For example, the guidance states

While inherently governmental functions necessarily involve the exercise of substantial discretion, not every exercise of discretion is evidence that such a function is involved. Rather, the use of discretion must have the effect of committing the Federal Government to a course of action when two or more alternative courses of action exist. . . . Determining whether a function is an inherently governmental function often is difficult and depends upon an analysis of the factors of the case, . . . such analysis involves consideration of a number of factors, and the presence or absence of any one is not in itself determinative of the issue. Nor will the same emphasis necessarily be placed on any factor at different times, due to the changing nature of the Government's requirements.

As if to acknowledge its own difficulties finding the bright line, OFPP leaves the final interpretation of whether an activity is or is not inherently governmental up to agencies alone. Thus, if the Department of Energy decided that writing congressional testimony for the secretary was not an inherently governmental function and could be done by a contractor, so be it.

THE DEFINITIONAL TANGLE. It is not enough to examine the two terms—commercial activities and inherently governmental functions—

separately; one must examine the intersection because the two terms interact to form separate zones for privatization, contracts, grants, and mandates, and full government involvement. Presumably, government should never privatize a noncommercial activity that is an inherently governmental function and should never retain a commercial activity that is not an inherently governmental function.

But a definitional tangle arises because an intersection is rarely definitive. Doing laundry for the U.S. Navy can be a purely commercial activity in home ports such as Norfolk, Virginia, but can become an inherently governmental function in the Persian Gulf. Testing ordnance equipment can be a commercial activity when the ordnance is an M-16 rifle but can become an inherently governmental function when calibrating a laser for a missile defense system. Building a communications satellite or rocket motor can be an entirely commercial activity unless building that satellite or rocket motor is top secret or essential to government's ability to oversee contracts for the commercial activity.

Where one sets the boundaries for each zone depends on more than context, however. It also involves politics, as has been made clear by the decision to allow government agencies to bid against private firms to perform commercial activities for other government agencies. The Reagan administration almost certainly would not have allowed the Department of Agriculture's National Information Technology Center in Kansas City to best IBM and Computer Sciences Corporation in a competition to build a $250 million Federal Aviation Administration data center, as it did in 1997. Nor would the Reagan administration have allowed the Department of Treasury to create a Center for Applied Financial Management that would compete with private firms to provide $11 million in administrative support to other government agencies in 1997, or the Department of Interior's Denver Administrative Support Center to win a contract from the Social Security Administration to provide payroll services in 1998.[19] Not only did the Clinton administration allow all three departments to bid and win, it openly encouraged departments and agencies to compete against private firms for administrative service contracts and won congressional approval for a five-year experiment with the franchise funds that allow agencies to

19. See Serlin (1997).

provide services to one another as part of the Government Management Reform Act of 1994.

Reshaping by Other Means

Given this definitional tangle, it is unclear just how big the federal civil service would be if all inherently governmental jobs that have been contracted out were drawn back into government, or how small the civil service could become if all commercial activities that have been kept in house were privatized. The central question for future downsizings, however, should not be how large or small the civil service should become, but rather how Congress and the president should sort the jobs that should stay from those that should go.

The government has tried and failed repeatedly to make the system based on the distinction between commercial and inherently governmental activities work. It is time to develop a system based on core competencies. Simply defined, a core competency is a skill required for the successful performance of an organization's mission. Although the term is more traditionally used by human resource professionals to describe the skills needed in a particular job, it can also be applied to broad organizational demands.[20] Instead of asking what individual employees need for superior performance, an organizational competency approach asks what a given unit needs to produce results of one kind or another.

The core competency approach is reminiscent of the zero-based budgeting (ZBB) model adopted by the Carter administration in the late 1970s. Like ZBB, a core competency assessment begins with a broad analysis of what a given organization seeks to accomplish, an analysis that is already embedded in the Government Performance and Results Act (GPRA) strategic planning process. With its goals, objectives, indicators, and measures already specified under OMB Circular A-11, a government agency could easily move forward with a detailed assessment of the human resource requirements for successful performance.

---

20. See National Academy of Public Administration (1996), for an example of how the core competency model might be used to build an effective human resource unit.

The five-year strategic plans of GPRA already require agencies to identify the general resources needed for success, as well as the mitigating conditions that might undermine results (for example, natural disasters, lower-than-expected economic growth), while the annual performance plans demand a "description of the organizational processes, skills, and technology, and the human capital, information, or other resources that will be needed to meet the performance goals." [21]

Most departments and agencies are still struggling to define their goals and objectives clearly. This has prompted House majority leader and former college professor Dick Armey to give government an "F" on the first round of plans. Nevertheless, a few have achieved a measure of success. The Department of Transportation earned uniform high grades at both ends of Pennsylvania Avenue. It was one of the few departments to establish measurable goals, using traffic-related deaths and severity of injuries as core indicators of actual performance. More to the point, the Transportation Department was also one of the few organizations to discuss the role of its work force in ensuring results. It was also the only major agency to set a human resource goal that was to "foster a diverse, highly skilled work force capable of meeting or exceeding our strategic goals with efficiency, innovation, and a constant focus on better serving our customers now and into the 21st Century."

Toward that end, the department promised to "conduct workforce planning across the Department to align human capital requirements with strategic goals," assess "how the Department's culture should be adapted to support a high performing organization characterized by a high degree of employee empowerment in decision making, risk taking, collaboration, and other related aspects of work," ensure "that the Department's workforce composition reflects the national workforce," eliminate "any artificial barriers to the advancement and full contribution of all employees, such as glass ceilings, discrimination, and sexual harassment," "recruit, develop, and deploy a diverse workforce with those 21st Century competencies needed to achieve the DOT's strategic goals," maintain the "continuity and institutional knowledge needed to provide strong leadership through better succession planning," cre-

---

21. Office of Management and Budget (1998).

ate "a continuous learning environment required of all high performing organizations by implementing policies, providing resources and opportunities, which enable all DOT employees to build the job competencies, computer and technology capabilities, work management skills, flexibility, and organizational knowledge required to achieve the Department's strategic goals," link department "awards and recognition programs to program outcomes, encouraging employees to work toward strategic goals and objectives, including innovation, costcutting, and enhanced customer service," and implement "worklife policies that support both employees in balancing work and personal priorities and the Department in meeting its goals."[22]

Much as one can admire the effort to link human resources to its more general goals, the department's plan missed one important point. Instead of looking at its work force as a collection of individual civil service jobs, it also needed to examine the mix of in-house versus external capacity. With an estimated contract and grant work force of more than 820,000, the department could have easily justified a detailed assessment of how its contractors and grantees would make sure their employees would be similarly empowered, while balancing work and personal priorities.

It could have also justified a thorough discussion of the appropriate mix of workers needed to achieve higher performance. To what extent, for example, could customer service be enhanced by bringing certain functions back in house or by contracting certain activities out to the private sector? To what extent could traffic fatalities be reduced by shifting jobs from grants to contracts or vice versa? To what extent could the severity of injuries be reduced by privatizing certain units? Such questions are hardly beyond the realm of analysis, particularly given the continued headcount pressure envisioned in other parts of Circular A-11.

Such an analysis would not start with basic questions about private versus public, however. It would start with a systematic assessment of what the agency needs to meet its statutory and performance obligations. Once its core competencies were defined, an agency could pro-

22. U.S. Department of Transportation (1997, pp. 62–63).

ceed to a more traditional review of commercial versus inherently governmental activities to determine which noncore activities might be pushed out and which should stay in because of lower cost. The result of this analysis would be a multitiered work force built around a relatively small center of civil servants who hold clearly identified core competencies, a larger group of civil servants who perform noncore functions for clearly defined reasons, and a still larger group of non-civil-service employees who perform noncore functions on behalf of the federal government under contracts, grants, and mandates.

Moving to this core competencies model would take more than new analytic capacity at OMB or OPM. It would take a basic change in how government views its work force. Instead of focusing on civil servants as the sole focus of its human resource activities, the federal government would have to adopt a much fuller definition of who constitutes an employee. Not only would such an approach require new data on who works for government under what instruments, it would also demand a new bridge between those who *hire* labor through civil service appointments, those who *purchase* labor through contracts and grants, and those who *create* labor through mandates.

Unable to define its core competencies, the federal government has engaged in fifty years of mostly random reshaping. Pick any two agencies, and one will find a mix of decisions that led one agency to keep certain jobs in house and the other to drive them outward and downward. The result is extraordinary unevenness across and within agencies, with a given unit's ability to do its job in-house largely dependent on the age and quit rates of its employees. Instead of a government that "works better and costs less," as Vice President Al Gore would put it, Americans get a government that is highly dependent on a work force that may or may not be accountable to Congress and the president.

Conclusion

There is no reason to believe that Congress or the president will soon abandon the headcount constraints that have done so much to alter the shape of the government work force over the decades, or that they will stop searching for ways to reduce the total civil service headcount.

To the contrary, both political parties are nearly certain to endorse further federal downsizing. The days of a fully self-contained government work force are long gone, never to return.[23]

Ample reasons exist for future presidents and Congresses to keep the civil service small. Presidents have come to prefer a small federal work force because it appears to strengthen their control over government against an increasingly reform-minded Congress; Congress because contractors and the jobs they create provide an essential source of ongoing campaign support and incumbency advantage; Democrats because a small civil service provides a defense against their image as the party of big government; and Republicans because contracting out strengthens their base of business support. Even civil servants have incentives to favor a small civil service, whether because it may increase public confidence or because it increases their responsibilities. Having a government that looks smaller but delivers at least as much also seems to increase incumbency advantages, whether that incumbent happens to be a Democrat or Republican, president or mayor.

So keeping government looking small is the work force policy that satisfies almost every political preference. By cutting federal headcount even as the program agenda remains steady or expands, the federal government gives the public exactly what it wants: the perception of efficiency and the benefits of an activist program agenda. It is also one way for America's elected and appointed leaders to reap the significant political benefits that are bestowed on those who claim progress in cutting costs.

There have been real cuts in both the federal headcount and the shadow work force, and real gains in productivity, service, and efficiency. The Clinton administration's procurement reform has clearly produced faster, cheaper, and smarter acquisitions, and innovation does appear to be on the rise. Thus, even as one can question the administration's claim that the era of big government is over, the evidence is abundant that government is working better today than it did at the beginning of the decade. The federal headcount may have returned to

---

23. For an excellent discussion of various theories of how government employment might change, see Hood, King, and Peters (1998).

1960 levels only in the most narrow sense, but the government has, almost certainly, become more effective.[24]

Short of some cataclysmic event such as a war or natural disaster, federal employment will stay down. Although the size of the contract, grant, and mandate work force will likely ebb and flow over time depending on the size of the defense budget, the civil service is going to get smaller. The question is not whether the federal government will continue to downsize, but whether future cutbacks will be used to reshape government deliberately or by accident. Without a work force planning system of some kind and a commitment to careful reshaping, change can only be accidental.

References

General Accounting Office. 1996a. *Federal Downsizing: Better Workforce and Strategic Planning Could Have Made Buyouts More Effective.* GAO-GGD-96-62 (August).

———. 1996b. *Federal Downsizing: The Costs and Savings of Buyouts versus Reductions-in-Force.* GAO-GGD-96-63 (May).

———. 1998. *OMB Circular A-76: Oversight and Implementation Issues.* GAO/T-GGD-98-146 (June).

Hood, Christopher, Desmond King, and B. Guy Peters. 1998. "Working for Government: Rival Interpretations of Employment Change in the Public Sector." Paper prepared for annual meeting of the American Political Science Association (September).

Kettl, Donald F. 1993. *Sharing Power: Public Governance and Private Markets.* Brookings.

———. 1998. *Reinventing Government, a Fifth-Year Report Card.* Brookings (September).

Leadership Directories. 1998. *Federal Yellow Book.* New York (Winter).

Light, Paul C. 1995. *Thickening Government: Federal Hierarchy and the Diffusion of Accountability.* Brookings and Governance Institute.

———. 1999. *The True Size of Government.* Brookings.

National Academy of Public Administration. 1995. *Effective Downsizing: A Compendium of Lessons Learned for Government Organizations.* Washington (August).

---

24. See Kettl (1998) for the grades, which include an A+ for effort, an A for procurement reform, and a B for downsizing.

————. 1996. *A Competency Model for Human Resources Professionals.* Washington (June).

————. 1997. *Downsizing the Federal Workforce: Effects and Alternatives.* Washington (April).

National Performance Review. 1993. *Transforming Organizational Structure.* Washington.

Office of Management and Budget. 1983. *Circular No. A-76, Revised.* Government Printing Office (August).

————. 1996. *Circular No. A-76, Revised Supplemental Handbook: Performance of Commercial Activities.* Government Printing Office (March).

————. 1998. *Preparation and Submission of Budget Estimates, Circular no. A-11,* revised. Government Printing Office (July).

Serlin, Michael D. 1997. "In the Ring." *Government Executive* 29 (September): 14–22.

U.S. Department of Commerce, Bureau of Economic Analysis. 1988. "Government Transactions." *Methodology Papers: U.S. National Income and Product Accounts.*

U.S. Department of Transportation. 1997. *A Visionary and Vigilant Department of Transportation Leading the Way to Transportation Excellence in the 21st Century.* DOT Strategic Plan, 1997–2002.

DONALD F. KETTL

13

The Three Faces
of Reinvention

FOR BETTER OR WORSE, two new realities emerged during the early years of the Clinton administration. First, the hazards that large-scale policy initiatives could pose for policymakers were underscored both by the stunning failure of the administration's health-care initiative and by the singular collapse of the 1995 Republican effort to simultaneously cut taxes and reduce the size of government. Having badly damaged one another in the battles, and faced with unforgiving budget constraints, the Democratic administration and the Republican Congress grew uncommonly cautious about ambitious policy changes. Short of a major crisis or a fundamental change in the balance of political power—such as a decisive end to divided-party government—future policy battles are likely to resemble World War I–style trench warfare, with many bloody skirmishes over small pieces of turf.

Second, with megapolicy initiatives ruled out, the soaring economy alleviating many traditional concerns of Washington lawmakers, and the cold war receding into history, management issues became far more important. With trust in the efficiency and efficacy of government programs at a low, the Clinton administration realized that governmental reform was a prerequisite to a more activist public sector. Under Vice President Al Gore's singular leadership, the administration committed itself to "reinventing government" in a quest for a smarter, cheaper, and more effective public sector. Management reform scarcely supplanted the big battles over policy. However, faced with political stalemate and the emergence of some big management problems, the administration realized that it had to find a way to address the management problems in government.

Other countries were experiencing the same problem. Indeed, since the mid-1980s public sector management reform has spread globally. Virtually all of the world's industrialized nations, and many developing nations as well, have launched some kind of "reinvention."[1] The political rewards from such reform, however, have been highly uncertain. While the *costs of failing* to detect and avoid management problems often proved large—the Republicans fiercely attacked the Clinton administration over its management of the Internal Revenue Service (IRS) in 1997—the *political gain* from reinvention was anything but clear.

Having initiated a significant effort at management reform, the Clinton administration was attacked both for doing it badly and for failing to do it seriously. The administration tried "creating a government that works better and costs less"[2] but found itself under attack for timidity, for a lack of success, and for attacking the wrong problems. Some critics contended that the effort was dangerous to democracy.[3] Others rejected the effort as meaningless. Peter Drucker concluded that steps Vice President Gore claimed as radical were, in fact, so trivial that in other institutions they "would not even be announced, except perhaps on the bulletin board in the hallway."[4]

Three Faces

Sorting out the conflicting claims and criticisms is no easy task because the Gore-led reform effort was, in its first five years, three different reinventions, not one. The initiative evolved, in part, to adjust to what the reinventers learned along the way, and, more important, to respond to lurching political counter pressures. In phase one, the administration

1. See Kettl (1997, pp. 446–62).
2. Gore (1993).
3. See, for example, Goodsell (1993, pp. 7–10); Segal (1993, pp. 18–23); Moe (1994, pp. 125–36). For a balanced analysis, see Arnold (1998, esp. chapter 12).
4. Drucker (1995, p. 50). See also Goddard and Riback (1998, pp. 33–49).

launched the effort and scored some important victories. In phase two, the reinventers scrambled to cope with the challenges of the Republican takeover of Congress following the 1994 midterm elections. And finally, in phase three, the reinventers worked to reinvigorate the initiative to help the vice president's 2000 presidential aspirations. While the shifting patterns of the effort make it hard either to characterize or to judge the reinventing government initiative, they chart the large issues defining the strategy.

Phase One: Works Better, Costs Less

Just six weeks after taking office in 1993, President Clinton put Vice President Gore in charge of an intensive six-month review of the federal government. The project, christened the National Performance Review (NPR), followed the pattern of a much-publicized initiative in Texas in which squads of reformers swept through government agencies to identify targets of waste and opportunities for improvement in management.

For "new Democrats" like Clinton and Gore, the launch of the reinventing government campaign was a natural first step toward their vision of a new progressivism.[5] The Clinton-Gore campaign manifesto had been bold: "It is time to radically change the way the government operates—to shift from top-down bureaucracy to entrepreneurial government that empowers citizens and communities to change our country from the bottom up. We must reward the people and ideas that work and get rid of those that don't."[6] The March 1993 reinventing government announcement put that campaign promise into play.

The administration recruited hundreds of federal employees, formed them into investigative teams, and dispatched them throughout the federal bureaucracy. Their proposals were assembled into a September 1993 report containing 384 recommendations, promising $108 billion in savings, and pledging to reduce the federal work force by 12 percent within five years.[7]

5. See Osborne and Gaebler (1992); and Osborne (1993).
6. Clinton and Gore (1992, pp. 23–24). Gore (1993, p. i).
7. Gore (1993).

The works better–costs less formula had, on the one hand, great appeal. It promised a more productive, more efficient government, founded on the idea that government needs to do important things and that public officials have a responsibility to ensure that it does them well. On the other hand, it embodied a profound tension. The works-better component envisioned motivating and empowering employees to do a better job and take more responsibility. The costs-less dimension, however, was threatening because it sought to slash away unneeded programs and people. The reinventers and White House political operatives calculated that their credibility depended on producing large savings. To produce large savings required big cuts— especially in the number of government employees—and that made it hard to motivate the employees.

By pursuing both courses simultaneously, the reform process risked being sheared apart. Should managers be freed from constraints and encouraged to follow their own heads? Or should they have strategic plans set for their work and then be held accountable through performance measures? These approaches required shifts in opposite directions. Unwilling to select one, the NPR's voice was muddled from the beginning, and inconsistent recommendations were issued.

The political realities were no easier. There was heavy pressure, both inside and outside the White House, to show that the NPR was real— that it was producing budget savings. The one action that could, clearly and quickly, produce substantial quantifiable savings was reduction in federal employment. So the NPR promised at first to eliminate permanently 252,000, and later 272,900, federal employees.

Although downsizing drove the debate, two other initiatives also proved important in phase one. In 1994 Congress passed the Federal Acquisition Streamlining Act. This act was the first major reform of the government's contracting rules in a decade and soon was hailed as one of reinventing government's most important accomplishments. The other initiative was a mandate that all federal agencies develop customer service plans.[8] While critics argued that people were citizens or owners, not customers, the customer-service initiative launched a major transformation of the way many federal government employees

8. Clinton and Gore (1994, 1995).

thought about and preformed their responsibilities. It encouraged them to focus on the needs of the citizens for whom government programs had been created. For the hundreds of thousands of government employees whose job was to help other government employees get their jobs done, the customer-service initiative encouraged them to focus on broader policy goals rather than on each agency's narrow concerns. Thus, while downsizing was the defining theme for phase one, procurement reform and customer service provided the subtext.

Phase Two: What Should Government Do?

By the early fall of 1994, the customer service initiatives were under way, Congress had passed procurement reform, and the administration had already significantly downsized the federal work force. Vice President Gore hailed "heroes of reinvention" who had championed better government and slashed red tape. But then in the 1994 elections, Republicans stunned the Clinton administration by gaining control of both houses of Congress for the first time in a generation. The new majority quickly launched a frenzied effort to shrink government even more radically.

The Republican initiative overwhelmed the administration's rhetoric of government improvement and shifted the focus of the debate from *how* government did its work to *what* government ought to do. Vice President Gore launched phase two of the NPR and challenged federal managers to "review everything you do"—even to consider the implications if their agency were eliminated.[9] Gore campaigned to devolve more power to state and local governments and to increase privatization, including selling off certain government assets. He proposed relying more on user fees to finance some government programs and pushed along the major reorganization under way at the National Aeronautics and Space Administration (NASA) and other agencies. In its 1995 report, the NPR felt obliged to include a discussion of "Why We Have a Federal Government" and "How Things Got Out of Hand."[10] While the downsizing of phase one had worried many government employees, phase two left them seriously unnerved.

9. Gore (1995b).
10. Gore (1995a, pp. 14–16).

The Republicans failed to get most of their more radical proposals enacted. The number of cabinet agencies remained the same, and the threatened massive extinction of federal programs never happened. Congress did pass significant budget cuts, but the president vetoed these bills, leading to two shutdowns of large portions of the government. In the end, the president escaped from the crisis by outflanking congressional Republicans. Despite the clash of grand rhetoric, the battle ended in a draw with little sorting out of government's functions, reorganizing of its operations, or shrinking of its role.

Phase two had plugged some of the holes in the political dike. With "hammer awards" (to celebrate breaking through bureaucratic barriers), Gore recognized the work of agency-level reinventers. The customer-service movement bore considerable fruit, especially in agencies like the Social Security Administration and the Customs Service. Procurement changes helped make the lives of government managers easier and made the federal government a better partner to its private contractors. The government's acquisitions work force shrank by one-third, and the Air Force Materiel Command claimed a 64 percent reduction in the number of pages in its acquisitions regulations. Assessing cost savings proved difficult; the NPR claimed savings of $12.3 billion in the effort's first four years.[11] But the battle over the budget dampened much of the enthusiasm that had surrounded phase one and further cemented downsizing and cost saving as the keystone of the NPR.

Phase Three: Search for Political Relevance

In early 1998 the vice president worked to restore the NPR's luster by shifting gears once again. He changed the National Performance Review to the National Partnership for Reinventing Government (the NPR with a silent G, wags suggested). To signal the reinvention of reinvention, Gore gave the NPR a new slogan, "America @ Its Best." He promised a stronger focus on an information-age government and even better customer service. But the new effort reached for even broader goals, such as building a "safe and healthy America," "safe communities," a "strong economy," and the "best-managed government ever."

11. See the NPR web site (www.npr.gov). See also Freedberg (1998, pp. 932–33); and General Accounting Office (1998).

The administration decided to invest 80 percent of its reinvention efforts in thirty-two "high-impact agencies" that dealt most directly with citizens, and where the failure to reform quickly—as in the case of the IRS—could compromise the NPR's other accomplishments. The administration, for example, committed the Occupational Safety and Health Administration (OSHA) to reducing worker injuries in the 50,000 most dangerous workplaces by 25 percent before the year 2000. The Food and Drug Administration was to cut the drug approval process to one year, and the Postal Service was to achieve overnight delivery of 92 percent of local first-class mail.[12]

Phase three sought to build on the demonstrable successes, like customer service, to prevent future crises like the 1997 IRS debacle. It also attempted to broaden the initiative's political appeal by focusing on the policy problems that Americans cared most about. If successful, the question, "What has reinventing government really accomplished for ordinary Americans?" could be answered by the Gore-for-President campaign.

The reinventers hoped that, in phase three, process reforms would motivate people on the inside while broad policy goals—safe communities and a strong economy—would excite people on the outside.[13] But this created a central dilemma. The inside-government game focused on improving the federal government's performance, building an information-age government that would be managed as well as America's best companies. At the same time, the external game promised results that the federal government had only a limited capacity to produce. Federal leverage over the economy is indirect at best, weak in the short term, and hard to measure in any event. It is local governments that police the streets, even if they are aided by extra police funded by federal grants. The health and safety of the nation as a whole is obviously everyone's first concern, but the forces that shape it are so complex that assigning responsibility (or, for that matter, blame or credit) is difficult indeed. And so, in seeking political relevance, phase three distanced itself from any realistic ability to achieve and measure its results.

Phase three thus risked making pledges on which it could not deliver. It focused government employees on problems they could not solve by themselves. The gap between megapolitics and front-line management

---

12. Stone (1998). Stone is deputy director of NPR.
13. For a sample of these arguments, see Gore (1997).

had already been a problem during phases one and two. In the search for political relevance, phase three threatened to make that gap unbridgeable. It was a long road indeed from better customer service and improved information technology to a strong economy and safe and healthy communities.

The Effects of Reinvention

What has the NPR accomplished? Clearly not all that it promised. But that should be expected given that the NPR's goals are part of an endless, never-to-be-completed quest. The twentieth century alone has seen eleven major government reform initiatives, including the Keep Commission (1905–09), the two Hoover commissions (1947–49, 1953–55), and the NPR.[14] Each reform has solved some problems but created new ones, problems that feed the need for further reforms. In the NPR's case, the promise has been a government that works better and costs less.

Works Better?

Under the NPR, energetic administrators throughout government developed some imaginative solutions. For example, managers in radiology departments at Veterans Affairs hospitals developed new electronic links that reduced the need for on-call radiologists. Postal workers in Newton, Massachusetts, saved $50 million with a movers guide and welcome kit that improved service and reduced costs. Through the mandate to develop customer service plans, all federal agencies had been forced to identify those they were in business to serve. Procurement reform streamlined the government's buying process. More than 570 government agencies and programs developed more than 4,000 customer service standards. About 325 "reinvention laboratories" were established to develop innovative approaches to public service delivery.[15]

Despite these accomplishments, large problems remain. The NPR had little effect in some agencies, and in many agencies morale was poor. A 1996 survey showed that only 37 percent of federal employees

14. See DiIulio, Garvey, and Kettl (1993, p. 8). See also Goddard and Riback (1998); and Arnold (1998). See especially Light (1997).
15. See the NPR web site (www.npr.gov).

believed that reinvention was a top priority at their organization. The NPR's goals for management improvement penetrated far less deeply in the Pentagon than in civilian agencies.[16] Only 20 percent of federal workers said that the NPR had brought positive change to government. Where the NPR was considered to be a top priority, 59 percent of employees thought productivity had improved; where it was not, only 32 percent thought productivity was better. Where the NPR's goals received emphasis, employees were three times as likely to think that government organizations made good use of workers' abilities and about one and one-half times as likely to believe that they were given greater flexibility.[17] The attitudes of government employees depended on how much top managers made reinvention a priority.

One of the most subtle, yet most important, failures of the NPR effort was the administration's failure to enlist many of its own political appointees in the cause even though the vice president maintained an unusual and constant enthusiasm for the initiative. Without strong political leadership from these appointees, many agencies did not connect with the NPR campaign. And so after five years the answer to the question of whether government worked better because of the NPR was, "It depends." On the procurement reform and customer service fronts there were clear victories, but the wide disparity across agencies makes it difficult to provide a generalized conclusion for the government as a whole.

Costs Less?

What about the NPR's claim that government costs less? The Clinton administration estimated that, if all of its recommendations had been adopted, the federal budget would have shown savings of $177 billion by fiscal year 1999. Actual savings, the NPR estimates, totaled $112 billion (see table 13-1). These claims, however, have not been audited—and, in fact, portions are unauditable.[18] Some—like the estimated savings from procurement, information technology, and administrative processes reforms—are ambiguous and hard to measure. Others—like

16. U.S. Merit Systems Protection Board (1998, p. vii).
17. U.S. Merit Systems Protection Board (1998, pp. vi–vii).
18. For the GAO's assessment of the problem, see General Accounting Office (1994).

Table 13-1. *The NPR's Claimed Savings, 1993–99*
Billions of dollars

Source of savings	Originally estimated savings	Actual savings
Phase I		
Downsizing the bureaucracy	40.4	54.8
Procurement reform	22.5	12.3
Savings from information technology	5.4	0.4
Reducing intergovernmental administrative costs	3.3	0.0
Agency-based initiatives	36.4	14.7
Phase II		
Total	177.4	111.8

Source: "National Performance Review Savings for NPR Recommendations Made in 1993 and 1995 as of October 15, 1997" (www.npr.gov/library/papers/bkgrd/97savci.html [June 21,1999]).

the work force reduction—are more straightforward. By November 1998 federal employment had been reduced by almost 350,000 positions. With fewer than 2 million civilian employees, the federal work force was smaller than at any time since the Kennedy administration.[19] Critics might debate the NPR's estimates of total savings, but with half of all claimed savings associated with the reduction in government employment, it is clear that the reinventing government initiative saved a substantial amount of money.

Where Did the Downsizing Occur?

The federal civilian work force (excluding the Postal Service and the Postal Rate Commission) shrank 15.9 percent from January 1993 through December 1998. Defense employment accounted for much of the reduction. Employment elsewhere in the bureaucracy shrank less, although reductions varied widely across agencies.

In the Pentagon downsizing began *before* the NPR's launch. Cynics contended that the NPR simply ratified reductions in the Defense Department's civilian work force that were going to occur anyway with the end of the cold war. Since the Pentagon was already in the process of

19. The number excludes employees of the U.S. Postal Service. See Office of Personnel Management (1999).

downsizing, since defense employment accounted for a disproportionate share of the NPR's work force reductions, and since work force reductions accounted for the bulk of the confirmed NPR savings, some critics argued that the NPR itself has accomplished little on this front. However, the NPR did accelerate the reduction in defense employment that had already started and spread it to the civilian agencies. The reductions were real and, for some government employees, extremely painful. Thus if the NPR accomplished nothing else, it certainly spurred a sustained reduction in federal employment—virtually across the board—of a magnitude never before seen in the federal government.

The impact of the work force reduction varied widely across the bureaucracy. Even though the overall work force was reduced by about one-sixth, the Justice Department grew 26.7 percent (largely as a result of the hiring of new prison guards). Some agencies and departments shrank only slightly. The work force of the Environmental Protection Agency declined just 2.1 percent and that of the Department of Health and Human Services was down 4.6 percent. Other agencies took much bigger hits. The Department of Housing and Urban Development downsized by 24.9 percent; the Department of Defense (DOD) by 26.5 percent; the General Services Administration by 31.5 percent; and the Office of Personnel Management (OPM) by 46.9 percent.[20] The important point is that the federal government's downsizing was not one phenomenon but many, with the reasons as varied as the agencies themselves. OPM transferred most of the government's personnel responsibilities to the agencies. DOD's reductions were part of the far larger, post–cold war downsizing of the military.

Downsizing in Middle Management

The Clinton administration committed itself not just to reducing the size of the overall work force but also to thinning the ranks of middle-level managers. This part of the strategy mirrored the private-sector reforms of the 1980s in which corporate transformations were dominated by "de-layering" initiatives and other measures to reduce the distance from top managers to front-line workers. The justification for this policy was straightforward. Top-level managers make the key policy

20. Office of Personnel Management (1999).

decisions. Front-line workers deliver the services. But mid-level managers only push paper and contribute to bureaucracy. Minimizing the number of bureaucratic layers and increasing the span of control (the number of employees each manager supervised), reformers believed, would focus organizations on their work and improve their responsiveness to customers.

There was, however, a big gap between rhetoric and reality. The biggest reductions in the federal government's employment came not in management ranks but on the front lines. The numbers of levels 1 to 4 General Schedule (GS) workers (low-level clerical and blue-collar workers) were cut about in half (see figure 13-1), the ranks of mid-level clerical workers (GS 5–8) shrank 19 percent, entry- and mid-level professional and technical workers (GS 9–12) were reduced by about 12 percent, and the number of managers (GS 13–15) actually inched up a bit.

What accounts for the disparity between rhetoric and reality? Virtually all personnel reductions were voluntary. The government made available payments up to $25,000, in addition to accrued retirement benefits, to workers who agreed to leave the government. That meant that the fit between the NPR's overall downsizing strategy and its long-term results depended far more on the calculations of individual workers than on the decisions of the NPR's chiefs. Even more important, the reductions depended on shifts in the federal government's management and policy strategies.

Much of the reduction in GS 1–4 came through defense downsizing. As military bases closed, the workers most likely to be affected were blue-collar support staff, from mechanics to janitors, who often were near the bottom of the federal government's pay scale and who, for the most part, moved to private-sector employment. In addition, the federal government markedly increased its contracting out for services, from the food services provided in cafeterias in federal buildings to planning for government programs. That reduced the numbers of GS 5–12 employees who previously had done this front-line work. However, more contracting out meant proportionately fewer front-line workers employed by the government and proportionately more higher-level managers who were needed to negotiate, write, and oversee the contracts. The NPR's downsizing thus reflected not so much the

Figure 13-1. *Federal Employment by GS Level, 1992, 1997*

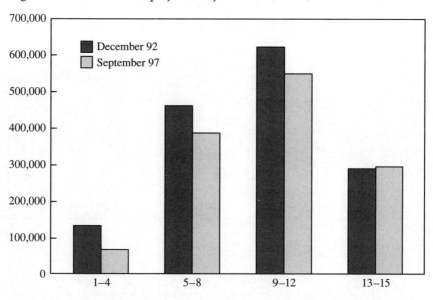

Source: Office of Personnel Managment Central Personnel Data File.

"reduce middle management" rhetoric as a shift in the way the federal government implemented its programs and activities.

The decline in the lower-level work force while the numbers of higher-level workers remained constant—or even increased—can be seen as part of the long-term pattern of grade creep (see figure 13-2). Over the past thirty years, the average grade level of federal employees has inched up from about a GS 7 in 1960 to more than a GS 9 at the end of the 1990s. Critics have pointed to this grade creep as evidence of the federal government's increasing bureaucracy. Some of it undoubtedly stems from the increasing "layering" of the federal establishment. Paul C. Light, who has shown that the federal government has accumulated more layers, especially at top levels of the bureaucracy, has argued that layering has reduced the government's responsiveness and impeded its effectiveness.[21]

Much of the grade creep flows directly from the changing nature of what the federal government does. Federal entitlement, grant, loan, and

21. Light (1995).

Figure 13-2. *Average Grade Trend for GS Employees, 1960–98*

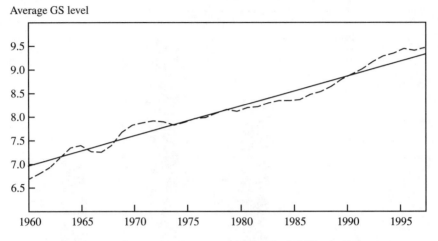

Average GS level

Source: Office of Personnel Management, *Pay Structure of the Federal Civil Service*. Various years.

regulatory programs have increased in importance, while direct service-delivery programs have steadily shrunk. The federal work force has adjusted accordingly. A government that delivers fewer services directly and relies more on private contractors, state and local governments, and nonprofit organizations to do the job instead will naturally have fewer lower-level workers and proportionately more higher-level managers.

The more difficult question to answer is whether the NPR *accelerated* the well-established trend. The numbers shown in figure 13-2 suggest that the NPR's downsizing and the move to contract out many services did shift the mix of government employment in the direction of top-level workers. What is difficult to separate is the contribution that defense downsizing made. The grade creep slowed during the defense buildup of the 1980s as the Pentagon added more workers in the field and more clerical staff to process contracts. Defense downsizing naturally reversed this and pushed grade creep forward again. Nevertheless, the NPR probably modestly accelerated the long-term trend of grade creep, which is being driven largely by changes in what the federal government does and how the government chooses to do it.

Probably the most notable failure of the NPR was its inability to deal with the layering problem, especially the proliferation of political appointees, 3,000 of whom encrust the top of the federal bureaucracy. This problem was compounded by the reluctance of many of the political appointees to embrace and aggressively lead the effort. Furthermore, the decision to contract out many functions in an effort to capture the efficiencies of the private sector made it harder for the NPR to deliver on its promise to downsize middle-level management en route to better customer service. When those who actually deliver the government's goods and services increasingly are private sector workers, it is difficult to reduce the distance from top managers to those on the shop floor.

To sum up, the NPR almost certainly produced some cost savings. The federal civilian work force was smaller than it was or would have been without the NPR, and this reduction will realize substantial salary and benefit savings over both the short and the long term. Partially offsetting these savings are the costs associated with the grade creep that was probably accelerated by the NPR. Other savings, in areas like procurement reform, are real but far harder to assess because it is difficult to know what the government costs would have been without the reforms. Finally, many claimed savings represent hopes and wishes whose value cannot be determined.

The Lessons of Government Reform

Whatever its economic and programmatic impact, the NPR has had one clear political consequence: it inescapably connected Vice President Al Gore with management reform. Despite reinvention's obvious lack of political sex appeal and the many other demands on his time, Gore was consistent and energetic in his pursuit of the program's goals. Along with environmental policy and high-tech initiatives, the NPR would be part of his identity as he geared up for the presidential campaign. Could it be used to his political advantage, or would it only reinforce his popular—if misplaced—image as a stiff techno-child of the information age?

The NPR effort to produce a government closer to the people was intended to help define a "new Democrat" approach to governance, one that would be broadly popular but appeal particularly to supporters of H. Ross Perot. Yet the initiative barely registered on the political radar screen, and voters put Republicans in charge of both houses of Congress for the first time in a generation. Furthermore, despite the investment of time and energy, the NPR failed to protect the administration from major management embarrassments like abuse of taxpayers at the IRS.

In many ways, the vice president's challenge of making management performance politically relevant is one all elected officials face. The squeeze between rising costs and citizen expectations, on the one hand, and taxpayer reluctance to pay more taxes on the other, has put elected officials in a bind. They cannot launch big new programs because the revenue base needed to support such initiatives is lacking. They must make government work better because the political repercussions from management failure are serious. So they face the difficult task of wringing ever-greater productivity from government programs to meet the demands for more services without bigger government or higher taxes.

But is there a political payoff for avoiding poor performance, wringing more from existing programs, and giving voters the additional government they crave even as they protest that government is already too big and burdensome? Will political survival in the twenty-first century require that politicians invest in management reforms even when they do not have political payoffs? Must they do so simply to avoid the political retribution that surely will accompany demonstrable administrative failures?

The experience of America's states and cities provides some insights into these questions. Many state capitals and city halls are being led by a new generation of pragmatists. In the nation's best-run states and cities, it is hard to identify a distinctly Republican or Democratic theme shaping the new approach to policy problems. An emerging class of state and local officials is defining success as getting things done. This scarcely means that political considerations and political parties are evaporating. But it does mean that state and local elected officials—especially the most successful ones—have made getting measurable results their primary focus. The triumph of pragmatism over partisanship has not only produced widely heralded successes—cheaper, more effective, more responsive government—it has also yielded clear political payoffs. Voters have looked to results more than party when casting their ballots and have returned to office leaders with demonstrated track records.

Transporting the political fruits of pragmatism from the states and cities to the national government is a tough job, however. The states and, especially, the cities actually *do* things directly for citizens. They build roads and educate children. They put out fires, arrest lawbreakers, and put criminals behind bars. They provide clean drinking water, and they process sewage. The federal government, meanwhile, invests most of its energy in managing *others* who do its work.

Mayors and governors have an easier time staking their futures on delivering results because, especially compared with the federal government, they are *responsible for delivering results*. For the president and members of Congress, the job is far tougher. Many of the goods and services the federal government funds are delivered by third parties. Much of what the federal government does directly—manage the air traffic control system, inspect the safety of food, deliver social security checks, and guard the borders—is low profile because the public expects these programs to run smoothly. They become an issue only when disasters or serious management failures occur.

The federal government's domestic policy stewardship is shaped by hundreds of detailed regulatory actions and tens of thousands of meetings. Much of the real work of the federal bureaucracy happens in the back rooms and side channels of the contracting and intergovernmental systems. For example, the Environmental Protection Agency (EPA) hammers out new regulatory reform pilot projects with the states; the Department of Health and Human Services tries to connect immunization programs with local schools; and the Defense Department embarks on a radical transformation of its management to squeeze out extra dollars for weapons modernization. Rarely do these actions rise to the level of major presidential or congressional policy debates.

How well this stewardship succeeds depends on how well the subtle regulatory changes and coordinating meetings work. Along the Potomac, where thousands of ears bend for news of presidential scandals or major new policy pronouncements, such details are just not the stuff of high politics. What the federal government actually does to help most domestic programs work rarely attracts the attention of congressional committees and seldom draws more than a yawn from the Washington media.

So not only is Washington increasingly removed from where the real action is taking place, but national policymakers also seem increasingly uninterested in using what limited leverage they might have to

shape domestic policy. Because this influence is exercised through subtle channels, it simply escapes most key policymakers. That, in turn, has
led federal officials to promote symbols because they often cannot find
the real levers of power.

President Clinton's bold promise in his 1997 State of the Union
Address that "the era of big government is over" reflects such a
response. Faced with a citizenry that wants lower taxes but shows little
willingness to accept a reduced level of government service, politicians
have responded by promising to make the government "smaller." This
has involved reducing government employment while making government's fundamental operation increasingly dependent on private, nonprofit, and intergovernmental institutions. The more government has
been downsized, the more interconnected it has become with other
institutions. The end of big government has blurred the boundaries
between government and the rest of civil society.

The evidence from abroad demonstrates how difficult it is for
national governments to grapple with the inescapable management
realities of this boundary blurring while seeking electoral success
through management reform. In the three countries with the most
established and widely recognized reforms—Australia, New Zealand,
and the United Kingdom—the political parties that launched the
reforms have been replaced by competitors with different ideas about
how to meet the challenge of public productivity. National officials, it
appears, have a harder time than subnational officials in winning electoral reward for reform. Farther from the front lines with less direct
control over results—and less direct contact with citizens—the links
between performance and politics are harder to establish.

Reforming the Reforms

Washington policymakers face some tough dilemmas. It is difficult for
them to exert tight control over program outcomes. Furthermore, the
federal government is organized, managed, and driven politically by
assumptions that no longer fit reality. Authority is organized along hierarchical lines, even though few federal programs work hierarchically.
Debates over management apply hierarchical models of authority. Congressional committees hold oversight hearings demanding that federal

managers explain costly failures, and television news magazines demand to know why federal managers allow bad things to happen.

Addressing the government's productivity challenge—getting more government service from less taxpayer money—will require overcoming the disconnect between assumptions and reality. Discovering sources of leverage over the politically important links between public policies and the results they produce will call for further reform. While the NPR did not succeed in tackling this central problem, it developed several strategies that could prove useful as the reforms are themselves reformed.

The Government Performance and Results Act

One such strategy is the Government Performance and Results Act (GPRA) of 1993. This legislation required all federal agencies to write strategic plans by 1997, and by March 2000 they must establish indicators for measuring the outcomes of these activities. Old hands may be jaded by the stream of previous reforms: Robert McNamara's promise in the 1960s to bring a planning-programming-budgeting (PPB) system to the Pentagon; Richard Nixon's transformed version, management by objectives (MBO); Jimmy Carter's effort to promote zero-based budgeting (ZBB); and organizational behavior reforms in the 1980s through total quality management (TQM). This alphabet parade of reforms—PPB, which begat MBO, which begat ZBB, which begat TQM—led to the GPRA. Cynics predicted that the ambitious new search for federal goals and outcomes would soon result in employment for thousands of consultants and yet another acronym to replace a failed strategy. Some government managers, cynical from the constant effort at reform, concluded that they could safely burrow in and allow this new effort to blow by.

There are, however, reasons to believe that the GPRA might prove different. First, unlike the previous efforts, all of which were the product of executive orders, Congress invested itself directly in the GPRA by passing it into law. Second, both Congress and the Clinton administration quickly found political value in the GPRA. In 1997 House Majority Leader Dick Armey realized that the GPRA provided a reason and a framework to bring executive-branch officials before congressional committees to answer for their programs. His GPRA "report cards" attracted media attention and embarrassed many senior federal managers. The Office of Management and Budget (OMB), for its part, began relying on the GPRA to shape agencies' activities. As entitlements and other mandatory spending programs absorbed a steadily larger share of the federal budget, OMB officials were eager for a tool that increased their leverage over the operations of federal agencies. These political incentives, of course, produced big political squabbles. But they also gave the GPRA greater prominence than earlier reforms ever enjoyed. Third, some agencies—the EPA, NASA, the IRS, and the DOD to name a few—have begun using the GPRA process to improve *internal* management. While these applications have, to date, been rudimentary, the GPRA will achieve greater staying power if managers find it a tool that helps them manage their agencies. Indeed, the principal weakness of its predecessors was the failure of the reform tools to become integrated with the internal management—and external political—processes.

Finally, the experience of the reforms in Australia, Canada, New Zealand, and the United Kingdom suggests that the GPRA might have more staying power than previous reform efforts. Like the GPRA, these reforms, which have been in existence for a number of years, rely heavily on performance measures to improve public management. The New Zealand government has depended on output measures for more than fifteen years. Over the years, these nations have found that performance measurement has proven valuable because it provides a mechanism for linking discussions of four key questions: What should government do? How should government go about doing it? What are the results of government programs? Are there better ways to produce these results?

A generation of experience teaches the need for caution in predicting the future of management reforms. But the GPRA is sufficiently different from its predecessors that it might well succeed where they failed.[22] And if the GPRA does succeed, even to some degree, it could provide part of the bridge between management reform and the broader political

---

22. Previous reforms, of course, did not fail completely. Each one has left behind a residue of ideas and tactics on which managers continue to rely.

realities of federal government politics: It could provide a language and a yardstick for focusing the conversation on what works, what does not, and why.

Information Technology

Vice President Gore has become at least as well known for his interest in information technology as in reinventing government. Indeed, for the Clinton reinventers, the NPR and information technology are inextricably connected. They see information technology as the central nervous system for the government of the future: a way to make tax filing easier, to make services more integrated, to make customer service better. In fact, the information-based "office of the future" was one of the signature pieces of the third phase of the NPR when it was launched in the spring of 1998.

To date, the NPR's information technology leadership has been more rhetorical than real, principally due to the NPR's tiny staff and the disparate nature of the federal government. The reformers' instincts to focus on information technology, however, offers great potential. The less hierarchy shapes public management, the more managers need tools to cross bureaucratic boundaries and to link interdependent operations. Moreover, reformers everywhere have sought to improve the integration of public services—to bring together, for example, the job training, day care, transportation, and job placement services on which welfare reform depends. Service integration means thinking spatially instead of functionally, thinking from the bottom up about how programs come together in one place and how they affect a single service recipient in contrast to the top-down view managers often have of programs.[23]

Information technology offers one of the few—perhaps the only—sets of tools to span bureaucratic boundaries and improve service integration. As the vast expansion of the Internet and world wide web have proven, information knows no bureaucratic bounds and can flow easily and rapidly where traditional hierarchy and authority cannot. Of course, providing information does not guarantee that anyone will use

---

23. Perri 6 (1997); National Academy of Public Administration (1998).

it, or that if they use it the result will improve delivery of services. But as traditional forms of organization, in both government and the private sector, become less useful, new forms of coordination will need to replace them. It is much too early in the information revolution to predict the course it will take, but the NPR's own experiments with information-age government have already demonstrated its potential.[24]

Civil Service Reform

One of the great paradoxes of the current reform effort is that the grand transformations that promised to reduce or streamline the work of government employees—new budget and performance systems, contracting out, and information technology, among others—have made government managers *more* rather than *less* important. Performance measurement means little if it is not integrated with the budgetary system. Contracting out can lead to massive fraud, waste, and abuse if government managers do not manage the contracts carefully. Information technology has often made information managers more important, as they have been enlisted to support the critical work of other government managers.

The General Services Administration's Office of Inspector General (OIG), for example, discovered that its officials balked at technological innovations like sophisticated voice-mail systems. Their internal surveys revealed that their "customers"—OIG workers around the country—had a hard time coping not only with the system but also with the queue that the system produced. Users with computer problems often needed quick help and became angry or frustrated when they discovered that they were number eighty in line. The information systems manager replaced the voice-mail system with a people-first policy. The goal was to have a real person answer all telephone calls by the second ring, even if it meant that the systems manager or his deputy had to pick up the phone. The managers discovered that most problems could be handled immediately over the phone, which gave users the quick answers they needed and decreased the waiting time for help on more complicated problems. The growing complexity of the OIG's

24. Gore (1997); Bellamy and Taylor (1998).

computer system made the personal touch of computer professionals more, rather than less, important. Tales from both the public and the private sector underline the message: dealing with technical complexity and bridging organizational boundaries are, at their core, people problems that demand more smart problem solvers.

If the NPR made some progress on the GPRA and information technology, it has proved far less successful in transforming the government's people policies through civil service reform. It is not that senior NPR officials did not believe that civil service reform was important. Rather, they chose not to act on their beliefs for two reasons. First, because of government downsizing, they already faced problems with the public employee unions, who fought to keep their members' jobs. The unions were an important source of political support for Democrats, and the Clinton administration was not eager to court even more opposition at the NPR's very start. Second, because of union opposition and long-standing concerns of congressional committees, NPR officials determined that it was unlikely that Congress would enact any serious civil service reform. They concluded instead that any reform would have to be piecemeal, fought out agency by agency, instead of through omnibus legislation.

The NPR thus set out to dismantle much of the Office of Personnel Management and to devolve to federal agencies the job of reforming their own personnel systems. With great fanfare, the OPM tossed its much-hated *Federal Personnel Manual* into a dumpster and celebrated the demise of its equally despised SF-171, the federal government's standard job application form for higher-level positions. In addition, the Clinton administration proposed that some agencies be designated performance-based organizations (PBOs) and given substantial personnel and operating flexibility in exchange for greater accountability for performance. Modeled on performance-based systems in New Zealand and the United Kingdom, the PBOs were to be part of the Clinton administration's strategy to break a few agencies loose from the civil service straitjacket. When Congress failed to approve the PBO plan, it reinforced the Clinton administration's judgment that agency-by-agency reforms were more likely to succeed than government-wide reforms.[25]

25. For a review of the problems of and possible remedies for the civil service system, see Kettl (1996).

The agency-based systems left ambitious agencies free to frame sweeping changes—and let the others do little more than adopt as their own the discredited and abandoned OPM manuals and forms. As a result, although devolved authority produced some significant changes, it increased the disparities among government personnel policies. The devolution strategy also significantly weakened the OPM. Indeed, save for the dramatic reductions in the Federal Deposit Insurance Corporation and the Resolution Trust Corporation that accompanied completion of the savings-and-loan bailout, the 46.9 percent reduction in the OPM's staff was the largest cut any federal agency suffered during the Clinton administration's downsizing.[26] The OPM lost most of its capability to train government employees and to engage in strategic work force planning. The training function was increasingly shifted to private contractors, and the planning has been largely abandoned.

While international comparisons can prove hazardous—even though ideas travel easily, the contexts that supported them do not—other nations that have championed management reform made civil service reform an integral part of their efforts. In particular, they invested in employee training and, especially in New Zealand, have paid increasing attention to strategic work force planning. It is one thing to exhort government's managers to squeeze extra productivity from their budgets, to create a government that works better and costs less. It is quite another to ask them to create an information-age government within a civil service system designed for the horse-and-buggy days. The Clinton administration's difficulty in pursuing an aggressive and comprehensive civil service reform in the end limited its ambitious works better–costs less objectives.

Conclusion

While the Clinton administration's reinventing government initiative encountered some serious problems, it achieved some genuine accomplishments as well during its first six years. It saved a significant amount

26. Office of Personnel Management (1999).

of money, brought substantial managerial reforms, especially in customer service and procurement processes, and promoted a more performance-based discussion about government's functions.

The NPR's shortcomings, though, are as instructive as its successes. President Clinton's bold proclamation about the end of "big government" missed the far more important, if much more subtle, transformation in the way government now works. The NPR demonstrated, in both its achievements and its failures, that the federal government is no longer organized for the job that the Constitution and legislation charge it to do. In particular, the federal government has not built the capacity needed to manage effectively a government that increasingly operates through proxies.

With the budget deficit transformed into surpluses, the defining reality of U.S. domestic policy since the late 1960s has evaporated. Nevertheless, two other deficits—quieter but just as important—remain: government's performance deficit—the gap between government's goals and results—and the confidence deficit—citizens' trust in government's ability to get its job done.[27] Management reform—improving government's ability to achieve its results—is the key to reducing the performance deficit. Reducing government's performance deficit, in turn, is the key to progress on the confidence deficit.

Making government work better thus is a goal that both political parties have little choice but to embrace. Government's top officials, for their own sakes as well as for the sake of reducing the deficit in public confidence in government, will continue to pursue administrative reforms especially now that both Democrats and Republicans have been burned politically on megapolicy initiatives. The public might not reward policymakers for improving the way government works—Americans expect their public services to work smoothly and often balk at rewarding government workers for doing their jobs. But government officials will, nevertheless, work hard to improve performance because embarrassing failures can have electoral repercussions and because every penny of increased productivity is a tax that does not have to be raised or an expenditure that does not have to be cut. That is what makes a continued effort to reinvent American government an inevitable if, perhaps, thankless task. A constant battle for management reform is the one sure bet in American politics.

References

Arnold, Peri E. 1998. *Making the Managerial Presidency: Comprehensive Reorganization Planning, 1905–96.* 2d ed. University Press of Kansas.

Bellamy, Christine, and John A. Taylor. 1998. *Governing in the Information Age.* Buckingham, England: Open University Press.

Clinton, Bill, and Al Gore. 1992. *Putting People First: How We Can All Change America.* Times Books.

———. 1994. *Putting Customers First: Standards for Serving the American People.* Government Printing Office.

———. 1995. *Putting Customers First '95: Standards for Serving the American People.* Government Printing Office.

DiIulio, John J., Jr., Gerald Garvey, and Donald F. Kettl. 1993. *Improving Government Performance: An Owner's Manual.* Brookings.

———. 1994.

———. 1995.

Drucker, Peter. 1995. "Really Reinventing Government." *Atlantic Monthly* (February): 49–61.

Freedberg, Sydney J., Jr. 1998. "Attention, Pentagon Shoppers!" *National Journal* 30 (April 25): 932–33.

General Accounting Office. 1994. *Management Reform: Implementation of the National Performance Review's Recommendations.* GAO/OCG-95-1 (December).

———. 1998. *Acquisition Reform: Implementation of Key Aspects of the Federal Acquisitions Streamlining Act of 1994.* GAO/NSIAD98-81 (March).

Goddard, Taegan D., and Christopher Riback. 1998. *You Won—Now What? How Americans Can Make Democracy Work from City Hall to the White House.* New York: Scribner.

Goodsell, Charles T. 1993. "Did NPR Reinvent Government Reform?" *Public Manager* 22 (Fall): 7–10.

Gore, Al. 1993. *From Red Tape to Results: Creating a Government That Works Better and Costs Less.* Government Printing Office.

———. 1995a. *Common Sense Government: Works Better and Costs Less.* Government Printing Office.

———. 1995b. Memorandum to heads of executive departments and agencies, "Second Phase of the National Performance Review." January 3, 1995.

———. 1997. *Businesslike Government: Lessons Learned from America's Best Companies.* Government Printing Office.

Kettl, Donald F. 1996. *Civil Service Reform: Building a Government That Works.* Brookings.

———. 1997. "The Global Revolution in Public Management: Driving Themes, Missing Links." *Journal of Policy Analysis and Management* 16 (Summer): 446–62.

Light, Paul C. 1995. *Thickening Government: Federal Hierarchy and the Diffusion of Accountability.* Brookings.

———. 1997. *The Tides of Reform: Making Government Work, 1945–95.* Yale University Press.

Moe, Ronald C. 1994. "The 'Reinventing Government' Exercise: Misinterpreting the Problem, Misjudging the Consequences." *Public Administration Review* 54 (March–April): 125–36.

National Academy of Public Administration. 1998. *Building Stronger Communities and Regions: Can the Federal Government Help?* Washington (March).

Office of Personnel Management, Office of Work Force Information. 1999. *Monthly Report of Federal Civilian Employment* (SF 113-A) (February 18).

Osborne, David. 1993. "Reinventing Government: Creating an Entrepreneurial Federal Establishment." In *Mandate for Change*, edited by Will Marshall and Martin Schram, 263–87. New York: Berkley Books.

Osborne, David, and Ted Gaebler. 1992. *Reinventing Government: How the Entrepreneurial Spirit Is Transforming the Public Sector.* Reading, Mass.: Addison-Wesley.

Perri 6. 1997. *Holistic Government.* London: Demos.

Segal, David. 1993. "What's Wrong with the Gore Report?" *Washington Monthly* (November): 18–23.

Stone, Bob. 1998. "Gore Official Discusses High-Impact Strategy." *GovExec Daily Briefing* (May 7, 1998) (www.govexec.com/dailyfed/0598/050798t2.htm [June 21, 1999]).

U.S. Merit Systems Protection Board. 1998. *The Changing Federal Work Force: Employee Perspectives.* Government Printing Office.

THOMAS E. MANN

14

The U.S. Campaign Finance System under Strain

THE 1996 U.S. presidential election resulted in a seemingly predictable and conventional outcome: the reelection of a president
strategically positioned in the political center during a time of peace
and prosperity. The controversies surrounding the financing of that
election, however, made it anything but business as usual. In the last
several weeks of the campaign, a flurry of news reports of potentially
illegal contributions to the Democratic National Committee may have
reduced President Clinton's electoral margin and hurt Democratic congressional candidates.

After the election, titillating details emerged of White House coffees
and Lincoln bedroom sleepovers, of Buddhist nuns and Chinese
conspiracies, adding lurid color to a growing list of possible criminal
violations. These infractions included fund raising from foreign
nationals, conduits used to mask impermissible contributions, the
improper use of public property for fund raising, the possible linkage
between public policy decisions and political contributions, and willful
circumvention of spending limits on publicly funded presidential
candidates. These charges and the anecdotal evidence lending credence
to them led to investigations in both houses of Congress and to
demands for the appointment of an independent counsel in the Justice
Department.

Concern about illegal foreign contributions and White House fund raising is understandable. Breaking laws to win elections is a serious matter. And such investigations in 1997 gave Republicans a golden opportunity to weaken a newly reelected Democratic president. But focus on scandal obscures a more fundamental point. Campaign finance regulations enacted years ago in reaction to the scandals surrounding the 1972 election have collapsed. Candidates, parties, and groups have found ways to raise and spend funds that are not subject to the limitations of the federal election law. The true scandal of 1996 was not illegal fund raising but what could be and was done quite legally. Practices supposedly outlawed by the act—the solicitation of six- and seven-digit political contributions by elected officials and the use of corporate and union treasuries to finance electioneering communications—returned with a vengeance in 1996 and 1998 and will doubtless appear in 2000. The legal framework to curb campaign finance has become little more than an annoyance, not a real constraint on the behavior of the contestants. The failure of the 105th Congress to enact campaign finance reform, in spite of the transparent abuse and the willingness of reformers to trim their ambitions to deal with the most egregious problems, underscores the daunting political obstacles facing any serious effort to overhaul federal election campaign law.

Campaign Finance Law: Theory versus Practice

Money in American politics has a long and notorious history. Mark Hanna, the Ohio political boss who masterminded William McKinley's 1896 presidential election victory with the help of a campaign kitty worth more than $100 million in today's dollars, once remarked, "There are two things that are important in politics. . . . The first is money and I can't remember what the second one is."[1] More than a half-century later, Jesse Unruh, the speaker of the California assembly and later state treasurer who built a political machine with funds extracted from lobbyists, said, "Money is the mother's milk of politics."[2]

1. Rosenkranz (1998b, p. 883).
2. Cited in Jacobs (1995, p. 88).

Campaign Finance Legislation

In the decades before and after 1900, political parties financed and ran campaigns for national office with large contributions raised from "fat cats."[3] During the Progressive Era early in the twentieth century, concern that the need to seek political contributions from corporations and wealthy individuals corrupted parties, candidates, and incumbents led to the first attempts to regulate private money in elections.[4] The Tillman Act of 1907 prohibited corporations and national banks from contributing to candidates for federal office. Later measures restricted the sources of campaign funds, limited spending, and provided for the disclosure of contributions. These laws were ineffectual. Statutes had gaping loopholes. Enforcement mechanisms were lacking. And a largely uninformed public tolerated relatively unconstrained campaign fund raising and spending.

The environment began to change in the late 1950s and early 1960s as campaigns became more candidate centered, television based, and costly. Worries about rising costs and wealthy challengers led Congress to enact the Federal Election Campaign Act (FECA) of 1971, which set limits on how much of their own personal wealth federal candidates could spend on their own campaigns, established ceilings for media expenditures, and required full public disclosure of campaign receipts and disbursements.[5] Revelations about the Watergate scandal focused attention on fund-raising abuses in the 1972 election and prompted Congress to rewrite the act in 1974.

The FECA amendments of 1974 constituted the first comprehensive regulation of campaign finance in U.S. federal elections.[6] The amendments retained the long-standing prohibition on contributions from corporations and unions and the limits on expenditures made by candidates from their personal or family funds that were part of the 1971 law but imposed new limits on contributions to federal campaigns by individuals and political committees. They also limited total spending by presidential, Senate, and House candidates and independent

---

3. Overacker (1932).
4. Corrado (1997, pp. 27–31).
5. Corrado (1997, pp. 31, 32, 52).
6. Corrado (1997, pp. 32–33, 53–55).

expenditures made on behalf of or in opposition to a federal candidate. The spending limits, but not the contribution limits, were indexed for inflation. The amendments strengthened the disclosure and enforcement provisions of existing law and established an independent agency, the Federal Election Commission, to administer the law. Finally, the legislation instituted voluntary public financing for presidential elections. At the nomination stage, public funds were to match private donations. Qualifying nominees could receive a public grant equal to the spending limit in force if they agreed to accept no private donations in the general election campaign.

Before this extraordinarily ambitious and comprehensive approach to political financing could take effect, the Supreme Court decided in *Buckley* v. *Valeo* (1976) that corruption or the appearance of corruption could justify regulation of campaign contributions but that the state interest was insufficient to justify limits on individual expenditures.[7] The Court explicitly rejected as unconstitutional the rationale provided by Congress to limit spending, namely, "to equalize the relative ability of [individuals and groups] to affect the outcome of elections." The Court found, "The concept that government may restrict the speech of some elements of our society in order to enhance the relative voice of others is wholly foreign to the First Amendment." *Buckley* gave Congress broad scope to limit contributions, as long as those limitations were needed to prevent corruption or the appearance of corruption. But it threw out mandatory limits on candidate spending, independent spending, and use of personal funds by candidates. The Court also narrowed the statute's coverage by insisting that it apply only to expenditures made that mention "explicit words of advocacy of election or defeat."

The Lid Is Off

Two decades later this restriction provided the constitutional rationale for the explosion of election-oriented issue advocacy.

The federal campaign finance law after *Buckley* was a hybrid, designed by no one, the residue of a statute subjected to withering con-

---

7. The text draws on Ortiz (1997, pp. 63–64). The decision is excerpted on pp. 67–77.

stitutional scrutiny. The Court left intact voluntary presidential campaign spending limits tied to the provision of public subsidies. Only 1 of 52 candidates opted out of that voluntary system in the presidential elections of 1976, 1980, 1984, and 1988.[8] Increases in campaign expenditures moderated. The fund-raising frenzy in presidential politics diminished. And expenditures on general election campaigns by candidates of the two major parties were roughly equal.[9] Money remained important in presidential elections, particularly in the nominating phase, but the situation seemed under control.

The legal framework remaining in place for congressional elections was much less effective. Without public subsidies to secure voluntary compliance with spending limits, nothing limited the demand for campaign funds. Indeed, the threat of a challenge from wealthy, self-financed candidates—real or imagined—intensified that demand. When coupled with this increased demand, the retention of contributions limits not indexed for inflation generated perverse pressures: an intensification of the money chase, rising prominence of fund raisers in the Washington community, a flow of private dollars to more accessible political channels, and the emergence of an underground economy in political financing.

The Spending Explosion

Not surprisingly, spending increased much more rapidly in congressional than presidential campaigns.[10] The trend was fueled in part by political action committees (PACs), whose numbers grew from 608 in 1974 to 4,009 in 1984 and whose contributions to congressional candidates grew during that decade from $12.5 million to $105.3 million.[11] The PACs could contribute up to $5,000 to candidates in both the primary and general election campaign, while the limit for individuals was $1,000. But the proliferation of PACs paused after 1984, and their share of contributions to congressional candidates stabilized, although

8. Maisel (1993, pp. 237–38).
9. Sorauf (1992, pp. 158–59).
10. Ornstein (1997, p. 7); Ornstein, Mann, and Malbin (1998, pp. 88–95).
11. Ornstein, Mann, and Malbin (1998, pp. 140–41); Souraf (1984, p. 38).

incumbents steadily increased their advantage over challengers in PAC fund raising until 1994.

Individual donors provided the majority of funds in congressional campaigns, and politicians sought new and more effective means of "dialing for dollars." Candidates made repeated pilgrimages to the most prosperous zip codes. Washington lobbyists became adept at delivering individual donors for their favorite elected officials, and the national political party committees made themselves increasingly useful in identifying generous donors. Between 1980 and 1996 the share of House campaign funding provided by PACs remained roughly constant while the part financed with donations of $500 or more doubled.[12]

The strains in the campaign finance system intensified after 1994 when the Republicans captured Congress and set the stage for a high-stakes political confrontation between a Democratic president and a Republican Congress. Determined to recover from his devastating 1994 political setback, President Clinton used every means available to become the first Democratic president reelected to a second term since Franklin Roosevelt. Speaker Newt Gingrich and other Republican leaders were equally determined to retain their congressional majorities and preside over the first Republican House since the 1920s to hold sway for two consecutive terms. Liberal allies of the Democratic minority in Congress, threatened by the conservative ascendancy in the House, were desperate to keep the Republican tenure short. This intensely competitive political environment created incentives for politicians, parties, and interest groups of all stripes to press their case with the public as aggressively as possible. All viewed funding, and new, unconstrained ways of spending those funds, as essential. Soft money and issue advocacy became the means to those ends.

Soft Money

The architects of the Federal Election Campaign Act did not envision soft money—funds raised by the parties for purposes other than directly influencing federal election campaigns—and such funds have no official standing in federal election law.[13] National and state party

12. Ornstein (1997, pp. 16–17).
13. Corrado (1997, pp. 167–77).

organizations have legitimate interests in state and local elections and in general party building. That provisions of the state campaign finance law should govern the collection and expenditure of such funds is quite reasonable. In many cases, however, those state laws are more permissive than federal law—no bans on corporate or union contributions, no limits on individual and PAC contributions to the parties. In addition, many political activities occupy a gray area between national politics and state or local politics, including voter registration, get-out-the-vote drives, and generic party advertising.

In a series of rulings beginning in 1976, the Federal Election Commission (FEC) authorized party organizations to maintain two sets of accounts—federal and nonfederal—and to allocate expenses, including overhead, between the two accounts. In effect, the FEC gave the parties permission to raise funds for nonfederal accounts directly from corporations and unions and in unlimited amounts from individuals, even though federal law explicitly prohibited such solicitations.

The national parties quickly seized this new opportunity. They raised an estimated $19 million in soft money in 1980 and $22 million in 1984 and worked hard to cover as many of their expenses as possible with soft—that is, unregulated—money. Subsequent rules issued by the FEC for allocating expenses between federal and nonfederal accounts permitted the parties legally to pay for a greater share of their expenses with soft money than before. Efforts to raise soft money intensified, and by 1992 the major party organizations raised more than $83 million. But all of this was simply a rehearsal for the 1996 election cycle, when the two parties raised and spent $262 million in soft money.

Issue Advocacy

The secret was a new way to spend soft money—financing issue advocacy ads that are designed to help presidential and congressional candidates but do not count as federal election spending because they do not expressly advocate the election or defeat of a federal candidate.[14] The Supreme Court in *Buckley* v. *Valeo* created this opportunity when it rejected as unconstitutionally vague the FECA's language regulating all spending "in connection with," or "for the purpose of influencing" a fed-

---

14. Potter (1997, pp. 227–38); Moramarco (1998).

eral election, or "relative to" a federal candidate. The Court insisted that
the law could apply only to speech that constituted "express advocacy" and
indicated in a footnote explicit words (such as "vote for," "elect," "defeat,"
"reject") that satisfied its express advocacy test. Years passed before federal
courts tried to apply the express advocacy test to actual communications.
By the mid-1990s most court rulings agreed that political communication
not expressly endorsing or opposing a candidate's election was issue advocacy and not subject to federal regulation. As a result, sponsors became
free to run an unlimited number of issue advocacy ads paid for in any
way they liked, including from sources and in amounts prohibited by
federal election law. Furthermore, sponsors do not have to disclose the
sources of financing or the expenditures themselves.

Political strategist Dick Morris reports that President Clinton readily
accepted his proposal to use issue advocacy ads to bolster the president's
public standing.[15] Morris argued that such ads would not count against
the spending limits imposed on presidential candidates who voluntarily accept public financing (an argument disputed later by FEC staff but
ultimately supported by commission members in a December 1998 ruling). Morris also claimed that such ads could be financed in part with
soft money. The aggressive solicitation of soft money by the president
and vice president, and the well-publicized abuses that were linked with
it, can be better understood in the context of issue advocacy.

Other political actors quickly followed suit. The AFL-CIO announced a $35 million issue advocacy campaign financed with union
treasury funds and targeted against potentially vulnerable Republican
House members. Both national party committees ran "issue ads" to
bolster their presidential nominees before the party conventions, when
regulated funds were running short. Dozens of groups, some formed
for this sole purpose, launched a barrage of ads attacking their political opponents but stopping short of using the magic words of express
advocacy. While the lack of disclosure makes a full accounting almost
impossible, a study of the Annenberg Public Policy Center reported that
at least $135 to $150 million were spent on issue ads in 1996 to influence federal elections.[16] These ads were notable, the study found, for

15. Morris (1997, p. 141).
16. Beck and others (1997).

their use of candidate names and images, their negativism and aggres-
siveness, and the absence of issue advocacy or content. No one, certainly
not their sponsors, doubted that their purpose was to help elect or
defeat federal candidates without the burden of being subject to laws
regulating sources and amount of contributions and requiring public
disclosure. The extensive use of party soft money and issue advocacy
in the 1998 congressional elections confirms that the 1996 experience
was less an anomaly than a harbinger of a new world of campaign strategy and finance.[17]

Ailments: Chronic and Acute

Developments in political financing since the adoption of a comprehensive regulatory scheme in 1974 have diminished the health of American democracy, with symptoms chronic and acute. The chronic
maladies are mostly connected with the money chase. The problem is
not simply vast sums spent in election campaigns—the $2.2 billion
dollars in direct spending by federal candidates and parties in 1996 does
not include election-oriented issue advocacy spending by various
groups[18]—or even the rate of increase in spending, which has greatly
outpaced the cost of living. Gaining the attention of 268 million citizens
in a sprawling nation subject to a continuous barrage of commercial
advertisements is neither easy nor inexpensive. The nation's many elec-
tive offices and the frequency of primary and general elections make
that challenge even more daunting.

The threat to the health of the American democracy stems rather from
what candidates and their supporters must do to raise the sums needed to
compete successfully. The cost of mounting a major campaign is a huge
disincentive to candidacy for people of ordinary means who lack the
stomach for nonstop fund raising. Money may be necessary for political
success, but it is no guarantee, as clearly demonstrated by the experience
of Al Checchi, who spent $40 million from his personal fortune in a futile
quest for the Democratic gubernatorial nomination in California.
Indeed, Checchi's experience is typical of the failure of most free-

17. Magleby with Holt (1999).
18. Center for Responsive Politics (1998).

spending wealthy candidates.[19] Nonetheless, the number of self-financed candidates is growing, and parties increasingly seek to recruit the ones who are able and willing to finance their own campaigns.

The money chase does more than discourage potential candidates. It structures how elected officials spend their time, where they travel, with whom they speak, and how they focus their legislative energies. White House documents released during the investigations of fund-raising practices of the 1996 Clinton reelection campaign offer sobering documentation of the demands on the time of the president and vice president (by most accounts willingly met) for fund raising.[20]

The impact of the money chase on Capitol Hill is even more striking. Congressional leaders must have their own PACs, spearhead the fund-raising drives of their party campaign committee, and constantly calculate how the legislative party agenda, scheduling, and committee assignment decisions might affect their colleagues' fund-raising prospects. Rank-and-file members of Congress who are facing the possibility of a serious challenge—or more likely working to ward one off—in the next election cannot afford to let many days pass without reeling in substantial campaign funds. Personal accounts of former members illustrate the myriad ways in which life in Congress is shaped by the constant quest for campaign funds.[21]

One need not be impressed with the many studies correlating PAC contributions and votes or accept the crudest quips about "The best Congress money can buy" to take those accounts seriously.[22] Most votes in the House and Senate are influenced primarily by party, ideology, and constituency interests, not campaign contributions. Donations from groups with legislative interests are more likely to follow votes in Congress than to determine them. Incumbents can often dominate their relationship with contributors, playing off competing interests and exploiting the risk-averse orientation of many donors. And yet who can doubt that politicians sometimes pay back contributors in the only coin

19. Todd S. Purdum, "Money Politics Wasn't Defeated in California," *New York Times*, June 7, 1998, p. 1.

20. U.S. Senate, Committee on Governmental Affairs (1998, pp. 34, 40–43).

21. Schram (1995).

22. Sorauf (1992, pp. 126–27, chap. 6); Hall and Wayman (1990, pp. 797–820); Rosenkranz (1998b).

they possess in abundance, or that large financial contributors enjoy preferential and inequitable access? In the countless decisions elected officials make every day—whose phone calls to return, whether to support or oppose amendments in committee or even be present when the vote is taken, or which matters to devote one's legislative energies to—dollars may well amplify the voices of important financial benefactors over those of ordinary citizens. Conflicts of interest and inequities are inescapable and would arise even if private money were banished from campaigns. But the money chase—the relentless quest for campaign funds by politicians—exacerbates these problems and feeds the popular suspicion that monied interests unfairly dominate public policy.

The problem is not only with how funds are raised but with how those funds are distributed. The campaign finance system rewards incumbents over challengers and members of the majority party in Congress over members of the minority. It thereby reduces the number of seriously contested races and even denies some voters a genuine choice of candidates. It heightens the reelection rates of incumbents and reduces the frequency of alterations in party control of Congress.

Another shortcoming of the present campaign finance regime—one as old as efforts to regulate money in politics—is the inadequacy of mechanisms to administer and enforce the law.[23] This characteristic reflects congressional intent. In creating the Federal Election Commission, Congress had no interest in a powerful independent agency that could impose severe and timely penalties for violations of campaign laws. Consequently, the FEC was hamstrung in various ways: with a membership structure—three Democrats and three Republicans—that is prone to partisan deadlock on controversial matters; with procedural requirements that virtually ensure years of delay in moving against violators; with no independent authority to impose sanctions or to conduct its own litigation; with a ban on random audits of candidates; and with an annual, instead of multiyear, budget that Congress niggardly supports despite the commission's expanding workload. It is hardly surprising that candidates in 1996 cavalierly flouted the law and that the FEC did not launch an investigation until months after the election.

23. Mann (1997, pp. 277–80).

All of these problems—the money chase, conflicts of interest, inequities in access and influence, the lack of competition, and weak enforcement—have persisted for years, like a low-grade fever, debilitating the body politic but not threatening its survival. The experiences of 1996 suggest that maladies of a more acute nature have developed. Practices that year egregiously violated the objectives of the law and challenged the legitimacy of the entire system. The explosion of soft money brought back the corrupting potential of huge unregulated contributions from corporations, unions, and wealthy individuals and the temptation for elected officials to use the power of the state to extort private resources for political purposes. The acceleration of soft-money raising in the 1997–98 period underscored how central expenditures of unregulated money have become to the electoral strategies of the congressional parties.[24]

The rise of electioneering masquerading as issue advocacy undermines laws requiring disclosure and prohibiting direct corporate and union financing of independent expenditures. It weakens the ability of voters to hold candidates accountable for what is said and done in campaigns. Issue advocacy is rapidly becoming the political communication tactic of choice for candidates, parties, and groups liberated from the constraints of disclosure and contribution limits. Consulting firms are moving quickly to offer a full array of services along these lines.

Taken together, soft money and issue advocacy make a mockery of campaign finance regulation and may soon precipitate a complete collapse of credibility for campaign finance laws that have been gamed beyond recognition. Prospects for financial integrity in the 2000 election are hardly encouraging.

Comparative Perspectives

The dependence of the U.S. campaign finance system on private money may be problematic, but money is not the root of all evil in politics. A major restructuring of campaign finance law would not dramatically

24. Parties raised $201 million in soft money during the 1998 election cycle, almost double the $102 million they raised in the previous (1994) midterm election. See Federal Election Commission, "Political Party Fund-raising Continues to Climb," press release, Washington, January 26, 1999.

reduce corruption and purify politics and governance. The experience of other democracies in grappling with similar problems suggests that political finance rules are important but secondary in shaping democratic accountability and governmental performance.[25] Money is a problem in the politics of all democracies, and efforts to deal with the problem have yielded disappointing results. Scandals have arisen in most countries in both their pre- and postreform stages. Levels of corruption are not closely connected to the extent of public subsidies or the intensity of regulation of party and campaign finance.[26] The institutional, legal, and political order in which the political financing system is embedded seems critical, not the rules governing campaign finance.

The political finance tools available to reformers—disclosure, contribution limits, spending limits, public subsidies, and regulation of campaign activity—often fail to reduce corruption, lessen the influence of monied interests, slow the increase in campaign expenditures, or increase electoral competition. Cross-national studies suggest that other policies and institutions are more important levers for combating corruption: broad economic policies—macroeconomic stabilization, public ownership, regulation, and taxes—that determine the discretionary authority of public officials; institutions and practices nurturing the rule of law; an independent judiciary; adequate pay and strong ethical requirements for politicians and civil servants; transparent budget and financial control systems; and party systems nurturing stable patterns of competition, accountability, and alteration of majorities.[27] The United States measures up well on these dimensions and has, in fact, become markedly less corrupt over the course of this century.

The appearance as well as the reality of corruption is a source of concern.[28] Perceived corruption can undermine the public consensus that undergirds legitimate politics and government. The *seeming* corruption of the U.S. campaign finance system is therefore a serious problem. Most Americans believe that campaign finance practices give special access

25. Mann (unpublished).

26. For example, money in politics has been especially problematic in Italy and Japan, two countries with substantial public financing and regulation.

27. Kaufmann (1997); Pope (1996).

28. Johnston (1993).

and influence to monied interests.[29] This belief arises in part from the new realities of an intensified money chase and the aggressive solicitation of large contributions. But, paradoxically, it also results from the increased transparency achieved in an earlier round of reform. Although disclosure curbs corruption, it has the unfortunate side effect of making odious practices appear the norm rather than the exception.

Not all campaign finance reforms are doomed to fail, but they are not miracle cures for the ills arising from money in politics. A tension between the reality of economic inequality and the ideal of political equality is inevitable in democratic societies. Political parties and candidates for public office need money and other resources to compete successfully in elections. Relatively few citizens have the personal means and desire to contribute to political campaigns. Under these circumstances, efforts to prevent concentrations of wealth from undermining political equality may conflict with bedrock freedoms of speech and association. The challenge is not to eliminate the tension but to manage it as well as possible given each society's complex constraints and other, sometimes competing, goals for the political system.

Alternative Approaches to Reform

Since the Supreme Court's ruling in *Buckley* v. *Valeo*, reform advocates in Congress have fought unsuccessfully to adapt a version of the campaign finance rules in presidential primaries—voluntary spending limits tied to partial public financing—for congressional elections. Frustrations with these repeated failures in Congress, with legal constraints imposed by *Buckley*, and with the unanticipated and often perverse consequences of campaign finance laws have led to new approaches to campaign finance reform.

Full Public Financing

Given the deadlock over changes in federal campaign finance law, most initiative in recent years has come from the states. Almost two-thirds

29. Princeton Survey Research Associates, "Money and Politics Survey: A National Survey of the Public's View on How Money Impacts Our Political System," conducted for Center for Responsive Politics, June 6, 1997 (http://www.opensecrets.org/pubs/survey/top.htm [May 19, 1999]).

of the states have enacted major campaign finance laws since 1979, one-third since 1990.[30] Like federal law, many contain disclosure requirements, contribution limits, and public financing that operates within the constraints of *Buckley*. More innovative proposals, including strict contribution limits (for example, $100), restrictions on out-of-district fund raising, and prohibitions on carrying over funds from one election cycle to another, have largely failed to withstand judicial scrutiny, as lower courts have applied the *Buckley* standard that laws must be narrowly tailored to prevent corruption or the appearance of corruption.[31]

One state-based approach—the Clean Money Option—departs radically from the congressional reform agenda but strives to comply with *Buckley*.[32] It seeks to institute voluntary full public financing by providing public grants to candidates in primary and general elections who agree to raise and spend no private dollars beyond a low qualifying threshold. This offer would be open to any candidate who raises the requisite number of small ($5.00) contributions in his or her district or state. Maine approved a version of this approach in 1996; it is scheduled to go into effect in 2000. Vermont approved a similar plan in 1997, as did Arizona and Massachusetts in 1998. All face judicial and funding challenges before they are implemented. A new advocacy group—Public Campaign—is organizing grass-roots campaigns in other states in support of this approach to campaign finance reform.

It is too early to judge whether this approach will work or be sustainable in the small, low-cost states of Maine and Vermont, adapt to more populous and contentious states that feature expensive, media-based campaigns, and eventually become the model for federal elections. But obstacles to its success are formidable. The first is that citizen support for publicly financed campaigns may prove evanescent. Survey evidence is mixed but suggests that the public might respond to arguments of politicians and others who oppose public financing and balk at providing the large sums needed to fully finance modern campaigns. Initial support may well evaporate when the public discovers that all qualifying candidates and parties, even fringe and patently

30. Malbin and Gais (1998, pp. 9–32).
31. Corrado and Ortiz (1997, pp. 337–40).
32. Donnelly, Fine, and Miller (1999, chap. 1).

offensive ones, receive the same amount of public funding. Furthermore, such even-handed treatment of marginal candidates and minor parties might harm the political process by creating political fragmentation and confusion among voters.

A second possible obstacle could arise from the accompanying complete shut-off of private funds. Experience in the United States and other democracies suggests that the ingenuity of candidates and contributors and the inherent porousness of democratic institutions will triumph over efforts to drastically reduce or eliminate private funds in election campaigns. The explosion of soft money and issue advocacy in the 1996 and 1998 elections supports the view that groups operating outside of the regulated arena could easily overwhelm a system financed entirely by public funds.

Even if it were possible to eliminate private funds from campaigns, doing so might not be desirable. Money in politics brings benefits as well as risks. The ability to raise money is one measure of a candidate's political support and of the intensity of preferences. And contributing money to campaigns is one important channel for organized political action, an essential element of representative democracy.

Deregulation

Another approach to reform would take the nation in the opposite direction—toward complete deregulation of campaign finance.[33] This approach is predicated on the belief that restrictions on private money in politics trample on the free speech guarantees in the Constitution and create a regulatory monster that exacerbates rather than mitigates the damaging consequences of the money chase. A bill sponsored by Representative John Doolittle (R-Calif.) would remove all restrictions on the sources and size of contributions to candidates and parties, end all public financing of presidential elections, and mandate electronic filing and timely disclosure on the Internet of reports on contributions to candidates for federal office. Doolittle offers an intellectually disarming and emotionally compelling vision of a political marketplace disciplined not by arcane rules and zealous regulators but by rational citizens exercising their franchise.

33. Mann (1998, pp. 20–21).

"Deregulate and disclose" is a seductive slogan in light of the widespread evidence of perverse effects and unanticipated consequences from previous efforts to regulate the flow of money in elections. But would policy based on this slogan have the desired effects? Would public indignation prevent campaign donations and expenditures from reinforcing or magnifying the influence of concentrated economic wealth and state power? To do so, voters would need to acquire full information on who was giving what to which candidates and parties; be able to differentiate among the opposing candidates or parties in the pattern of campaign contributions; and have a strong incentive to cast their ballots on a single basis: to punish at the polls candidates or parties who accept funds from repugnant sources. That is a mighty tall order for a citizenry that rationally limits its time invested in pursuing information about politics.

Furthermore, the Doolittle bill does nothing to require disclosure of campaign activity disguised as issue advocacy—the most rapidly growing, the most negative, and the least accountable form of political communication. Voters would find it difficult to use the ballot to discipline extravagant candidates, particularly when large economic interests invest heavily in both parties or contribute to winning candidates after the election, or when each party or candidate attracts campaign contributions from different, but equally offensive, sources. Finally, voters would be unlikely to disregard factors such as party identification, peace and prosperity, political ideology, or the candidate's character and instead focus exclusively and quixotically on the struggle to contain the harmful effects of money in politics.

In the unlikely event that the campaign finance system were fully deregulated—its appeal is currently limited to a small minority of politicians and voters—the unrestrained use of economic wealth and state power in the electoral process would almost certainly lead to insistent public demands to restore regulation.

Alternatives to Buckley v. Valeo

Other reforms require circumventing the restrictions laid down in the Buckley v. Valeo decision, a condition that could be reached through a constitutional amendment that gives Congress and the states authority to set reasonable limits on the funds expended, including contributions, to influence the outcome of elections. This approach is open to serious objections. It would weaken the free speech guarantee of the Constitution and give elected officials the power to enhance the advantages of incumbency. The courts would still have to determine whether specific spending limits and the definition of covered expenditures enacted by statute were "reasonable." In any case the two-thirds majorities in the House and Senate needed to send the amendment to the states for ratification are nowhere in sight.

The Century Foundation and the Brennan Center for Justice at the New York University School of Law are spearheading another, more intriguing, route to a post-*Buckley* world.[34] They are trying to persuade the Supreme Court to overrule the parts of the *Buckley* decision that prevent legislatures from enacting reasonable limits on campaign spending. Adherents of this approach concede that campaign spending deserves full First Amendment protection, but they argue that "judges should uphold carefully tailored regulations of such spending that are supported by compelling governmental interests."[35] Besides reducing corruption or the appearance of corruption, such interests might include expanding the pool of candidates who can run for office, preserving the time of incumbents to serve the public, restoring public confidence in the democratic process, equalizing the voices of citizens, reducing the disproportionate influence of concentrated wealth, and promoting the constitutional rights to vote and to petition. A strategic campaign—involving litigation, legislation, scholarship, and public education—is being launched to persuade the courts to rectify their past mistakes and loosen judicial constraints on campaign finance reform.

Even if *Buckley* were to fall, however, there is no guarantee that a framework permitting regulation of campaign spending would replace it. Just the opposite could result—a ruling rejecting regulation of contributions as well as of expenditures. Federal court decisions since *Buckley* suggest that champions of a constitutional doctrine favorable to the regulation of campaign spending have a long, uphill battle before them.[36] In 1996 the Supreme Court found in *Colorado Republican Fed-*

---

34. Rosenkranz (1998a).
35. Rosenkranz (1998a, p. 3).
36. Ortiz (1997, pp. 64–66).

eral Campaign Committee et al. v. *Federal Election Commission* that political party expenditures that were independent of its candidates could not be limited, and it left open the question of whether limitations on party expenditures that are coordinated with a candidate are constitutional.[37] It would not be surprising if the courts threw out all limits on what political parties can spend in coordination with their candidates. In fact, the U.S. District Court for Colorado subsequently ruled such limits on parties unconstitutional, a decision now on appeal to the Tenth Circuit.[38]

On another front the courts are being asked to overrule the FEC requirement that issue advocacy by parties be paid for with some hard as well as soft dollars.[39] This action would effectively remove all restraints on electioneering that does not meet the strict definition of express advocacy. Taken together, two such rulings could turn political parties into devices for avoiding all remaining federal restrictions on campaign spending. Such a result is a far cry from the aims of those who are mobilizing to topple *Buckley*.

Adjustments to the Regulatory Model

One or more of these approaches might bear fruit in the years ahead. State experimentation, including the Clean Money Option, may reveal national options not now in sight. Continuing litigation questioning limits on coordinated spending by political parties and the lawsuits challenging the legitimacy of FEC's allocation rules governing issue advocacy by parties could result in a far more deregulated system. In spite of the daunting odds, the intellectual energy of the "anti-*Buckley* brigade" may stimulate a major doctrinal rethinking of the relationship between campaign spending and free speech. But for the immediate future, Washington reformers will focus on making much-needed adjustments to the current federal election regulatory framework. To do so, they must deal with the critical problems that threaten a collapse of that framework and the chronic ills that have plagued the system for many years. They must find ways to curb soft-money fund raising by

37. U.S. Supreme Court (1996).
38. U.S. District Court (1999).
39. Philip B. Heymann and Donald J. Simon, "Parties to Corruption," *Washington Post*, June 25, 1998, p. A23.

the parties and to bring electioneering that masquerades as issue advocacy within the regulatory system. They should restore the real value of contribution limits eroded by twenty-five years of inflation, ease the restrictions on what parties can do with hard money on behalf of their candidates, and provide public subsidies to candidates, directly—with cash grant or matching funds—or indirectly—with tax credits, free mailings, voter brochures, and free broadcast time. Such adjustments to the regulatory model should also include stronger disclosure requirements and enforcement rules.

Soft Money

The highest priority of most reformers is to curb soft money. What began as a reasonable way of paying for general party building and coordinated campaigns involving federal, state, and local elections has degenerated into a frenzy of aggressive solicitation of megacontributions from corporations, unions, and wealthy individuals; ever more creative ways to spend those dollars to advance the election prospects of federal candidates; and dizzying transfers and trades of soft and hard dollars between national and state parties. The simple truth is that soft money makes a mockery of the contribution limits in federal election law.

A bill sponsored in the 105th and 106th Congresses by Senators John McCain (R-Ariz.) and Russell Feingold (D-Wisc.) and by Representatives Christopher Shays (R-Conn.) and Martin Meehan (D-Mass.) would ban soft money at both national and state levels.[40] National parties would be prohibited from maintaining more than one set of (hard money) accounts. All expenditures and transfers to state parties and nonprofit organizations would have to be financed with contributions subject to federal regulations. Federal officeholders, candidates for federal office, and national party officials and their agents would be barred from raising or steering funds not subject to federal contribution limits. Finally, state parties would be prohibited from raising and spending nonfederal funds on party activities that in any way benefit candidates for federal office.

40. S. 25 (105 Cong., 1997) and H.R. 3526 (105 Cong., 1998). S. 26 (106 Cong., 1999); H.R. 417 (106 Cong., 1999).

A variation on this approach would prohibit national parties and federal candidates from raising and spending soft money and prohibit transfers of nonfederal funds among state parties but continue to let state law govern state parties. This change, which was part of the bill sponsored in the 105th Congress by a bipartisan group of House freshmen and subsequently endorsed as part of a package of reforms recommended by the Committee for Economic Development, would allow state parties to finance their share of general party activities or coordinated campaigns with contributions governed by state law.[41] This approach respects federalism but would permit some contributions from corporations, unions, and wealthy individuals to support activities that might conceivably help candidates for federal office. Like the first approach, however, it would effectively return federal campaign finance practice to the situation in which federal officeholders and candidates face strict limits on the sources and size of contributions they solicit on behalf of their parties.

Another reform track would concede the legitimacy of soft money but set limits on how it is raised and spent. For example, Congress might cap contributions to the nonfederal accounts of national party committees at $50,000 or $75,000. Such limits would eliminate the notorious six- and seven-figure contributions but preserve a capacity for parties to invest more easily in general activities not tied specifically to federal candidates. With the forbearance of the courts—by no means ensured—Congress might also prohibit parties from using soft money to finance electioneering messages—defined more liberally than express advocacy—or any messages coordinated with federal candidates. Laws along these lines would prevent much of the willful circumvention of spending limits on publicly funded presidential campaigns that was so evident in 1996.

Issue Advocacy

If soft money is the most important item on the reform agenda, issue advocacy is the most difficult. By restricting federal regulation to political communications involving express advocacy, the courts have enabled parties, candidates, and groups to avoid federal dis-

41. H.R. 2183 (105 Cong., 1998).

closure requirements and contribution limitations. That loophole permitted candidates and parties in elections since 1996 to avoid legal strictures. Issue advocacy ads have become a major campaign instrument.

The challenge is to control election-oriented issue advocacy without trampling on constitutionally guaranteed free speech. The increasing reliance on this method of shaping public opinion makes meeting this challenge more difficult and more important. The Supreme Court was properly concerned about the vagueness and excessive breadth of the language Congress used in 1974. One strategy is to codify, by statute or regulation, a definition of express advocacy that reflects the realities of electioneering better than the "magic words" test of *Buckley*.[42] The FEC tried to do just that by issuing an express advocacy regulation that adopts the "reasonable person" approach taken by the Ninth Circuit in *Federal Election Commission* v. *Furgatch* (1987). Under the FEC regulation, express advocacy includes not only communications that contain the magic words but also those that "when taken as a whole and with limited reference to external events, such as the proximity to the election, could only be interpreted by a reasonable person as containing advocacy of the election or defeat of one or more clearly identified candidate(s)." Moreover, that election advocacy must be "unmistakable, unambiguous, and suggestive of only one meaning."[43]

The legal standing of this approach is at best uncertain. The First Circuit upheld a district court decision overturning the regulation as too broad and unconstitutionally vague and therefore likely to have a chilling effect on speech.[44] Although the Supreme Court has not yet spoken, the weight of judicial opinion in other cases suggests that it will side with the First Circuit.

An alternative is to find another bright-line test of express advocacy, as clear and unambiguous as the magic words, that brings obvious electioneering communications within the reach of the law.[45] For example,

42. Potter (1997); Moramarco (1998); Corrado and Ortiz (1997, p. 381).

43. 11 C.F.R. § 100.22 "Expressly Advocating (2 U.S.C. § 431 [17])," *Federal Register*, vol. 60 (July 6, 1995), pp. 35304–305.

44. *Maine Right to Life Committee, Inc* v. *Federal Election Commission*, 914 F. Supp. 8 (D. Me. 1996). See Corrado and others (1997, p. 235).

45. *Maine Right to Life Committee, Inc.,* v. *Federal Election Commission*, 914 F. Supp. 8 (D. Me. 1996).

any paid communication with the general public that uses a federal candidate's name or likeness within, say, thirty or sixty days of an election could be deemed express advocacy. Although this approach may sweep in advertisements designed solely to influence debate on an issue, it provides clear guidelines to genuine issue advocacy groups on how to avoid having their educational communications treated as express advocacy. In any case, the point of this reform strategy is not to squelch speech but to make it more likely that communications clearly and unambiguously designed to influence a federal election are subject to disclosure of funding sources and are not financed, directly or indirectly, from corporate or union treasuries.

Even if Congress patched the soft money and issue advocacy leaks that turned into gushers in 1996 and 1998, serious problems with the finance system for congressional elections would remain. The solution of choice for much of the reform community during the past two decades—voluntary spending limits tied to the provision of public subsidies—failed to garner the necessary support when Democrats controlled both ends of Pennsylvania Avenue. It is not even on the Republican congressional agenda.[46] The most promising line of reform may be to make it easier for congressional candidates to raise the money needed to run competitive campaigns.

Contribution Limits

The most obvious, though controversial, step is to raise contribution limits, which have been frozen for a quarter century. If limits on contributions from individuals and political committees were reasonable when enacted in 1974, restoring their real value and indexing them for future inflation should be equally reasonable and acceptable. Since prices have tripled since 1974, this step implies an immediate threefold increase. An additional step—setting higher contribution limits for the first $100,000 or $200,000 raised—would make it easier for challengers to raise the seed money critical for launching a serious candidacy.

---

46. Voluntary spending limits on House and Senate candidates who accept public funding, albeit limits higher than those proposed in recent reform bills, are among the recommendations proposed by the Committee for Economic Development (1999).

Party Spending

Current law limits the contributions from political parties to their candidates and spending by parties on behalf of those candidates. In 1996 the combined limit on contributions and coordinated spending by national and state parties was $101,820 for House candidates and ranged for Senate candidates from $161,140 in small states to $2,855,998 in California.[47] These limits enabled parties to finance barely 10 percent of the average cost of races by successful House challengers. The *Colorado* v. *Federal Election Commission* case mentioned earlier will test the constitutionality of limits on party-coordinated spending. The crux of the matter is whether such spending should be treated as a contribution (and thus subject to regulation) or as a form of constitutionally protected spending. If the limits on coordinated spending are upheld, Congress could raise them or end them, perhaps along with a ban of soft money and an increase in limits on hard-money contributions to parties.

Having the parties play a larger role in the financing of congressional campaigns, beyond the simple displacement of some fund-raising burden from candidates, would bring several benefits. Parties are strategic: they have incentives to channel funds to potentially successful challengers, not just to entrench incumbents. Parties could also steer resources to candidates facing free-spending opponents. They provide some insulation between contributors and politicians. And parties exert some counterpressure—in the form of party image and policy coherence—on the candidate-centered character of American elections.

Having parties play a larger role in the financing of congressional elections is not risk free, however. Modern U.S. political parties are instruments of incumbent politicians more than they are independent grass-roots organizations. As such, they can launder contributions and increase the leverage of interest groups and individuals on policymaking.

Public Subsidies

Direct public funding of federal campaigns is currently limited to presidential elections. Congressional candidates receive no explicit public

---

47. Ornstein, Mann, and Malbin (1998, p. 107).

subsidies for campaign activities, although incumbents surely benefit relative to their challengers from salary, staff payroll, and official expense funds given to members of Congress. Public funds could be used to support candidates of both major and qualifying minor party candidates. Such support could be contingent on the candidate's agreement to spend no more than, say, $50,000 of personal funds.[48] Partial public financing would ease the burden of fund raising and would likely attract better candidates, thereby increasing the competitiveness of congressional elections. A public grant to qualifying general election candidates would be much easier to administer than a matching fund system in place for both primary and general elections.

Public subsidies need not be in the form of direct cash assistance. Qualifying candidates could receive vouchers for the purchase of broadcast time, financed by an appropriation of public funds or by broadcasters as part of their public interest obligations. They could also be provided with free or subsidized mailings, possibly financed with the election-year budget for the congressional frank. Voter brochures could be prepared and distributed to citizens. And candidates could be given a strong incentive to raise small contributions in their own states through the provision of a 100 percent tax credit or a government match based on contributions smaller than some threshold.

These measures alone would not remove the incentives for ever higher spending in potentially competitive races. Combined with effective controls on soft money and issue advocacy advertising, however, they would reduce current excesses.

Disclosure and Enforcement

Improved disclosure of campaign contributions and expenditures and strengthened enforcement of the law are necessary elements of a reform in campaign finance regulations. Improved disclosure should include mandatory electronic filing, with posting on the Internet and a disclosure requirement for election-oriented issue ads. Improved enforcement requires strengthening of the Federal Election Commission.

---

48. Public subsidies could also be contingent on candidates adhering to voluntary spending limits, as recommended most recently by the Committee for Economic Development (1999).

Constructive steps would include a single, eight-year term for commissioners, a permanent nonvoting chairman, independent litigating
authority for the commission, a private right of legal action, increased
appropriations, and a multiyear budget cycle.[49]

The Politics of Campaign Finance Reform

If there was any doubt about the political difficulty of enacting modest
changes in the current regulatory framework, one need only look at
the tortuous and ultimately futile odyssey of campaign finance reform
in the 105th Congress. Because Watergate triggered the last major
restructuring of federal campaign finance regulation, it was reasonable
to hope that the fund-raising scandals of the 1996 election cycle and the
collapse of campaign finance regulation would lead to reform of the
laws governing how money is raised and spent in federal elections. The
flexibility of reformers should also have improved prospects, as they
set aside controversial proposals to limit spending in congressional elections and focused on features of the 1996 campaign that politicians on
both sides of the aisle acknowledged were at the root of the 1996
imbroglio—soft money and election-oriented issue advocacy. When
the sponsors of the major legislative vehicle for reform—John McCain
and Russell Feingold in the Senate, Christopher Shays and Martin Meehan in the House—reintroduced their bill in the fall of 1997, controversial provisions to limit spending, provide free or reduced-cost
broadcast time to complying candidates, abolish PACs, and restrict out-
of-district fund raising were dropped. Yet the opposition of the Republican leadership in both houses remained implacable—leading to a
filibuster in the Senate and maneuvers in the House designed to prevent
passage. The tactics in the House backfired, however, as Representatives
Shays and Meehan built a bipartisan coalition that overcame numerous parliamentary hurdles to achieve a stunning victory.

In the end, the bill failed in the Senate, as supporters could attract
only fifty-two votes, eight short of the supermajority needed to end
the filibuster mounted by opponents. Sufficient pressure never developed from a reform-minded but cynical and inert public to overcome

49. Mann (1997).

the rational calculations of self-interested politicians and the adamant opposition of key interest groups in the Republican coalition. While numerous polls and focus groups substantiated the widespread public disgust with the money in politics system, they also underscored for politicians the relatively low priority the public places on campaign finance reform and the absence of any consensus on a reform agenda.[50] Few members of Congress were bombarded with mail or confronted in their constituencies by citizens demanding campaign finance reform. Expressions of outrage were mostly confined to the editorial pages. This public indifference or feeling of hopelessness gave members of Congress leeway to talk about reform without feeling an obligation to act.

The Republican leadership was reluctant to tamper with a campaign finance system that seemed likely to favor their party over the long haul. Although Democrats had proved more competitive in soft- than hard-money party fund raising, Republicans calculated that their natural advantage with corporations and wealthy individuals, reinforced by their control of Congress and eventual return to the White House, would pay them handsome soft-money dividends in the years ahead. And while Bill Clinton and the AFL-CIO had set the standard for successfully exploiting the issue advocacy loophole, Republicans also figured that their party committees and support groups would be able to take fuller advantage of this feature of the law in the future. Opposition to any restrictions on issue advocacy by the National Right to Life Committee, the National Rifle Association, the Christian Coalition, and other key groups in the Republican coalition reinforced this view.

As the new congressional minority, Democrats discovered a devotion to changing the rules of the campaign finance game that had been well hidden when they controlled Congress and could have reformed the system. Even as the minority party, some Democrats were lukewarm to an outright ban on soft money. Their almost unanimous embrace of McCain-Feingold/Shays-Meehan legislation seems to have been as much an exercise in position taking as legislating.

50. Saad (1997, pp. 11–14); Princeton Survey Research Associates, "Money and Politics Survey"; Gallup Poll, "Americans Not Holding Their Breath on Campaign Finance Reform," October 11, 1997 (http://www.gallup.com/poll/releases/pr971011.asp [July 9, 1999]); Gallup/CNN/USA Today Poll, June 4–5, 1999 (http://www.pollingreport.com/issues.htm# Election Issues [June 25, 1999]).

This experience in the 105th Congress and the halting efforts to reignite the reform process early in the 106th Congress underscore the daunting obstacles to enacting new campaign finance law. Politicians' self-interest, low public salience, partisanship, the supermajority requirement in the Senate, and limits imposed by the courts constrain the ability of reformers to achieve their goals.

But remove these factors and politicians would still find it difficult to pass a campaign finance reform bill. Conflicts among desirable goals produce legitimate disagreement on how best to proceed. Restraining politicians' financial dependence on individuals and organizations with substantial public business can diminish freedom of speech and association. Increasing the role of small donors can intensify the money chase. Limiting the sources and amounts of funding available to political parties can weaken their role in elections relative to candidates and interest groups.

It is not surprising that politicians with contrasting ideologies set different priorities on these conflicting objectives. Forging compromises requires a willingness to listen to and respect the views of those members with different values and perspectives, hardly a quality that characterizes the current partisan Congress. And even if successful, that process of deliberation and amendment will have to repeat itself time and again, as tensions built into the law produce undesirable consequences and campaign professionals find ever more creative ways of evading its reach.

References

Beck, Deborah, and others. 1997. *Issue Advocacy Advertising during the 1996 Campaign.* Series 16. University of Pennsylvania, Annenberg Public Policy Center (September).

Center for Responsive Politics. 1998. *Who's Paying? Stats at a Glance on the Funding of U.S. Elections.* Washington.

Committee for Economic Development. 1999. *Investing in the People's Business: A Business Proposal for Campaign Finance Reform.* New York.

Corrado, Anthony. 1997. "Money and Politics: A History of Federal Campaign Finance Law." In *Campaign Finance Reform: A Sourcebook*, edited by A. Corrado and others, 25–60. Brookings.

Corrado, Anthony, and Daniel R. Ortiz. 1997. "Recent Innovations." In *Campaign Finance Reform: A Sourcebook*, edited by A. Corrado and others, 335–92. Brookings.

Donnelly, David, Janice Fine, and Ellen S. Miller. 1999. *Money and Politics: Financing Our Elections Democratically*. Beacon Press.

Hall, Richard L., and Frank W. Wayman. 1990. "Buying Time: Moneyed Interests and the Mobilization of Bias in Congressional Committees." *American Political Science Review* 84 (September): 797–820.

Jacobs, John. 1995. *A Rage for Justice: The Passion and Politics of Phillip Burton*. University of California Press.

Johnston, Michael. 1993. "The Political Costs of Corruption." Paper presented at Primera Conferencia Latinoamericana de Lucha contra la Corrupcion Administrativa. Bogota, Columbia (November).

Kaufmann, Daniel. 1997. "Corruption: The Facts." *Foreign Policy* (Summer): 114–31.

Magleby, David B., with Marianne Holt. 1999. "Outside Money: Soft Money and Issue Ads in Competitive 1998 Congressional Elections." Brigham Young University.

Maisel, L. Sandy. 1993. *Parties and Elections in America: The Electoral Process*. 2d ed. McGraw-Hill.

Malbin, Michael J., and Thomas L. Gais. 1998. *The Day after Reform: Sobering Campaign Finance Lessons from the American States*. Albany, N.Y.: Rockefeller Institute Press.

Mann, Thomas E. 1997. "The Federal Election Commission: Implementing and Enforcing." In *Campaign Finance Reform: A Sourcebook*, edited by A. Corrado and others, 275–334. Brookings.

———. Unpublished. "Comparative Perspectives on Money and Politics: Lessons for the U.S."

———. 1998. "Deregulating Campaign Finance: Solution or Chimera?" *Brookings Review* 16 (Winter): 20–21.

Moramarco, Glenn. 1998. *Regulating Electioneering: Distinguishing between "Express Advocacy" and "Issue Advocacy."* Campaign Finance Reform series. New York University School of Law, Brennan Center for Justice.

Morris, Dick. 1997. *Behind the Oval Office: Winning the Presidency in the Nineties*. Random House.

Ornstein, Norman J. 1997. *Campaign Finance: An Illustrated Guide*. Washington: AEI Press.

Ornstein, Norman J., Thomas E. Mann, and Michael J. Malbin. 1998. *Vital Statistics on Congress 1997–1998*. Washington: Congressional Quarterly.

Ortiz, Daniel R. 1997. "The First Amendment at Work: Constitutional Restrictions on Campaign Finance Regulation." In *Campaign Finance Reform: A Sourcebook*, edited by A. Corrado and others, 61–92. Brookings.

Overacker, Louise. 1932. *Money in Elections.* Macmillan.

Pope, Jeremy, ed. 1996. *The Transparency International Source Book: Analytical Framework; Applying the Framework.* Berlin: Transparency International.

Potter, Trevor. 1997. "Issue Advocacy and Express Advocacy." In *Campaign Finance Reform: A Sourcebook,* edited by A. Corrado and others, 225–74. Brookings.

Rosenkranz, E. Joshua. 1998a. *Buckley Stops Here: Loosening the Judicial Stranglehold on Campaign Finance Reform*, Report of the Twentieth Century Fund Working Group on Campaign Finance Litigation. New York: Century Foundation Press.

———. 1998b. "Faulty Assumptions in 'Faulty Assumptions': A Response to Professor Smith's Critiques of Campaign Finance Reform." *Connecticut Law Review* (Spring): 867–96.

Saad, Lydia. 1997. "No Public Outcry for Campaign Finance Reform." *Gallup Poll Monthly* (February): 11–14.

Schram, Martin. 1995. *Speaking Freely.* Washington: Center for Responsive Politics.

Sorauf, Frank J. 1984. *What Price PACS?* Report of the Twentieth Century Fund Task Force on Political Action Committees. New York: Twentieth Century Fund.

———. 1992. *Inside Campaign Finance: Myths and Realities.* Yale University Press.

U.S. District Court. 1999. *Federal Election Commission v. Colorado Republican Federal Campaign Committee et al.,* No. 89 1159 (D. Colo.).

U.S. Senate, Committee on Governmental Affairs. 1998. *Investigation of Illegal or Improper Activities in Connection with the 1996 Federal Election Campaigns.* Final Report of the Committee on Governmental Affairs, vol. 1. Senate Report 105–167. 105 Cong. 2 sess. Government Printing Office.

U.S. Supreme Court. 1996. *Colorado Republican Federal Campaign Committee et al.* v. *Federal Election Commission,* 518 U.S. 604.

Contributors

Henry J. Aaron is currently Bruce and Virginia MacLaury Senior Fellow in the Economic Studies program at Brookings. From 1990 through 1996 he was director of the program. His most recent book, coauthored with Robert D. Reischauer, is *Countdown to Reform: The Great Social Security Debate* (Century Foundation, 1999).

Gary Burtless is a senior fellow in the Brookings Economic Studies program. He has worked as an economist in the Office of the U.S. Secretary of Labor and in the Office of the Secretary of Health, Education, and Welfare.

I.M. Destler is a professor and director of the Center for International and Security Studies at the School of Public Affairs at the University of Maryland. He is also a visiting fellow at the Institute for International Economics.

John J. DiIulio Jr. is Fox Leadership Professor of Politics, Religion, and Civil Society and professor of political science at the University of Pennsylvania and nonresident senior fellow at Brookings. He is a senior fellow at the Manhattan Institute and senior counsel to Public/Private Ventures.

WILLIAM GALE is Joseph A. Pechman Fellow in the Brookings Economic Studies program. He is coeditor, with Henry Aaron, of *Economic Effects of Fundamental Tax Reform* (Brookings 1996).

BRUCE KATZ is a senior fellow at Brookings and director of the Brookings Center on Urban and Metropolitan Policy. He was chief of staff at the U.S. Department of Housing and Urban Development from 1993 to 1996.

DONALD F. KETTL is a nonresident senior fellow at Brookings and professor of public affairs and political science at the University of Wisconsin-Madison. He is the director of a Brookings project on the Clinton administration's reinventing government project and author of a forthcoming book on the global reform movement in public management.

PAUL C. LIGHT is Douglas Dillon Senior Fellow and founding director of the Center for Public Service at Brookings. He is also a research professor at Georgetown University and adjunct professor of practice at Harvard University's John F. Kennedy School of Government. His most recent book is *The True Size of Government* (Brookings, 1999).

THOMAS E. MANN is W. Averell Harriman Senior Fellow in American Government at Brookings. He was director of the Brookings Governmental Studies program from 1987 to 1999. His most recent book is *Campaign Finance Reform: A Sourcebook* (Brookings, 1997).

MICHAEL O'HANLON is a senior fellow in the Brookings Foreign Policy program. He specialized in national security issues and foreign aid issues at the Congressional Budget Office from 1989 until 1994.

PAUL R. PORTNEY is president of, and a senior fellow at, Resources for the Future. He has served as chief economist at the Council on Environmental Quality in the Executive Office of the President and has been a visiting lecturer at the University of California at Berkeley and at Princeton University.

DIANE RAVITCH is a historian of education, research professor of education at New York University, and a nonresident senior fellow at Brookings. She was assistant secretary for research in the U.S. Department of Education from 1991 to 1993.

ROBERT D. REISCHAUER is a senior fellow in the Brookings Economic Studies program. From March 1989 until March 1995 he served as director of the Congressional Budget Office. His most recent book, coauthored with Henry J. Aaron, is *Countdown to Reform: The Great Social Security Debate* (Century Foundation, 1999).

ISABEL V. SAWHILL is a senior fellow in the Brookings Economic Studies program. She serves as president of the National Campaign to Prevent Teen Pregnancy and was an associate director of the Office of Management and Budget.

JAMES SLY researched tax and budget issues at Brookings and is currently a research assistant at the Center on Budget and Policy Priorities.

Index